1993
THE GUIDE TO COOKING SCHOOLS

Fifth Edition

SHAWGUIDES, Inc.
625 Biltmore Way, Suite 1406
Coral Gables, Florida 33134
(305) 446-8888

Library of Congress Catalog Card Number 88-92516
ISSN 1040-2616
ISBN 0-945834-16-0

INTRODUCTION

The Guide to Cooking Schools is the only comprehensive source of information about cooking courses, apprenticeships, tours, and culinary arts schools worldwide. This fifth annual edition, the largest to date, contains information about 664 programs — a ten percent increase over the fourth edition. Whether you cook for pleasure or profit, *The Guide* will help you find the programs that fit your interests, schedule, and budget. Schools range from cookware shops, restaurants, resorts, and individuals offering classes primarily for the nonprofessional cook, to private institutions, community colleges, trade schools, and earn-as-you-learn apprenticeships for those pursuing a culinary career or seeking to improve their professional skills. More than 150 of the schools offering career training report a job placement rate of 90% to 100% for graduates. Their administrators state that many more jobs are available than can be filled.

• **New to this edition are School Rankings by Tuition Costs** and **School Rankings by Percentage of Applicants Accepted.** These rankings of career programs are general guidelines provided to assist the prospective student in identifying schools best suited to his or her financial and academic situation.

• **Section I, Cooking and Culinary Arts Schools,** contains the following detailed information about 345 schools (44 new to this edition) in 39 states and 22 countries: year established, subjects taught, method of instruction, schedule of classes, months of operation, maximum number of students per class, description of facilities, faculty credentials, tuition, payment and refund policies, school location or tour itinerary, and contact name, address, and telephone/fax numbers. All schools provide instruction in English. The length of a listing depends largely on the amount of information provided by the school and is not intended to reflect the merit of its faculty or curriculum. **A Currency Conversion Table** is provided for calculating the approximate tuition at schools outside the United States.

• **Section II, Vocational Schools and Community Colleges,** contains the following vital statistics for an additional 192 culinary arts programs offered by junior and community colleges and vocational-technical schools in 42 states, Canada, and Australia: year established, length of programs, degrees awarded, admission dates and requirements, total enrollment and student to teacher ratio, percentage of applicants accepted, availability of paid externships, financial aid, and scholarships, percentage of graduates obtaining jobs, tuition, size of faculty, accreditation, and specialties.

• **Also in Section II is a description of the three-year National Apprenticeship Training Program for Cooks,** which is administered by the Educational Institute of the American Culinary Federation and registered with the U.S. Department of Labor. More than 2,600 apprentices are earning an income while receiving on-the-job training in foodservice establishments throughout the United States. Contact information is provided for the 128 programs currently available in 40 states, Puerto Rico, and the Bahamas.

• **Section III, Culinary and Accrediting Organizations,** describes the goals and objectives, publications, activities, dues, and services of 13 organizations. Two of these — the American Culinary Federation Educational Institute (ACFEI) and the Career College Association (CCA) — are officially recognized by the U.S. Department of Education as accrediting agencies. Page-referenced lists of ACFEI and CCA-accredited schools are on pages 280 and 283. A third organization, the International Association of Culinary Professionals (IACP), endorses those cooking schools that adhere to specific requirements. A page-referenced list of IACP-endorsed schools is on page 287.

• **Section IV, Appendix,** contains five indexes to the schools in Section I. **The Specialty Index** groups schools into 17 cuisines and topics, such as "Baking, Pastries, Desserts", "Microwave Cookery", and "Vegetarian, Healthy". Those interested in a cooking vacation should refer to the index of **171 Travel & Vacation Programs** and individuals pursuing a culinary career should consult the index of **91 Professional Programs. Indexes of 47 children's courses and 51 restaurant-affiliated schools** are also included.

All listings that appeared in the previous two editions were returned to the schools for updating. Program descriptions appearing for the first time in this edition were prepared from information provided by the school officials, who had an opportunity to verify their listings prior to publication. The programs are not endorsed by the publisher nor do schools pay to be listed in *The Guide.*

Although we've strived to make each listing as accurate and complete as possible, changes do occur. Call or write to the schools to confirm costs, schedules, and programs before enrolling or making travel plans. Please let us know if you feel that any listing is an inaccurate representation of a school's program or if you are acquainted with schools that should be listed in future editions.

The editors and publisher thank the school and organization administrators for their cooperation and assistance and wish you enjoyment and success in all your culinary endeavors.

ShawGuides

CONTENTS

I

COOKING &
CULINARY ARTS
SCHOOLS

ALABAMA

MARRIOTT'S GRAND HOTEL WINE AND COOKING WEEKEND
Point Clear, Alabama

February

This annual event features informal cooking classes, wine tastings and lectures, evening receptions and banquets, a session on aquaculture (farm-raised fish and seafood), and tours of the culinary facilities and herb garden.

Specialties: A variety of topics.

Faculty: Grand Hotel culinary staff, headed by Executive Chef Robert Bach and wine instructor Gregory Imbach. Wines provided by Robert Mondavi Winery.

Costs, Accommodations: Cost is approximately $200 per couple per night, which includes double occupancy lodging, continental breakfasts, dinners, and all planned activities.

Location: Point Clear is 23 miles south of Mobile.

Contact: Marriott's Grand Hotel, Hwy. 98, Pt. Clear, AL 36564; (800) 544-9933 *or* (205) 928-9201.

SOUTHERN LIVING COOKING SCHOOL
Birmingham, Alabama and locations in the South

Spring and Fall

Since 1975, *Southern Living* magazine has presented cooking shows co-sponsored by nationally recognized food brands, such as Hormel, Kikkoman, Heinz, Pillsbury, Campbell's, and Dole, and local newspapers who publish notices of the event. Each year, approximately 120,000 attend the two-hour show held at more than 40 locations throughout the South. Shows are scheduled at 10 am and/or 7 pm and feature the demonstration of 16 recipes, each containing a sponsor's product. Attendees receive a recipe book and gift bag of coupons.

Specialties: A variety of Southern dishes featuring name brand products.

Faculty: Professional home economists from *Southern Living* magazine.

Costs: Admission ranges from $1 to $10, depending on location.

Location: Auditoriums and community centers in southern cities.

Contact: *Southern Living* Cooking School, P.O. Box 2581, Birmingham, AL 35202; (205) 877-6000.

ARIZONA

LES GOURMETTES COOKING SCHOOL
Phoenix, Arizona

October-May

Founded in 1982, this school offers approximately 10 guest chef specialty classes and three 3-session seasonal cooking courses quarterly. A variety of cuisines are taught in the school's country French kitchen, although French and Southwest dominate, and students may enroll in one class or a series of three. The

2½ to 3-hour demonstrations, each limited to 15 students per instructor and two assistants, begin at 9:30 am and 6:30 pm and conclude with a full meal. Culinary trips have been scheduled to San Francisco, New York, France, and Greece.

Specialties: A variety of topics, including French and Southwest cuisines; guest chef and cookbook author specialties.

Faculty: School proprietor and instructor Barbara Fenzl, CCP studied at the Cordon Bleu, L'Ecole LeNotre, and with James Beard, Simone Beck, Julia Child, and Michel Guerard. Guest instructors have included chefs Pierre Fauvet, Chris Gross, and Vincent Guerithaut; and cookbook authors Giuliano Bugialli, Hugh Carpenter, Ken Hom, Deborah Madison, Lydie Marshall, Jacques Pépin, Barbara Tropp, Paula Wolfert, and Martin Yan. The school is endorsed by the IACP.

Costs: Guest chef classes range from $40 to $85; three-sessions are $95. Advance payment is required and refund or class credit is granted cancellations.

Location: Central Phoenix, near the downtown area and the freeway system.

Contact: Barbara Fenzl, Les Gourmettes Cooking School, 6610 N. Central Ave., Phoenix, AZ 85012; (602) 240-6767, Fax (602) 266-2706.

THE HOUSE OF RICE STORE
Scottsdale, Arizona

Year-round

This retail store and school, founded in 1977, offers 22 one and three-session demonstration/participation courses (limit 12 students) in Chinese, Japanese, and Vietnamese/Thai cuisine. The two-hour afternoon and evening sessions are scheduled five to seven times a week. In addition to basic and advanced Oriental cuisine, topics include appetizers, hot and spicy foods, sushi, mu shu pork, stir-fry wok, and Vietnamese/Thai. Private group classes can be arranged.

Specialties: Chinese, Japanese. and Vietnamese/Thai cuisines.

Faculty: School owner Kiyoko Goldhardt, Chau Liaw, and Lan Nguyen.

Costs: Ranges from $13 for a class to $40 for a three-session course. Pre-payment is required and refunds are granted cancellations one week prior.

Location: One mile east of downtown Scottsdale, near fine shopping.

Contact: Kiyoko Goldhardt, The House of Rice Store, 3221 N. Hayden Rd., Scottsdale, AZ 85251; (602) 947-6698 *or* (602) 949-9681.

SCOTTSDALE CULINARY INSTITUTE
Scottsdale, Arizona

Year-round

Founded in 1986, this private school offers an accelerated 11-month course leading to a restaurant or catering career. Classes are held in six modern, full-service kitchens and offer personalized instruction with an average student to teacher ratio of 10 to 1 in all practical classes. Prior to admission students submit an application and essay and approximately 70% of applicants are accepted. New classes begin every six weeks. Job placement assistance is available and 97% of graduates find employment. The school has a total enrollment of 140 students and is accredited by the CCA (NATTS) and the ACFEI.

The comprehensive course covers all aspects of food preparation and presentation, safety and sanitation, and inventory and purchasing. Portions of the course are spent in the student-run L'École Restaurant, where students learn restaurant management and front-of-the-house operations (dining room service, menu design, advanced wines, restaurant management). The final eight weeks are spent in a paid externship program. Students are evaluated on the basis of class participation, practical skills, professionalism, and practical and written exams.

Specialties: A 65 credit-hour Associate of Occupational Studies degree in Culinary Arts & Sciences and Restaurant Management.

Faculty: Founder and director Elizabeth Leite developed and implemented a commercial food trades curriculum at Scottsdale Vocational Technical Institute. Her teaching staff consists of 16 professionals with higher education and practical experience. An advisory board of distinguished executive chefs, food and beverage directors, and restaurant owners recommends curriculum.

Costs, Accommodations: Tuition for the 11-month course is $9,790. A nonrefundable (unless applicant is rejected) fee of $50 must accompany application and full tuition must be paid prior to first day of class unless other arrangements are made. Federal financial aid is available. Housing adjoins the campus.

Contact: Admissions Director, Scottsdale Culinary Institute, 8100 E. Camelback Rd., Scottsdale, AZ 85251; (602) 990-3773 *or* (800) 848-2433.

THE TASTING SPOON
Tucson, Arizona

September-May

Founded in 1978, this school offers three to four $2^1/2$ to $3^1/2$-hour classes and two to three one-hour Lunch and Learn sessions (limit 10 students) each month, two diploma courses in spring and fall, and a ten-week International Series. The Diploma I course, 12 weekly evening three-hour classes, covers the techniques of food handling, why ingredients react as they do, and correct cooking vocabulary. Those who complete this course may enroll in the ten-session Diploma II course, which covers advanced subject matter and techniques. The ten-session International Series includes nine different cuisines and a final class in which students prepare dinner. Demonstration sessions by local chefs at their restaurants are also offered and participation courses for youngsters are scheduled at holiday time.

Specialties: A variety of topics; classes for children.

Faculty: School proprietor Virginia Selby, Judith Berger, Amalia Ruiz Clark, Marilyn Davison, Rosemary Emory, Edith Gregg, Carol A. Grimm, Robert Leopardi, Donald Luria, Karen Lustig, Rita Rosenberg, Rob Selby, Susan Shafer, Katie Valenzuela, and chefs Jeff Azersky and Donna Nordin.

Costs: Classes range from $25 to $40, Lunch and Learn sessions are $12, and the Diploma I, Diploma II, and International Series cost $350 to $375 each. Full payment is required with registration and full refund is granted cancellations more than 48 hours prior to class. Credit cards (VISA, MasterCard) accepted.

Location: On Tucson's northwest side.

Contact: Virginia Selby, The Tasting Spoon, P.O. Box 44013, Tucson, AZ 85733-4013; (602) 327-8174.

CALIFORNIA

AMY MALONE SCHOOL OF CAKE DECORATING
La Mesa, California

Year-round

Founded in Virginia in1977, this school offers approximately 20 two or three-hour morning and evening participation (limit 14 students) and demonstration (limit 30) classes each quarter. Garnish classes feature a variety of creative food presentations, such as vegetable flower bouquets, cucumber whales and turtles, carrot centipedes, pear rabbits, egg yolk chicks, roses made from sliced meat, and honeydew swans. Decorating classes include wedding cakes, cupcake carica-tures, icing flowers, chocolate artistry and gingerbread houses. Other classes cover catering, napkin folding, and candymaking.

Specialties: Cake decorating, creative garnishes, and related topics.

Faculty: Amy Malone is a graduate of the Wilton, Betty Newman May, John McNamara, Mary Howard, and Josepha Barloco schools of cake decorating and served as guest instructor at L'Academie de Cuisine and the BICC.

Costs: Range from $15 to $75 per class. A $10 deposit is refundable for cancellations more than five days prior.

Location: East of San Diego.

Contact: Amy Malone, Amy Malone School of Cake Decorating, 4212 Camino Alegre, La Mesa, CA 91941; (619) 660-1900.

ACADEMY OF COOKING — BEVERLY HILLS
Beverly Hills, California

Year-round except January and August

Established in 1990, this school for home cooks offers six to eight classes monthly on a variety of topics, including afternoon tea, buffet and brunch menus, and California, international, and vegetarian cuisines. The four-hour participation sessions (limit 10 students) are scheduled days (11:30 am) and evenings (6 pm) and include a complete meal of the foods prepared.

Specialties: A variety of topics.

Faculty: Chef-instructor Meredith Jo Mischen studied with chefs at New York's Plaza and Waldorf Astoria Hotels and operates a catering business, Meredith's Marvelous Morsels.

Costs: Classes are $50. Credit is granted cancellations more than 72 hours prior.

Contact: Meredith Jo Mischen, Director, Academy of Cooking-Beverly Hills, 400 S. Beverly Dr., #214, Beverly Hills, CA 90212; (310) 275-0268.

BED AND BREAKFAST IN TUSCANY (page 210)

BRISTOL FARMS COOK 'N' THINGS PROFESSIONAL COOKING SCHOOL
South Pasadena and Manhattan Beach, California
Year-round

This cookware store and school began offering classes in 1985, established a professional program in 1990, and opened a second school in Manhattan Beach in 1992. About five three-hour demonstration (limit 30 students) and participation (limit 16) sessions are scheduled each week in the fully-equipped teaching kitchen, which has an amphitheatre with individual work areas, a Jade range with 12 burners, and a video monitor system. Topics include specialty series on a variety of cuisines, 8-session participation and 12-session demonstration courses in cooking fundamentals, courses for professionals, and food history classes.

Specialties: A variety of topics for nonvocational and professional cooks.

Faculty: Director Claudia McQuillan, CCP, and such guest chefs as Bruce Aidells, Hugh Carpenter, Julia Child, Jim Dodge, George Germon, Johanne Killeen, Lynne Rosetto Kasper, Nick Malgieri, Jacques Pépin, Wolfgang Puck, Stephan Pyles, Michel Richard, and Martin Yan. The school is affiliated with the IACP, AIWF, and Southern California Culinary Guild.

Costs: Range generally from $45 to $55 per session, payable at least four days in advance. Cancellations more than 24 hours prior receive class credit.

Location: Next door to the South Pasadena Market, 15 minutes from Los Angeles near I-110; in the Manhattan Beach Market, 10 minutes west of I-405.

Contact: Claudia McQuillan, CCP, Director, Bristol Farms Cook 'N' Things Professional Cooking School, 606 Fair Oaks Ave., S. Pasadena, CA 91030; (818) 441-5588, Fax (818) 441-8994. 1570 Rosecrans Ave., Manhattan Beach, CA 90266; (310) 643-5229, Fax (310) 643-5258.

CALIFORNIA CULINARY ACADEMY (CCA)
San Francisco, California
Year-round

This private institution, accredited by the ACFEI and CCA (NATTS), was founded in 1977 to provide technical and professional chef training for individuals desiring an entry-level position or advancement as a cook, chef, or baker. The school offers a 16-month career program and a variety of continuing education classes for both novices and professionals. Approximately 80% of applicants are accepted and 88% of graduates obtain employment. Facilities include two pastry shops, a bakery, a confiserie, a butchery, two garde manger kitchens and three hot food kitchens, including one for Pacific Rim/Asian cooking, one demonstration kitchen, three instructional dining rooms, one classroom for food and wine pairing and one classroom for food and beverage management instruction. Two of the three student-staffed restaurants are open to the public: The Carême Room serves Classical/Modern cuisine, The Academy Grill serves American regional dishes.

The 16-month program, enrolling more than 540 students and modeled after the European system of closely monitored apprenticeships, trains students in the art of professional cooking. Emphasis is on classic and modern cooking techniques and nutritional cooking, as well as culinary theory. The course of study is predetermined for four 16-week terms and students serve a one-month externship during their senior year. Students are admitted in January, February, April, June, September, and October, and classes are scheduled daily from 2:30 to 9:30 pm during the freshman and senior terms and from 7 am to 2 pm during the sophomore and junior terms. The 2,035-hour program consists of 31.25 hours of instruction per week or 6.15 contact hours per day. The 23 lab courses and 12 lecture courses cover Skill Development, Demonstration Kitchen, Product Identification/Purchasing. Professional Cooking Development, Introduction to Culinary Arts, Meat Identification/Butchery, Safety and Sanitation, Food Chemistry, Nutrition, Banquet/Buffet Catering, Introduction to Table Service, International Cooking, Wine Appreciation, Wine and Food Affinities (both classes with a winery field trip), Kitchen Management, Introduction to Garde Manger, Introduction to Baking and Pastry, Introduction to Classical Cooking, Advanced Tableservice, Advanced Baking and Pastry, Service Management, Menu and Facilities Planning, Human Resource Management, Cost Control, Advanced Garde Manger, Classical Pastry, and Classical Tableservice. During the last three terms, students rotate through all kitchen and dining room stations at the school's three restaurants. An Associate of Occupational Science degree is issued to all students who graduate from the 16-month program. A full-time placement office assists students in pursuing part-time employment and alumni with career placement.

The Continuing Education Program offers 80 classes a year for novice and professional cooks and a 12-week Baking and Pastry Course for individuals interested in learning the pastry arts. Topics include professional cooking, professional baking, shellfish cooking, food show competition, and various ethnic cuisines. Most short courses are held from 9 am to 1 pm on Saturdays or 6 to 9:30 pm weekdays. Students who complete a three-course series receive a Continuing Education Certificate. Special courses for large groups can be custom-designed.

Specialties: Full time 16-month professional chef training program emphasizing classic and modern cooking techniques; continuing education weekend and evening avocational courses and a 12-week baking and pastry course.

Faculty: A full-time staff of 20 professionally trained European, American, and Asian chefs averaging 15 years of experience, a full-time staff of 4 professionally-trained maitre's d'hotel, 6 part-time faculty, and a visiting faculty of area professionals. The CCA Educational Advisory Board includes Julia Child, Robert Mondavi, Jeremiah Tower, Richard Swig, and Martin Yan.

Costs: Tuition for the 16-month course is $4,770 per term. Additional costs include a nonrefundable application fee, a nonrefundable registration fee, an acceptance deposit, a supply package fee, and for seniors, a graduation fee. Admission is competitive and open to those who have a high school diploma or equivalency. Prospective students should apply four months prior to start of semester and are notified of acceptance three months prior. Tuition is due the first day of class and deferred payment plans are available. Financial aid and veterans aid assistance are provided to qualified applicants. Refund policy conforms to CCA (NATTS) requirements. Continuing education single session course fees range from $50 to $95. Payment must accompany registration and full refund is granted cancellations more than three days prior to class.

Location: Near Civic Plaza, two blocks from City Hall, one block from Opera Plaza, and convenient to public transportation.

Contact: California Culinary Academy, 625 Polk St., San Francisco, CA 94102; (415) 771-3536 *or* (800) 229-2433.

LA CARAVANE ADVENTURES IN FOOD AND TRAVEL (page 228)

CAROLE BLOOM, PÂTISSIÈRE
Carlsbad, California

Year-round

Since 1978, Carole Bloom has taught demonstration (limit 16 students) and participation (limit 8) classes in pastry and desserts. The three to five-hour day and evening sessions are scheduled two to three times weekly in the specially-equipped professional kitchen. Topics include Swiss, French, Italian, and Austrian pastries and desserts with emphasis on chocolate work, pralines, wedding and occasion cakes, pastries, and ice creams. Private instruction is available.

Specialties: Pastries, desserts, chocolate, truffles and candies, ice creams, and afternoon teas.

Faculty: Carole Bloom studied at La Varenne, The Cordon Bleu Cookery School, and the Wilton School and has served as assistant pastry chef at The Stanford Court Hotel in San Francisco and pastry chef at Hotel Le Beau Rivage Palace in Switzerland. She writes for *Chocolatier* and *Food & Wine*, is author of *Truffles, Candies, & Confections*, is executive producer and on-air chef for an instructional cable television cooking show, and is an IACP Certified Culinary Professional.

Costs: $75 per class must accompany reservation. Refunds are granted cancellations at least 48 hours prior to class.

Location: About 15 miles north of San Diego on the Pacific coast.

Contact: Carole Bloom, 6832 Maple Leaf Dr., Carlsbad, CA 92009; (619) 931-5920.

CHINA ADVOCATES (PAGE 158)

COOKS AND BOOKS COOKING SCHOOL
Danville, California

September-June

Established in 1991, this cookbook store and school offers one to four-session demonstration/participation courses (limit 35 students), local gourmet shopping excursions, and culinary tours abroad. More than 100 classes a year are scheduled in the school's 1,600-square-foot teaching facility, which has one fully-equipped kitchen with three partially-equipped stations. Topics include international cuisines, seasonal and holiday menus, nutritious foods, and guest chef specialties. A trip to France is planned in 1994.

Specialties: A variety of topics.

Faculty: In-house instructor Elizabeth Thomas is a Cordon Bleu graduate. Other instructors are San Francisco-area chefs, teachers, and cookbook authors.

Costs: Classes range from $35 to $50 each. Payment by check or credit card

(VISA, MasterCard) is required with registration. Cancellations more than seven days prior receive a refund; store credit is granted 72 hours to seven days prior.

Location: Thirty miles east of San Francisco.

Contact: Beverly Sheperd, Cooks and Books, 482 Hartz Ave., Danville, CA 94526; (510) 831-0708.

CUISINE SUR LA MER
Manhattan Beach, California
February-June and September-November

This gourmet shop and school, established in 1980, offers 15 to 20 demonstration classes (limit 18 participants) quarterly. The 2½-hour sessions begin at 7 pm and include a meal. Wine tasting and private group lessons are available.

Specialties: A variety of topics.

Faculty: Include caterer Cheryl Tarango, author Susan Mitchell, Tarla, and Cathy Thomas and Sue Young, who studied at the Cordon Bleu and La Varenne.

Costs: Cooking classes are $30, wine tasting lessons are $20. Credit card (MasterCard, VISA, American Express) registrations accepted. Credit is granted cancellations more than 72 hours prior.

Location: The Los Angeles area, on the Pacific Coast.

Contact: Cuisine Sur La Mer, 919 Manhattan Ave., Manhattan Beach, CA; 90266; (310) 374-3103.

CULINARY ADVENTURES, INC.
Malibu, California and Other Locations
Year-round

These day-long tours, designed to educate serious cooks about food products, include lectures, cooking demonstrations, visits to specialty food markets, growers, and manufacturers, and product tastings. Tours usually run from 9 am to 5 pm and are limited to 25 participants. Consultations and private tours can be arranged. Extended tours to such locations as Napa/Sonoma, New Orleans, Santa Fe, and Hong Kong/Bangkok are also offered.

Specialties: Food-related tours.

Faculty: Tour leader Doris Felts, a cooking instructor since 1976, has conducted tours for organizations and consults with food professionals for products and sources in the Southern California area.

Costs: Day tours range from $65 to $95, including lunch and transportation. Consultation and private tour costs on request.

Location: Culinary places of interest in the Greater Los Angeles area.

Contact: Doris Felts, Culinary Adventures, Inc., 23908 DeVille Way, Malibu, CA 90265; (213) 456-2484.

EPICUREAN COOKING SCHOOL
Los Angeles, California

Year-round

Established in 1985, this school offers a variety of one to four-session courses, culinary tours, and a seven-month professional chef training program. More than 40 three to four-hour demonstration (limit 30 students) and participation (limit 16) classes are scheduled during each four-month period. The professional chef training course, which emphasizes classic French culinary methods, offers four hours of practical and theoretical class in the morning or evening, one day a week, and consists of Pro Chef I (Classic French, 18 weeks), Pro Chef II (Contemporary, 10 weeks), and Pro Chef III (Restaurant/Extern Program, 10 weeks). The curriculum covers techniques and the preparation of meat, fish, fowl, stocks and sauces, vegetables, breads, and pastries. Business aspects of food costing and accountability are also covered. Students may supplement their training with optional attendance and assistance at the school's other classes, at no additional cost. All applicants are accepted and a job placement service is available for graduates. Approximately 40% to 60% desire employment.

Specialties: A variety of topics, including ethnic cuisines, basic skills, and chef specialties; professional course in classic French cuisine.

Faculty: School proprietor is Shelley Janson. The professional program is taught by graduates of the Culinary Institute of America.

Costs: Single sessions range from $50 to $60. Credit card (VISA, MasterCard) registrations accepted. Cancellations more than 48 hours prior receive school credit. Cost of the professional programs is $2,500 (Pro Chef I, $1,300; Pro Chef II, $600; Pro Chef III, $600).

Contact: Shelley Janson, Epicurean Cooking School, 8759 Melrose Ave., Los Angeles, CA 90069; (310) 659-5990.

EXPLORING THE KITCHENS OF ASIA WITH JOYCE JUE (page 134)

FLORENTINE COOKING SCHOOL
Saratoga, California

Year-round

Established in 1990 by Ernestine Del Monaco, founder of the Florentine Restaurants, this school offers more than 50 participation (limit 14 students) and demonstration (limit 18) classes four times a week throughout the year. The emphasis is on Italian specialties and contemporary cuisine and each class deals with a specific subject. Programs include one-hour Friday Lunch and Learn classes, Tuesday evening Supper Samplers, three-hour Thursday evening participation classes, and a weekly series in October (Nonna in the Kitchen), in which a grandmother prepares her family's favorite recipe in front of the group.

Specialties: Italian and contemporary cuisine.

Faculty: Includes native Italian Franca Coletta, who specializes in recipe development and whose family owned a restaurant in Abruzzi. Some classes feature guest speakers or guest appearances by Mrs. Ernestine Del Monaco.

Costs: Single sessions range from $15 to $40. Credit cards (MasterCard, VISA) are accepted and refunds are granted cancellations more than 48 hours prior.

Location: Saratoga's Restaurant Row on Big Basin Way.

Contact: Franca Coletta, Florentine Cooking School, 14510 Big Basin Way, Saratoga, CA 95070; (408) 741-1777.

GOURMET SCHOOL OF COOKING AND ENTERTAINING
Los Angeles, California

September-June

Founded in 1971, this school offers about a dozen one to six-session participation courses each year in Judythe Roberts' home kitchen. Courses are limited to 10 to 12 participants and meet once weekly, Tuesday or Wednesday evening from 7 to 9:30, after which students dine on the foods prepared. Topics vary each season and a six-session Basic French Cooking course is repeated each year.

Specialties: A variety of topics; French and other ethnic and regional cuisines.

Faculty: School proprietor Judythe Roberts is a second generation alumna of the Cordon Bleu in Paris. Guest instructors conduct classes in special subjects.

Costs: Tuition is $180 for six sessions, $135 for five sessions, $50 for two sessions, and $35 to $40 for a single session.

Location: The hills above Los Angeles.

Contact: Judythe Roberts, Gourmet School of Cooking and Entertaining, 3915 Carnavon Way, Los Angeles, CA 90027; (213) 666-5080.

THE GREAT CHEFS AT THE ROBERT MONDAVI WINERY
Oakville, California

Spring and fall

Since 1976, the Robert Mondavi Winery has hosted two and three-day weekend events that feature 2 to 2½ hours of morning or afternoon daily cooking demonstrations by noted chefs and culinary experts, winery tours and tastings, and gourmet lunches and dinners in an environment designed to embody the art of good living. The presentation of wine and food is enhanced by the use of special tableware and linens, fresh cut flowers, and an ever-changing room decor with appropriate entertainment at each meal to suit the mood, from casual theme lunches to the Saturday night gala dinner. Four events are offered during the year, two in spring and two in fall, and attendance is limited. The program begins on Friday for the long weekend, Saturday for the weekend with a private morning tour of the Winery, and concludes with a late farewell luncheon at the Winery on Sunday. Participants also attend seminars on such topics as table settings and flower arrangements, nutrition, and food and wine pairing.

Since 1992, the Winery has offered an intensive, one-day single session — A Day with the Great Chefs — designed for area professionals and serious amateurs and held the Monday following each weekend event. The program includes a cooking demonstration of a full menu, a winery tour with tasting, discussion of wine and food pairing, and luncheon of the foods prepared.

Specialties: International cuisines.

Faculty: The faculty changes each year. Previous guest chefs have included Barbara Tropp, Stephan Pyles, Lydia Shire, and Michel and Claude Troisgros.

Costs, Accommodations: Vary depending on program format and if local transportation and lodging is included. Costs range from $650 for a two-day weekend excluding transportation and lodging to $1,550 for the three-day weekend, all inclusive. Accommodations for the long weekend events are based on double occupancy (single supplement is available). One-day session ranges from $95 to $175, depending on guest chef. Payment must accompany application and credit card (VISA, MasterCard) registrations are accepted. Cancellation charge ranges from 10% of full payment (six weeks prior) to 50% (within six weeks).

Location: In California's Napa Valley.

Contact: Axel Fabre, Director, The Great Chefs at the Robert Mondavi Winery, P.O. Box 106, Oakville, CA 94562; (707) 944-2866, Fax (707) 944-8517.

JC'S KITCHEN COMPANY
San Diego, California

Year-round

Established in 1991, this gourmet cookware store and school offers more than 60 one to three-hour demonstration classes (limit 24 students) quarterly in its specially-designed teaching kitchen. Topics include international and regional cuisines, guest chef specialties, and cooking for health.

Specialties: A variety of topics.

Faculty: Local and celebrity guest chefs, including Giuliano Bugialli, Mark Miller, and Jacques Pépin.

Costs: Range from $20 to $40 per class.

Contact: Jana Cason, JC's Kitchen Co., 4223 Genesee Ave., #110, San Diego, CA 92117; (619) 541-1990, Fax (619) 541-2237.

THE JEAN BRADY COOKING SCHOOL
Santa Monica, California and Italy

October-August

Established in 1971, this school offers mostly demonstration classes (limit 17) that emphasize techniques and guest chef specialties. The two-hour sessions, scheduled at 10 am and 7 pm, are held in Jean Brady's commercially-equipped home kitchen, featured in *Bon Appétit* magazine. Group and children's birthday classes can be arranged, and one-week summer programs can be scheduled for a private group. Culinary tours of Italy are planned for the spring and fall.

Specialties: Ethnic and regional cuisines, guest chef specialties.

Faculty: Proprietor Jean Brady studied with Lydie Marshall, Jacques Pépin, and Paula Wolfert and attended the Cordon Bleu and La Varenne. Guest chefs include Lydie Marshall, Paula Wolfert, and area chefs in their restaurant kitchens.

Costs: Single classes range from $35 to $75; a series of seven classes is $225.

Location: Jean Brady's glass and redwood kitchen is situated on a stream in a wooded canyon above the Pacific Ocean, 20 minutes from Beverly Hills.

Contact: The Jean Brady Cooking School, 680 Brooktree Rd., Santa Monica, CA 90402; (310) 454-4220.

JUDITH ETS-HOKIN'S HOMECHEF COOKING SCHOOL
San Francisco, California

Year-round

Founded in 1972, this gourmet store and school offers a 14-week basic cooking course and one to four-week sessions on a variety of topics. Demonstration (limit 45 students) and participation (limit 20) workshops are held week nights at 6:30 or mornings at 10 and may be taken singly, space allowing. The basic course covers cooking methods, concepts, and techniques. Emphasis is on the science of cooking — why and how things work — and students are given homework assignments to reinforce the concepts learned in class. The course covers stocks, sauces, soufflés, pastries, custards, mousses, and cooking methods. Those who complete the full course receive a Certificate of Attendance. Private group sessions can be arranged. A reduced tuition program is offered student assistants, who are chosen on a first-come basis and receive individual supervision.

Specialties: A variety of topics, including basics, ethnic cuisines, light cooking, vegetarian, and food processor techniques.

Faculty: Founder Judith Ets-Hokin, author of the *The Dinner Party Cookbook and The Homechef, Fine Cooking Made Simple*, is a Certified Culinary Professional and holds certificates from cooking schools in England, France, and Italy. Principal instructor is Rebecca Ets-Hokin.

Costs: The basic course is $392 (assistants $185); single classes are $35 each. Short courses range from $35 for a single session to $125 for four sessions (assistants $15 to $60). Credit card registrations accepted.

Contact: Homechef Cooking School, Laural Center, 3525 California St., San Francisco, 94118; (415) 668-3191, Fax (415) 668-0902.

KAKE KREATIONS
Canoga Park, California

Year-round

This cake decorating and candy making store and school offers a variety of one to eight-session courses. Multi-session courses include the eight-lesson beginning, intermediate, and advanced cake decorating courses, the four-lesson flower course (16 types of flowers), and two-lesson courses in panoramic egg, rolled fondant, and cake crafting (three-dimensional designs). One-session classes include candy train, cocoa painting, brush embroidery, gingerbread, and marzipan. All sessions are two hours except the all-day wedding cake workshop.

Specialties: Cake decorating and candy making.

Costs: One-lesson classes are $8.50 to $15, two and four-lesson courses are $20 to $25, and eight-lessons are $40. Supplies are additional. Hands-on candy classes are $20 to $25, including supplies.

Location: A Los Angeles suburb in the San Fernando Valley.

Contact: Kake Kreations, 21835 Sherman Way, Canoga Park, CA 91303; (818) 346-7621.

KAY PASTORIUS SCHOOL OF INTERNATIONAL CUISINE
Laguna Beach, California and Other Locations

September-May

Founded in 1975, this school offers four-session participation courses once a month. The three-hour sessions, scheduled one morning a week in Kay Pastorius' home kitchen, are limited to 12 students, who dine on the full meal they've prepared. The emphasis is on Southwestern cuisine as well as ethnic and regional specialties. A two-week culinary trip to Europe is scheduled each year (May, 1993) and cooking tours to Mexico and Santa Fe are planned from time to time. Additional one-week cooking tours for 1993 include Oaxaca, Mexico (Jan.) and southern Italy (Feb.)

Specialties: Mexican, French, Italian, Oriental, California, and other ethnic cuisines, regional specialties, holiday menus; culinary trips.

Faculty: Kay Pastorius has studied at cooking schools in Mexico, the Cordon Bleu and Ritz-Escoffier schools, and with Madeleine Kamman, Lorenza de' Medici, Jacques Pépin, Diana Folinari, and Enrico Franzese.

Costs: The four-session course is $180. Students may enroll in an individual class for $50 on a space available basis. Those who cancel more than one week prior to class receive a class credit. One-week tour to southern Italy is $2,000.

Location: In Bluebird Canyon in the Pacific Coast community of Laguna Beach, midway between Los Angeles and San Diego.

Contact: Kay Pastorius, Kay Pastorius School of International Cuisine, 1075 Dyer Pl., Laguna Beach, CA 92651; (714) 494-1774.

KITCHEN WITCH GOURMET SHOP
Encinitas, California

September-December, February-July

Founded in 1981, this gourmet shop and school offers 40 to 45 two to three-hour demonstration classes monthly, usually scheduled at both 11 am and 6 pm and limited to 14 students. Friday Learn-a-Lunch sessions are from noon to 1:15 pm and Friday after-school classes for children, ages 5 to 7 and 8 and over, cover ethnic meals, holiday treats, and brown bag lunches. Private group lessons can be arranged.

Specialties: Include ethnic and regional cuisines, vegetarian, holiday menus, pastry, breads, microwave and food processor techniques; classes for children.

Faculty: Includes pastry chefs Carole Bloom and Milo Safarik, cookbook author Phillis Carey, children's cooking specialist Suzy Eisenman, research chemist Evelyn Sudora, restaurant consultant Dee Biller, Italian cooking instructor Nadia Frigeri, teacher Sadhana Gandhi, preserving specialist Janet Chatfield, nutritionist Nancy Brown, food specialist Kay Pastorius, and caterer Didier Petak.

Costs: Learn-a-Lunch classes are $12.95; children's classes are $16; other classes range from $22 to $30. Credit card (VISA, MasterCard) registration accepted. Refunds are granted those who cancel at least three days prior to class.

Location: North of San Diego, on the Pacific Coast.

Contact: Marie Santucci, Kitchen Witch Gourmet Shop, 127 N. El Camino Real, Suite D; Encinitas, CA 92024; (619) 942-3228.

LET'S GET COOKIN'
Westlake Village, California
Year-round

This gourmet store and school, under the present ownership since 1983, offers more than 50 different three-hour demonstration and participation classes each quarter, classes for children, 5 to 12-session demonstration courses in fundamental, intermediate, and advanced creative cooking techniques, a 24-session professional cooking series, a 6-session catering course, culinary day trips, and gourmet cooking tours abroad. Celebrity chef classes, children's birthday party classes, and private instruction are also offered. Classes are usually scheduled at 10:30 am or 6:30 pm and cover a variety of topics. Children's hands-on two-hour classes, for ages 6 to 9 and 10 to 14, are limited to 12 students and feature holiday and ethnic menus, food preparation technique, and safety. The creative cooking techniques courses cover the techniques of preparing classic and contemporary cuisine. Each session is devoted to a different food group and three to five recipes are demonstrated with a discussion of a variety of cooking methods. Students receive a certificate on completion.

The 24-session professional series, is divided into three parts, each a combination of lectures, demonstrations, and hands-on instruction. The first part covers beef, poultry, fish, vegetables, breads, pastries, sauces, equipment, health and sanitation, nutrition, food science, quantity and quality control, costing, menu planning, and presentation. The second part covers shellfish, game, egg dishes, salads, appetizers, cakes, and desserts, with information about wine and exploration of part one topics in greater depth. The third part covers exotic vegetables, pastas, pizzas, ethnic cuisines, and more complex preparations and concludes with a graduation meal. Sessions meet once weekly for four hours and are limited to 12 students. On completion of the series, students receive a certificate and assistance in finding a job. The professional catering series covers party and menu planning, proposals and contracts, marketing and advertising, purveyors, business aspects, recipes, and quantity cooking.

Specialties: A variety of topics, including ethnic cuisines, holiday and seasonal dishes, guest chef specialties; career courses; classes for children.

Faculty: The more than 25-member guest and regular faculty includes owner Phyllis Vaccarelli; food writer Nancie McDermott; pastry chef Carole Bloom; cookbook authors Hugh Carpenter and Jim Dodge, and guest chefs Jane Butel, Mark Miller, Jacques Pepin, and Julie Sahni. Cecilia De Castro, who coordinated professional chef programs for UCLA and Ma Cuisine Cooking School, teaches the professional cooking series and Ann Bernstein, IACP-Certified Culinary Professional, teaches creative cooking.

Costs: Individual classes range from $45 to $75; children's classes are $25; the creative cooking techniques courses average $45 per session and students may register for a single session at $50 on a space available basis; the 24-session course is $1,950; and the catering series is $250. Students in the 24-session course are eligible for the Student Assistant Program, in which they assist in some classes in exchange for free tuition in others. Credit card (VISA, MasterCard, American Express) registrations are accepted and cancellations received at least 48 hours prior to class receive a credit.

Location: Westlake Village is a 30-minute drive from Los Angeles.

Contact: Phyllis Vaccarelli, Let's Get Cookin', 4643 Lakeview Canyon Rd., Westlake Village, CA 91361; (818) 991-3940.

LILY LOH'S CHINESE COOKING CLASSES
Solana Beach, California

Fall, winter, spring

Since 1976, Lily Loh has taught Chinese cooking in her home kitchen. Her six courses are limited to nine students and meet once weekly for three-hours on Tuesday mornings or Wednesday evenings. Each session includes a lecture, demonstration, and some participation, concluding with a sit-down dinner. The five-week Beginner's Class covers cooking techniques, seasonings and spices, and the preparation of dishes using easy-to-find ingredients; the four-week Intermediate Class emphasizes quick and easy menus and one-dish meals; the four-week Advanced Class covers Peking Duck and Moo Shu Pork, such Chinese ingredients as golden needle and black fungus, and the preparation of formal dinners; the four-week Seafood and Vegetable course covers a variety of cooking methods for preparing fish, shellfish, tofu, and vegetable combinations; the four-week Specialty Class covers dim sum and other appetizers and advanced cooking techniques using the wok, steamer, and fire pot; and the four-week Teenage Class features healthy menu planning and basic cooking techniques.

Specialties: Chinese cuisine.

Faculty: Lily Loh was born in Shanghai, China, and holds a home economics degree from Purdue University and masters degree from Cornell University. She is an IACP-Certified Culinary Professional and author of *Lily Loh's Chinese Seafood and Vegetables*.

Costs: The tuition for each course is $180. A nonrefundable $50 deposit is required to reserve a space, with the balance payable on the first day of class.

Location: Solana Beach is situated near San Diego.

Contact: Lily Loh, P.O. Box 1232, Solana Beach, CA 92075; (619) 755-5345 (phone and fax).

MICHAEL'S WATERSIDE
Santa Barbara, California

Year-round

Chef Michael Hutchings has conducted demonstration classes at his well-known French restaurant since it opened, in 1984. During fall and spring he offers one 3-hour demonstration session a month for home cooks and occasional master classes and two-day sauce intensives for professionals. Classes are held in the teaching area of the restaurant solarium or the kitchen and are limited to 20 students, who sample the foods prepared, accompanied by appropriate wines. Occasional "cook and dine" classes are followed by a complete meal in the restaurant. Emphasis is on the techniques of modern French cuisine, including such topics as salmon, petit fours, canapés, potatoes, and small game birds. Sessions are usually held at either 9 am on Saturdays or 5:30 pm Mondays.

Specialties: Modern classic French cuisine.

Faculty: Chef Michael has more than 25 years experience in the culinary field. He trained at Chez Cary in Orange and La Serre and L'Orangerie in Los Angeles and worked for three years for Albert and Michel Roux at Great Britain's Michelin three-star Le Gavroche, where he served as second chef.

Costs: Classes range from $35 to $50. A full refund is granted those who cancel more than one week prior to class or if a substitute is found.

Location: The restaurant is situated across from the André Clark Bird Refuge in a Victorian cottage built in 1872. It's south of downtown Santa Barbara off U.S. Highway 101.

Contact: Michael Hutchings, Michael's Waterside, 50 Los Patos Way, Santa Barbara, CA 93108; (805) 969-0307.

MONTANA MERCANTILE
Santa Monica, California

Year-round

This culinary retail store and cooking school, founded in 1976, is dedicated to providing an education in traditional cooking as well as exploring new trends and ethnic cuisines. Classes are conducted in the store's fully-equipped kitchen, which accommodates 30 students. Courses include a ten-session Cooking Fundamentals program that focuses on specific topics, a four-session basic cooking course taught in Spanish, as well as a variety of demonstration and participation classes.

Specialties: A variety of topics, including ethnic and regional cuisines, seasonal foods, fundamental cooking techniques, and California cuisine.

Faculty: Local and visiting chefs and well-known cooking professionals.

Costs: Costs are approximately $500 for the ten-session course, $300 for the four-session course, $60 for participation classes, and $50 for demonstrations. Telephone credit card (VISA, MasterCard, American Express) enrollments are accepted. Store credit is granted cancellations at least 72 business hours prior.

Location: The school is in a fine shopping area, 15 blocks from the ocean.

Contact: Rachel Dourec, Montana Mercantile, 1500 Montana Ave., Santa Monica, CA 90403; (213) 451-1418.

NAPA VALLEY COLLEGE CULINARY ARTS
Napa, California

Year-round

Established in 1990, this school offers more than 50 courses on a variety of topics each year as well as culinary trips and an annual catering seminar. The demonstration (limit 22 students) and participation (limit 14) classes meet for one to five sessions and cover such topics as regional, international, and seasonal menus. Most classes run from three to five hours with some scheduled over a weekend. A two-part Basics of Cooking is offered as well as a wine-tasting course and Fundamentals of Food Writing, a one-day workshop devoted to historical and practical instruction and application. Strategies for Successful Catering, a four-day summer participation program, covers staffing and supervision, marketing and sales, pricing, site logistics and crisis control, menu planning, food preparation, and table, buffet, and floral design. Students cook each day and prepare a buffet on the final class day. Recent day and evening trips included a walking tour of San Francisco's North Beach and a ten-course meal at a noted Chinese restaurant. A two-week culinary and cultural tour of Thailand features visits to less populated regions and optional cooking classes in Bangkok.

Specialties: A variety of topics, including European, Asian, and American regional cuisines; healthful and vegetarian menus; food and recipe writing; wine tasting; catering.

Faculty: Includes cookbook authors Carolyn Dille, food columnist Holly Rudin-Braschi, sausage-maker Bruce Aidells, food editor Elaine Corn, caterer Diane Clark, and chefs John Ash, Jan Birnbaum, Heidi Krahling, Marlee Rodrique, and Sally and John Schmitt.

Costs: Courses range from $40 to $70 per session. Full payment is required with registration; credit cards accepted.

Location: Classes are held at wineries and other Napa Valley locations, about a one-hour drive northeast of San Francisco.

Contact: Sue Farley, Program Coordinator, Napa Valley College, Culinary Arts, 2277 Napa-Vallejo Hwy., Napa, CA 94558; (707) 253-3377 or (707) 963-4861.

NORTHERN CALIFORNIA CENTER FOR THE CULINARY ARTS
San Francisco and Northern California

January-July, September-November

Established in 1992, the NCCCA organizes and promotes chefs conducting cooking classes in their own establishments and provides periodic financial assistance to local culinary academic institutions. The Renowned Chefs of Northern California features more than 20 four to five-hour classes each season. The late morning hands-on sessions (limit 8 to 16 participants) are held in the chef's restaurant kitchen and conclude with a four-course meal. Mini class tours and tastings include bakeries, sausage makers, and wineries. Weekend get-aways at fine resorts are also offered.

Specialties: Well-known chef's specialties.

Faculty: Includes John Ash (John Ash & Co.), Lissa Doumani (Terra), Scott Gmazel (The Elite Cafe), Joyce Goldstein (Square One), Robert Helstrom (Kuleto's), Hubert Keller (Fleur de Lys), Jacky Robert (Amelio's), Juan Serrano (Masa's), and Matt Wyss (Cafe Majestic).

Costs: Chefs' classes range from $75 to $140; mini classes begin at $15. Full payment is required with registration. Full refund (class credit) is granted cancellations more than seven days (three to six days) prior to class. When classes are held at inns, special room rates are available.

Location: San Francisco and Northern California locations, including Napa, Marin, and Sonoma counties, the East Bay, San Mateo, and Santa Clara county to Monterey.

Contact: Northern California Center for the Culinary Arts, 44 Montgomery St., 5th Flr., San Francisco, CA 94104; (800) 773-7979 *or* (415) 397-7345, Fax (415) 397-6309.

P. K. SHELDON CULINARY TOURS
Southern California

Year-round

Since 1986, freelance cook and food writer Pamela K. Sheldon has arranged and conducted cooking classes and culinary tours that feature visits to restaurants, wineries, and private homes. Programs range from individual instruction to demonstrations for up to 150 students; participation classes are limited to 15. Day-tours include Santa Barbara with a cooking class and visits to Temecula wineries; Catalina Island with a cooking class; an herb farm with a class in organic gardening; and Los Angeles produce and flower markets. Culinary tours for 1992-93 include Italy, Ireland, and Greece.

Specialties: A variety of topics, including basic techniques, restaurant specialties, low cholesterol foods, international and California cuisines.

Faculty: Pamela K. Sheldon, a Certified Culinary Professional by the IACP, has served as director of Ma Cuisine Cooking School in Newport Beach and assistant chef at Max au Triangle in Beverly Hills.

Costs: Average class/day-tour price is $40, not including transportation. Full refund is granted cancellations more than one week prior.

Location: Tours are held within the area between San Diego and Santa Barbara; classes are conducted in Los Angeles, Santa Barbara, and Orange Counties.

Contact: P.K. Sheldon, Box 14834, Long Beach, CA 90803; (310) 423-2856.

PEGGY RAHN COOKS
Pasadena, California

Year-round except Christmas

Founded in 1974, this school offers one to four single workshops weekly and a five-session technique class. The demonstration and participation (limit eight students) classes meet for one or two 3-hour morning or evening sessions in the teaching kitchen of Peggy Rahn's 1918-vintage California home. She also offers private and custom classes, leads small group excursions to markets, restaurants, chef classes, and ethnic areas in such locales as Rancho Santa Fe, Santa Barbara, and Tijuana, and conducts an annual two-week overseas culinary tour.

Specialties: Ethnic cuisines, spa cooking, technique classes, pastry, dinner menus, holiday class; culinary travel.

Faculty: Peggy Rahn is a food and travel columnist, cookbook and restaurant reviewer, and co-host of CBS's "Meet the Cook". She is an IACP Certified Culinary Professional, teaches at UCLA, and has studied at La Varenne, Cordon Bleu, The Oriental Bangkok, and Maria's Cookery in Hong Kong. Guest faculty has included Giuliano Bugialli, Madeleine Kamman, and Paula Wolfert.

Costs: Each class session ranges from $35 to $70.

Location: Ten minutes from downtown Los Angeles, 30 minutes from the beach, and 90 minutes from San Diego and Santa Barbara.

Contact: Peggy Rahn Cooks, 484 Bellefontaine St., Pasadena, CA 91105; (818) 441-2075, Fax (818) 577-1769.

SARAH MONICK CULINARY TOURS (page 197)

SAUCE FOR THE GOOSE, ETC.
Fresno, California
Year-round except August and December

In 1990, this gourmet kitchenware store began offering four to eight-session demonstration courses (limit 35 to 50 students) that emphasize techniques and the hows and whys of French cuisine. The courses, which meet for three hours three evenings a week and include wine tastings, are Classic French Cuisine I (soups and stocks, poaching and sauteing, puff pastry, crepes and souffles), Classic French Cuisine II (deep frying, pastry, vegetables, pates, advanced techniques), Classic French Desserts (pate brisee, pate a choux, genoise, chocolate), Holiday Entertaining-Classic French Cuisine, California cuisine, and Italian cuisine. Approximately 100 sessions are scheduled annually in the store's modern teaching kitchen with Wolf range and video monitors.

Specialties: French classic and regional cuisines, California cuisine, Italian cuisine, wine selection.

Faculty: Chef and store manager Charles Conklin-Chase Hiigel is a member of the IACP and studied with Anne Willan at La Varenne U.S.A. and the Paris Cordon Bleu. He also teaches in California and Texas for Williams-Sonoma.

Costs: $35 per session, $280 for a series of eight. No refunds.

Location: North Pointe Center.

Contact: Charles Conklin-Chase Hiigel, Manager, Sauce for the Goose, 6747 N. Palm Ave., Fresno, CA 93704; (209) 436-1010.

SCHOOL FOR AMERICAN CHEFS
Beringer Vineyards
St. Helena, California
Year-round

This school, opened in 1989 at Beringer Vineyards, offers tuition-free graduate studies for professional chefs working throughout the United States and at U.S. military bases. Four chefs study simultaneously at Beringer Vineyards' Culinary Arts Center during eight two-week sessions annually. The chefs are chosen as a result of their applications and a competition based on menu/recipe design and a statement of goals as regards the future of food professions in the United States. Approximately 20% of applicants are accepted each year, and all must be at least 21 years of age, have a high school diploma or equivalent, and have at least two years of experience as a working chef.

Specialties: Scholarship programs for professional chefs.

Faculty: School Director Madeleine Kamman was born in Paris and spent much of her youth working at her aunt's Michelin-starred restaurant in the Loire Valley. She has taught French cuisine in the United States since 1960 and is the author of six cookbooks, including her latest, *Madeleine Kamman's Savoie*. She stars in PBS-TV's "Madeleine Cooks".

Costs: There is no tuition charge.

Location: Beringer Vineyards is located in the Napa Valley, California's wine country, 75 minutes north of San Francisco.

Contact: Debra Murphy, Administrator, Beringer Vineyards, P.O. Box 111, St. Helena, CA 94574; (707) 963-7115.

SIAMESE PRINCESS RESTAURANT
Los Angeles, California

October-May

Since 1987, executive chef and cookbook author Victor Sodsook has taught demonstration/participation classes (limit 24 students) in Royal Thai cuisine. Classes are held in the restaurant's dining room and kitchen on Sundays, from 1:30 to 4:30 pm. Each student has an individual work area.

Specialties: Royal Thai cuisine.

Faculty: Restaurant co-owner Victor Sodsook, author of *I Love Thai Food* and *The Art of Authentic Thai Cooking*, taught Thai cooking at the Montana Mercantile School in Santa Monica and the Epicurean Cooking School in West Hollywood. The Siamese Princess Restaurant received the Three-Star Award from the California Restaurant Writers Association, 1985-1992.

Costs: Classes are $40 and include wine. Credit cards accepted.

Location: West Los Angeles.

Contact: The Siamese Princess, 8048 W. Third St., Los Angeles, CA 90048; (213) 653-2643.

A STORE FOR COOKS
Laguna Niguel, California

Year-round

This cookware store and school offers 25 to 30 morning and evening demonstration classes each quarter and Lunch and Learn classes once a week. All sessions are limited to 25 students.

Specialties: A variety of topics, including ethnic and regional cuisines, holiday and seasonal foods, menus for entertaining, guest chef specialties.

Faculty: Proprietor and cookbook author Susan Vollmer, executive chef Hugh Carpenter of Chop Stix Cafe, Cathy Thomas and Sue Young of The Tasting Spoon, Tarla Fallgatter, Kay Pastorius, Phillis Carey, and local restaurant chefs.

Costs: Lunch and Learn classes are $10; morning and evening demonstration classes range from $28 to $60. Telephone credit card (VISA, MasterCard, American Express) reservations accepted. Refunds are granted cancellations at least 72 hours prior.

Location: On the Pacific coast between San Diego and Los Angeles.

Contact: Susan Vollmer, A Store for Cooks, 30100 Town Center Dr., Suite R, Laguna Niguel, CA 92677; (714) 495-0445.

SUGAR 'N SPICE CAKE DECORATING SCHOOL
San Francisco, California
Year-round

Established in 1973, this specialty baking supply store and school offers more than 50 one to six-session participation courses (limit 14 students) annually in cake decorating and candy making. Most sessions are two or three hours, scheduled at 10 am or 7 pm, with occasional all-day classes in candy making. Several times a year, the school also offers five-session courses in beginner, intermediate, and advanced cake decorating. Other courses cover gum paste roses, Australian and Nirvana methods, writing and airbrush techniques, and confections for holidays and celebrations.

Specialties: Cake decorating and candy making.

Faculty: Jeanné Lutz is a graduate of the Edith Gate's Cake Decorating School and has studied with several professionals. Guest instructors are featured from time to time.

Costs: Range from $20 for one session to $75 for a six-session course. A $15 deposit must accompany registration with balance due on first day of course. Cancellations at least 48 hours prior to class receive a refund.

Contact: Sugar 'n Spice Cake Decorating School, 3200 Balboa St., San Francisco, CA 94121; (415) 387-1722.

TANTE MARIE'S COOKING SCHOOL
San Francisco, California
Year-round

Founded in 1979, this cooking school offers daytime, evening, and weekend demonstration (limit 38 students) and participation (limit 16) courses and culinary travel programs for beginning to professional cooks. Two six-month courses begin in March and September. The six-month culinary certificate course is scheduled from 10 am to 4 pm, Monday through Friday, and covers the basic techniques of French cooking, pastries and desserts, ethnic cuisines, purchasing and handling foods, menu planning, and refining one's sense of taste. The six-month professional pastry course is scheduled part time. One-week courses allow individuals to attend class with the full-time certificate students any week of the school year and sometimes focus on a specific theme, such as pastry making or regional cooking. During a typical day, students (limit 16) spend the morning in a full-sized kitchen preparing classical recipes that they eat for lunch. The afternoon is devoted to a step-by-step demonstration by a guest chef. Six-session weekly evening participation courses on a variety of topics, limited to 12, are held Tuesday, Wednesday, or Thursday evenings, from 6 to 10 pm, and conclude with a three or four-course meal prepared by students. Those who wish to attend a single class, either day or evening, may do so on a space available basis. Saturdays and Sundays feature demonstration or participation classes that focus on a single specialty. Approximately 95% of applicants are accepted and 95% of graduates obtain employment.

Specialties: Professional and nonprofessional courses in various aspects of food preparation, including the basics, ethnic and regional cuisine, pastries and desserts, and catering.

Faculty: School founder Mary Risley is the primary teacher and instructs most of the morning classes. She has studied at the Cordon Bleu and La Varenne and taught in the U.S. and Canada. The guest and evening faculty varies each season and may include Giuliano Bugialli, author of *Classic Techniques of Italian Cooking*; Jim Dodge, pastry chef at the Stanford Court Hotel; Deborah Madison, author of *The Greens Cookbook*; and Alice Medrich, founder of Cocolat.

Costs: Tuition is $10,000 for the six-month culinary certificate course, $4,000 for the six-month part-time pastry course. One-week courses are $500; six-session evening courses are $390; afternoon demonstration classes are $35 (5 classes for $150); and participation classes are $65. Weekend one-day classes range from $35 to $100. The deposit of $75 for the six-month course is nonrefundable; $100 deposit for one-week and evening courses is refundable if cancellation is more than four weeks prior. Students who cancel within four weeks receive a credit and no refunds are granted for afternoon demonstrations or after the course has started. Credit cards (VISA, MasterCard) accepted.

Location: By the Bay on historic Telegraph Hill, within walking distance of Fisherman's Wharf and convenient to cable car and bus transportation.

Contact: Tante Marie's Cooking School, Inc., 271 Francisco Street, San Francisco, CA 94133; (415) 788-6699.

LE TROU RESTAURANT AND COOKING SCHOOL
San Francisco, California and Deux Sevres, France

Year-round

Aux Gastronomes, the cooking school of Le Trou restaurant, offers full-time culinary apprenticeships as well as one and two-week courses in San Francisco and France. Professional training in cooking and food-related fields, offered since 1983, is patterned after the French model in which study and work occur within the context of a restaurant. Twelve-week and six-month apprenticeships in San Francisco meet eight hours daily Tuesday through Saturday. Regional, classic, and modern French cuisines are examined, as well as menu planning, kitchen and business management, dining room service, wines, and other practical skills.

Eight-week fall, winter, and spring apprenticeships in France are limited to four to six serious culinary students. The daily routine includes planning, marketing, classes, and preparation, with focus on skills, theory, and themes. Master classes are also offered. Individuals and small groups desiring a cooking vacation can enroll for one or two-week classes and tours to France and Italy.

Specialties: Regional, classic, and modern French cuisines.

Faculty: Robert Reynolds, the French-trained chef of Le Trou Restaurant and Cooking School, is co-author with Josephine Araldo of *From A Breton Garden*. He participated in the Great Chefs Teaching Series, contributed to various cookbooks, is recipient of an honor from Gault Millau, and is a certified Educational Supervisor in California.

Costs, Accommodations: The 12-week San Francisco apprenticeship is $4,500; course in France depends on the exchange rate. Approximately 25% of applicants are accepted and 100% of graduates obtain employment. Class and tour programs are $950 per week. Apprentices in France are offered the opportunity to live with townspeople in Niort and become part of the community. Hotels and inns are also available. A 25% deposit is required with balance due the first day of class. Full refund, less $100 fee, is granted cancellations 30 days prior; no refunds thereafter.

Location: Deux Sevres, area of rolling farmland, bordered by Poitiers to the east, Cognac and Bordeaux to the south, and the Venise Vert canal area to the west.

Contact: Robert Reynolds, Le Trou Restaurant and Cooking School, 1007 Guerrero St., San Francisco, CA 94114; (415) 550-8169.

TWO BORDELAIS (page 199)

UCLA EXTENSION DIVISION OF CULINARY ARTS
Los Angeles, California
Year-round

UCLA Extension, a tuition-supported division of UCLA, offers courses, classes, and seminars for professionals, aspiring professionals, and home cooks. Four certificate programs — Professional Cooking, Professional Catering, Professional Baking, and Fine Wine— and a variety of courses and seminars are designed for professional chefs, cooks, caterers, and sommeliers. Most courses meet for 3 1/2 to 4 hours once weekly for 10 to 12 weeks and can be taken on a week night or Saturday morning. Participation courses are limited to 20 students, demonstrations to 30, lectures to 100. Avocational courses for beginning to experienced cooks cover a variety of topics and are taught by local professionals. Essentially 100% of applicants are accepted to entry level courses and 100% of graduates who earn a certificate obtain employment.

Professional Cooking consists of nine courses: Principles of Cooking I, Principles of Cooking II, Principles of Cooking III, Advanced Cooking Techniques, Introduction to Pastry & Baking, Introduction to Fine Wine, Sanitation, Safety, Nutrtion and Menu Planning, and Mixology & Bar Management. Students must also participate in a 400-hour externship, where they gain practical, hands-on experience. Catering, which consists of seven required courses and two electives, can be completed in three quarters. Required courses include the first three professional cooking courses, Food Production and Management, Professional Practices in Catering, Event Planning, and The Art and Science of Catering. The student can select electives from 20 different courses and seminars. The Wine certificate program, the only such program affiliated with a major university, consists of three core courses and two electives. The three core courses —Vintage I, II, and III — are devoted to viticulture, enology, history, marketing, economics, and serving of wine and include extensive tasting.

Each quarter, Extension also provides approximately 20 one to ten-session demonstration courses and one-day seminars for cooks of all levels. Topics include culinary tours, guest chef lectures, holiday entertaining, professional food styling, and wine appreciation. A series of three-hour Monday evening workshops emphasize a "quick fix" in such disciplines as bagel making, pasta production, preserving, truffles, and risotto.

Specialties: Certificate programs in Professional Cooking, Catering, Baking, and Fine Wine; a variety of avocational programs, including ethnic and regional cuisines, guest chefs, and wine appreciation.

Faculty: Local restaurant chefs, culinary specialists, and graduates of the CIA and CCA, including CCA graduates Kathryn King, Denise Vivaldo, and Laura Weinman; CIA graduates Greg Gevurtz, Bart Goldberg, David Keith, and Beth Taddeo; corporate event planner Mary Ann Reilly; NRA spokeswoman Terri Woodard-Polster; and two-time finalist, Sommelier of the Year Award, Paul Ellis.

Costs: The nine-course Catering Certificate Program is approximately $3,600, the Professional Cooking courses are $595, other courses range from $45 to $60 per session. Students enrolling in the certificate courses must file an application accompanied by a nonrefundable $75 application fee. Credit card (MasterCard, VISA) registrations accepted. Written cancellations at least three days prior to course receive a full refund, less $75 for certificate courses, $20 for other courses.

Location: Professional classes are taught in West Los Angeles and Santa Monica. Courses for the public are taught in private homes and local facilities.

Contact: Culinary Arts Program, UCLA Extension, 10995 Le Conte Ave., Room 222, Los Angeles, CA 90024-0901; (213) 206-8120.

VALLEY OAKS COOKING SCHOOL
Fetzer Vineyards
Hopland, California

March-July, October

Established in 1991, this school offers Saturday classes (limit 30 students) once a month. The schedule features demonstrations and participation sessions, seminars on wine and food pairing, a tour of Fetzer's bio-dynamic organic garden, where more than 1,000 varieties of produce are grown, a tasting of seasonal produce, and a presentation by a well-known culinarian. Each class is devoted to a different topic, such as soups and stews, seafood, game cookery, Oriental cuisine, and Italian specialties.

Specialties: A variety of topics, with emphasis on fresh produce.

Faculty: Culinary Director John Ash and guest chefs.

Location: In Mendocino County, north of San Francisco.

Contact: Joel Clark, Hospitality Director, Fetzer Valley Oaks Food & Wine Center, P.O. Box 611, Hopland, CA 95449; (707) 744-1250.

WEIR COOKING
San Francisco, California

Year-round

This school, established by Joanne Weir in 1989, offers courses, three and five-day intensives, and an annual culinary tour of San Francisco. Participation courses (limit eight students) are offered in Ms. Weir's specially designed professional kitchen and consist of day (10 am to 2:30 pm) or evening (6 to 10 pm) sessions, concluding with a three or four-course meal. Topics include the classic and provincial cuisines of France, Italy, and other Mediterranean countries as well as regional foods of the U.S., especially California. Three and five-day intensives, geared to out-of-towners, focus on a single country or region. The seven-day, spring or fall San Francisco tour (limit 8) features meals at fine restaurants, private winery tours, and a cooking demonstration at Tante Marie's Cooking School.

Specialties: French, Italian, Mediterranean, and American regional cuisines.

Faculty: Joanne Weir teaches at Tante Marie's Cooking School in San Francisco and was a cook at Alice Water's Chez Panisse restaurant in Berkeley. She studied full-time for a year with Madeleine Kamman, teaches at various locations in the U.S., Canada, New Zealand, and Australia, and is author of *Mediterranean First Courses* (to be published in 1993).

Costs, Accommodations: Tuition ranges from $60 to $80 per day or evening session. Nonrefundable payment for one session must accompany registration, with balance due at first session. Tuition for intensives is $200 for three days, $375 for five. A 50% deposit, half of which is refundable for cancellations more than two weeks prior, must accompany registration. The cost of the San Francisco tour is $1,595, which includes double occupancy lodging in a first class hotel, ground transportation, and all meals. Single supplement is $325. A $350 deposit must accompany reservation with balance due eight weeks prior to departure. Cancellations more than eight weeks prior receive full refund less $50; no refunds thereafter.

Contact: Joanne Weir, Weir Cooking, 2107 Pine St., San Francisco, CA 94115; (415) 776-4200, Fax (415) 924-7939.

YAN CAN INTERNATIONAL COOKING SCHOOL
Foster City, California

Year-round

Founded in 1985 by Martin Yan, host of the "Yan Can Cook" television show, this school offers approximately 20 individual demonstration and participation classes per quarter. The $2\frac{1}{2}$ to 5-hour classes, which usually start at 10 am or 7 pm and average 18 participants, cover Chinese cuisine and a variety of culinary topics. Facilities include two full kitchens, an overhead mirror, and counter space for hands-on sessions. Every month Martin Yan conducts a San Francisco Chinatown Walking Tour, which includes a dim sum lunch. Other walking tours visit Asian and ethnic markets in Oakland and East Bay public markets.

Specialties: Chinese and ethnic cuisines and a variety of culinary topics.

Faculty: The more than 15-member faculty includes Martin Yan, sausage maker Bruce Aidells, caterer Peggy Fallon, and cookbook authors and *San Francisco Chronicle* columnists, including Flo Braker, Jay Harlow, and Joyce Jue. Guest chefs have included Jacques Pepin and former White House chef René Verdon.

Costs: The $2\frac{1}{2}$ to 3-hour classes range from $35 to $50; 4 to 5-hour sessions and celebrity chef classes range from $45 to $75. Credit card (VISA, MasterCard) registrations accepted. For most classes, cancellations more than 48 hours prior receive a full refund. Spouse programs and private classes may be arranged.

Location: Ten minutes from the San Francisco airport and 25 miles south of San Francisco on Route 92/101.

Contact: Susan Yan, School Director, Yan Can International Cooking School, Charter Square, 1064 G Shell Blvd., Foster City, CA 94404; (415) 574-7788.

COLORADO

ALTAMIRA TOURS—FOODS OF SPAIN (page 232)

COOKING SCHOOL OF THE ROCKIES
Boulder, Colorado

Year-round

Established in 1991, this school for home cooks offers primarily participation (limit 10 students) as well as demonstration (limit 30) courses in French techniques, pastry, baking, nutrition, and Mediterranean cuisines. The emphasis is on creativity, organization, and presentation, and each session culminates with a four-course meal. French Techniques I and II, both five-session courses, meet for five hours once a week. The school also offers classes in pastry, baking, and bread making and schedules summer week-long intensives for out-of-towners. Classes are held in a new, specially-designed 2,000-square-foot facility.

Specialties: French culinary and pastry techniques; guest chefs; Italian cookery.

Faculty: Director and teacher Joan Brett participated in the professional program at Peter Kump's New York Cooking School, apprenticed with Chef Boris Bless at the small Wonder Cafe in Boulder, studied with Julia Child and Jacques Pépin, and is a member of the IACP. Pastry chef and teacher Mary Copeland is a graduate of the Culinary Arts program of the Cordon Bleu Cookery School in London.

Costs: The Techniques courses are $295 each, demonstrations range from $25 to $60. Nonrefundable deposits range from $25 to $100; balance due at first session.

Location: In the foothills of the Rocky Mountains, 25 miles northwest of Denver.

Contact: Joan Brett, Cooking School of the Rockies, 637H S. Broadway, Boulder, CO 80303; (303) 494-7988.

LA CUCINA AL FOCOLARE (page 212)

HEALY-LUCULLUS SCHOOL OF FRENCH COOKING
Boulder, Colorado

Irregularly throughout the year

This school, which was founded in New Haven, Connecticut, in 1978 and moved to Boulder in 1980, offers intensive, five-day Nouvelle Pâtisserie workshops for food professionals and gourmet cooks. These full-participation master classes are limited to five students, who meet for six hours daily in the school's professionally-equipped teaching kitchen. Using classic techniques and theory as background, students examine modern trends and techniques. Emphasis is on fillings and mousses; simplified methods of assembling and decorating gâteaux and charlottes; jellyrolls, multilayered cakes, and cheesecakes; and the use of chocolate, fruits, and caramelization in the presentation of desserts.

Specialties: French pastries.

Faculty: Bruce Healy holds a Ph.D. in theoretical physics from the Rockefeller University, trained in French pastry at Pâtisserie Clichy in Paris, and co-authored

Mastering the Art of French Pastry. He is a member of the Confédération Nationale des Pâtissiers, Glaciers, et Confiseurs de France.

Costs, Accommodations: Cost for the five-day workshop is $695, which includes all instruction and materials and light lunch each day. A $125 nonrefundable deposit is required with application and balance due four weeks prior to workshop. No refunds are granted unless space can be filled. The school can assist students in finding accommodations.

Location: Boulder is 30 miles northwest of Denver and a one-hour drive from the Rocky Mountain National Park.

Contact: Bruce Healy, Healy-Lucullus School of French Cooking, 840 Cypress Drive, Boulder, CO 80303; (303) 494-9222.

CONNECTICUT

CONNECTICUT CULINARY INSTITUTE (CCI)
Farmington, Connecticut

Year-round

This year-round private cooking school, founded in 1988 and certified by the Connecticut Department of Education, offers day and evening 360-hour professional training programs, career advancement courses for professional cooks, and a wide variety of courses for beginning to experienced home cooks. Courses are taught in the school's custom-built, 4,500-square-foot facility, which houses two modern, fully-equipped kitchen-classrooms, a student lounge, and gourmet deli. The school also offers its 12-week Professional Training Program at a modern, fully-equipped facility in downtown New Haven. CCI designs cooking courses to accommodate tour, social, and professional groups and also offers a gourmet foods catering service.

The professional training program emphasizes the preparation of fine international cuisine. Day courses start in September, January, March, and June and students attend classes for 12 weeks, from 10 am to 3 pm, Monday through Friday. Evening courses start in September and February and students attend classes for 20 weeks, from 6 to 11 pm, three evenings a week. Home assignments and extracurricular research are required. Class size is limited to 14 students, who practice planning and preparing daily menus and study and participate in all aspects of fine food preparation. The curriculum includes kitchen organization, food identification and purchasing, vegetable, poultry, fish and seafood cookery, meat butchery and cookery, soups and sauces, salads and cold foods, eggs, baking and pastry, catering, and buffets. Graduates receive assistance in obtaining employment and about 92% find jobs. Career advancement courses, which are designed for food service professionals, are coordinated on a group basis and include sanitary food handling, low cholesterol cooking, profiting from party pleasers, wine service instruction, and such basic topics as sautéing, braising, and poaching. These programs can be customized to fit specific training goals and can be held at the food service location, if desired.

Approximately 15 to 20 one to ten-session demonstration (limit 40 students) and participation (limit 12) courses for nonprofessional cooks are scheduled each month. A variety of topics are covered, including ethnic and regional cuisines, nutritional foods, seasonal and party menus, three five-day (15-hour) intensive courses in the techniques of French cuisine, and three ten-session courses in wine appreciation. Sessions range from 2 to 5 1/2 hours and are scheduled at 10 am, 2 pm and 6:30 pm. Classes for children, ages eight and over, are also offered. Most classes conclude with tastings or a complete meal. The school also schedules open houses and other special cooking events throughout the year.

Specialties: Professional 360-hour culinary training program; continuing education courses for professional cooks; courses for nonprofessionals covering such topics as ethnic and regional cuisines, nutritional foods, seasonal and party foods, wine appreciation; classes for children.

Faculty: In addition to administrative personnel, the CCI has 25 part-time chef/instructors, a director of education, staff instructors, a registrar, group coordinators, and educational supervisors. Tad Graham-Handley is the school's general manager and Leslie Hickey is manager of the Professional Training Program.

Costs: Tuition for the 360-hour professional program is $5,300 plus $345 for materials and a $100 nonrefundable fee, which must accompany application. A $750 deposit is due within 10 days of acceptance, a $2,500 payment is due 30 days prior to class, and balance is due one week prior. Students who are accepted and cancel within three days of submitting tuition deposit and enrollment agreement receive a full refund of deposit. Penalty charge for withdrawal ranges from 10% of tuition for those who cancel during the first week to 100% of tuition for those who cancel after the sixth week. Financial aid is available to eligible students. Applicants must have a high school diploma or equivalent and pass a CCI interview. Continuing education classes range from $75 to $95 per session, with special group rates, and nonprofessional classes range from $25 to $55 per session. The five-day courses in Fine Techniques of Cooking are $325 each. Credit card (VISA, MasterCard) registrations are accepted. Full payment is required to hold a place and is nonrefundable but transferable to another course or person if written notice is received at least 10 days prior to class.

Location: A suburban location in the Farmington Valley, 10 miles west of Hartford off Interstate 84, Exit 39 on Route 4; and downtown New Haven, a block from the New Haven Green and near Yale University.

Contact: Connecticut Culinary Institute, Loehmann's Plaza, 230 Farmington Ave., Farmington, CT 06032; (203) 677-7869.

HAY DAY COOKING SCHOOL
Greenwich and Ridgefield, Connecticut

Year-round

This country farm market and year-round cooking school, established in 1984, offers approximately 40 demonstration (limit 40 students) and participation (limit 15) classes annually on a variety of topics. The three-hour sessions begin at 7 pm and conclude with serving of the foods prepared accompanied by wine. Facilities include a well-equipped professional kitchen and demonstration area with overhead mirror.

Specialties: A variety of topics, including ethnic and regional cuisines, guest chef and restaurant specialties, nutritional cooking, breadmaking and baking.

Faculty: Has included well-known culinary personalities Giuliano Bugialli, Nathalie Dupree, Larry Forgione, Marcella Hazan, Nicholas Malgieri, Wolfgang Puck, Anne Rosenzweig, and Patricia Wells. The school is a Certified Member of the IACP and an active member of the AIWF.

Costs: Classes range from $40 to $75. Major credit cards are accepted. Refund granted cancellations at least two weeks prior; thereafter a substitute may be sent.

Location: The Riverside section of Greenwich, a 45-minute drive from New York City, and Old Main St. in Ridgefield, a 70-minute drive.

Contact: Hay Day, Inc., 1071 Post Rd. East, Westport, CT; 06880 (203) 221-0100.

RONNIE FEIN SCHOOL OF CREATIVE COOKING
Stamford, Connecticut

Spring and fall

Ronnie Fein has taught both demonstration and participation classes (limit 10 students) since 1970. Sessions, which emphasize an understanding of ingredients and techniques to encourage creativity, are scheduled at 10 am and 7:30 pm in her fully-equipped home teaching kitchen. Approximately 15 to 20 different 2½-hour classes are offered each season and private instruction is available year-round.

Specialties: A variety of topics, including ethnic and regional cuisines, holiday and entertaining menus, food gifts, and guest chef specialties.

Faculty: Ronnie Fein is a freelance writer for food publications and has a weekly food column in the *New Canaan Advertiser*, *Stamford Advocate*, and *Greenwich Time*. She conducts cooking demonstrations, tests kitchen equipment, is a free lance writer for food-related publications, has hosted a radio talk show about cooking, and served as a cooking contest judge.

Costs: Classes range from $45 to $50. Full refund granted cancellations at least 48 hours prior to class; class credit thereafter.

Location: The Ridges section of North Stamford, about a 15-minute drive from Stamford Town Center.

Contact: Ronnie Fein School of Creative Cooking, 438 Hunting Ridge Rd., Stamford, CT 06903; (203) 322-7114.

THE SILO COOKING SCHOOL
New Milford, Connecticut

March-December

Founded in 1972 by former restaurateur Ruth Henderson and her husband, New York Pops founder and music director Skitch, this country kitchen and gourmet foods store, art gallery, and cooking school each year offers more than 70 three to four-hour classes and several two to four-session courses. Housed in a former cattle barn with twin silos and designed to preserve the barn-like ambience, The Silo, which is a member of the IACP, has a well-equipped teaching kitchen with exposed beams and high ceilings. The demonstration (limit 30 to 35 students) and participation (limit 14) sessions are scheduled mornings, afternoons, and evenings and cover a variety of topics. The school also offers more than a dozen classes for 6 to 14 year olds and sponsors a five-day summer cooking camp for children ages eight and older. Custom group classes are available and can be designed teach a favorite food or to celebrate a special occcasion.

Specialties: A variety of topics, including ethnic and regional cuisines, holiday and entertaining menus, baking, breadmaking, master and restaurant chef and cookbook author specialties; wine selection; children's classes.

Faculty: Has included well-known chefs Giuliano Bugialli, Skitch Henderson, Madeleine Kamman, Albert Kumin, Lydie Marshall, Lorenza de' Medici, Jacques Pepin, Richard Sax; restaurant chefs Christopher Idone, Christopher Pardue; cookbook authors Rose Levy Beranbaum, Diana Kennedy, Karen Lee, Sheila Lukins, Perla Meyers, Julie Sahni; magazine columnist David Rosengarten.

Costs: Approximately $75 to $85 for master chef classes, $45 to $75 for other classes. Payment must accompany application and refund or transfer is granted cancellations at least 14 days prior to class. No refund or transfer thereafter. Credit card (VISA, MasterCard, American Express) registration accepted.

Location: Eighty miles from New York City on the Henderson's 200-acre Hunt Hill Farm in the Litchfield Hills of northwestern Connecticut, an area known for its historic houses and museums, antique shops, galleries, inns, recreational facilities, and resorts.

Contact: Sandra Daniels, Director, Silo Cooking School, Upland Rd., New Milford, CT 06776; (203) 355-0300.

DISTRICT OF COLUMBIA

PARIS COOKS
Washington, D.C.

October-April

Elizabeth Esterling has taught intermediate and advanced French cuisine since 1976. The five 2^1/2-hour session demonstration and participation courses, limited to four or five students, stress easy, elegant, do-ahead menus and conclude with a meal of foods prepared. Facilities consist of a small kitchen with seating for four to five students.

Specialties: French cuisine; food processor and microwave techniques; special subjects as requested.

Faculty: Elizabeth Esterling holds a degree from La Varenne and is Chevalier du Tastevin, Clos Vougeot. She has written the bilingual *Le Cookbook* and contributed to *Small Feasts and Simple Feasts*.

Costs: Five 2^1/2-hour lessons are $150.

Contact: Elizabeth Esterling, Paris Cooks, 1619 34th St., N.W., Washington, DC 20007; (202) 333-4451.

TASTE OF ITALY (page 222)

LA VARENNE (page 200)

FLORIDA

ARIANA'S COOKING SCHOOL
Miami, Florida
Year-round

Founded in 1976, this gourmet cookware store and school offers more than 50 demonstration and participation (limit 28 students) classes each quarter with varying seasonal and holiday themes, as well as guest chef events and sessions for children. Free demonstrations, scheduled at 2 pm on Saturdays, feature such topics as microwave cooking, soufflés, dressings, and salads. Three-hour morning (10 am) and evening (7 pm) classes cover a variety of topics. Once a month or so a guest master chef presents a two or four-session morning and evening workshop and local chefs and caterers teach their restaurant specialties. Classes for singles and couples are also scheduled and two-hour Saturday morning classes for youngsters, ages 10 to 14, cover foods, equipment, recipe-reading techniques, and safety. Birthday party and bridal shower classes are available. The teaching facility is an enclosed 400-square-foot kitchen with ample island space, overhead mirror, and double appliances.

Specialties: A variety of topics, including ethnic and regional cuisines, seasonal and holiday menus, desserts, wine appreciation, guest chef specialties, nutritious foods; children's classes.

Faculty: The more than 15-member faculty includes cooking teachers and food specialists Wendy Kallergis, Carole Kotkin, and Ariana Kumpis; caterers Mark Gibson and Mario Martinez; Claire Griffin, *Gourmet Magazine* columnist Sarah Benson, Ann Chassen, baker Lucila Venet de Jimenez, Tania Sigal, and Dexter Tom. Well-known guest chefs include Giuliano Bugialli, Nicholas Malgieri, Jacques Pépin, and chefs from fine South Florida restaurants.

Costs: Classes are $25 to $40; guest chef programs range from $50 to $100 for a two-session course to $300 for a four-session series and students may sign up for a single class on a space available basis. Payment must accompany application and full refund is granted cancellations at least five days prior to class; class credit is issued thereafter. Credit card (VISA, MasterCard) registrations accepted.

Location: In South Miami near the University of Miami.

Contact: Ariana M. Kumpis, Ariana's Cooking School, 7251 S.W. 57th Ct., Miami, FL 33143; (305) 667-5957.

CAPTIVA COOKING SCHOOL
South Seas Plantation Resort & Yacht Harbour
Captiva Island, Florida

Since 1988, this resort has conducted cooking school weekends that combine instruction, demonstration, and hands-on experience, culminating in a seven-course dinner on Saturday evening. The four-day (Thursday evening to Sunday afternoon) courses, offered twice a year, include Florida Seafood Sensations Cooking School, which covers how to buy, clean, cook, and sauce seafood; and Holiday Cooking School, which focuses on food for entertaining, pies, pastries, and other desserts. Food decoration and presentation are also emphasized. The weekend begins with a Meet the Chef reception and concludes with a Sunday graduation brunch.

Specialties: Florida seafood, menus for holidays and entertaining.

Faculty: Guest chefs have included television weatherman Willard Scott, author of *The Willard Scott Great American Cookbook.*

Costs, Accommodations: Rates are $366 to $570 per person, double occupancy, with accommodations ranging from a hotel room to a two-bedroom Land's End Village unit. Included are an opening reception, continental breakfast, two dinners, and Sunday brunch. Each student receives a chef's hat, apron, and recipe book. Full payment must accompany reservation and full refund is granted cancellations at least seven days prior.

Location: The 330-acre South Seas Plantation Resort & Yacht Harbour is situated on Captiva Island, off Florida's southwest coast. Resort amenities include tennis, golf, boating, swimming, and fishing.

Contact: Your travel agent *or*: (800) 237-3102, (800) 282-3402 in Florida, *or* (813) 472-5111.

CHARLOTTE ANN ALBERTSON'S COOKING SCHOOL (page 104)

CHEF ALLEN'S
North Miami Beach, Florida

Spring, summer, fall

Since 1986, Chef Allen Susser has been teaching personalized, one-on-one classes at his popular, 103-seat restaurant, which specializes in regional American and South Florida cuisine. The demonstration and participation session usually lasts four to five hours, beginning at 3 pm and concluding at 7 or 8 pm with the student working along with the kitchen staff. Topics include food quality and selection, preparation of fresh fish, seafood, and produce, breadmaking, pastries, and soufflés. The student may also assist in composing the menu for the day and have a daily special named after him or her. Arrangements can be made for group classes and a newsletter is available.

Specialties: Personalized to the student's needs and interests, with emphasis on Florida's fresh fish and tropical produce.

Faculty: Chef Allen Susser is a graduate of Florida International University's School of Hospitality and Restaurant Management and a professor on the faculty. He studied classical French cuisine at Le Cordon Bleu and served as chef at the Bristol Hotel in Paris and Le Cirque in New York prior to opening his restaurant.

Costs: An individual session is $195. Reservations should be made three weeks in advance.

Location: In North Miami Beach, one block east of Biscayne Boulevard.

Contact: Chef Allen Susser, Chef Allen's, 19088 N.E. 29th Ave., N. Miami Beach, FL 33180; (305) 935-2900.

COOKING WITH STEVEN RAICHLEN (page 68)

CUISINE CLASSICS COOKING SCHOOL
Sarasota, Florida

June

Established in 1974 by Sally Fine, this school offers about a half dozen three-session courses each summer in international and regional cuisines. The demonstration (limit 10 students) and participation (limit 6) classes meet in a large, professionally-equipped home kitchen from 10 am to 2 pm on Tuesdays or Fridays and include a seated lunch.

Specialties: Classic French, Italian, international, and new American.

Faculty: IACP-Certified Food Writer Sally Fine.

Costs: $50 for participation classes, $35 for demonstrations.

Location: Sarasota is on Florida's west coast, 50 miles south of Tampa and 100 miles west of Disney World.

Contact: Sally Fine, Cuisine Classics Cooking School, 401 Burns Ct., Sarasota, FL 34236; (813) 349-7626.

FLORIDA CULINARY INSTITUTE
New England Institute of Technology at Palm Beach
West Palm Beach, Florida

Year-round

Established in 1982 and accredited by the ACFEI and CCA (NATTS), the Florida Culinary Institute offers Specialized Associate Degrees in the Culinary Arts and International Baking as well as various short courses for both professional and nonprofessional cooks. Students are admitted every quarter to this full-time program, which consists of six 11-week quarters that are normally completed in 18 months. Instruction is split between classroom theory presentation and practical application in the specially designed teaching kitchens that simulate modern commercial kitchens. Total enrollment is approximately 400 students, with a student to teacher ratio of 18 to 1. The school offers job placement assistance and 95% of students obtain employment upon graduation.

The first quarter, Introduction to Culinary Arts, focuses on cooking basics, sanitation, terminology, and the preparation of breakfast items, salads, stocks, soups, and sauces. The second quarter, Cooking, covers meat and poultry, complicated menu procedures, starches and vegetables, and the purchase, storage, and preparation of fish and shellfish. In the third quarter, International and Classical Cooking, students learn to prepare the cuisines of Spain, the Middle East, Asia, Latin America, France, Italy, and Germany. The fourth quarter, Garde Manger, is devoted to cold foods, including sauces, salads and dressings, pâtes, galantines, mousses, and the design and presentation of cold food platters. Artistic creations, such as tallow and salt dough sculptures and edible and inedible centerpieces, are also taught. In the fifth quarter, Baking, students learn the theory and practical techniques of bread, pastry, and cake preparation and receive extensive hands-on experience in decorating pastries and cakes. The sixth quarter,

Culinary Arts, presents concepts in table service, nutrition, wine appreciation, hospitality management, facilities planning, and menu design.

Specialties: Full-time 18-month programs leading to Specialized Associate Degrees in Culinary Arts and International Baking.

Faculty: Sixteen instructors, who are ACF-Certified with have B.A. and/or Associate Degrees, and a 10-member support staff.

Costs: Annual tuition is $13,050. High school diploma or equivalent and admission test are required and 87% of applicants are accepted. Financial aid and scholarships are available.

Contact: Florida Culinary Institute, 1126 53rd Court and Australian Ave., W. Palm Beach, FL 33407-9985; (800) 826-9986 *or* (407) 842-8324.

HARRIET'S KITCHEN WHOLE FOODS COOKING SCHOOL
Winter Park, Florida

September-June

Established in 1987, this school offers 30 to 35 classes each quarter in healing macrobiotic and gourmet vegetarian cuisines featuring whole grains, fresh vegetables and fruits, and simple proteins (no dairy or sugar). The two to four-hour sessions are held mornings, afternoons, and evenings in a 500-square-foot teaching kitchen and include the nine-session Healing Macrobiotic Series, the four-session 60-Minute Healthy Gourmet series, and individual classes on such topics as bread making, pasta, fish cookery, desserts, and regional recipes. Both demonstration (limit 35 students) and participation (limit 16) classes are offered and all sessions include a meal of the foods prepared. Weekend Art of Life Intensives at a "naturally oriented" bed and breakfast are geared to facilitating a lifestyle change. The school plans to offer week-long programs, which will include visits to Walt Disney World, Sea World and Universal Studios.

Specialties: Macrobiotic and whole food cookery.

Faculty: Director Harriet McNear, a Kushi certified teacher and licensed nutrition counselor, studied at the Kushi Institute and the Natural Gourmet Cookery School. Other faculty includes Kushi certified senior teacher and counselor Wendy Esko, macrobiotic cookbook author Meredith McCarty, and area chefs Tim Rosendahl of Walt Disney World, David Yates of Sheraton World, and Mark Rodriguez and Clair Epting of Jordon's Grove.

Costs: Individual classes range from $20 to $40, the nine-session course is $180, and the weekend intensive is $500. A 50% deposit is required with balance due at class. Full refund is granted cancellations at least five days prior. Spouses may attend at a 30% discount; cost of meal only is $10. Work-study and assistantship positions are available.

Location: Central Florida, near Walt Disney World.

Contact: Harriet's Kitchen, 1136 Oaks Blvd., Winter Park, FL 32789; (407) 644-2167.

JOHNSON & WALES UNIVERSITY (page 111)

THE SOUTHEAST INSTITUTE OF CULINARY ARTS (SICA)
St. Augustine Technical Center
St. Augustine, Florida

Year-round

Established in 1970 and accredited by the ACFEI and the Southern Association of Colleges and Schools, this school offers one-year (1,080 hours) Certificate and two-year (2,160 hours) Diploma programs in Commercial Foods and Culinary Arts. Several Specialized Certificates can be earned for completion of portions of the course outline. Students are admitted to the full-time day program every nine weeks, beginning the last week in August; short-term and part-time morning courses begin at specific times. Total enrollment is 719 and the student to teacher ratio is 15 to 1. The job placement service obtains employment for 85% of graduates, who can also enroll in the Daytona Beach Community College Hospitality Management Program and earn up to 30 college credits toward an A.S. degree. Apprenticeship and cooperative education programs are available for those who wish to earn money while they're enrolled.

The curriculum blends classroom theory with practical experience in basic areas that introduce students to the profession and help them determine their strengths. After rotating through each area, the student may then participate in intensified courses in a specific topic. In addition to the core courses on sanitation, terminology, nutrition, and computer literacy, the curriculum covers pantry items (sandwiches, salads, dressings, and relishes), breakfast, fast foods, cafeteria foods, continental foods (American, classical, and international cuisines), table service (dining room and front-of-house operations), epicurean service (tableside preparation), cold buffet (vegetable and fruit carvings, ice and tallow sculptures), bakeshop, pastry shop, and purchasing and receiving. A nine-week externship completes the diploma program.

Specialties: One-year Certificate and two-year Diploma programs in Commercial Foods and Culinary Arts.

Faculty: Twenty-three instructors, all of whom are ACF-Certified, and three laboratory assistants.

Costs: Annual tuition (full-time) is $800 for in-state students, $1,600 for out-of-state students. Nonrefundable registration fee is $15 and annual book deposit fee is $50. Full refund is granted applicants who have not attended a class and send a written request within 30 days of application. Applicants must be at least 16 years of age. Financial aid and scholarships are available.

Location: St. Augustine, the nation's oldest city and home of the American Culinary Federation, is situated on Florida's northeast coast.

Contact: Chef Harold Holanchock CEC, CCE, The Southeast Institute of Culinary Arts, 2980 Collins Ave. at Del Monte Dr., St. Augustine, FL 32095-9970; (904) 824-4401, ext. 291 *or* (904) 824-8128.

GEORGIA

DIANE WILKINSON
Atlanta, Georgia

Diane Wilkinson has taught cooking since 1974 and has escorted European culinary travel excursions since 1977. Her mostly demonstration one to five-session courses are limited to eight students and cover a variety of topics. Sessions usually last from three to four hours and are scheduled at various times throughout the day. A five-day intensive techniques course meets from 10 am until 6 pm, Monday through Friday, with a 90-minute mid-day break. Each day's session is equally divided between demonstration and participation and the course concludes with the awarding of certificates at the graduation dinner.

Specialties: A variety of topics, including seasonal foods, French cuisine, wine appreciation, and guest chef specialties.

Faculty: Diane Wilkinson studied at the Paris Cordon Bleu, with Marcella Hazan, has spent time in various kitchens in France and Italy, and is certified by the IACP. Guest chefs have included food scientist Shirley Corriher.

Costs: Individual classes are $45, five sessions are $225, and the five-day intensive is $425.

Contact: Diane Wilkinson, 4365 Harris Trail, Atlanta, GA 30327; (404) 233-0366.

KITCHEN FARE COOKING SCHOOL
Atlanta, Georgia

Year-round

This year-round school for nonprofessional cooks, founded in 1983, offers demonstration classes four evenings a week in its large, home-style kitchen. The 2 to 2¹/₂-hour sessions begin at 7 or 7:30 pm and are limited to 25 students.

Specialties: A variety of topics, including ethnic and regional cuisines, recipes for entertaining, and desserts.

Faculty: Revolving staff of local chefs and professionals.

Costs: Each class is $20. Cancellations prior to noon on the day before class receive class or store credit. No cash refunds. Credit card registrations (VISA, MasterCard) accepted.

Contact: Kitchen Fare, 2385 Peachtree Rd., NE, Atlanta, GA 30305; (404) 233-8849.

URSULA'S COOKING SCHOOL, INC.
Atlanta, Georgia

January-May, September-November

This school, founded in 1966 by Ursula Knaeusel, offers four-session demonstration courses (limit 38 students) in international cooking. The three-hour sessions, which emphasize timesaving methods and advance preparation, meet every other week and can be taken any day, Monday through Thursday, at either 10 am or 6:30 pm. Three courses are scheduled each year from January through March, April through May, and September through November. Classes are held in a three-level classroom designed around Ursula's overhead mirrored teaching kitchen. Children's and holiday classes are also offered and Ursula has a catering service and operates The Oak Tree House for special occasions and parties.

Specialties: International cuisine.

Faculty: Ursula Knaeusel has over 35 years of professional experience. She has supervised kitchens, managed guest houses, operated restaurants in Europe and the U.S., and taught cooking in Central America and the Caribbean.

Costs: Tuition is $75 for the four-session course. Refunds are granted cancellations made prior to course.

Location: A mile from Interstate 75 and 85, four miles from downtown Atlanta.

Contact: Ursula, Ursula's Cooking School, Inc., 1764 Cheshire Bridge Rd., N.E., Atlanta, GA 30324; (404) 876-7463.

HAWAII

CUISINES OF THE SUN
The Mauna Lani Bay Hotel and Bungalows
Kohala Coast, Island of Hawaii

Mid-July

This annual five-day program, first held in 1990 and limited to 175 participants, offers cooking demonstrations, tastings, and wine seminars with emphasis on the ingredients, histories, and similarities and differences of equatorial cuisines. Each year the focus moves westward, from Southwestern, California, and Hawaiian cuisines in 1990, to the foods of the Pacific Rim, Thailand, and Hong Kong in 1991, to specialties of the South of France in 1992, to "flavors from four worlds" (Hawaii, Caribbean, Bali, and Sicily or Sardinia) in 1993. The program begins with a Saturday evening reception and buffet featuring the cuisine of each participating chef. Cooking demonstrations and tastings and wine and beer tastings are held on Sunday and Monday mornings and afternoons and Tuesday morning. The event concludes with a Tuesday evening farewell dinner and dancing.

Specialties: Cuisines of the hot islands.

Faculty: Noted chefs from Los Angeles, New York City, and the islands featured. Alan Wong of the Mauna Lani Bay Hotel.

Costs, Accommodations: The program cost of approximately $600 includes planned activities, receptions and some meals; a special four-night room rate beginning at $800 is available to program participants.

Location: The big island of Hawaii.

Contact: Catering Dept., Cuisines of the Sun, The Mauna Lani Bay Hotel and Bungalows, P.O. Box 4000, Kohala Coast, Hawaii, 96734-4000; (800) 367-2323 or (808) 885-6622.

ILLINOIS

CHARIE'S KITCHEN AT BEAUTIFUL FOOD
Glenview, Illinois

January-March and September-November

Since 1973, Charie MacDonald has offered cooking instruction that emphasizes fresh foods and basic techniques. She now teaches approximately 20 three-hour participation classes a year with each class limited to 20 students. Sessions are conducted in the 2,800-square-foot commercial kitchen of Beautiful Food, Ms. MacDonald's catering and wholesale specialty food business. A two-week tour to Provence, France is scheduled during the spring.

Specialties: A variety of topics, including breads, pastas, pastries, soups, and low-cholesterol foods.

Faculty: Charie MacDonald studied at Le Cordon Bleu, the Ecole des Trois Gourmands (Provence), and with Simone Beck. A charter member of the IACP, she founded Beautiful Food in 1982.

Costs: Class fee is $40, payable by cash in advance.

Location: Glenview is northwest of Chicago, near O'Hare International Airport.

Contact: Beautiful Food, 1872 John's Dr., Glenview, IL 60025; (708) 657-8403.

CHEZ MADELAINE
Hinsdale, Illinois

Fall, winter, spring

Founded in 1977, this school offers approximately 50 demonstration and participation classes annually. The four to five-hour sessions, each limited to six students and held in a private kitchen, begin at 10 am and include an hour for lunch to sample the meal that has been prepared.

Specialties: A variety of topics, including ethnic cuisines, seasonal and holiday menus, preserving, soups and stocks, baking, and a series for beginners.

Faculty: Owner-teacher Madelaine Bullwinkel received the Diplome from L'Academie de Cuisine in Bethesda, is author of *Gourmet Preserves, Chez Madelaine,* and is a member of Les Dames d'Escoffier and the AIWF. She publishes a bimonthly newsletter, *Madelaine's Kitchen Secrets.*

Costs: Range from $50 to $65. Payment must accompany application and credit or refund is granted if space can be filled.

Location: Hinsdale is located 20 miles west of Chicago.

Contact: Madelaine Bullwinkel, Chez Madelaine Cooking School, 211 N. Washington St., Hinsdale, IL 60521; (312) 325-4177.

CLEA'S CASTLE COOKING SCHOOL
Chicago, Illinois

Year-round

Established in 1974, this school offers twelve-session courses in International Cuisine, two-session courses in Special Ice Carving, and five-session courses in

Cake Decorating (buttercream flowers, filigree, needle work, borders, all-occasion cakes), Advanced Cake Decorating (foreign methods with royal icing, flowers on wires, gum paste, rolled fondant, wedding cakes), Baking (genoise, sponge, chocolate, and white wedding cakes, frostings), Advanced Baking (cookies, tortes, mousses, petit fours), Buffet Catering (appetizers, dips, salads, mousses, pates, carved fruits and vegetables), Advanced Buffet Catering (galantines, molded and complex items, centerpieces, dessert buffets), and Gum Paste. The International Cuisine course covers French, Arabic, German, Italian, Polish, Spanish, Mediterranean, American, and Creole specialties. Classes meet weekly for four hours and conclude with a meal. The five-session courses meet weekly from 9 am to 3 pm and the two-session ice carving course meets weekly from 6 to 10 pm. A 30-hour Supervisory Development and Nutrition course is also offered as well as a five-session Sanitation and Safety course for state certification.

Specialties: Baking, cake decorating, buffet catering, ice carving, international cuisine; sanitation, safety, and other aspects of restaurant management.

Faculty: Cleatis V. Wilcox, CCE, CEPC, CWC, AAC, is a member of the Escoffier Society and the Professional Pastry Guild. Other instructors include gum paste expert Bernice Oliveres and medal-winning ice carver Jose Luna, CEC.

Costs: Costs are $125 for the baking, decorating, catering, and ice carving courses; $200 for the cuisine and gum paste courses; and $135 for the sanitation and safety and supervisory courses. Tools and supplies are additional.

Contact: Clea's Castle Cooking School, 1201 Fair Oaks Ave., Oak Park, Illinois 60302; (708) 383-8245, (708) 848-1161, or (312) 889-6320, Fax (708) 848-8580.

THE COOKING AND HOSPITALITY INSTITUTE OF CHICAGO (CHIC)
Chicago, Illinois
Year-round

Established in 1983 and accredited by the CCA (NATTS), CHIC offers a two-year associate degree in culinary arts and certificate programs in professional cooking, baking and pastry, restaurant management, and beverage management as well as various culinary classes for nonprofessional, professional, and aspiring chefs and bakers. Total enrollment is 700 students per year and student to teacher ratio is 20 to 1. Approximately 80% of applicants are accepted and the school's placement service obtains employment for 95% of the graduates.

The 600-hour certificate program in professional cooking is devoted to qualitative and quantitative cooking and development of technical proficiency. The focus in the latter portion of the course shifts to quantity food preparation and involvement with the school's on-site restaurant. Curriculum covers poultry, meat, fish composition and storage, menu planning, ethnic foods, recipe development, sanitation, and job search techniques. Full-time 21-week classes start every six weeks and a part-time one-year program starts three times each year. The 600-hour certificate program in baking and pastry begins with the basic concepts of baking science and techniques of qualitative production. The second half of the program emphasizes using food as an art form and the principles of quantitative cooking. Subjects include yeast breads, puff pastries, pies, tarts, cakes, cookies, soufflés, mousses, decoration, and display. Full-time classes meet Monday through Thursday and part-time classes are held Wednesday evenings and all day Sundays. A 300-hour certificate Restaurant Management program covers Purchasing, Menu and Facility Planning, Accounting, and Supervision.

More than a dozen one or two-session courses for nonprofessionals are offered for 2½ to 3 hours on Saturday afternoons and at 6:30 pm weekdays. Topics include seafood, herbs, and pasta and all-day sessions cover charcuterie and catering. An eight-session demonstration course, Putting It All Together, focuses on different aspects of a six-course meal. At the final session, students prepare the meal and dine on it. Each of the sessions may be taken individually.

Specialties: Associate degree program in culinary arts and professional certificate programs in cooking, baking, pastry, and restaurant management; nonprofessional courses in baking and pastry, preparation of meat, poultry, and fish, and other topics.

Faculty: School founder Linda Calafiore is a past state coordinator of local vocational training programs. Instructors include Mark Facklam, formerly executive chef at Cricket's, and Monique Hooker, formerly of Monique's cafe. Celebrity chefs are occasionally featured.

Costs: Tuition for the two-year (69 credit-hour) degree program is $12,075. Students applying for the certificate courses must submit a $100 registration fee with application. Tuition, which includes registration fee plus books, materials, and insurance, is $4,800 for each certificate program. High school diploma or equivalent is required for admission. The refund policy on certificate programs follows CCA standards. Pell grants and guaranteed student loans are available and information can be obtained from the financial aid officer following completed registration. Costs for the culinary classes and seminars are $300 for the eight-session Putting It All Together course, $125 to $150 for the all-day workshops, and $40 for the evening sessions. Class credit is granted cancellations.

Location: All classes are held at the school in Chicago, in one of two new, fully-equipped instructional kitchens or the on-site restaurant.

Contact: The Cooking and Hospitality Institute of Chicago, 361 W. Chestnut, Chicago, IL 60610; (312) 944-0882.

THE CULINARY SCHOOL OF KENDALL COLLEGE
Evanston, Illinois

Year-round

This division of Kendall College, founded in 1985, offers a 21-month program in culinary arts leading to an Associate in Applied Science degree. The curriculum includes both practical cookery and theory, with emphasis on learning by doing in an apprenticeship environment, to prepare students for positions as cooks or apprentice chefs. A maximum of 40 students are admitted to the program quarterly, in September, January, March, and June. Modern facilities include a demonstration kitchen, a production kitchen, a display kitchen, three professional kitchens, a baking and pastry kitchen, and a dining room and banquet area. Graduates may avail themselves of the services of Kendall College's Office of Career Planning and Placement and 100% obtain employment. The college also offers two and four-year programs in Hospitality Management for those desiring a hospitality career in a restaurant, hotel, or institutional setting. The Culinary School of Kendall College is accredited by the ACFEI and Kendall College is fully accredited by the North Central Association of Colleges and Schools.

The 21-month program consists of six 11-week terms of study and an approved 13-week externship between the third and fourth terms. The course of study involves lecture/demonstration, skill development, and practical application. Students are expected to master certain areas of professional cookery and complete a minimum number of weeks working in the school's cafeteria, a white tablecloth restaurant serving lunch and dinner, a bakery and pastry shop, and a banquet and catering service. During the first three semesters they study professional and culinary skills, stocks and sauces, meat and product identification, sanitation, storeroom and cost control, nutrition, communications, garde manger, management principles, and menu planning. The externship consists of 500 hours of approved salaried employment in the foodservice industry. The final three semesters are devoted to advanced culinary skills, baking, pastries, and desserts, restaurant theory, wines, spirits, and beverage control, garde manger and banquet organization, dining room service, classical cuisine, and facilities planning and advanced cost control. Advanced students work in The Dining Room, the college's open-to-the-public fine dining restaurant. The menu features a contemporary approach to food preparation based on classical cooking techniques with emphasis on the use of fresh and seasonal products.

Specialties: Two-year Associate in Applied Science degree in Culinary Arts, which can become a baccalaureate degree in Hospitality Management with 21 more months of study. Culinary certificates and part-time classes are also available.

Faculty: The professionally trained faculty includes 18 chef/instructors and hospitality specialists as well as visiting lecturers.

Costs, Accommodations: Tuition, which includes instruction, uniforms and laundering, student activities fee, and two meals daily, five days a week, is $10,602 the first year (terms 1-3), $10,620 the second year (terms 4-6). The basic admission requirements are a high school diploma or equivalent and some experience in the foodservice industry. Application must be accompanied by a $30 nonrefundable fee and a $150 nonrefundable tuition deposit is due within 30 days of acceptance. Those who withdraw within the first week of class receive a full refund less $100; those who withdraw during the second week receive a two-thirds refund of tuition less $100; no refunds thereafter. A variety of sources of financial aid are available. Room and board charges are $1,007 per term double room, $1,742 per term single.

Location: In the greater metropolitan Chicago area, 35 minutes from Chicago's Loop by express train, which stops two blocks from the Kendall College campus. The numerous Chicago restaurants provide adjunct instructors and externship opportunities.

Contact: The Culinary School of Kendall College, 2408 Orrington Ave., Evanston, IL 60201; (708) 866-1300.

FOOD FESTS
Hotels and resorts in or near Chicago, Milwaukee, Minneapolis, Phoenix, Pittsburgh, and other locations

Weekends at various times of year

Established by public relations specialist Gail Guggenheim in 1984, Food Fests are cooking school weekend getaways that feature four 90-minute demonstration classes by local chefs and culinary experts, alternating with seminars and tastings. The programs begin on Friday evening and conclude at noon on Sunday. Class topics might include menus for entertaining and at home, a variety of international and regional cuisines, and such new food trends as healthy eating and quick cuisine. Demonstrations are held in the hotel ballroom, which is set up as a complete kitchen with stove, refrigerator, overhead mirrors, and in-house video with monitors. Seminars presented by local producers, writers, and food authorities cover such subjects as using fresh herbs, new food products and equipment, and new cookbooks. All recipes prepared in class are tasted and local food producers provide products for sampling and purchase.

Specialties: A variety of topics, including entertaining and holiday menus, international and regional cuisines, and new food trends.

Faculty: Instructors are well-known area chefs and experienced cooking teachers, usually Certified Members of the IACP.

Costs, Accommodations: Most Food Fests are about $169 to $189 per couple, which includes double occupancy lodging for two nights, continental breakfasts, and all classes and tastings. Refund policy varies with location.

Location: Food Fests have been held at The Kahler Hotel in Rochester, Minnesota (November and March); Inn of the Dells in Wisconsin Dells, Wisconsin (April and November); Sheraton San Marcos Resort in Chandler, Arizona (August); Lakeview Resort in Morgantown, West Virginia (January); Marc Plaza Hotel in Milwaukee, Wisconsin (November and March); and in the Chicago area.

Contact: Food Fests, 125 Country Lane, Highland Park, IL 60035; (708) 831-4265 (to be placed on mailing list, state geographic area of interest), Fax (708) 831-4266.

KITCHEN CONSERVATORY
Belleville, Illinois and St. Louis, Missouri

Year-round

This gourmet shop and school, established in 1984, offers 25 to 30 demonstration and participation classes (limit 16 students) and local day trips quarterly at each of its two locations. The 2½ to 3-hour classes are usually scheduled in the morning or evening and cover a variety of topics. Lunch & Learn sessions are scheduled from noon until 1 pm and two-hour Junior Gourmet classes for 7 to 14-year-olds are held on Saturday mornings. Local tours visit such culinary attractions as the Westerfield House, the St. Louis Italian Hill District, and restaurants and shops in Kimmswick, Missouri.

Specialties: Include ethnic and regional cuisines, appetizers, main courses, desserts, seasonal and entertaining menus, guest chef specialties; local tours; classes for children.

Faculty: Instructors include proprietor Carol Hess, local chefs, executive chefs, restaurateurs, caterers, dietitians, home economists, and members of the IACP. Guest instructors have included Betsy Oppenneer, pastry chef Nicholas Malgieri, Marlene Sorosky, Jude Theriot, Hugh Carpenter, Merle Ellis, Martin Yan, and Joanne Weir.

Costs: Classes range from $20 to $50, Lunch & Learn are $15, and Junior Gourmet sessions are $16. Credit card (VISA, MasterCard, American Express) reservations accepted. Refunds are granted cancellations at least two weeks prior to class.

Location: The Belleville store is 15 minutes from downtown St. Louis; the St. Louis store is minutes from downtown.

Contact: Kitchen Conservatory, Shopland Center, 6930 W. Main St., Belleville, IL 62223; (618) 398-2665. 8021 Clayton Rd., St Louis, MO 63117; (314) 862-2665.

MARIA BATTAGLIA — LA CUCINA ITALIANA (page 217)

ORIENTAL FOOD MARKET & COOKING SCHOOL, INC.
Chicago, Illinois
Year-round

Established in 1971, this market, catering service, and school offers year-round one and six-session demonstration courses (50 students maximum) in Chinese cooking techniques . The one-session courses are held on Saturdays from noon to 2:30 pm and feature such topics as the theory of Chinese cooking, desserts, soups, cold dishes, appetizers, and Japanese, Thai, and Szechuan specialties. The six-session courses are held weekly from 6:30 to 8:30 pm on Wednesdays and cover soups, appetizers, and main dishes in Mandarin, Hunan, Szechuan, and Cantonese cuisines. At the end of class, students dine on the meal prepared.

Specialties: Oriental cooking techniques and nutrition.

Faculty: Pansy and Chu-Yen Luke have operated the market and school since its inception.

Costs: The six-session evening course costs $85, payable in advance with no refunds or makeups, and each Saturday class costs $21.

Contact: Oriental Food Market and Cooking School, 2801 West Howard St., Chicago, IL 60645; (312) 274-2826.

LA VENTURÉ
Skokie, Illinois
November-May

Founded in 1980, this school offers six-session participation courses (limit 10 students) in Chinese, French, and Italian cuisine, basic and advanced candy making, and cake decorating. Chinese cooking courses cover wok and vegetable preparation and other dishes; the French cooking course covers preparation techniques, stocks, sauces, crepes, soufflés, and croissants; typical Italian course recipes are eggplant and veal parmesan, chicken fricassee, pasta, and tortes. The basic candy making course covers dipping techniques, caramels, and fondants; the advanced course features lollipops, truffles, and peanut brittle. The cake decorating courses teach flowers, borders, and decorating and drawing techniques, rings, color flow drawing, and tear cake arrangements.

Specialties: French, Italian, and Chinese cuisines; candy making and cake decorating; baking.

Faculty: Director-owner Sandra Bisceglie attended the French School Dumas Pere and Harrington Institute of Interior Design and has a certificate of completion from the National Institute for the Foodservice Industry.

Costs: The courses in French, Italian, and Chinese cuisine are $189; the candy making and cake decorating courses are $259; baking courses (six classes) are $359. Refund for cancellations if notice is received 10 days prior to class.

Location: Skokie is adjacent to Chicago.

Contact: Sandra Bisceglie, La Venturé, 5100 West Jarlath, Skokie, IL 60077; (708) 679-8845.

WHAT'S COOKING
Hinsdale, Illinois and Locations in the Far East

Established in 1980, this school offers demonstration and participation courses in Asian cooking and conducts culinary tours to the Far East twice each year. Classes are limited to 15 students and cover the cuisines of China, Thailand, Singapore, Malaysia, Indonesia, India, Korea, the Philippines, and Japan. Asian Culinary Adventure, a two-week tour, features cooking classes with professional chefs, gourmet dining, sightseeing, and visits to food markets in Thailand, Singapore, Jakarta, Bali, Indonesia, and India.

Specialties: Asian cuisine; culinary tours to the Far East.

Faculty: School proprietor and instructor Ruth Law, a Certified Member of the IACP, is author of *The Southeast Asia Cookbook* and *Dim Sum—Fast and Festive Chinese Cooking*.

Location: Hinsdale is a suburb of Chicago.

Contact: Ruth Law, What's Cooking, P.O. Box 323, Hinsdale, IL 60522; (708) 986-1595, Fax (708) 655-0912.

WILTON SCHOOL OF CAKE DECORATING AND CONFECTIONARY ART
Woodridge, Illinois

February-November

This school, founded by candy-maker Dewey McKinley Wilton in 1929, offers a variety of career-oriented participation courses in cake decorating and candy making for students with beginning to advanced decorating skills. The Wilton Method stresses creativity and self-expression, efficient workmanship, and perfection of execution through continuous practice. Courses are offered February through November at the school's 2,200-square-foot facility, which includes a classroom, teaching kitchen, student lounge, and retail store. Offerings include The Master Course, Pulled Sugar Course, and Chocolate Artistry. Students with a basic knowledge and skill in cake decorating may enroll in the Lambeth

Continental Course, the Australian Method Course, and Cakes for Catering. Most classes start at 8 am and are conducted on consecutive days with weekends free. Students who complete the courses are awarded a Wilton Diploma.

The 10-day, 70-hour Master Course provides individualized instruction in basic decorating techniques, flowers and borders, painting in icing with color flow, decorating accessories, novelties and sugar molds, figure piping, and cake design. The final preparation is a decorated, tiered wedding cake. Classes are scheduled Monday through Friday from 7:30 am to 2:30 pm. Those enrolled in the Master Course may also enroll in the 4-day, 12-hour Introduction to Gum Paste course and the 3-day, 9-hour Pulled Sugar Course. The Gum Paste Course covers flowers, bouquets, and floral arrangements. The Pulled Sugar Course includes flowers, candy dishes, ribbons, bows, and covering a wedding cake. Both courses meet immediately after the Master Course is finished for the day, from 3 to 6 pm. The 3-day, 15-hour Pulled Sugar Course covers the same material as the 9-hour Pulled Sugar Course, with extra time to work on an individual project. The 5-day, 30-hour Chocolate Artistry course, devoted to making and decorating candy, covers melting, molding, decorating with chocolate, hollow molding, center making, hand dipping, fondant, truffles, and cups. The 5-day, 40-hour Lambeth Continental Course teaches the Old World method of using intricate, dimensional overpiping of borders on royal icing and rolled fondant covered cakes. The Australian Course, which teaches rolled fondant and royal icing lacework and embroidery, can be taken alone as a 5-day, 40-hour course or as a 10-day, 80-hour course along with Advanced Gum Paste and English and South African methods. Cakes for Catering, a 5-day, 40-hour course, covers wedding and other tiered cakes, sheet cakes, large rounds and squares, petit fours, and theme party cakes.

Specialities: Cake decorating and candy-making.

Faculty: The teaching staff includes Sandra Folsom, Susan Matusiak, Amy Rohr, Wesley Wilton, and Elaine Gonzalez, author of *Chocolate Artistry*.

Costs, Accommodations: Tuition ranges from $125 for the 12-hour Introduction to Gum Paste course to $525 for the 10-day courses. A registration fee of $25 to $75 must accompany application and a full refund is granted those who cancel in writing within 14 days of enrollment and more than 14 days prior to course. Those who withdraw after the start of course forfeit their registration fee and tuition refund is prorated. The school brochure lists area motels.

Location: A southwestern suburb about 25 miles from downtown Chicago.

Contact: School Secretary, Wilton School of Cake Decorating and Confectionary Art, 2240 W. 75th St., Woodridge, IL 60517; (708) 963-7100, ext. 211.

INDIANA

COUNTRY KITCHEN
Fort Wayne, Indiana

Year-round

Founded in 1964, this school offers cake decorating courses three times a year and more than 35 two to three-hour classes, both demonstration (limit 60 students) and participation (limit 25), on candies, desserts, and a variety of topics. The eight-session basic, intermediate, and advanced cake decorating courses meet weekly for two hours and cover flowers, borders, bulb and star work, theme painting, clowns, wedding cakes, and airbrush techniques. Demonstration sessions on such topics as desserts, coffee cakes, pies, and brunches meet at various times. The school also offers candy and cake decorating classes for clubs, groups, and children's parties. New facilities include a classroom with tiered work and observation seating.

Specialties: Cake decorating, candy making, desserts, and a variety of topics.

Faculty: More than ten instructors teach the courses.

Costs: The basic and intermediate cake decorating courses are $65 each and the advanced course is $70, which covers all supplies. Demonstrations range from $10 to $30. Full payment must accompany registration and refunds are granted cancellations at least one week prior.

Location: One block from the Children's Zoo and accessible to the Civic Center, Old Fort, and the Botanical Gardens.

Contact: Vi Whittington, Country Kitchen, 3225 Wells St., Fort Wayne, IN 46808; (219) 482-4835.

THE EIGHT MICE COOKING SCHOOL
Lafayette, Indiana
Year-round except January and August

This school, restaurant, wine bar, market, and cookware shop, which began classes in 1975, offers five to ten 2-hour evening and Sunday afternoon sessions monthly. The mostly demonstration sessions (limit 20 students) are held in the shop's mirrored teaching kitchen and cover a variety of topics. Market trips, classes for men and couples, wine tastings, and private parties are also offered.

Specialties: Include ethnic and regional cuisines, menus for holidays and entertaining, appetizers, main courses, desserts, and wine tastings.

Faculty: Director Isabella Williams. Local and visiting chefs are also featured.

Costs: From $15 to $25. Cancellations at least two days prior receive refund.

Location: In Lafayette's Market Square Shopping Center, approximately 60 miles northwest of Indianapolis.

Contact: Isabella Williams, Director, The Eight Mice, Market Square, Lafayette, IN 47904; 317-447-5255.

KITCHEN AFFAIRS
Evansville, Indiana
January-November

Established in 1987, this cookware store and school offers demonstration sessions (limit 15 students) on such topics as basic techniques, gourmet menus, ethnic and regional specialties, appetizers, salads, and desserts. The $2^{1}/_{2}$ to 4-hour sessions are scheduled mornings, afternoons, and evenings and more than 100 different classes are scheduled each year. Classes for children (limit 12) are also offered. Facilities include a 180-square-foot home-style kitchen with front-row counter seating for each student.

Specialties: A variety of topics; classes for children.

Faculty: Restaurant chefs, regional cooks, professional cooking instructors, cookbook authors, and school owners Shelly and Mike Sackett. The school and many of its instructors are members of the IACP.

Costs: Class fees, which must accompany registration, range from $12 to $60. Credit cards are accepted. Cancellations more than 10 days prior receive refund.

Location: Across from Evansville's largest shopping mall.

Contact: Kitchen Affairs, Woodland Center, 4610 Vogel Rd., Evansville, IN 47715; (812) 474-1131.

IOWA

COOKING WITH LIZ CLARK
Keokuk, Iowa

Year-round

This school, opened in 1977, offers year-round demonstration (limit 20 students) and participation (limit 12) classes for home cooks and a five-day intensive technique series (eight hours of instruction each day) in August limited to eight serious cooking enthusiasts. Approximately 10 four-hour classes are offered each quarter, scheduled at various times in Elizabeth Clark's completely renovated antebellum home, which also houses her fine restaurant. A five-day cooking and etiquette course for children ages 10 and up is held during the summer and weekend intensives are offered at various times. College credit is available.

Specialties: A variety of topics, including seasonal and holiday menus and guest chef specialties; children's classes.

Faculty: Liz Clark has studied in Italy and France, received her diploma in the Cours Intensifs from La Varenne, and studied at the Moulin de Mougins with Roger Vergé and at The Oriental in Bangkok. Other instructors include Barbara Kafka, *Chicago Tribune* food writer Bill Rice, and cookbook author Janeen Sarlin.

Costs, Accommodations: Classes are $36 to $60 each, the technique series is $250, and the children's course is $100. Students from out-of-town can be housed overnight for $30. Credit or refund is granted cancellations.

Location: Keokuk is located near the restored Mormon City of Nauvoo, Mark Twain's Hannibal, and Iowa's well-known Amana colonies. Several restored steamboat villages are a short drive away.

Contact: Southeastern Community College; (319) 752-2731, Fax (319) 524-3221, ext. 40.

KANSAS

BARON OF BARBEQUE SCHOOL OF PITMASTERS
Shawnee Mission, Kansas

Year-round

Kansas City's Baron of Barbeque, a purveyor of fine barbecue products, sponsors monthly demonstration/participation courses for cooks (limit 25) of all levels. The four-session courses meet for a total of ten hours. Weekend courses can be arranged for groups.

Specialties: Barbecue.

Faculty: Chef Paul Kirk, CWC, PHB, was named Chef of the Year (1990) by the Kansas City Chapter of the ACF and has won more than 350 awards, including the World Barbeque Champion (1989, 1990). He is a board member of the not-for-profit Kansas City Barbeque Society and inductee to their Hall of Fame.

Costs: Course fee is $125 in Kansas City, $150 per student plus expenses elsewhere. Major credit cards are accepted and full refund is granted cancellations at least one week prior.

Location: Shawnee Mission is a part of Greater Kansas City, twin city of Kansas City, Missouri, home of the Kansas City Barbeque Society. A tour of local barbecue houses can be arranged.

Contact: Baron of BBQ School of Pitmasters, Box 1394, Shawnee Mission, KS 66222; (913) 321-0222, Fax (913) 321-4628.

KENTUCKY

THE COOKBOOK COTTAGE
Louisville, Kentucky
Year-round

Established in 1986, this cookbook store and school offers more than 150 demonstration (limit 20 students) and participation (limit 10) classes a year on a variety of topics, including herb and spice cookery, breadmaking, international and regional cuisines, holiday and seasonal menus, appetizers to desserts, and guest chef specialties. The 2$^{1}/_{2}$-hour classes are scheduled mornings and evenings in the 1,200-square-foot classroom, which seats 30 and has overhead mirrors.

Specialties: A variety of topics for the cooking enthusiast.

Faculty: Proprietor/instructor Stephen J. Lee earned a degree in Culinary Arts from the University of Kentucky, is food columnist for *Louisville Entertainer* and a member of the IACP, and specializes in herb cookery and edible flowers. Other faculty includes local cooking teachers and chefs and noted guest chefs.

Costs: Range from $15 to $30 for most classes, $48 for guest chefs. Advance registration and payment is required and no refunds are granted for cancellations after the closing date for each quarter. Credit cards accepted.

Contact: Stephen J. Lee, Proprietor, The Cookbook Cottage, 1279 Bardstown Rd., Louisville, KY 40204; (502) 458-5227.

THE NATIONAL CENTER FOR HOSPITALITY STUDIES
Sullivan College
Louisville, Kentucky
Year-round

Founded in 1987 as a division of Sullivan College, which is accredited by the Commission on Colleges of the Southern Association of Colleges and Schools, The National Center for Hospitality Studies offers an 18-month Culinary Arts program and Baking & Pastry Arts Program leading to an Associate of Science Degree. Its Culinary Arts Program is accredited by the Accrediting Commission of the ACFEI. The school operates on a quarterly calendar with admission dates in January, April, June, and September. Approximately 75% of applicants are accepted and 100% of graduates obtain employment.

The curriculum consists of 78 credit hours of major (culinary) and core requirement (business, accounting, communications) courses and 24 credit hours of general studies in humanities/fine arts, natural science/mathematics, and social/ behavioral sciences. Culinary arts subjects include theory and skills, regional cuisine, purchasing and cost containment, sanitation, nutrition and meal planning, bakery and garde manger, menu design and layout, buffet and catering, international and American cuisine, and culinary arts, which includes 400 hours in off-premise practicum. Students attend classes Monday through Thursday with Friday free for individual study, practice, or assistance from instructors. Facilities include an à la carte kitchen, three bakery labs, international lab, garde manger lab, and basic skills lab. The school provides a job placement service for life and allows graduates to review any course taken previously, at no charge.

Specialties: An 18-month career program leading to an Associate of Science Degree in Culinary Arts or Baking & Pastry Arts.

Faculty: The 34-member resident faculty includes President Steve Coppock, Ed.D., Culinary Chairman Chef Tom Hickey CEC, CCE, Baking and Pastry Chairman Chef Walter Rhea CMPC, CEC, CCE, Chef John Castro CWC, Chef Alan Fitch, Chef Derek Spendlove CEPC, CCE, and Chef Carol Gott CWC. The school also has a 32-member adjunct faculty.

Costs, Accommodations: Nonrefundable application fee is $100, tuition for both in and out-of-state residents is $13,980 ($6,990 per nine-month period), and the comprehensive supplies fee is $3,450 ($690 per lab). Applicants must have a high school diploma or equivalent and can apply for financial assistance from several state and federal programs. Modern air-conditioned apartments for students are available nearby for $240 per month and daily transportation is provided. For married students, the College assists in finding housing.

Location: In Sullivan Centre, situated at the corner of the Watterson Expressway and Bardstown Road in suburban Jefferson County.

Contact: The National Center for Hospitality Studies, Sullivan College, Sullivan Centre Campus, Watterson Expressway at Bardstown Rd., P.O. Box 33-308, Louisville, KY 40232; (800) 844-1354 *or* (502) 456-6504.

LOUISIANA

COOKIN' CAJUN COOKING SCHOOL
New Orleans, Louisiana
Year-round

This school was established in 1988 by Lisette Sutton and her brother, Kenneth Verlander, in Creole Delicacies, a 30-year-old firm specializing in Cajun and Creole gift and gourmet items. Two-hour demonstration classes (limit 50 to 80 students) in Cajun and Creole cooking are scheduled at 11 am daily, Monday through Saturday, in a theatre-style mirrored kitchen overlooking the Mississippi River. Following the class, students are served a complete meal, such as Oysters

Rockefeller, Sausage Jambalaya, Mardi Gras Salad, and Bananas Foster. Three menus are rotated and written recipes provided. Private classes, parties, and fish classes for anglers can be scheduled mornings or evenings, seven days a week.

Specialties: Cajun and Creole cuisine.

Faculty: Daily classes are taught by Susan Murphy and Inez Hayden; other instructors are Lee Barnes and Poppy Tooker.

Costs: $15 per class. Advance reservations are required.

Location: The school is in the Riverwalk Marketplace adjacent to the New Orleans Convention Center.

Contact: Cookin' Cajun Cooking School, #1 Poydras, Store #116, New Orleans, LA 70130; (504) 523-6425.

CULINARY ARTS INSTITUTE OF LOUISIANA (CAILA)
Baton Rouge, Louisiana

Year-round

Established in 1988, this private school for those pursuing a career as cook, chef, caterer, or food service manager offers a 48-week, four-semester day and evening program of study in Professional Cooking Skills and Restaurant Management. A new session begins each month and the program is completed in one year with four weeks off between 12-week sessions. The 1,440-clock-hour curriculum consists of courses in culinary theory and technique, hands-on laboratory classes, and general education courses with emphasis on communications and science. The school is licensed by the Department of Education and grants certification in Sanitation, Nutrition, and Restaurant Management, as recognized by the Educational Divisions of the ACF and the NRA. Students provide catering services and run a full service restaurant that serves breakfast and lunch to the public. Total enrollment is 40, the student to teacher ratio is 10 to 1, 95% of applicants are accepted, and 100% of graduates have obtained employment.

Specialties: A 48-week certificate in Professional Cooking and Restaurant Management.

Faculty: Founder and president Violet Harrington, who received an M.B.A. from U.C.L.A., teaches restaurant management and operations and sanitation; culinary arts instructors are chefs Tony Jean-Claude Cantin, Marc D'Antonio, and Robert Esseltine; local guest chefs demonstrate their specialties.

Costs, Accommodations: Tuition is $10,500, which includes the daily main meal, uniforms, cutlery, liability insurance, and job placement while in school and upon graduation. A $25 refundable fee must accompany application. Scholarships are available. Student housing at the Riverview Suite Hotel, a five-minute drive from the Institute, ranges from $250 per month double occupancy to $500 per month single, based on an annual contract.

Contact: Vi Harrington, Director, Culinary Arts Institute of Louisiana, 427 Lafayette St., Baton Rouge, LA 70802; (800) 927-0839 *or* (504) 343-6233.

KAY EWING'S EVERYDAY GOURMET
Baton Rouge, Louisiana

Year-round

After teaching in her home for three years, Kay Ewing began in 1988 to teach participation classes at The Panhandler, a gourmet kitchen store. Classes are limited to six students and emphasize everyday cooking featuring various cuisines and cooking methods. Approximately eight to ten three-hour morning classes are offered quarterly. Private and group sessions can be arranged.

Specialties: A variety of topics, including ethnic and regional cuisines, seasonal and holiday foods, menus for entertaining, food processor techniques, breadmaking; classes for children.

Faculty: Kay Ewing, a member of the IACP, teaches all classes.

Costs: Tuition is $25 for adults, $15 for children. Payment is due one week prior to class and refund is granted cancellations at least 48 hours prior.

Location: Baton Rouge, the state capitol and home of Louisiana State University, is 80 miles from New Orleans.

Contact: Kay Ewing, c/o The Panhandler, 9259 Florida Blvd., Monterrey Plaza, Baton Rouge, LA 70815; (504) 927-4371.

THE NEW ORLEANS SCHOOL OF COOKING
New Orleans, Louisiana

Year-round

This year-round school for cooking enthusiasts and New Orleans visitors was founded in 1980 and moved to Jackson Brewery in 1984. Demonstration classes are held from 10 am until 1 pm, Monday through Saturday, in the school's large mirrored kitchen, which accommodates 60 persons and is situated behind the Louisiana General Store. Students are seated at tables and served a full meal, usually jambalaya, gumbo, bread pudding with rum sauce, pralines, and iced tea and beer. Those who send the school a letter stating that they have prepared the recipes receive a hand-lettered diploma. Classes for private groups and tours can be scheduled during the afternoons and evenings.

Specialties: Cajun and Creole cuisine.

Faculty: The classes are conducted by school proprietor Joe Cahn and other Louisiana chefs. Joe Cahn is a native of New Orleans, a self-taught cook, television personality, and spokesperson for several food-related industries.

Costs: The class is $15. Payment is made at the end of the session. Credit cards (VISA, MasterCard, American Express) accepted.

Location: On the river in the French Quarter at the Jackson Brewery.

Contact: The New Orleans School of Cooking, 620 Decatur St., New Orleans, LA 70130; (504) 525-2665, Fax (504) 482-3922. Group reservations: Jo Rivers, (504) 482-3632.

WOK AND WHISK, INC.
Baton Rouge, Louisiana

February-May, September-November

Established in 1975, this school offers approximately 20 evening demonstration (limit 30 students) and participation (limit 10) courses a year. A variety of topics are covered in the mostly one-session courses, including international and regional cuisines, appetizers to desserts, and guest chef specialties. A six-session course in Chinese cooking concludes with Peking Duck and classes for children feature holiday treats and breakfast fare. Facilities include an overhead mirror and two 4x8-foot islands for participation classes.

Specialties: A variety of topics; children's classes.

Faculty: Includes president Barbara C. Peterson and guest chefs Giuliano Bugialli, Shirley Corriher, Tim Creehan, Nicholas Malgieri, and Poppy Tooker.

Costs: Single sessions range from $25 to $75, six-class series are $125 to $150, and children's classes are $15. Advance payment is required and refunds are granted cancellations at least 48 hours prior to class. Credit cards (VISA, Mastercard) accepted.

Location: In the southern section of Baton Rouge.

Contact: Barbara Peterson, Wok and Whisk, Inc., 6301 Perkins Rd., Baton Rouge, LA 70808; (504) 769-5122.

MAINE

THE WHIP AND SPOON
Portland, Maine

January-April and September-November

This gourmet foods and cookware store, established in 1980, offers nonprofessional cooks approximately 15 to 20 demonstration classes (limit 20 to 25 students) each quarter in its well-equipped teaching kitchen. Most of the two to three-hour sessions begin at 6 pm, Tuesday and Thursday, and are limited to 20 to 25 students. Free food processor and beermaking demonstrations are sometimes scheduled on Saturday mornings.

Specialties: A variety of topics, including ethnic and regional cuisines, healthful foods, food processor, beermaking, guest chef specialties.

Faculty: Instructors, who are local chefs, caterers, and people who enjoy cooking and teaching, include caterers Rosemarie DeAngelis and Barbara Gulino, restaurateur Cheryl Lewis, natural foods specialist Rick Perry, and television chef Avis Layman.

Costs: From $12 to $15 per class. Cancellations at least 48 hours prior receive a full refund. Credit cards (VISA, MasterCard) accepted.

Location: In the Old Port Exchange on Portland's waterfront.

Contact: The Whip and Spoon, 161 Commercial St., P.O. Box 567, Portland, ME 04112; (207) 774-4020.

MARYLAND

L'ACADEMIE DE CUISINE
The Academy of Culinary Arts
Bethesda, Maryland
Year-round

This school for cooking enthusiasts and aspiring and professional cooks, founded in 1976 and certified by the Maryland Board of Education, offers instruction in the classic French style with emphasis on purchasing, preparation, palate, and presentation. All professional courses are approved by the Maryland Higher Education Commission. About 90% of applicants are accepted for admission and the student teacher ratio averages 15 to 20:1. Facilities consist of a 30-seat demonstration classroom and a 22-station practice kitchen equipped with modern appliances, both gas and electric, and overhead mirrors. For the aspiring or professional chef, the school offers a full-time 48-week Culinary Career Training program and a part-time 26-week Pastry Course, 9-month Theory and Technique Course and Practical Skills Course, and 4-week Catering Course. During the summer the Theory and Technique Course and Practical Skills Course, the Catering Course, and some Advanced Professional Pastry Courses are offered as condensed intensive programs along with other Basic and Advanced Intensive cooking classes. Throughout the year the school offers a variety of demonstration (limit 30 students) and participation (limit 22) courses and classes for cooks of all levels and children. The school also sponsors one-week culinary programs at La Bastide Gasconne in Barbotan Gascony, located in France's Armagnac region.

The 48-week Culinary Career Training Diploma program, which begins in July and January, is designed for those interested in operating a small fine restaurant or in food research, writing, teaching, or catering. It consists of two 24-week phases scheduled from July to January and January to June over a one-year period. The first phase is devoted to theoretical skills and techniques of fine food planning, preparation, and presentation. Classes are scheduled weekdays from 9 am to 4:30 pm, during which students attend practical sessions from 9 am to 1 pm and theory classes from 1:30 to 4:30 pm and complete research projects in their area of interest. In the second phase they advance to a 30 to 36-week paid externship in a restaurant selected by the school and continue theory studies one day a week. Subjects include equipment, safety, sanitation, herbs and condiments, appetizers, soups, stocks and sauces, eggs, meat, poultry, fish and shellfish, garde manger, vegetables, fruits, cheeses, breads, pastries and desserts, sugars, chocolate, wine and spirit selection, catering, menu planning, kitchen and restaurant management, business and legal aspects, and assessing the job market. Approximately 85% of graduates obtain employment and a placement board assists students in obtaining positions, preparing resumés, and providing a letter of reference.

The 26-week Pastry Certificate Course, which begins each fall, meets twice weekly (Mondays from 6:30 to 10:30 pm and Saturdays from 1 to 5 pm) and covers equipment, doughs, batters, pastry cremes and filling, decoration and presentation, ice carvings, calligraphy, chocolate work, sugar work, desserts, petits fours, and French pastries. Advanced courses in marzipan, wedding cakes, sugar, and chocolate are offered occasionally.

The 9-month (36-session) Theory and Technique Certificate Course, which begins each fall, covers the same topics as the 48-week course and is designed to provide an understanding of French classic techniques and theory as well as basic and refined methods of food planning, preparation, and presentation. Students attend a three-hour demonstration class each Monday morning or evening. The Practical Skills Certificate Course, usually taken concurrent with the Theory and Technique Course, enables students to practice techniques hands-on. Six sessions each are devoted to basic techniques, stocks, soups, and vegetables, fish and shellfish, meat and poultry, bread and pasta, and pastries and desserts.

The 4-session Catering Course, offered at various times during the year, is designed for those who want to start a catering business. The course covers food purchasing, preparation, presentation, business aspects, government and health regulations, marketing, and menu-planning. A one-week condensed Catering Course is held in the summer as a four-day (10 am to 1 pm) program.

Courses for nonprofessionals include the four-session Basic Techniques of Cooking (participation), classes covering international and American regional cuisines, nutritional foods, basic and advanced pastry, wine and food pairing, low cholesterol/high fiber, bread baking, and The French Cooking Course, an ongoing series of weekly three-hour demonstrations. Students may register for a single session of some courses. The Great Luncheons, Great Dinners, and Friday Night Specials sessions feature the demonstration of a complete meal, which is served to students. Individual demonstration and participation classes, offered weekday evenings and all day Saturdays, cover a variety of topics. Cooking classes and summer cooking camps for children, ages 9 to 14, are scheduled on Saturday mornings and private birthday parties are on Friday afternoons. Private dinners, guest chef demonstrations, and culinary travel programs to nearby cities are also offered from time to time.

Specialties: Professional courses in French cuisine, pastry, and catering; courses for nonprofessionals on a variety of topics; children's classes.

Faculty: School president François Dionot, who teaches the theoretical component of all the professional courses, graduated from L'Ecole Hotelière de la Societé Suisse des Hoteliers in Switzerland and served apprenticeships at the Hotel Meister in Lugano and the Hotel le Relais in Gap, France. He served as food consultant to Time-Life Books and is a founding member and former president of the IACP. Pascal Dionot, a graduate of the Hotelfachschule D. Speiser in Germany, teaches the practical component of all the professional courses. Nancy Hight, a graduate of the school, teaches basic pastry, food service management, and sanitation. The school has approximately 18 instructors as well as guest chefs that have included Giuliano Bugialli, Shirley Corriher, Jean Louis Palladin, Gerard Pangaud, and Roland Mesnier, White House Executive Pastry Chef, who oversees the Pastry Course.

Costs, Accommodations: A $100 enrollment fee must accompany registration for all part-time professional courses. The total cost for the Culinary Career Training Program is $10,500, which does not include a $50 application fee, uniforms, and personal equipment. Applicants must have a high school diploma or equivalent. Tuition is payable at the start of each semester, unless monthly installment plan is chosen. Those who cancel within seven days after submitting enrollment agreement and $425 tuition deposit receive a full deposit refund;

cancellations after seven days but prior to first class forfeit deposit and application fee; refund is pro-rated thereafter. Tuition is $3,975 ($4,300 for installment plan) for the Pastry Course, $2,200 ($2,376 for installment plan) for the Theory and Technique Course, $2,400 ($2,592 for installment plan) for the Practical Skills Course, and $250 for the Catering Course. Payment in full must accompany registration for short courses and classes (individual sessions are $25 to $70). Credit card (American Express, VISA, MasterCard) registrations are accepted. The school has a house with rooms for rent that can accommodate five full-time students; several nearby hotels offer student discounts. An Assistants Program is available to those who wish to receive a 50% tuition discount.

Location: The school is 2¹/₂ miles northwest of Washington, D.C., and five miles southwest of Rockville, Maryland.

Contact: Patrice W. Dionot, Administrative Director, L'Academie de Cuisine, 5021 Wilson Lane, Bethesda, MD 20814; (301) 986-9490, Fax (301) 652-7970.

BALTIMORE INTERNATIONAL CULINARY COLLEGE (BICC)
Baltimore, Maryland

Year-round

Founded in 1972 and accredited by the CCA (NATTS), this two-year, private, not-for-profit college offers four hospitality majors, each leading to the associate of arts degree or certificate, and four admission dates a year, in winter, spring, summer, and fall. The two-year single-degree majors are designed for those who wish to concentrate on one area of expertise: Professional Baking and Pastry, Professional Cooking, Restaurant/Foodservice Management, and Innkeeping. All two-year degree programs include at least three weeks of study at the College's European Educational Centre in Ireland (page 207) as well as a six-month externship. The College also offers second-degree programs that combine two single-degree prorams for those who desire additional career flexibility. Those with prior industry, work, and/or college experience may qualify for one of the College's accelerated programs. Accelerated programs compact the same courses of study into 12 or 15-month schedules, which may be supplemented by study at the College's European Educational Centre. BICC graduates are eligible to earn their Bachelor of Science degree in Hospitality Management from Southeastern University at BICC's campus in Baltimore. The four A.A. degree majors transfer into the B.S. degree program, which can be completed within an additional 12 to 15 months. The College's more than 400 full-time students attend technical classes, which are demonstration, participation, or both, as well as academic classes. The 90,000 square feet of modern facilities include training kitchens, bakeshops, a lecture theater and cooking demonstration theater, academic class-rooms, library, computer lab, college bookstore, and student dining room. Stu-dents gain practical experience in the College's Baltimore Baking Co. (restaurant, deli, and bakery) and Park Hotel-Deer Park Lodge, all open to the public. The Student Employment and Career Development Office maintains files of current job opportunities, arranges on-campus recruiting, and sponsors job fairs for students. Approximately 98% of applicants are accepted and the job placement rate exceeds 95%.

The Baking and Pastry program, designed for those who aspire to careers as retail bakers and pastry chefs, builds from a foundation of basic culinary theories and techniques and proceeds to advanced techniques and special projects, supervised by the chef instructors. The business side of the field, including menu costing and pricing, are also covered. The Professional Cooking program, for those who plan to be cooks, chefs, and caterers, begins with the study of fundamental culinary theories and techniques along with laboratory classes that focus on skill development and practical application. Students produce their daily meal in foodservice production classes, and progress to preparation of à la carte cuisine for The Baltimore Baking Co. restaurant or for the dining facilities at the Park Hotel-Deer Park Lodge. The Restaurant/Foodservice Management program, for those seeking careers as restaurant managers and administrators, caterers and banquet managers, food and beverage cost controllers, personnel administrators and convention managers, offers practical experience in the culinary arts and lectures in dining room skills, equipment and facilities maintenance, purchasing, restaurant and club administration, and accounting. In addition to equipping individuals with the above skills, the Innkeeping major focuses development on managerial and operational skills for careers in the lodging industry. Students are taught managerial theory and practice, budgeting, and forecasting. Property operations, front desk operations, and guest services are learned in combined lecture/laboratory environments in three months of operations at the Park Hotel-Deer Park Lodge, part of the College's European Educational Centre.

Specialties: Hospitality majors include four single-degree programs and ten second-degree options. All two-year degree students study in Europe for at least three weeks.

Faculty: The 55-member faculty includes Certified Executive Chefs, Certified Working Chefs, Certified Master Pastry Chefs, and Certified Culinary Educators, all professional recognitions of the ACF. Academic faculty members hold degrees through the doctorate level.

Costs, Accommodations: Tuition for the two-year (five-term) degree program ranges from $2,691 to $3,540 per term, which includes accident insurance, library fees, and three weeks of study at the European Educational Centre (includes airfare allowance, housing, and three meals per class day). Costs for additional study at the European Educational Centre range from $730 to $1,940 for housing and three meals per class day. Candidates for admission must have a high school diploma or equivalent. A $25 nonrefundable fee must accompany application and a $100 tuition deposit is required to reserve a space in class. Refund of tuition deposit is granted students who withdraw within three days of signing enrollment agreement. Those who withdraw during the first week of class forfeit $350. Student housing is available in college-owned apartments. Housing costs range from $825 to $1,875 per term.

Location: In Baltimore's Inner Harbor area and within walking distance of the Meyerhoff Symphony Hall, Lyric Opera House, Walters Art Gallery, Center Stage, National Aquarium, and Maryland Science Center.

Contact: Admissions Dept., BICC, 25 S. Calvert St., Rm. 208, Baltimore, MD 21202; (800) 624-9926 *or* (410) 752-4710, ext. 208.

CAKE COTTAGE, INC.
Baltimore and Bel Air, Maryland
Year-round

Founded in 1977, this candy shop and school offers participation courses (limit 30 students) in basic and advanced cake decorating and demonstration (limit 50) and participation classes in candies, cake writing, puff pastry, petit fours, butter cream flowers, air brush decorating, and party foods. Sessions are scheduled in the morning, afternoon, and evening in both the Baltimore (Perry Hall Crossing) and Bel Air (Bel Air Harford County) stores. The basic cake decorating course is offered from 11 am to 1 pm or 7 to 9 pm once weekly for six weeks, or from 10 am to 3 pm once weekly for three weeks; the seven-session advanced course is offered once weekly from 11 am to 1 pm or 7 to 9 pm; and the children's (ages 8 to 16) three-session course is held once weekly from 11 am to 1 pm. Individual classes are two to three hours each.

Specialties: Cake decorating for adults and children, candies, party foods.

Faculty: Carole, the instructor, has been teaching cooking and decorating for more than 20 years. She has attended many courses, including those at the Wilton School.

Costs: The basic cake decorating course is $35, the advanced course is $40, and the children's course is $25. Single-session classes range from $8 to $40. Full nonrefundable payment must accompany registration.

Location: The store, located in the northeast section of Baltimore off Beltway Exit 32 North, is 20 minutes from Inter-Harbor-downtown.

Contact: The Cake Cottage, Inc., 8716 Belair Rd., Baltimore, MD 21236; (410) 529-0200 *or* Bel Air Harford County, 110 N. Tollgate Rd., Bel Air, MD 21014; (410) 838-6260.

THE CHINESE COOKERY, INC.
Silver Spring, Maryland
Year-round

Founded by cooking educator and biochemist Joan Shih in 1975, this school offers seven levels of Chinese participation and demonstration courses: basic, advanced, gourmet I, gourmet II, gourmet III, Szechuan, and Hunan. Each course is limited to five students and consists of five weekly two-hour evening sessions that emphasize authentic recipes and techniques. Facilities consist of a classroom/lab equipped for Chinese hands-on cooking. Certificates are awarded to those who complete all seven levels and pass an exam. The school also offers a class in Japanese sushi that meets on Saturday from 11:30 am to 1:30 pm and classes for teenagers. Private lessons for professional cooks are available by appointment.

Specialties: Chinese and Japanese cuisines.

Faculty: Joan Shih has a background in chemistry and medical technology and is a chemist at the National Institute of Health. She received a certificate in Chinese cuisine in Taiwan and has taught Chinese cooking and Japanese sushi on television and in public and private schools. She is listed in *Who's Who in the World, 1992-1993*, and *Who's Who of American Women, 1992-1993*.

Costs: The Chinese cooking courses are $120 (five lessons) and the Japanese sushi class is $35 per lesson. A nonrefundable deposit of $25 is required. All classes are arranged by appointment only, two weeks in advance.

Location: North of Washington, D.C., about 40 minutes from downtown.

Contact: Joan Shih, The Chinese Cookery, Inc., 14209 Sturtevant Rd., Silver Spring, MD 20905; (301) 236-5311.

MASSACHUSETTS

BOSTON UNIVERSITY
SEMINARS IN THE CULINARY ARTS
Boston, Massachusetts

Year-round

This school for professional and nonprofessional cooks offers a four-month Certificate Program in the Culinary Arts and participates in all Seminars in the Culinary Arts. Approximately 30% of applicants are accepted for admission. Sessions are taught by practicing local and well-known guest chefs in the Culinary Center's modern teaching facility, which has an overhead mirror in the demonstration room and eight fully-equipped restaurant stations in the laboratory kitchen. The Certificate Program, started in 1989, is dedicated to training students in the basic classic and modern techniques and theories of food production and the careful handling of food. Ethnic, regional, and historical information are also a part of the curriculum as well as proper dining room theory and practice and purchasing ingredients. Students are required to participate in the Seminars in the Culinary Arts. Sessions begin in January and September and are each limited to 12 students. Placement assistance is provided and 100% of graduates obtain employment. The Seminars in the Culinary Arts program, started in 1986, features a variety of topics and guest chefs who teach their specialties. Some sessions begin at 6 or 7 pm and end at 9 or 10; others are scheduled from 9 am to 4 pm. Enrollment in hands-on cooking classes is limited to approximately 24 students, who dine on the foods prepared. Tours are are scheduled to such locations as Provence, the Cote D'Azur, Tuscany, and the Veneto.

Specialties: Four-month professional certificate program and courses covering a variety of topics.

Faculty: Recent faculty and guest chefs have included Odette Bery, Julia Child, Jim Dodge, Albert Kumin, Lorenza de' Medici, Mark Miller, Jacques Pépin, Julie Sahni, Nina Simonds, and Jasper White.

Costs: Tuition for the certificate course is $4,900, which includes linens and supplies. Refunds are granted according to University policy. Single-session seminars range from $10 for a two-hour seminar to $125 for a four-hour demonstration; full-day classes and three-session courses range from $150 to $300. A 5% to 10% discount is granted dual enrollments. Payment must accompany registration and full refund is granted cancellations more than 48 hours prior to seminar.

Location: In Kenmore Square.

Contact: Boston University Metropolitan College, Seminars in the Culinary Arts, 808 Commonwealth Ave., Room 109, Boston, MA 02215; (617) 353-9852.

THE CAMBRIDGE SCHOOL OF CULINARY ARTS (CSCA)
Cambridge, Massachusetts
Year-round except summer

Established in 1974, licensed by the Commonwealth of Massachusetts Department of Education, and accredited by the CCA (NATTS) and IACP, this school offers a full-time, ten-month Professional Chef's Program for those desiring a career in the food industry. The 700-clock-hour program, which runs from September to June or January to January (with 12 weeks summer vacation), provides a European approach to culinary education with emphasis on French and Italian cuisines. About 90% of applicants are admitted and class size is limited to 32 students for demonstrations and lectures and to 15 students for hands-on cooking. The primary classes (twice weekly $7^1/_2$ to 8-hour sessions) are baking (15 weeks) and food basics (14 weeks); provincial French (8 weeks), intensive French (10 weeks), Italian (12 weeks), American (6 weeks), and Nouvelle (4 weeks) cuisines. Secondary classes (once weekly three-hour sessions) are food management (9 weeks), sanitation (5 weeks), food history, butchering, and introduction to wine (4 weeks each), Eastern cuisine (3 weeks), and graduate panel, cheeses, herbs and spices, the restaurant business, and chocolate workshop (1 week each). Day and evening classes are available, allowing students to maintain full-time jobs while attending. Facilities and equipment, which are continually upgraded, consist of commercial appliances, including gas and electric ovens and gas burner stoves.

Specialties: Ten-month full-time (flexible) Professional Chef's Program.

Faculty: President, founder, and executive chef Roberta Avallone Dowling has traveled extensively and received diplomas from Julie Dannenbaum, Marcella Hazan, Madeleine Kamman, and Richard Olney. A member of the ACF, the IACP, the Academy of Chefs, and Les Amis d'Escoffier Society, she has taught professional chefs and restaurateurs from the Greater Boston area and other U.S. locations. Her catering company, DeGustibus, Inc., has served well-known individuals, corporations, and organizations. Instructors are master chefs and experienced teachers.

Costs, Accommodations: The tuition is $7,950, which can be paid in four interest-free installments. Applicants must be at least 18 years old and have a high school diploma or equivalent. Admission is based on application, personal statement of background, interests, and goals, two letters of reference, transcripts, resume, and physician's certificate of health. Personal interview may be waived for applicants outside the Boston area. Upon acceptance, enrollment is completed by submission of an Enrollment Agreement and $100 tuition deposit. Written cancellations within five days (but prior to start of course) receive full refund; after five days (but prior to start of course), cancellation penalty is $50. Thereafter, refund policy is in accordance with the CCA directives. Apartments and rooms are available in Cambridge and surrounding towns. Counseling and placement assistance are provided and 90% of graduates obtain employment.

Location: Within walking distance of public transportation, the school is on Massachusetts Avenue, which runs from downtown Boston (a 20-minute drive and 15 minutes by MBTA Rapid Transit) to Lexington and Concord. The area offers a wide variety of cultural attractions and recreational facilities.

Contact: The Cambridge School of Culinary Arts, 2020 Massachusetts Ave., Cambridge, MA 02140; (617) 354-3836.

CHILLINGSWORTH INN
Brewster, Massachusetts

July-December

This Cape Cod school, founded in 1981, offers about four demonstration (limit 25 students) and participation (limit 10) classes from September through December and occasional guest chef sessions in the summer. The 2½-hour classes, held in this fine French restaurant's kitchen, feature such specialties as sauces, pastries, and French cuisine.

Specialties: French cuisine, pastries, sauces, guest chef specialties.

Faculty: Instructors are all French-trained chefs.

Costs: Classes range from $35 to $40. Credit card (VISA, MasterCard, American Express) registrations are accepted. Those who cancel at least 24 hours prior to class receive a full refund.

Location: The Inn is situated a 90-minute drive from Boston, in the midst of Cape Cod's many attractions.

Contact: Pat Rabin, Chillingsworth Inn, 2449 Main St., Brewster, MA 02631; (617) 896-7482.

THE COUNTRY KITCHENS OF GASCONY (page 187)

THE KUSHI INSTITUTE
Becket, Massachusetts

Year-round

This nonprofit educational facility, founded by Michio and Aveline Kushi, offers seminars and conferences on natural, whole foods cooking and macrobiotic healing arts. The one-week Macrobiotic Residential Seminar, scheduled two or three times a month, is designed for those who wish to improve their well-being as well those with a specific health concern. Each seminar is limited to 18 participants and includes daily hands-on cooking classes as well as lectures on the theory and practice of macrobiotics. Students are taught how different foods affect health and prepare dishes using freshly hulled grains, organic vegetables, and specialty foods produced on the premises. Personal dietary and way of life interviews with a Kushi Certified Teacher are available. The Institute also offers a Leadership Program for those pursuing a career, a one-week summer conference of more than 120 classes and events, and a series of seminars on the practical, philosophical, and spiritual aspects of macrobiotics.

Specialties: Macrobiotic cooking.

Faculty: The Kushi Institute cooking staff.

Costs: Fee is $895 ($695 for accompanying spouse or guest), which includes meals and shared lodging in the Institute's country home. A $100 deposit is required with balance due on arrival. Credit cards (VISA, MasterCard) accepted. Airport pick-up is $50 one way.

Location: In the Berkshires, a three-hour drive from Boston and New York City and 90 minutes from the airports in Hartford, CT, and Albany, NY.

Contact: The Kushi Institute, P.O. Box 7, Becket, MA 01223; (413) 623-5741.

MARGE COHEN
Needham Heights, Massachusetts

September-June

Marge Cohen has taught demonstration and participation courses in her home kitchen since 1980. Her five-session Basic, Intermediate, and Advanced courses, limited to eight students, cover Chinese and other ethnic cuisines. She also teaches a five-session course for men only and The World, which features a variety of cuisines. Each class lasts 2¹/₂ hours and includes a meal of the foods prepared. Marge also teaches private classes and conducts a three hour Cook's Tour of Chinatown and other culinary excursions.

Specialties: Chinese and other ethnic cuisines, local excursions.

Faculty: Marge Cohen has certificates from the Cordon Bleu in London and Weichuan Cooking School in Taiwan. She has studied with many chefs and hosted a cable television program, "Marge's Cookery".

Costs: Each five-session course is $85; culinary tours are $25. No refunds are granted but a substitute may be sent.

Location: Twenty minutes west of Boston.

Contact: Marge Cohen, P.O. Box 53, Needham Heights, MA 02194; (617) 449-2688.

NEWBURY COLLEGE
Brookline, Massachusetts

Year-round

Established in 1962 and accredited by the New England Association of Schools and Colleges, this school offers a two-year Associate of Applied Science degree in culinary arts. Enrollment in the program is approximately 300, of which two thirds are day students and one third are continuing education students. Student to teacher ratio is 17 to 1 and 66% of applicants are accepted. In addition to theory and hands-on training in the preparation and presentation of breads, soups, sauces, salads, cold foods, desserts, and international and regional cuisines, instruction covers equipment operation, sanitation, safety, customer relations, nutrition, menu planning, and the food and beverage industry. English, mathematics, management, humanities, and other general education courses are also emphasized. Facilities include seven professionally-equipped production kitchens and the College's Mitton House Dining Room, where second year students prepare international and classic haute cuisine for friends and faculty of Newbury College and local residents. Terms begin in September and January and a 480-hour required supervised externship, arranged through the Career Planning and Placement Office, is conducted between the first and second years. Job placement rate is 99%.

Specialties: Two-year program leading to the A.A.S. degree.

Faculty: Culinary arts program chairman George Anbinder received a B.S. degree from Boston University and an A.O.S. from Johnson & Wales University. The 11 full-time faculty members are active industry professionals.

Costs: Annual tuition is $9,030. Financial aid and scholarships are available and students can earn $8 to $9 per hour during their externship.

Location: A suburban setting, 3½ miles from downtown Boston.

Contact: Newbury College, Admissions Center, 129 Fisher Ave., Brookline, MA 02146; (617) 730-7007.

THE SUMMER HOUSE COOKING SCHOOL
Siasconset, Massachusetts

April, May, October

Established in 1992, this school offers six week-long courses each year that focus on the preparation of classic and innovative French and Northern Italian cuisines. The schedule includes five two-hour demonstration/participation classes (limit 12 students) in the Summer House's professional kitchen, instruction in floral arrangements, a traditional New England beachside clambake, dinners at the Waterfront Home and an historic Nantucket home, tours of island historical sites and antique shops, whale watching, and visits to a vineyard, the Nantucket Whaling Museum, and Mariah Mitchell Observatory.

Specialties: Classic and innovative French and Northern Italian cuisine.

Faculty: Chef Charles François Salliou trained under Paul Bocuse, Claude Barnier, and Jacques Febway. He was fourth nationwide in France in 1976 and was awarded the Gold Medal from the Education Ministry.

Costs: All-inclusive cost is $3,000 double, $3,300 single occupancy in The Summer House cottages. A $400 deposit is required with balance due 30 days prior to course. Refunds are granted cancellations at least 30 days prior.

Location: Near the Nantucket village of Siasconset on a bluff overlooking the ocean. The Summer House amenities include antique furnishings, a surfside pool, and a bungalow restaurant.

Contact: Judy Terrell, 7707 Willow Vine Ct., Ste. 219, Dallas TX 75230; (214) 373-1161, Fax (214) 373-1162.

TERENCE JANERICCO COOKING CLASSES.
Boston, Massachusetts

September-June

Established in 1965, this school offers one and six-session demonstration (limit 12 students) and participation (limit 6) courses. The six-session courses, which meet one morning or evening a week and are scheduled five to eight times a year, are: Gourmet Cooking, Baking, American Regional Cooking, French Provincial Cooking, Italian Provincial Cooking, and Chinese and Asian Cooking. Single-session techniques classes, which can be taken in the morning or evening and are offered two to six times a year, are: Crepes and Omelets, Terrines and Pates, Meringues, Strudel and Phyllo Dough, Hors D'Oeuvre, Pasta, and Soups, Stews and Breads. All sessions run for three hours and include a meal.

Specialties: International and American regional cuisines, basics, baking, and a variety of special techniques.

Faculty: Terence Janericco has operated a catering business for more than 25 years and teaches at adult education centers in Boston and at cooking schools in New England and Michigan. His recipes have appeared in *Better Homes and Gardens* and *The New York Times* and he is author of 12 books, including *The Book of Great Hors d'Oeuvre, The Book of Great Soups, Sandwiches and Breads, The Gourmet Galley*, and *Fabulous Fruit Desserts*.

Costs: Six-session courses are $300, single-session classes are $55. A $50 deposit is required with balance due at first class; full refund one week prior.

Contact: Terence Janericco Cooking Classes, 42 Fayette St., Boston, MA 02116; (617) 426-7458.

TRAVEL CONCEPTS (page 182)

MICHIGAN

KITCHEN GLAMOR
Redford, West Bloomfield, and Rochester, Michigan
Year-round

This gourmet cookware store and cooking school, founded in 1949, offers two to three-hour demonstration (limit 125 students) and participation (limit 25) courses on a variety of topics. Approximately three to five demonstration, no pre-registration sessions per month are scheduled at 1 pm and 7 pm in each location's kitchen auditorium, which has a 12-foot work counter, two four-range burners, an overhead mirror, and seats 125. About 15 to 20 pre-registration "private" classes (limit 12 to 16 students) and professional guest chef classes are offered each season, with the format ranging from demonstration to full participation. Sessions are scheduled at 11 am, 12:30 pm and 6:30 pm. A four-session course in cake decorating is also offered.

Specialties: A variety of topics, including baking, cake decorating, holiday menus, and chef specialties.

Faculty: Includes award-winning cake decorator Mary Ann Hollen and food authority Marcia Sikarskie. Local chefs include Milos Cihelka, Brian Polcyn, and Jimmy Schmidt. Noted guest chefs have included Giuliano Bugialli, Nicholas Malgieri, Jacques Pépin, and Marlene Sorosky.

Costs: The no pre-registration demonstrations are $3 each, $30 for 12; pre-registration "private" classes are $40 for the professional guest chef classes, $25 to $35 for others; the cake decorating course is $30; well-known guest chef demonstrations range up to $80 per session. Credit card (VISA, Discover, MasterCard) registrations accepted. No refunds.

Location: The West Bloomfield School is in the Orchard Mall; the Rochester school is in the Great Oaks Mall, Walton at Livernols; the Novi location is at the Novi Town Center. The closest major city is Detroit; Canada is across the bridge.

Contact: Kitchen Glamor, 26770 Grand River, Redford Township, MI 48240; (313) 537-1300.

NELL BENEDICT COOKING CLASSES
Birmingham, Michigan

Year-round except June and July

Since 1970, Nell Benedict has taught two-hour evening demonstration classes (limit 45 students) in the newly renovated teaching kitchen at Birmingham Community House. A European culinary tour is offered each summer.

Specialties: A variety of topics, including ethnic cuisines, breadmaking, and restaurant specialties.

Faculty: Nell Benedict has studied at the Cordon Bleu, La Varenne, and L'Arts Culinara and with James Beard, Richard Olney, Julie Dannenbaum, Jacques Pépin, and Roger Vergé. She has taught on television and is a Charter Member of the IACP.

Costs: Each session is $16. A full refund is granted those who cancel at least 48 hours prior to class.

Location: Approximately 8 miles north of Detroit.

Contact: Nell Benedict, The Community House, 380 S. Bates St., Birmingham, MI 48009; (313) 644-5832 *or* International Cuisine, 18769 Alhambra, Lathrup Village, MI 48076.

MINNESOTA

BYERLY'S SCHOOL OF CULINARY ARTS
St. Louis Park, Minnesota

Year-round

Founded in 1980, this school offers 20 to 25 demonstration (limit 25 students) and participation (limit 14) classes each month on a variety of topics. The two-hour sessions are scheduled in the mornings, afternoons, and evenings in the school's teaching kitchen equipped with overhead mirror. Private classes and 90-minute children's birthday party classes (limit 14) can also be arranged.

Specialties: Include ethnic and regional cuisines, holiday menus, guest chef specialties; couples and parent-child classes.

Faculty: The more than 20-member faculty includes school manager Mary Evans, who studied at La Varenne and Lenôtre in Paris; caterers Sue Erickson and Dan Johnson; Paulette Mitchell, author of *The 15-Minute Vegetarian Gourmet*; syndicated columnist Joyce Battcher; food columnist Mary Carroll; restaurateur Antonio Cecconi; food writer Deidre Schipani; and chef Larry Kime.

Costs: Most classes range from $14 to $25. Credit card (VISA, MasterCard) registrations accepted. Full refund is granted cancellations at least three days prior to class.

Location: St. Louis Park is a suburb of Minneapolis.

Contact: Byerly's School of Culinary Arts, 3777 Park Center Blvd., St. Louis Park, MN 55416; (612) 929-2492.

COOK'S OF CROCUS HILL
St. Paul, Minnesota

Year-round

Founded in 1976, this cooking equipment store and school offers one, three, and five-session demonstration and participation courses for beginning cooks and 15 to 20 demonstration and participation classes each month for beginning to experienced cooks. The three-session Boil Water 101 course, designed for those who have never cooked, covers kitchen organization, basic cooking methods, and easy-to-prepare recipes. The five-session Pro Approach to Basics of Cooking course covers techniques for preparing fish, vegetables, soups, meats, and poultry. Two to three-hour classes cover a variety of topics and guest chef specialties. Attendance is limited to 12 in participation classes and 25 in demonstrations and classes are usually scheduled at 6:30 pm weekdays or 10 am Saturdays. At the end of class, students dine on the food they've prepared. Saturday classes for children ages 8 to 14, scheduled from 10 am to noon and 1 to 3 pm, feature holiday treats. Private group classes can be arranged.

Specialties: Include basics, ethnic cuisines, holiday menus, and guest chef specialties; children's classes.

Faculty: The 17-member faculty includes owner Martha Kaemmer, Bobbie Carpenter, food authority Lynne Rossetto Kasper, baker Raleigh Foss, children's teacher Colleen Miner, and Janice Cole, Lois Lee, and Yvonne Moody. Guest chefs include Hugh Carpenter, Marcia Fox, Nick Malgieri, and Jacques Pépin.

Costs: The three-session course is $90 and the five-session course is $150. Individual classes range from $18 to $40. Payment is required within five working days of registration and refunds are granted cancellations more than three working days prior. Credit cards (VISA, MasterCard, American Express) accepted.

Contact: Lois Lee, Director, Cook's of Crocus Hill, 877 Grand Ave., St. Paul, MN 55105; (612) 228-1333.

SARAH MONICK CULINARY TOURS (page 197)

MISSISSIPPI

THE EVERYDAY GOURMET
Jackson, Mississippi

January-November

This gourmet cookware store and school, established in 1982, offers approximately 12 demonstration (limit 24) and participation (limit 12 to 15) classes each month . Classes are usually scheduled from 6:30 to 9:30 or 10 pm in the store's kitchen, which has an overhead mirror. Local and guest chefs, lunch sessions, and classes for children ages 4 to 7 and 8 to 12 are also scheduled each month.

Specialties: A variety of topics, including ethnic and regional cuisines, seasonal and holiday dishes; classes for children.

Faculty: Includes Cissy Coleman, Martha McIntosh, Gayla Stone, Cheryl Welch, and school director Chan Patterson. Guest chefs include Giuliano Bugialli, Ann Clark, Shirley Corriher, Merle Ellis, Anne Greer, Emeril Lagasse, Nick Malgieri, Jean-Louis Palladin, Jacques Pépin, Marlene Sorosky, and Susan Spicer. The school is a member of the IACP.

Costs: Adult classes range from $20 to $40, children's classes are $15. Advance payment is requested and refund is granted cancellations at least 48 hours prior. Credit cards (VISA, MasterCard, American Express) accepted.

Location: In Woodland Hills, near downtown Jackson.

Contact: The Everyday Gourmet, Inc., 2905 Old Canton Rd., Jackson, MS 39216; (601) 362-0723 *or* (800) 898-0122 in Mississippi.

MISSOURI

DIERBERGS SCHOOL OF COOKING
Creve Coeur, Ellisville, St. Louis, and St. Peters, Missouri
Year-round

Founded in 1978, these four St. Louis-area schools offer more than 200 informal two-hour demonstration and participation classes for adults and more than 80 one or two-hour participation classes for youngsters each quarter. Additional children's classes are offered in the summer. The schools, located in Dierbergs Supermarkets, are bright, sound-proof enclosures that allow for maximim visibility and interchange. Classes are scheduled at 10 am and 6:30 pm and are limited to 18 students. Children's classes are divided into age groups: the classes for petite chefs (ages 5 to 6) are highlighted by a story-reading with related recipes, junior chefs (ages 7 to 11) and young chefs (ages 10 to 14) learn teenage favorites and ethnic foods. Classes for couples and parent-child sessions are also scheduled and children's birthday party classes can be arranged.

Specialties: A variety of topics, including ethnic and regional cuisines, microwave and food processor techniques, guest chef specialties; children's classes.

Faculty: In addition to the more than 30-member faculty of home economists and cooking instructors, guest teachers include restaurateurs, cookbook authors, traveling chefs, and food industry spokespersons.

Costs: Adult classes range from $12 to $20, guest chef classes begin at $20, and cookbook author demonstrations are $20 to $40, which includes cookbook. Children's and family classes range from $6 to $10. Payment is due within three days of enrollment and refunds or transfers are granted cancellations at least four days prior to class. Credit cards (MasterCard, VISA) accepted.

Location: The four schools are located in the suburbs of St. Louis.

Contact: Dierbergs, 11481 Olive St. Rd., Creve Coeur, MO 63141; (314) 432-6561/6505. 1322 Clarkson/Clayton Center, Ellisville, MO 63011; (314) 394-2254/9504. 12420 Tesson Ferry Rd., St. Louis, MO 63128; (314) 849-3600/3698. 290 Mid Rivers Dr., St. Peters, MO 63376; (314) 928-1117.

SUZANNE CORBETT — CULINARY RESOURCES, INC.
St. Louis, Missouri
Year-round

Since 1976, Suzanne Corbett, who specializes in foods from the past, has taught one to five-session courses on a variety of topics in her home kitchen, in vocational classrooms, colleges, and at historic sites. The two to three-hour demonstration (limit 50 students) and participation (limit 10 to 16) sessions combine lecture, demonstration, and hands-on cooking. Culinary tours are planned from time to time and private and group classes are available.

Specialties: A variety of topics, including historic American foods, baking (emphasis on hearth-style, sourdough, and stone ground breads), regional dishes, international cuisines, and wok cookery.

Faculty: Cooking teacher, food historian, and consultant Suzanne Corbett has been a home economics instructor and a contributing editor to Rodale Press and *Victoria Magazine* and writes a weekly column. She is a certified instructor for vocational foodservice and a Certified Culinary Professional by the IACP.

Costs: Prices start at $15 per class. Refund granted for cancellations at least 48 hours before class.

Contact: Suzanne Corbett — Culinary Resources, Inc., 5850 Pebble Oak, St. Louis, MO 63128-1412; (314) 487-5205, Fax (314) 487-5335.

TAKE PLEASURE IN COOKING!
Kansas City, Missouri
Year-round

This school, founded in 1988 by Gloria Martin, operates in her home teaching kitchen equipped with overhead mirror. Approximately three $2\frac{1}{2}$-hour demonstration classes (limit 20 students) and three to four workshop participation classes (limit 6) are offered each month. Demonstrations emphasize techniques, ease of preparation, use of quality ingredients, and creative presentation. Each session concludes with a meal of the foods prepared. Participation classes cover the preparation of yeast doughs and use of the food processor. Special group classes can be arranged.

Specialties: A variety of topics, including culinary herbs, American regional cuisines, holiday foods, menus for entertaining, and food processor recipes.

Faculty: Gloria Martin has studied with Giuliano Bugialli, Helen Fletcher, Anne Greer, Madeleine Kammann, Peter Kump, Perla Myers, and Anne Willan. She prepares a recipe monthly on a local television show and is an IACP member.

Costs: The cost of most classes is $20 for demonstrations and $30 for participation workshops, payable in advance by check. Refunds are granted cancellations at least 24 hours prior to class.

Location: In the southeast Kansas City suburb of Raytown, 15 miles from downtown and 10 miles from the Country Club Plaza, a tourist center.

Contact: Gloria Martin, Take Pleasure in Cooking!, 8612 E. 84th St., Kansas City, MO 64138; (816) 353-6022.

NEW HAMPSHIRE

COOKING WITH STEVEN RAICHLEN
Snowville, New Hampshire and St. Barts, French West Indies

February, April-July, November

Since 1981, Steven Raichlen has offered hands-on culinary instruction in vacation settings and an annual gastronomic tour. All programs are limited to 10 students and each class concludes with a meal of the foods prepared. Five-day programs culminate with a "final exam", in which students prepare a complete meal without supervision or recipes. The April (Cooking in Paradise) program is held at the Seahorse Hotel in St. Barts and the February (Cook and Ski), May, and November (High-Flavor, Low-Fat) programs are held at the Snowvillage Inn in Snowville. Special session for groups of eight or more can be arranged.

Cooking in Paradise, a one-week course, features Creole, Caribbean, and French dishes such as St. Bart's bouillabaise, seafood gazpacho, accras (spicy cod fritters), and tropical fruit tarts. Other planned activities include dinners at local restaurants, a sailing cruise, and a picnic. Cook and Ski, a four-day course, features two hands-on classes and demonstrations for preparing healthy winter country cooking, including such dishes as wild mushroom strudels, Basque fish stew, and low fat chocolate soufflé. Students receive two lift tickets and cross country ski instruction. High-Flavor, Low-Fat, offered as a weekend course, is based on Raichlen's new book, *High-Flavor, Low-Fat Cooking*. Afternoons are free for exploring the White Mountains. Cooking at a Country Inn, also offered as a weekend and a five-day course, emphasizes basic techniques and seasonal and regional American and French cuisine. Tour destinations include France, Thailand, and Brazil.

Specialties: High flavor, low fat cooking; Creole, Caribbean, French, and regional American cuisines.

Faculty: Cooking teacher, food writer, and syndicated columnist Steven Raichlen contributes to *Bon Appétit* and *Eating Well* magazines, The New York Times Syndicate, The Los Angeles Times Syndicate, and *The Washington Post*. He is author of six books.

Costs, Accommodations: Cost, which includes double (single) occupancy resort lodging and planned activities, is $1,995 ($2,295) for Cooking in Paradise, $475 to $525 ($575) for Cook and Ski, and $325 ($425) for weekend courses. The rate is discounted for a non-cooking guest. A deposit of $150 to $500 is required and balance is due 30 days prior. Credit cards (VISA, MasterCard) accepted. Special sessions can be arranged for groups of eight or more.

Location: The Seahorse Hotel, overlooking the ocean in St. Barts, has ten bungalows, a swimming pool, and a garden terrace. Snowville Inn, in New Hampshire's White Mountains, has flower gardens, a clay tennis court, hiking and cross country ski trails, and swimming, canoeing, and ice skating on nearby Crystal Lake.

Contact: Cooking with Steven Raichlen, 4073 Park Ave., Coconut Grove, FL 33133; (305) 665-0363, Fax (305) 665-0390.

THE PASQUANEY INN COOKING SCHOOL
Bridgewater, New Hampshire

February-December

Established in 1989, this school offers approximately 40 weekend demonstration sessions (limit 36 students) a year. Each weekend features four hours of instruction in basic French cuisine, including how to cut and cook vegetables, make stocks and sauces, use thickening agents, debone a chicken, and select wines. Most sessions are held in spring and fall, limited instruction is provided in July in August, and advanced courses, for those who've completed the basic course, are scheduled in June and September. Facilities include a 400-square-foot demonstration classroom and 15-foot counter with overhead mirror.

Specialties: French cuisine.

Faculty: Bud Edrick, chef/owner of the Pasguaney Inn, was trained at the French Culinary Institute and was sous chef at Flamand, a French-Belgian restaurant in New York City, before purchasing the Inn in 1987.

Costs, Accommodations: Cost, which includes two breakfasts, one dinner, and double (single) occupancy lodging and private bath for two nights, ranges from $112 to $127 ($179 to $202); shared baths from $99 to $110 ($159 to $175). A 50% deposit is required. Cancellations more than two weeks prior forfeit $10.

Location: The Pasquaney Inn on Newfound Lake, built in 1840, is one hour northwest of the Manchester airport, one hour east of Lebanon, two hours northwest of Boston, and four to five hours north of New York. The Inn nas a 300-foot private beach and dock and nearby attractions include the White Mountains, antique shops, and discount shopping.

Contact: Pasquaney Inn Cooking School, Star Rte. 1, Box 1066, Bridgewater, NH 03222; (603) 744-9111.

A TASTE OF THE MOUNTAINS COOKING SCHOOL
Bernerhof Inn
Glen, New Hampshire

Year-round except summer

Founded in 1980, this school offers weekend and five-day courses for cooks who want to broaden their practical knowledge of healthful cooking and creative cuisine. All courses emphasize the basics of cooking, as well as sauces, pastries, garnishes, and cake decorating. A wine-tasting seminar and session on sugar pulling are also featured. The five-day course (limit ten students), which begins Sunday evening and concludes with a Friday afternoon buffet, consists of daily three-hour participation sessions ending with a meal. A demonstration class is also held during the week and the schedule is arranged to allow a free morning or afternoon each day. Weekend students arrive Friday evening for a wine tasting and Swiss fondue and depart following a farewell ceremony Sunday afternoon. The program consists of three-hour participation classes and a demonstration class features a complete meal. A Wednesday morning series featuring local guest chefs is offered throughout the winter months.

Specialties: Healthful and creative cuisine; wine tasting.

Faculty: Chefs Stephen James and Richard Spencer, both ACF Chef of the Year recipients; Mt. Washington Valley area guest chefs.

Costs, Accommodations: Rates, which include lodging, continental breakfasts, five-course gourmet luncheons and dinners each day, and wine-tasting seminar, range from $750 (double occupancy/shared bath) to $850 (single occupancy/ private bath) for the five-day session and from $260 to $320 for the weekend course. Costs for day students (space permitting) are $475 for five days and $185 for the weekend or $40 for one three-hour class and meal. Meal-only for guests is $15 and alumni receive a 10% discount. A 50% deposit must accompany reservation with balance due 30 days prior to arrival. Refunds are subject to evaluation of situation. Credit cards accepted.

Location: The historic Bernerhof Inn is seven miles north of North Conway, three hours north of Boston, and 90 minutes west of Portland, Maine. Built in the 1890s, the Inn has 11 bedrooms with private baths and spa tubs available. Recreational facilities include hiking, golf, tennis and indoor racquet sports, horseback riding, skiing, canoeing, fishing, swimming, and bicycling.

Contact: A Taste of the Mountains Cooking School, Box 240, Glen, NH 03838; (603) 383-4414 *or* (800) 548-8007 (out of state).

NEW JERSEY

ACADEMY OF CULINARY ARTS
ATLANTIC COMMUNITY COLLEGE
Mays Landing, New Jersey

September-May

The largest culinary academy in New Jersey, part of Atlantic Community College, was founded in 1981 to meet the need for highly skilled chefs and foodservice professionals for the Atlantic City hospitality industry. The Academy enrolls 350 students (100% of applicants are accepted), most from southern New Jersey, and offers a two-year program leading to the Associate in Applied Science degree in Culinary Arts and a six-month Cook's Training Program in entry level skills. Facilities include six teaching kitchens with overhead mirrors, a bake shop, and classrooms. A new $4.6 million facility includes teaching kitchens, classrooms, a restaurant, banquet room, and offices.

Students attend classes five hours daily, mornings or afternoons, and 75% of their training is hands-on. Classes run on a semester basis, September-December and January-May, and five 15-day blocks are scheduled each semester. The curriculum is designed to provide an understanding of basic food tastes and combinations and preparations that enhance food consumption; to teach the skills required for the preparation and presentation of food garnishes, ornate sculptures, and pastry; to impart an understanding of the tools, layout, and production techniques used in the kitchen; and to offer a broad-based liberal arts education. Courses cover culinary arts and skills, food and baking fundamentals, garde manger, dining room operations, basic and classical pastry preparation, institutional foodservice and catering, purchasing and cost controls, hot food preparation, table service, wines, menu and facilities designs, international food preparation, and gourmet dining room operations. The student to teacher ratio is 20 to 1. Carême's, a 60-seat open-to-the-public gourmet restaurant on Atlantic Community College's Mays Landing campus, is operated by the students as part of their curriculum. The Academy has a job placement service and has placed 100% of the students who have used it.

Specialties: Two-year program leading to the Associate in Applied Science degree in the Culinary Arts; six-month Cook's Training Program.

Faculty: Students are taught by a 15-member international faculty.

Costs, Accommodations: The cost of the two-year program is approximately $9,000. Full refund, except for the preliminary $300 deposit, is granted for cancellations prior to the first day of semester and 50% refund up to the end of the second week of classes. Off-campus housing is guaranteed. Applicants must have a high school diploma or equivalent and participate in an information session. Financial aid is available.

Location: Atlantic Community College, a 537-acre campus in the heart of New Jersey's Pinelands, is 17 miles west of Atlantic City's boardwalk, 45 miles from Philadelphia, and 115 miles from New York City.

Contact: Admissions Office, Atlantic Community College, 5100 Black Horse Pk., Mays Landing, NJ 08330-2699; (609) 343-4922 *or* (800) 645-2433.

COOKINGSTUDIO
Short Hills, Bedminster, and Verona, New Jersey
Year-round

This school offers 30 to 35 one to eight-session demonstration and participation courses each month at its Short Hills, Bedminster and Verona locations. Classes are two to three hours and cover a variety of topics. The eight-session Principles of Cooking Diploma Course (limit 14 students) meets once weekly at 10:30 am or 6:30 pm for four hours and covers stocks and sauces, roasting, egg cookery, broiling and grilling, moist heat cooking, and sautéing. Those who pass a written test may enroll in the five-session Advanced Principles of Cooking Course (limit 14), which covers menu planning, pastries, patés, cream sauces, mousses, and garnishes. Other multi-session courses cover cakes, meats, microwave basics, and Italian fundamentals. The school also offers Sunday With a Chef classes, celebrity chef demonstrations, classes for couples and singles, and weekend classes for children, ages 4 to 14.

Specialties: Include techniques, nutritional foods, holiday menus, ethnic cuisines, microwave cookery; classes for children.

Faculty: The more than 15-member resident and guest faculty includes microwave author Christa Craig, caterer Rick Rodgers, food editor Kathleen Kenny Sanderson, baking specialist Carole Walter, and authors Norman Weinstein and Jean Yueh. Guest chefs have included Giuliano Bugialli, Nicholas Malgieri, Lorenza de'Medici, Jacques Pépin, and Martin Yan. The school is a member of the IACP.

Costs: The eight-class Principles course is $450, the Advanced Principles course is $275, some individual sessions are free and others range from $10 to $40, children's classes are $25 to $35. Full payment must accompany registration. Credit card (VISA, MasterCard) registrations accepted. Those who cancel at least three days prior receive full refund.

Contact: Arlene Sarappo, Manager, Cookingstudios, 2 Dedrick Place, West Caldwell, NJ 07006; (201) 575-3320, ext. 415.

COOKTIQUE
Tenafly, New Jersey

February-July, September-December

Established in 1976, this school offers approximately 150 three-hour evening demonstration (limit 25 students) and participation (limit 14) sessions a year, including five-session techniques courses for beginning and intermediate cooks, three-session saucier's and fish courses, and classes in beginning and intermediate cake decorating, ethnic and regional cuisines, holiday and seasonal menus, healthful foods, guest chef specialties, and other topics. Children's classes are held about one Saturday a month. Facilities include a 400-square-foot demonstration kitchen with overhead mirror.

Specialties: A variety of topics.

Faculty: Culinary professionals and master chefs. Guest chefs have included Guiliano Bugialli, Nicholas Malgieri, Betsy Oppenneer, Jacques Pepin, Joanne Weir, and Martin Yan.

Costs: Sessions range from $35 to $45; guest chef classes are $90 to $100. Payment is required with registration and cancellations more than 10 days prior to class receive a refund. Credit cards accepted.

Location: Tenafly is six miles from the George Washington Bridge and 16 miles from New York City.

Contact: Cathy McCauley, Director, Cooktique, 9 W. Railroad Ave., Tenafly, NJ 07670; (201) 568-7990.

THE GLORIA ROSE GOURMET
LONG LIFE COOKING SCHOOL
North and central New Jersey

Year-round

Established in 1984, this school offers three and four-session programs (limit ten students) for individuals concerned with weight control and/or sound nutrition as well as those suffering from diabetes, high cholesterol, hypertension, heart disease or other conditions requiring a modified diet. The objective of each three-hour demonstration session, which includes a five-course meal, is to provide personalized nutritional counseling and teach gourmet cooking without added salt, sugar, fats, or oils. Speed and ease of preparation are stressed and vegetarian diets, cultural and ethnic foods, analysis of product labels, and food selection when dining out are also covered. Day and evening classes are conducted in a 300-square-foot teaching kitchen.

Specialties: Nutritional education and preparation of foods without added salt, sugar, or fat.

Faculty: Gloria Rose is author of *Enjoying Good Health*, which is included in the program materials. Instructors are Registered Dietitians or Nurses affiliated with New Jersey hospitals.

Costs: Ranges from $300 (three sessions) to $500 (four sessions).

Location: The central New Jersey school is eight miles from Newark and the north Jersey school is 30 minutes from Manhattan.

Contact: Gloria Rose Gourmet Long Life Cooking School, 48 Norwood Rd., Springfield, NJ 07081; (201) 376-0942.

NEW MEXICO

JANE BUTEL TEX-MEX COOKERY SCHOOL
Santa Fe, New Mexico and Woodstock, New York
Year-round

Southwest regional cooking authority and cookbook author Jane Butel teaches five-day courses (limit 15 students) each August and selected other times in Santa Fe and weekend courses (limit 8) in spring, summer, and fall in the fully-equipped kitchen in her Woodstock home. These participation programs, developed by Ms. Butel in 1960, are tailored to the cook who wants to learn New Mexican and Southwestern cuisine. Graduate and Southwestern cuisine classes are also offered. The five-day course covers techniques, chiles, native breads, traditional soups and stews, appetizers and desserts, and such dishes as fajitas, chile rellenos, chimichangos, flautas, and empañadas. Students attend class from 9 am to 2 pm daily, preparing 10 to 15 dishes each session, after which they lunch on the foods prepared. Afternoons and evenings are free with the exception of two dinners at restaurants noted for their regional specialties. The weekend course features three 4-hour cooking sessions followed by dinner and lunches of the foods prepared. Saturday and Sunday evenings are free.

Specialties: New Mexican and Southwestern cuisine.

Faculty: Jane Butel is author of 10 Southwestern cookbooks, including *Fiesta* and *Hotter Than Hell*. She is founder of the Pecos Valley Spice Company, a manufacturer of chiles and seasonings for Southwestern cuisine. Southwesterner Gordon McMeen, an experienced teacher, chef, and caterer, helps conduct the classes. Experienced teachers also assist.

Costs, Accommodations: The $1,695 fee for the five-day course includes classes, lunches and two dinners, and lodging at the Inn of the Governors in downtown Santa Fe. Single supplement is $320. The $375 fee for the weekend course includes classes, two lunches, and one dinner. The registration deposit of $350 ($200 for Woodstock) is nonrefundable.

Location: Santa Fe attractions include the internationally known Indian Market, the Santa Fe Opera, and a wide range of cultural and recreational activities. Woodstock, located in the Catskill Mountains approximately 110 miles nothwest of New York City, offers galleries and arts and crafts stores as well as cultural activities.

Contact: Jane Butel Associates, P.O. Box 46, Mt. Tremper, NY 12457; (914) 679-2312, Fax (914) 679-2361.

LA ROMITA SCHOOL OF ART, INC., (page 220)

SANTA FE SCHOOL OF COOKING
Santa Fe, New Mexico
Year-round

Established in 1989, this school and regional food market offers 2½ to 3-hour demonstration classes (limit 44 students) several times weekly and smaller participation classes that include shopping at the Farmer's Market. The sessions, which include a full meal, focus on New Mexican and contemporary Southwestern cuisines as well as vegetarian cookery. Classes are conducted in a Santa Fe-style kitchen with overhead mirrors. A five-day culinary tour, scheduled for February, 1993, includes classes, meals at fine Santa Fe restaurants, chile seminars, and field trips to surrounding areas.

Specialties: New Mexican and contemporary Southwestern cuisines, vegetarian.

Faculty: Resident chefs include local cookbook authors and restaurant chefs specializing in Southwestern cooking; visiting chefs include Mark Miller of Coyote Cafe, Tracey Ritter of the Golden Door, and cookbook authors Jacqueline Higuera McMahan and Deborah Madison.

Costs: Basic classes begin at $25; specialty classes and culinary tours vary.

Location: Centrally located in the historic downtown district on the upper level of the Plaza Mercado Mall.

Contact: Susan Curtis, owner/director, Santa Fe School of Cooking, 116 W. San Francisco St., Santa Fe, NM 87501; (505) 983-4511, Fax (505) 983-7540.

NEW YORK

L'AMORE DI CUCINA ITALIANA (page 209)

ANNA TERESA CALLEN ITALIAN COOKING SCHOOL
New York, New York
September-May

Since 1979, Anna Teresa Callen has taught regional Italian cooking and conducted culinary tours of Italy. Her demonstration/participation classes are limited to eight students. Each class lasts four hours and includes a meal with wine.

Specialties: Regional Italian cuisine.

Faculty: Anna Teresa Callen, a Certified Member of the IACP and the New York Association of Cooking Teachers, is author of *The Wonderful World of Pizzas, Quiches, and Savory Pies,* and *Anna Teresa Callen's Menus for Pasta.* She has written for *Gourmet, Cook's, BonAppétit, Food & Wine,* and *The New York Times,* and also teaches at New York University, The New School for Social Research, and Peter Kump's New York Cooking School.

Costs: Five classes are $625. A $125 deposit must accompany registration.

Location: Classes are conducted in the well-equipped kitchen at 59 West 12th Street. Culinary tours are planned for New York University.

Contact: Anna Teresa Callen Italian Cooking School, 59 W. 12 St., New York, NY 10011; (212) 929-5640.

ANNEMARIE VICTORY ORGANIZATION, INC (page 182)

A LA BONNE COCOTTE
New York, New York

Year-round

Founded in 1971, this school offers beginner, intermediate, and advanced four-session participation courses (limit 10 students) in French cuisine. The $3\frac{1}{2}$ to 4-hour sessions are held in a large country kitchen and meet once weekly on Monday or Tuesday evenings at 5:30 or Thursdays at 9:30 am. Topics range from simple regional recipes to haute cuisine and classes are organized so that students work on simple to more complicated dishes according to their level of experience. Emphasis is on sauces, pastries, and the techniques of French cuisine. Students dine on the meal they've prepared.

Specialties: French cuisine.

Faculty: Mme. Lydie Pinoy Marshall, author of *Cooking with Lydie Marshall* and *A Passion for Potatoes*, teaches all classes.

Costs: Fee for a series of four classes is $370 and a $100 deposit must accompany application. Money-back refund policy for cancellations.

Contact: Mme. Lydie P. Marshall, A La Bonne Cocotte, 23 Eighth Ave., New York, NY 10014; (212) 675-7736.

CAROL'S CUISINE, INC.
Staten Island, New York

Year-round

Founded in 1972, this school offers 135 to 150 participation (limit 15 students) and demonstration (limit 25 to 35) courses in its large teaching kitchen with overhead mirror. The one to six-session courses meet weeknights from 7:45 to 10:45 pm and cover a variety of topics, including seasonal and holiday themes and guest chef specialties. Two 6-session courses, Techniques and Theory I and II, cover various dishes as well as the fundamentals of haute cuisine. Gourmet cooking courses for youngsters ages 7 to 16, taught at noon on Saturdays and Sundays, focus on appealing and nutritious menus. Private lessons, birthday parties for children, and parties for five to eight couples can be arranged.

Specialties: A variety of topics, including techniques, ethnic cuisines, breadmaking, cake decorating, holiday menus, and desserts; children's classes; catering.

Faculty: Owner-director Carol Frazzetta, a Certified Member of the IACP, holds an advanced certificate from Cordon Bleu and studied at La Varenne, Marcella Hazan's School, John Clancy's School of Baking, and the CIA. Guest instructors include Nicholas Malgieri, Len Pickell, and chef Jack Ubaldi.

Costs: Single sessions range from $35 to $50, two sessions from $68 to $76, three sessions $105, four sessions $150, five sessions $175, and six sessions $204. Complete payment of single sessions must accompany registration. A $35 deposit is required for two and three-session courses and a $70 deposit for four to six-session courses. Credit card (VISA, MasterCard, American Express) registrations accepted. No refunds granted.

Location: One hour from Manhattan by ferry or bus.

Contact: Carol Frazzetta, Carol's Cuisine, Inc., 1571 Richmond Rd., Staten Island, New York, NY 10304; (718) 979-5600.

THE CHOCOLATE GALLERY
New York, New York

Year-round

Founded in 1978, this school is for those interested in cake decoration and pastry at all levels. Areas of study include the Wilton Method of cake decoration on the beginning level; intermediate courses in focused areas of confectionery, such as holiday chocolate decoration and international decoration techniques; and more advanced courses in gum paste, Lambeth method, blown sugar, and advanced chocolate. Baking classes, first offered in fall of 1992, cover cake bases, petit fours, tarts, and hotel and restaurant desserts. The mostly hands-on sessions range from two hours to full days to full-week intensives. Demonstrations in wedding cake techniques and by well-known guest lecturers are also featured. The Wilton courses meet for two hours each session and new courses begin each month, year-round. Students may attend one class weekly for four consecutive weeks or enroll in intensive courses meeting daily for four consecutive days. Course I (Discover Cake Decorating) covers borders, writing, flowers, icing, and coloring. In Course II (Icing Flowers and More), students perfect the basics and learn a variety of new borders and flowers, decorating a basket cake as the final project. Course III (Fancy Lace & Tiered Cakes) covers border principles, lacework, and string work, culminating in a tiered cake. Other introductory classes include Chocolate, Gum Paste, Airbrush and Drawing, Cookies, Buttercream Flowers, Marzipan, and Decorating with Fresh Flowers. Other intermediate and advanced courses include Special Occasion Cakes, Australian and South African Gum Paste Specialties, Lambeth, Chocolate, and Pulled Sugar and Brown Sugar.

Specialties: Cake decoration, chocolate, baking.

Faculty: Owner-teacher Joan Mansour has studied with master cake decorators in the U.S. and abroad for more than 15 years and is a certified Wilton Cake Decorating Instructor, receiving the 1991 Award for National Enrollment and 1991 Northeast Teacher of the Year. Guest lecturers include Marithe de Alvarado, Elaine Gonzales, Gloria Griffin, Gunther Heiland, Albert Kumin, Jeanette Van Neekerk, Betty Van Norstrand, Carole Walter, and Adrian Westrope.

Costs: The four-session Wilton Method of Cake Decorating courses are $80 each and the international intensive classes are $100 per day. Intermediate and advanced workshops range from $35 for two hours to $500 for a full week course. Full payment must be received two weeks prior to first class.

Contact: Joan Mansour, The Chocolate Gallery, 34 W. 22nd St., New York, NY 10010; (212) 675-2253.

CLUB CUISINE
New York, New York and culinary trips abroad
Year-round

This cooking club, founded in 1985, sponsors wine tastings, guest chef demonstrations (20 to 30 students), seminars and classes, food-related events, and culinary travel programs. Participation classes for eight to ten students are held in the club's model recipe-testing kitchen, which is also used for photo and television sessions. Seminars are held at private homes, restaurants, and other locations. Cooking programs have included a six-week French conversation and cooking course, a gourmet gift workshop, table etiquette classes, series of Italian and French cooking classes, and food and wine seminars. Food-related events have included an early breakfast at Fulton Fish Market, visits to a food photographer's studio, and yacht excursions. Culinary trips to such locations as France, Italy, and the Orient are regularly scheduled. The club publishes a bi-monthly newsletter and organizes fund-raising food-related events.

Specialties: A variety of cooking and food-related activities, including guest chef demonstrations, courses in ethnic cuisines, food and wine seminars, and culinary travel programs.

Faculty: Club Cuisine founder and president Michèle Lyster is a French native who trained at La Varenne in Paris and Roger Vergé in Mougins. A food stylist and former tour director with American Express, she serves on the staff of the Culinary Arts Program of the New School for Social Research. Wine classes are taught by Len Pickell, Chapter Director of Les Amis du Vin. Guest instructors have included author Anna Teresa Callen, food photographer Nancy McFarland, and "Great Performances" caterers.

Costs: Annual membership is $60. Classes range from $25 to $100 and payment is due one week prior. Those who cancel at least three days prior receive a full refund less $5. Credit cards (VISA, MasterCard, American Express) accepted.

Location: The club is located in midtown Manhattan. Events are held at various locations in the city.

Contact: Michèle Lyster, Club Cuisine, Inc., 244 Madison Ave., #2, New York, NY 10016; (212) 557-5702, Fax (212) 286-0214.

COOKHAMPTON — SILVIA LEHRER
Water Mill, New York and Tuscany, Italy
June-August, October-November

Established in 1988, this school offers one to four-session demonstration (limit 20 students) and participation (limit 8) courses and culinary tours. The four to five-hour evening sessions, which are held in the school's 400-square-foot teaching kitchen and conclude with a meal, cover a variety of topics. Some three-session courses are held on three consecutive days in order to accommodate out-of-towners.

A biennial 10-day culinary tour of Italy, scheduled for April-May, 1993, and accompanied by Ms. Lehrer and Giuliano Bugialli, features four days of hands-on cooking classes with Mr. Bugialli at his school in Florence, visits to Assissi,

Torgiano, Montalcino, and Siena, and a tour of the cheese and prosciutto factories in Parma.

Specialties: French and Italian cuisines, pasta, grilling, guest chef specialties.

Faculty: IACP-Certified instructor Silvia Lehrer, former owner of Cooktique in Tenafly, New Jersey, is author of *Cooking at Cooktique* and studied with James Beard, Simca Beck, Giuliano Bugialli, and Jacques Pépin. Guest chefs include Giuliano Bugialli and Jacques Pépin.

Costs: Single sessions are $85 per person, $150 per couple, $100 to $125 for guest chefs; courses range from $250 for three sessions to $325 for four. Full payment must accompany registration for single sessions, $100 deposit is required for courses, and full refund is granted cancellations at least 10 days prior. Tour cost is about $4,000 ($3,600 for nonparticipant guest), including first class hotel lodging, most lunches and dinners, ground transportation, and planned activities.

Location: The summer resort area of Southampton township.

Contact: Silvia Lehrer, Cookhampton, P.O. Box 765, Water Mill, NY 11976; (516) 537-7831.

COOKING WITH JOHN DOHERTY AT THE WALDORF
The Waldorf-Astoria
New York, New York

February-June, October-November

Since 1990, Waldorf Executive Chef John Doherty has conducted demonstrations (limit 20 students) that feature the preparation of a complete meal prepared in a contemporary French manner, incorporating Chef Doherty's personal style. Approximately 25 classes are held annually, scheduled on alternate Saturdays (9:30 to 12:30 am) or Wednesdays (5:30 to 8:30 pm). Each session begins with a reception and tour of the Waldorf's kitchens, followed by demonstration and full course meal.

Specialties: Contemporary French and Italian cuisine.

Faculty: John Doherty is a graduate of the CIA and has been executive chef of the Waldorf since 1985.

Costs: $65 for one class. Tuition is payable in advance and cancellations at least five days prior receive full refund.

Location: The Waldorf-Astoria is situated on Park Ave. in mid-Manhattan.

Contact: Cooking with John Doherty, Chef's Office, The Waldorf-Astoria, 301 Park Ave., New York, NY 10022; (212) 872-4866.

CORNELL'S ADULT UNIVERSITY (CAU)
Ithaca, New York

July and August

Established in 1968, Cornell's Adult University offers an annual on-campus four-week summer program consisting of one-week workshops and courses. Subjects include cooking, history, current events, ecology, music, literature, and architecture and art. The Culinary Workshop, which is offered every year, focuses on menu planning know-how and the necessary kitchen skills to make (or keep) cooking fun and to create appetizing and nutritionally sound meals. Mornings are spent in the lab preparing soups, salads, vegetables, meats (especially poultry and fish), yeast, quick breads, and some desserts. Afternoon sessions with Cornell food scientists cover healthful eating topics. The summer programs are open to all, with enrollment ranging from 12 to 20 participants. Courses meet mornings and afternoons from Monday through Friday and lectures, plays, and special events are scheduled in the evenings. A fully-supervised youth program for 3 to 16-year-olds features activities and courses geared to five age groups.

Specialties: A variety of subjects, including cooking.

Faculty: All programs are taught by Cornell University faculty and staff.

Costs, Accommodations: Cost of the summer program is approximately $700 per week for adults and $250 to $350 for children, which includes tuition, double occupancy dormitory lodging (single supplement available), 16 meals, and planned activities. A $30 materials fee is additional. A $25 nonrefundable deposit reserves a space with balance due 30 days prior.

Location: The 13,000-acre campus is in New York's Finger Lakes region.

Contact: Cornell's Adult University, 626 Thurston Ave., Ithaca, NY 14850-2490; (607) 255-6260.

LA CUISINE SANS PEUR
New York, New York

Year-round

This cooking school for professionals and amateurs, founded in 1978, offers small, intensive courses in classic and regional French cuisine for the serious student who wishes to learn how to cook well, easily, and with style, without consulting recipes. The more than 20 courses taught throughout the year include the basic course, three intermediate courses, a baking course, and two advanced courses. Specialty courses include The Dessert Course, Fish and Game Courses, and several Alsatian and Provençal courses. All courses are five 4-hour sessions with the exception of the basic course, which is six sessions. Classes are limited to four students, who meet from 10 am to 2 pm or 6:30 to 10 pm. A light lunch or dinner is served. A one-year apprenticeship program is also available to anyone acceptable to the school director following an in-person interview.

Specialties: Regional and classic French cuisine, featuring the dishes of Alsace and Provence.

Faculty: Caterer and restaurant consultant Henri-Etienne Lévy, Cuisinier/Proprietaire of La Cuisine Sans Peur, instructs most classes. Guest instructors include working chefs from New York French restaurants.

Costs: All courses are $400; $350 per person for three students enrolling as a group. Missed classes may be repeated (at the school's discretion) at no additional cost. When the school determines that a technique needs more work, students are invited back, gratis, for additional sessions. Courses are scheduled to meet the needs of students and class starting date and place is confirmed upon receipt of full fee four weeks prior to the first class. No cash refunds are given but credits are issued. Courses outside New York are subject to different terms and conditions.

Location: The school is on Manhattan's Upper West Side, close to subway and bus lines, 10 minutes from Lincoln Center and the Metropolitan Museum of Art, and about 15 minutes from the theatre district and other cultural attractions.

Contact: Henri-Etienne Lévy, cuisinier/proprietaire, La Cuisine Sans Peur, 216 W. 89th St., New York, NY 10024; (212) 362-0638.

THE CUISINE, WINES, AND CULTURE OF THE ISLANDS OF THE WESTERN MEDITERRANEAN (page 225)

CULINARY ARTS AT THE NEW SCHOOL
New York, New York

Year-round

Founded in 1919 as a center for "discussion, instruction, and counseling for mature men and women", the New School for Social Research offers a comprehensive culinary program including courses of study in cooking, baking, career training, and wine appreciation. Professional level courses are offered for cooking and foodservice professionals as well as those aspiring to careers in the culinary arts, and short term courses are offered for beginning to experienced home cooks who wish to expand their repertoire. The school also offers classes for children and sponsors a variety of culinary events, including field trips to restaurants and markets, weekend workshops, and out-of-town travel. Classes are held in a restored landmark townhouse that features indoor and outdoor dining areas and a fully equipped instructional kitchen, designed for maximum student participation.

For those desiring a professional career, the School offers three Master Class participation courses once each trimester. Each course is limited to 12 students and is scheduled from 8 am to noon, Monday through Friday. Students receive a Certificate of Completion. All certificate students in professional level courses are able to obtain apprenticeship placement. The 25-session Master Class in Cooking stresses high-quality rather than quantity cooking and provides a comprehensive introduction to basic culinary skills, including use of knives and culinary tools; stocks, soups, and sauces; vegetables and salads; meat, poultry, game, fish, and shellfish butchering and preparation; desserts and pastries; charcuterie and hors d'oeuvres; garnishing and presentation; and recipe development. The 14-session Master Class in Baking emphasizes the preparation of fine pastries, dough work, and breadmaking and includes measuring techniques, tarts and pies, meringue, soufflés and buttercreams, pâte à choux, cake assembly and decoration, and chocolate work. The 12-session Professional Catering Master Class focuses on both the culinary and operational aspects of a catering business and provides students with the knowledge and experience to market their services. The course includes hands-on cooking and baking instruction as well as lectures on business management, menu development, kitchen organization, cost accounting, service, rentals, storage, transportation, and strategies for dealing with clients. Students plan and prepare a cocktail party and buffet. About 15 one to twelve-session professional-level courses (limit 25 to 35 students) are scheduled each trimester, from 7:45 to 9:45 pm weeknights or 10 am to 4 pm weekends. Topics include restaurant management, commercial cake decorating, professional food styling, how to create and sell a new food or beverage, and how to get a cookbook published.

More than 50 two to eight-session cooking and baking participation courses for cooking enthusiasts are offered each trimester. Classes are limited to 14 students and cover ethnic and regional cuisines, holiday menus, culinary techniques, the chemistry of cooking, wild game preparation, cooking for singles and couples, appetizers, main courses, and desserts. A complete meal is served in most courses. Demonstration sessions (limit 10 to 20 students) conducted by New York chefs in their restaurants are scheduled 10 to 15 times each trimester and weekend workshops with well-known master chefs and bakers (limited 12 students) are scheduled from 10 am to 4 pm Saturday and Sunday. The three or four workshops offered each trimester cover spa cooking, chocolate desserts, and pastries. Additional culinary events include a series of lectures on culture and cuisine by guest experts, French and Italian cooking taught in the native tongue, and a weekend workshop in food styling. Participation classes for youngsters, ages 8 to 12, include a gingerbread house workshop and holiday cookie class. About 10 one to four-session wine courses are taught each trimester by wine authorities.

Specialties: An extensive variety of courses for culinary and foodservice professionals, those who aspire to a culinary arts career, beginning to experienced home cooks, cooking and wine enthusiasts, and children.

Faculty: The 50-member professional faculty, headed by well-known food and restaurant consultant Gary A. Goldberg and co-founder Martin Johner, includes cookbook authors Jack Ubaldi, Arlyn M. Hackett and Joanne Lamb Hayes; wine director and authority Harriet Lembeck; chefs Karen Snyder-Kadish, Richard M. Glavin, Lisa Montenegro, Miriam Brickman, and Henry Hugh; caterers Shirley King and Deborah Jensen; and food and wine consultants Leonard Pickell, Robert W. Posch, Lisa Chodosh, and Carmen Cook.

Costs: The Master Class in Cooking is $1,925 (plus $425 for materials); the Master Class in Baking is $1,050 (plus $190); and the Professional Catering Master Class is $915 (plus $225). Most other professional level courses are $40 per session (plus $5 to $14). Courses for cooking enthusiasts average $55 per session (plus $12 to $20) and children's classes are $25 (plus $8). Restaurant demonstrations are $60, lectures are $15, and weekend workshops are $315. Wine courses range from $30 to $35 per session (plus $12 to $23). Credit card (VISA, MasterCard) registration accepted. Mail registrations must be postmarked at least two weeks before class. Full refund, less $20 fee, is granted written cancellations prior to class. A kitchen assistant program and work/study program are open to selected applicants who may enroll at no cost in exchange for their services.

Location: Classes are held at 100 Greenwich Avenue, located between 12th and 13th Streets, in Manhattan's historic Greenwich Village district.

Contact: New School Culinary Arts, 100 Greenwich Ave., New York, NY 10011; (212) 255-4141 (New School Culinary Arts), (800) 544-1978, ext. 25 (for New School Bulletin), (212) 229-5690 (for registration).

THE CULINARY INSTITUTE OF AMERICA
Hyde Park, New York

Year-round

This private, not-for-profit institution was founded in 1946 to provide quality technical and practical culinary education to those seeking careers in the foodservice and hospitality industry. The school moved to its present 80-acre campus in 1972 and currently enrolls more than 1,900 full-time students in its two 21-month programs leading to an Associate's Degree in Occupational Studies (A.O.S.) in either culinary arts or baking and pastry arts. The Continuing Education Department offers both a year-round schedule (except the first two weeks of July and the last week of December) of one, two, three, nine, and thirty-week courses in cooking, baking and pastry, and food and beverage education and custom-designed programs for groups of six or more. These short courses are designed to help the foodservice professional expand skills, learn new techniques, and gain fresh ideas. The school's facilities include 36 commercially equipped production kitchens — including a fish kitchen, Oriental kitchen, experimental kitchen, three bakeshops, three pastry shops, six garde manger kitchens and a charcuterie kitchen — eight instructional dining rooms, a food production/demonstration auditorium, a food and sanitation laboratory, two meat cutting facilities, and a commercial storeroom. The Institute runs four student-staffed restaurants that are open to the public: The Escoffier Restaurant serves classical French cuisine, The American Bounty Restaurant showcases American food and wine, The Caterina de Medici Dining Room offers modern and traditional regional Italian cuisine, and St. Andrew's Cafe features contemporary cuisine in a casual atmosphere. Other on-campus facilities include a learning resources center, bookstore, and a 38,000-volume library. The General Foods Nutrition Center, opened in 1989, houses a state-of-the-art kitchen specially designed for nutritional cooking, a nutrition resource center and classroom, and a bakeshop. The School of Baking and Pastry, opened in 1990, is a 15,000-square-foot facility dedicated to baking and pâtisserie instruction. It includes three bakeshops and three pastry shops, each furnished with modular workstations. The Institute holds an Absolute Charter issued by the New York State Board of Regents and is approved for veterans training under the G.I. Bill of Rights. The curricula are registered with the New York State Education Department and the school is accredited by the CCA (NATTS).

The culinary arts program enrolls a new class of approximately 70 students 16 times each year, and the baking and pastry arts program starts eight times per year. Both programs are divided into four 15-week instructional semesters and an 18-week externship scheduled between the second and fourth semesters. The programs' common objective is to provide a broad culinary education with a balance of hands-on teaching of cooking and baking skills and culinary theory. Courses cover sanitation and safety, nutrition, culinary math, meat identification and butchering, purchasing and stewarding, cost control, foodservice business law, culinary skills development, seafood cookery, garde manger, American, Oriental, Italian, and classical French cuisines, charcuterie, baking skills and pâtisserie, wine and spirits, hospitality management, and banquet service. A rotation through each of the four public restaurants is scheduled for the fourth semester. Students are assigned to groups of 18 per instructor and attend classes approximately 6¹/₂ hours daily, either in the morning or the afternoon. The externships consist of a minimum of 600 hours in each program at a salaried position in a commercial foodservice establishment approved by the school. To graduate, a student must successfully complete the entire course of study. The school awards one-semester or one-year fellowships to a limited number of graduates who receive a weekly stipend and assist faculty members in kitchens, dining rooms, and bakeshops. The school's Career Services Office assists in finding employment opportunities and publishes a biweekly listing of job openings. Each graduate receives an average of three to four job opportunities.

The Continuing Education Department offers 47 different courses throughout the year for professional cooks, bakers, food supervisors and managers, restaurateurs, and culinary instructors. Two sessions are scheduled daily, Monday through Friday or Tuesday through Saturday: the morning session begins at 6:45 and the afternoon session begins at 1:30. A majority of the cooking courses are five days long and include lecture, demonstration, and hands-on practice. Topics include food show competition, use of new equipment, fish and shellfish, meat cutting, foodservice management, wine merchandising, food styling, baking and pastry, and a variety of cuisines. A 45-day comprehensive program covers basic cooking and baking methods. Baking and pastry courses, taught via lecture, demonstration, and hands-on practice, include the comprehensive Certificate Baking and Pastry Program, two 15-day courses, Professional Baking Fundamentals and Pâtisserie, a five-day pastry production course, Food Show Competition: Baking and Pastry, Artistic Decoration, Kitchen Desserts, Bread Baking, and Chocolate and Candies courses. Continuing Education Units (CEUs) are awarded those who successfully complete a course. During the spring and fall, the Continuing Education Department also offers a variety of courses for food enthusiasts, including two courses just for youngsters. Four-session courses, which meet once weekly for four consecutive weeks, include Breakfast and Brunch, Cooking Fundamentals, Culinary Math, Fun With Baking, International Cuisine, and Wines of the World. All courses are taught by Institute chef-instructors and conducted at the Hyde Park campus kitchens, bakeshops, and dining rooms.

Specialties: Full-time 21-month professional courses for cooks, apprentice chefs, bakers and apprentice pastry chefs; continuing education courses covering cooking, baking and pastry, and food and beverage education.

Faculty: The school's international faculty of more than 100 chefs, pastry chefs, maîtres d'hôtel, and food and beverage educators represent over 20 countries and have more than 2,500 combined years of experience.

Costs, Accommodations: The estimated total cost (tuition, fees, two meals a day) of the 21-month program is $21,705. Candidates for admission are required to have a high school diploma or equivalent and three to five months' of kitchen experience in a non-fast-food restaurant. Applications, accompanied by a nonrefundable $30 application fee, should be submitted 4 to 6 months prior to the date the applicant wishes to enter the program. An advance deposit of $150 is due 90 days prior to registration, half of each semester's tuition is due 60 days prior to the start of the semester, and the balance is due by registration day. Those who cancel at least 90 days prior to registration or within three days of signing enrollment agreement receive a full tuition refund. Refund ranges from full tuition less $150 for those who withdraw before the first week of each semester to no refund for those who withdraw after the eighth week. Financial aid is available from several sources, including scholarships for second-year students. The school has on-campus dormitory facilities for 1,100 students. Dormitory fees (per semester) range from $1,155 for a quadruple room to $2,385 for a single room with bath. Tuition (which includes two meals per day) for continuing education courses averages $495 for five-day courses, $1,250 for 14-day courses, $3,375 for 42-day courses. A nonrefundable $150 deposit must accompany application and balance is due two weeks prior to course. For longer courses, refunds are computed on a sliding scale. Guest rooms on campus are available at competitive rates.

Location: The school is located on U.S. Route 9 in Hyde Park, approximately a two-hour drive from New York City and one hour from Albany. It is three miles north of the Poughkeepsie railroad station, which is served hourly by Metro-North train service from New York City's Grand Central Terminal.

Contact: The Culinary Institute of America, 433 Albany Post Rd., Hyde Park, NY 12538-1499; (914) 452-9600. Continuing Education Dept.: (800) 888-7850.

DE GUSTIBUS AT MACY'S
New York, New York

September-June

Each fall and spring, Macy's Herald Square offers approximately a half dozen one to five-session cooking series taught by well-known chefs and cookbook authors. The mostly demonstration $2^{1}/_{2}$ to 3-hour sessions, held in the department store's professionally-equipped eighth floor kitchen, usually begin at 5:30 pm, although some start at 1 or 2 pm. Demonstration sessions are limited to 65 students and participation classes to 20. The school, founded in 1980, also offers Wine Intensive Seminars and a Recipe Writing Course for Chefs and Food Professionals on Saturdays from 1 to 4 pm. A one-day course for professional dining room staff, the New York Professional Service School, covers service skills and in-depth food and wine taste-training. A Gastronomic Tour to Belgium was first offered in 1992.

Specialties: Regional American cuisine, French/Italian cuisines, wine selection, menus for entertaining, guest chef specialties.

Faculty: Includes David Bouley, Giuliano Bugialli, Bobby Flay, Perla Meyers, Debra Ponzek, Alfred Portale, Wolfgang Puck, Stephan Pyles, Anne Rosenzweig, Alain Sailhac, André Soltner, Brendan Walsh, and Paula Wolfert. Karen MacNeil conducts the professional service program.

Costs: Series range from $55 for one session to $200 for a series of four. Individual sessions are $55 to $65, on a space available basis. The Professional Service School course is $125, with discounts available to several participants from the same restaurant. Credit cards (Macy's, American Express, MasterCard, VISA) accepted. Those who cancel receive class credit.

Location: Macy's Herald Square is located at 34th Street and 7th Avenue. Classes are also available at Roosevelt Field, Long Island.

Contact: Arlene Feltman, De Gustibus at Macy's, 343 E. 74 St., Apt. 9G, New York, NY 10021; (212) 439-1714.

DINNER IS SERVED COOKING SCHOOL
Brooklyn, New York

February-June, September-December

Established in 1989 by Louise Hoffman, this school offers demonstration (limit 16 students) and participation (limit 8) classes that feature whole foods and dairy-free and sugar-free vegetarian cuisine. Approximately six 3-hour classes are offered each month, with series running three to four weekly sessions. Classes are held in a brownstone apartment that has a fully-equipped teaching kitchen with two stoves and ovens.

Specialties: International dairy-free and sugar-free vegetarian and whole foods.

Faculty: Louise Hoffman is a graduate of the CIA and the Teachers Training Program of The Natural Gourmet Cookery School in New York City, where she serves as an instructor. She has cooked professionally for 14 years at restaurants in New York and New Orleans.

Costs: Tuition ranges from $35 to $45 per class and payment must accompany registration. Class credit is granted cancellations at least two days prior to an individual class. For a series, a substitute may be sent.

Location: The school is in Park Slope, near the 7th Avenue "F" train exit.

Contact: Louise Hoffman, Dinner Is Served, 434 Third Street, Brooklyn, NY 11215; (718) 499-3195.

ECOLE DES ARTES CULINAIRES ET DE L'HOTELLERIE (page 188)

EPICUREAN GALLERY, LTD.
New York, New York

Year-round

Founded in 1971, this school offers four 6-session participation courses (limit five students): Northern Italian, French, Slimming French, and Gilda Latzky's Famous Baking Course. The aim of each course is to provide the expertise needed to modify existing recipes, create new dishes, and plan menus. Sessions meet once weekly at 7 pm in the school's kitchen and include a dinner of the foods prepared.

Specialties: French, Italian, new American cuisine, baking, party catering.

Faculty: School owner-manager Gilda Latzky has taught French and Italian cooking and the art of baking for more than 19 years in New York City. She has studied in France and Italy and at the CIA.

Costs: Each six-session course is $350. A $75 deposit is required with registration and no refunds are granted.

Contact: Gilda Latzky, Epicurean Gallery, Ltd., 808 Broadway, New York, NY 10003; (212) 460-8243.

THE FRENCH CULINARY INSTITUTE (FCI)
New York, New York

Year-round

This professional cooking school, established in 1984 and accredited by the CCA (NATTS), is the result of a collaboration between the Chambre de Commerce et d'Industrie de Paris (CCIP) and Apex Technical School of New York, which was founded in 1961 as a private trade school specializing in technical training programs. FCI offers a 600-hour course that is evenly divided into two sections: an introduction to the basic techniques of French cuisine and an advanced course in French restaurant service. The curriculum was developed by Le Centre de Formations des Metiers de l'Alimentation (Ferrandi), a well-known cooking school in France. During the first half, students concentrate on learning techniques in the basic kitchen. They then move into the main kitchen where they prepare a wide variety of dishes for the Institute's dining room, L'Ecole, which is open to the public. During this period they learn 12 basic menus containing 72 separate items and also create original dishes. Final evaluation is based upon development and presentation of a creative, four-course menu, a written examination, and preparation and presentation of classic dishes to a panel of judges. Students may attend full-time for six months (from 8:30 am to 2:30 pm, Monday through Friday), or part-time for nine months (from 5:30 to 11 pm on Monday, Wednesday and Friday). Day and evening classes, with a student to teacher ratio of no more than sixteen to one, begin every six weeks. Graduates may utilize the school's placement service (employment rate is 91%) and are also eligible to attend the Ecole Superieure de Cuisine Française, a two-year program in advanced techniques offered at Ferrandi, in Paris.

Specialties: A 600-hour professional training course in French cuisine.

Faculty: Includes Jacques Pépin, Dean of Culinary Studies.

Costs, Accommodations: Total cost of the 600-hour course is $13,500, which includes tuition, uniforms, supplies, insurance, and a $50 registration fee. Students who cancel more than three days after signing the enrollment agreement forfeit the registration fee. Those who withdraw during the first week of class receive a full tuition refund (less uniforms, supplies, and registration fee). The withdrawal charge ranges from 10% of tuition during the first quarter of the course to 100% of tuition after the last half. A variety of sources of financial aid are available. Applicant must have a high school diploma or equivalent. Previous foodservice experience and knowledge of French are desirable but not mandatory. A list of nearby housing facilities that offer discounts to FCI students is provided, and the Admissions Office will assist out-of-town students with housing.

Location: On the corner of Grand and Broadway in New York's SoHo district.

Contact: Admissions Department, The French Culinary Institute, 462 Broadway, New York, NY 10013; (212) 219-8890.

THE GIULIANO BUGIALLI COOKING CLASSES IN NEW YORK
New York, New York

November and January

In addition to his Cooking in Florence program (page 214), Giuliano Bugialli conducts four-session participation courses (limit 12 students) that meet for three to four hours once weekly in a large reproduction of a Tuscan country kitchen. Two series are offered: the First Series consists of Guiliano's basic techniques; the Continuation Series presents new menus each season. Morning classes begin at

10 am, evening classes begin at 6 pm, and all classes culminate in a four-course meal of the dishes prepared, accompanied by appropriate wines. Recipes include pastas, soups, risotti, antipasti, sauces, desserts and pastries, bread making, and techniques for preparing, boning, and stuffing meat, fish, and fowl. Three-day weekend workshops, which cover hearth cooking and brick oven baking, are available to individuals and groups.

Specialties: Italian regional cuisine..

Costs: Cost of each course is $400. A $100 deposit is required with balance due 60 days prior to start of classes. Cancellations more than 60 days prior forfeit $10.

Contact: Giuliano Bugialli, P.O. Box 1650, Canal St. Station, New York, NY 10013; (212) 334-6430.

GRITTI PALACE COOKING COURSES (page 215)

ITALIAN COUNTRY COOKING WITH DIANA FOLONARI (page 216)

JANE BUTEL TEX-MEX COOKERY SCHOOL (page 73)

JANE THOMPSON'S COOKING SCHOOL
Pawling, New York

Year-round

Established in 1988, this school offers one to three-day technique courses and one-day specialized classes on request. The participation sessions (limit six students), which emphasize classic French and Italian cuisine, are conducted in the professionally equipped kitchen of Thornhill, the Thompson's 250-year-old Dutchess County farmhouse. The course meets from 10 am until 2 pm and concludes with a meal of the foods prepared, accompanied by wine. Classes feature dinner menus, brunch, and one day is devoted to fish. Students are taught how to make fresh pasta, bone poultry and fish, and prepare stocks, sauces, and pastries. One-day classes are scheduled any day, by arrangement, and are frequently offered at area gourmet stores.

Specialties: Classic French and Italian cuisine.

Faculty: Jane Thompson is managing editor of *Master Chef* magazine and has studied with Simone Beck, Jacques Pépin, Madeleine Kamman, Giuliano Bugialli, and Alice Waters.

Costs: The three-day courses are $235 and discounts are available for groups of five or more. A $100 deposit is required with balance due 14 days prior to course. Credit cards (VISA, MasterCard, American Express) accepted. Cancellations at least 14 days prior receive full refund less $20; no refunds thereafter but date can be changed. One-day classes range from $43 to $85.

Location: Pawling is 90 minutes from New York City.

Contact: Jane Thompson's Cooking School, P.O. Box 484, Pawling, NY 12564; (914) 855-3859/3406.

JULIE SAHNI'S INDIAN COOKING
Brooklyn Heights, New York, and Other U.S. locations

Year-round

Julie Sahni offers four year-round intensive participation courses for professional and nonprofessional cooks. Each course is limited to four students who meet over a weekend — 6 to 7 pm on Friday, 10 am to 4 pm on Saturday, and 11 am to 5 pm on Sunday— in the specially designed teaching/recipe tasting kitchen in her home. The courses, which include a trip to an Indian grocery and a complete meal, emphasize cooking techniques, appropriate use of spices, herbs, and seasonings, and planning healthful, balanced meals. Historical and cultural background and religious ideologies behind cuisines are also covered. Ms. Sahni offers the courses in any private kitchen located in the U.S. as a condensed day-long session, from 10 am to 6 pm, limited to six students (does not include trip to Indian grocery).

The courses are: Chemistry of Herbs & Spices— the science of combining spices and herbs with ingredients, the secret of Indian cooking; Classic Indian Cooking — the royal court, also known as Moghul or "classic" cooking of India, with emphasis on meat, poultry, and seafood, suited for entertaining; Regional Indian Vegetarian Cooking— emphasizing the Southern Brahmin and Western Jain cuisines, noted for low calorie, low salt dishes made with homemade cheese, lentils, vegetables, and fruits; and Indian Baking: Breads and Snacks— Indian breads made with whole meal flours using special techniques for kneading, rolling and cooking (griddlebaking, steam baking, dry heat baking, fire roasting, shallow frying, and deep frying) and famous Indian snacks.

Specialties: Indian cuisine.

Faculty: Award-winning cookbook author, food consultant, and columnist Julie Sahni was executive chef of two restaurants and proprietor of Julie Sahni's Indian Cooking School, all in New York City. She serves on the faculty of New York University and Boston University, is a regular contributor to the *The New York Times*, writes for *Bon Appétit, Food & Wine*, and other food magazines, is author of *Classic Indian Cooking, Classic Indian Vegetarian and Grain Cooking*, and *Moghul Microwave*, and is featured in *The Book of Bests*.

Costs: Three-session courses are $700; a private day-long class is $1,500 (travel and accommodations for locations outside a 100-mile radius of N.Y.C. are extra). A $150 nonrefundable deposit must accompany application. Course credit is granted cancellations.

Location: Near the Brooklyn entrance to the Brooklyn Bridge, overlooking the Wall Street area.

Contact: Julie Sahni, Julie Sahni's Indian Cooking, 101 Clark St., Brooklyn Heights, NY 11201; (718) 625-3958.

KAREN LEE IMAGINATIVE COOKING CLASSES & CATERING
New York, New York

Year-round

Since 1972, Karen Lee has conducted year-round participation classes in Chinese cuisine for cooks of all levels. Twice a year she offers two 5-day courses for out-of-towners, Nouvelle Chinese Cuisine and Basic Chinese Cuisine, three 4-session courses that meet once weekly — Nouvelle Chinoise, Basic Chinese Cuisine, and Soup, Salad, and Pasta Innovations — and weekend seminars, with subjects determined by participants. Italian cooking classes are also offered. Attendance in each course is limited to eight or nine participants, who conclude the session with a meal of the recipes prepared.

In the Nouvelle Chinese Cuisine course, students prepare such dishes as goat-cheese-filled won tons and Sichuan-peppercorn roast duck. Basic Chinese Cuisine is devoted to cooking and cutting techniques and the preparation of such dishes as spring rolls, shrimp in garlic sauce, barbecued roast duck, and steamed dumplings with spicy sauce. Classes meet from 10 am to 3 pm and include a tour of Chinatown's markets. Nouvelle Chinoise pairs French and Chinese ingredients and techniques to produce such dishes as parchment salmon with ginger saffron sauce, grilled tuna with tomato lime sauce, and Sichuan steak au poivre. Soup, Salad, and Pasta Innovations features menu planning and preparation of Egyptian chick pea soup, porcini veal sauce alla Parma, and scallop and caviar salad. Weekly sessions meet from 10 am to 2 pm or from 6 to 10 pm; weekend courses are from 5 to 10 pm Friday and 10 am to 5 pm Saturday and conclude with a shopping tour and lunch on Sunday. Topics include low salt/low fat dishes, grain recipes, and grilled specialties.

Specialties: Chinese and Italian cuisine.

Faculty: School owner Karen Lee teaches all classes. She apprenticed with Madame Grace Zia Chu and is author of *Nouvelle Chinese Cuisine, Chinese Cooking Secrets, Chinese Cooking for the American Kitchen,* and *Soup, Salad and Pasta Innovations*. She also operates a catering business.

Costs: Tuition, which includes a copy of Karen Lee's latest book, is $630 for the five-day course, $430 for the four-session course, and $280 for the weekend course (does not include Sunday lunch). A $150 nonrefundable deposit must accompany application. In the event of cancellation the deposit may be applied to future courses.

Location: On Manhattan's West Side, near Lincoln Center.

Contact: Karen Lee Imaginative Cooking Classes & Catering, 142 West End Ave., New York, NY 10023; (212) 787-2227.

THE KING'S CHOCOLATE HOUSE
Ozone Park, New York

Year-round except summer

The Ultimate Chocolate Candy Class, a five-day participation course scheduled four times a year, is designed to give students confidence in using different techniques and brands of chocolate. Sessions meet Monday through Friday, from 9 am to 4:30 pm, and cover such topics as apricot roses, hand-dipped fruits, truffles, fondant, English toffee, hard candy, mints, tempering, woven baskets and baby dolls, hollow and solid molding, marshmallow, and molded liqueur.

Specialties: Chocolate creations.

Faculty: School proprietor and instructor Joan Lipkis studied with Rose Levy Beranbaum, Vivian Blotter, Mildred Brand, Chris Dalquist, Elaine Gonzales,

Ruedi C. Hauser, Shirley Jackson, Albert Kumin, Mel Lopez, Meta McCall, and Westly Wilton.

Costs: Course fee is $775. A deposit of $375 must accompany registration with $400 due three weeks prior to course. Written cancellations at least three weeks prior forfeit $193.75 (25% of fee); no refunds thereafter.

Location: Between JFK International Airport and LaGuardia Airport in Queens. A list of nearby lodging is provided.

Contact: Joan Lipkis, The King's Chocolate House, 112-09 Rockaway Blvd., Ozone Park, NY 11420; (718) 848-8564.

KOSHER COOKING SCHOOL
92nd Street YM-YWHA
New York, New York

February-April and September-November

Established in 1978, this nonvocational school offers 10 to 15 demonstration (limit 18 students) and participation (limit 15) classes a year in kosher international cooking. The two to three-hour evening sessions are held in restaurant and synagogue kitchens, some of which have overhead mirrors.

Specialties: Kosher international cuisine.

Faculty: Director Batia Plotch is author of *The International Kosher Cookbook*.

Costs: Range from $50 to $60 per session.

Location: Facilities on Manhattan's East and West Side.

Contact: Batia Plotch, Kosher Cooking School, 92nd Street YM-YWHA, 1395 Lexington Ave., New York, NY 10128; (212) 415-5599, Fax (212) 415-5578.

MARCELLA HAZAN SCHOOL (page 218)

MARY BETH CLARK — INT. COOKING SCHOOL (page 219)

THE NATURAL GOURMET COOKERY SCHOOL
Institute for Food and Health
New York, New York

Year-round

Founded in 1977, this school offers a Chef's Training Program, an Assistant's Program, two-week intensive day and evening courses, a one-week advanced intensive, demonstration (limit 30 students) and participation (limit 15) classes covering a variety of nutritional culinary topics, and lectures on food and health-related topics. The school's philosophy is to teach people how to choose and prepare delicious food that improves or contributes to health, and understand the relationship between food and healing. The school also has a bookstore and a Friday Night Dinner Club, where a natural, healthful, five-course dinner for $18 is served each Friday at 6:30. Catering is also available.

No prior culinary knowledge is required for the Chef's Training Program, designed for those desiring a cooking career in natural foods establishments or as a private cook or caterer. The curriculum emphasizes the preparation of well-balanced meals according to Oriental and Western principles and includes whole grains, beans, vegetables, fish, soy products, sea vegetables, condiments, herbs and spices, and sugar-free desserts. Students are taught menu planning, special diet cookery, quantity cooking, and business skills. The course, limited to 16 students, includes 600 hours of theory, hands-on cooking, skills practice, and an externship. The daytime program begins each January, May, and September and the evening program begins in February, meeting two nights per week and three Saturdays per month. The school offers a job referral service. Approximately 98% of applicants are accepted and employment rate is 100%.

The two-week summer intensive, designed for out-of-towners, consists of eighteen $2^1/2$-hour classes covering herbs and spices, beans and grains, vegetables, soups and salads, dressings, whole-grain bread baking, sea vegetables, medicinal cooking, tofu, tempeh and seitan, utensils and equipment, buying and storing produce, and adapting ordinary recipes using healthful ingredients. Classes are scheduled daily, Monday through Friday, from 10 am to 4 pm. A textbook and lunches are included. An evening two-week intensive consists of 10 three-hour classes with a full meal served at each class. The one-week advanced intensive, which features hands-on and specialty cooking, meets Monday through Friday from 10 am to 4 pm and includes lunches.

Approximately 50 cooking courses, many with several sessions, are offered each trimester from 6:30 to 9:30 pm and include tastings or a meal; weekend classes are scheduled at various times. Lecture classes and series cover such health-related topics as kitchen pharmacy, Chinese herbology, and holistic health care for pets. A 13-session series, Food and Healing, East and West, meets once weekly and covers fundamentals of nutrition, the Chinese 5-phase theory, and the uses of food for healing. Students are required to read eight books, write a short paper, and give an oral presentation. A certificate of completion is awarded. Students may sign up for a single class in any series on a space available basis. The one-year Assistant's Program, for those who've completed two introductory classes, allows participants to observe and assist in one or more classes per week, help set up and clean up, and pay a flat fee. Programs begin in January, April, and September.

Specialties: Courses for all levels and classes in natural, health supportive, and nutritional cookery; ethnic cuisines adapted to natural foods.

Faculty: School founder and director Annemarie Colbin, C.C.P., C.H.E.S., is a syndicated columnist and author of three books—*The Book of Whole Meals*, *Food and Healing* and *The Natural Gourmet*; associate director Lissa De Angelis, C.C.P., has owned a bakery and has private cooking, restaurant, and catering experience. Other faculty include Louise Hoffman, a CIA graduate; natural foods chef Jenny Matthau; and Martin Goldstein, D.V.M.

Costs: Tuition is $7,500 for the Chef's Training Program, $1,060 for the summer intensive, $530 for the evening two-week intensive, $590 for the advanced intensive, $55 for single cooking classes, and $25 for lectures. Series of six classes are $285. The fee is $2,750 for the one-year Assistant's Program. Full payment for classes under $100 or 50% deposit for those that cost more is required with registration and balance is due by the first class. Tuition is refunded, minus a 10% fee, for cancellations more than five business days prior. No refunds thereafter but deposit or tuition, less a 20% withdrawal fee, may be applied to another course.

Persons over 65 receive a discount of 20% on Friday Night Dinner Club meals and 10% on classes. A work-study program is available. Credit cards (VISA, MasterCard) accepted.

Location: On 21st Street between 5th and 6th Avenues, accessible to any subway that stops at 23rd Street. Parking is available nearby.

Contact: Lissa DeAngelis, Associate Director, The Natural Gourmet Cookery School/Institute for Food and Health, 48 W. 21st St., 2nd Floor, New York, NY 10010; (212) 645-5170.

NEW YORK RESTAURANT SCHOOL
New York, New York

Year-round

Founded in 1980, this school for professional cooks offers a 6-month Culinary Arts course for those desiring a cooking career, a 10-month Cooking and Restaurant Management course, a 10-month Restaurant Management program for those who plan to operate a high-quality, small-to-medium-sized restaurant, and a Pastry Arts program for those pursuing a professional baking career. New courses start every month except August and December and are held in the school's four kitchens and two lecture classrooms. The Placement Office provides interview preparation classes, resumé writing assistance, and arranges for job interviews. Graduates may utilize the services of the Placement Office at any time and may return to retake any courses at no additional cost. Approximately 90% of applicants are accepted and 95% of graduates obtain employment.

The Culinary Arts course is designed to provide the student with an in-depth knowledge of basic food preparation, cooking, and baking techniques as well as to develop dexterity in knife skills, speed, timing, and coordination. Sanitation, recipe math, chemistry of cooking, career planning, and menu writing are also covered. During the first four months students attend kitchen classes seven hours daily, five days a week. The last two months are devoted to an externship at a selected restaurant, catering company, executive dining room, or gourmet food store, during which the student gains practical experience in an environment that fits his or her career interests. Schedule varies depending on the establishment but is likely to include a lunch (8:30 am to 4:30 pm) or dinner (3 to 11 pm) shift, five or six days a week. Students may also take the course in the evenings or on weekends. The Cooking and Restaurant Management course consists of cooking, baking, and management classes, with emphasis on personal hygiene and proper food-handling techniques. Students are assigned to groups of 18 and attend classes five days a week for seven hours each day, divided between $3\frac{1}{2}$ hours in the kitchen and $3\frac{1}{2}$ hours in management lectures, with eight weeks devoted to an externship. The Restaurant Management program focuses on principles of management, costs, controls, and marketing.

Specialties: Courses for foodservice professionals include a ten-month culinary arts course, a cooking and restaurant management course, a restaurant management program, and a pastry arts program.

Faculty: The 24 faculty members are selected for both their culinary training and industry experience.

Costs, Accommodations: Tuition, which includes food, books, and registration fee, is $11,979 for Culinary Arts, $17,795 for Cooking and Restaurant Management, $7,971 for Restaurant Management, and $6,276 for Pastry Arts. Applicants must have a high school diploma or equivalent and no previous foodservice experience is necessary. Students may arrange for installment payments or apply for financial aid through student or parent loans, Pell grants, or industry scholarships. Full refund is offered for cancellations within seven days after signing the Enrollment Agreement and the school retains the $40 registration fee for withdrawals after the seven-day grace period and up to the first week of class. The Admissions Office provides assistance in obtaining nearby housing.

Location: The school is in Manhattan, just off Fifth Avenue.

Contact: New York Restaurant School, 27 W. 34th St., New York, NY 10001; (212) 947-7097.

NORMAN WEINSTEIN'S BROOKLYN COOKING SCHOOL
Brooklyn, New York

September-June

Since 1974, Norman Weinstein has taught Oriental cooking techniques to cooks of all levels. The one to three-session participation courses (limit eight students) meet from 7 to 10 pm in Hot Wok Catering's 150-square-foot kitchen and cover such topics as knife skills, basic techniques, dim sum, Thai cuisine, Hong Kong specialties, and one pot dishes. Approximately 15 courses are offered during the year and private classes are available. Tasting dinners at New York area restaurants and Chinatown walking tours are scheduled regularly.

Specialties: Oriental cuisine.

Faculty: Certified Culinary Professional Norman Weinstein is author of two cookbooks and editor of The Hot Wok Newsletter. He has operated Hot Wok Catering for more than 15 years.

Costs: Courses range from $40 to $50 per session. A 50% deposit is required with balance due at first class. Cancellations more than two weeks prior receive a full refund less $5 fee.

Location: Brooklyn's Kensington area, accessible via subway from Manhattan.

Contact: Norman Weinstein's Brooklyn Cooking School, 412 E. 2nd St., Brooklyn, NY 11218; (718) 438-0577.

PATRICIA GAMBARELLI COOKING CLASSES
Glen Cove, New York

October-April

Patricia Gambarelli has taught one to four-session courses in Italian cuisine, pasta, breads, desserts, and wine appreciation in the kitchen of her home since 1979. The four-hour monthly participation classes (limit 8 students) are usually scheduled at 10 am and conclude with lunch. The four-session Italian Cooking Series is held once weekly and includes appetizers, pastas, sauces, risotto, soup, meat, fish, poultry, and desserts. Special workshops are devoted to holiday baking and wine appreciation and private classes can be arranged.

Specialties: Italian cuisine and holiday specialties.

Faculty: Patricia Gambarelli has studied with Giuliano Bugialli and Marcella Hazan and teaches Italian cooking for the Great Neck School of Continuing Education. She is a member of the IACP and the New York Association of Cooking Teachers.

Costs: Range from $40 for a demonstration to $225 for a four-session participation course. A 50% deposit, or full amount for a single session, must accompany registration. Refund is granted those who cancel at least ten days prior to class.

Location: On Long Island, about one hour from New York City.

Contact: Patricia Gambarelli, 170 Elm Ave., Glen Cove, NY 11542; (516) 676-6398.

PAUL SMITH'S COLLEGE
Paul Smiths, New York

Year-round

Founded in 1937 to provide a practical education with a liberal arts foundation and accredited by the Middle States Association of Colleges and Schools, Paul Smith's College began offering a Culinary Arts Program in 1980 and a Baking Certificate Program in 1989, both part of the College's Hospitality Management Division. Courses are held in the four campus Foods Laboratories, which include a full-scale à la carte kitchen and 60-seat dining room. The total College enrollment is approximately 800 students and the student to teacher ratio is 12 to 1. About 85% of applicants are accepted; a job placement service is available and 99% of graduates obtain employment or transfer to a four-year institution.

The two-year Culinary Arts Program admits students in September and January and emphasizes training for entry level culinary management. In addition to lecture and practical courses in cookery and management, students are required to complete a core of liberal arts courses in English, mathematics, science, social sciences/humanities, and physical education. After completing the first-year course work on campus, students are assigned one of the remaining semesters in the College's Hotel Saranac, where they receive training in food preparation with the evening meal in the hotel's dining room the primary responsibility. Another semester is devoted to the externship, obtained through recruiters from the hospitality industry.

The Bakery Certificate Program, which admits students in September, January, and May, offers two academic semesters on campus in a hands-on curriculum devoted to the skills necessary for a journeyman baker. Students learn advertising, merchandising, and management and produce a variety of goods, from breads and rolls to tortes and confections, for an on-campus bakery outlet. The program is open to students with industry experience or those who have completed the Culinary Arts Program at Paul Smith's or a similar program at another college.

Specialties: Two-year Culinary Arts Program (awards A.A.S. degree); one-year Bakery Certificate Program.

Faculty: The College has 66 full-time and 12 part-time faculty members. The Chef Training Program faculty includes Robert Brown CM, and Paul Sorgule CCE, 1988 Olympic Gold Medalist.

Costs, Accommodations: Annual tuition is $8,790, housing averages $1,930 per year, and board is $2,190 per year. The Culinary Arts Program comprehensive fee (laboratory, student activities) is $500 per semester. Applications are accepted up to one month prior to start of semester and must be accompanied by high school transcript or G.E.D., (SAT or ACT scores are recommended, but not required), and a $20 application fee. Several scholarships and financial assistance programs are offered and approximately 80% of the students receive financial aid and qualify for a 10-month payment plan.

Location: The rural campus is situated on the north shore of the Lower St. Regis Lake, surrounded by 13,100 acres of college-owned forests and lakes in the heart of the Adirondack Mountains.

Contact: Admissions Office, Paul Smith's College, Paul Smiths, NY 12970; (800) 421-2605 *or* (518) 327-6227.

PETER KUMP'S NEW YORK COOKING SCHOOL
New York, New York
Year-round

Founded in 1974 and dedicated to teaching cooking as a fine art in the European tradition, this school offers a variety of programs for both career cooks and nonprofessionals. Professional programs include the school's two core courses — Techniques of French Cooking and the Professional Pastry Program — as well as the Extern Program, French Apprenticeships, and Work Scholarship Program. Approximately 75% of applicants who meet requirements (a minimum of two years of college) are accepted and 90% of graduates obtain employment. Programs for all levels include five-day intensives, once-a-week Techniques and Pastry sessions, weekend workshops (suited to New York visitors), master classes, and daily demonstrations. All classes are taught in the school's four modern kitchens.

Techniques of French Cooking, offered several times a year and limited to 14 students, meets weekdays from 9 am to 5 pm for 12 weeks, or on Monday, Wednesday, and Thursday from 6 to 11 pm for 20 weeks. Each day includes a lecture, participation class culminating with a four-course meal, and a two-hour afternoon demonstration, which is open to the public. Monday sessions feature guest chef specialities, Tuesdays focus on butchering, pastry, or fish and shellfish, Wednesdays are Italian or Oriental cuisine, Thursdays are devoted to food styling, Mexican, spa cuisine, or restaurant management and sanitation, and Fridays feature a wine tasting. The first half of the course stresses techniques; the second half covers presentation, classic French recipes, one week of bread baking, and two weeks of pastry. Upon completion of the program students extend their training for six weeks in the school's Extern Program. They are placed in a professional setting of their choice, which may be catering, restaurant cooking, pastry, corporate dining rooms, or food writing, styling or teaching. The 36-week Work Scholarship Program enables students to pay their tuition by working at the school in various capacities and allows for repetition of major parts of the course as teaching assistants. A Professional Diploma is awarded to those who complete the courses and pass examinations. The 12-week Professional Pastry Program, offered year-round, meets weekdays from 9:30 am to 5 pm with two weeks devoted to bread baking. The daily schedule includes lectures, demonstrations, and hands-on classes. The school offers individually tailored French apprenticeship programs for those who complete either the Techniques or Pastry programs. Students spend one month in Paris learning French and are then placed in Michelin-starred restaurants or fine pastry shops.

Two 5-session catering courses, The Business of Catering and Cooking for Catering, are offered in the summer as an intensive five-day course (from 10 am to 2 pm and 6 to 9 pm for the business course) or in the winter as a once-a-week course from 6 to 10 pm. Throughout the year, the Techniques of French Cooking I-VIII and the Pastry and Baking courses I-IV are offered as individual five-session certificate courses that meet for five consecutive days (9:30 am to 5 pm including the afternoon demonstration classes) or on a once-a-week basis (10 am to 3 pm or 6 to 11 pm). Designed for nonprofessional cooks, the sessions follow the same format as the professional courses and must be taken in sequence. Five-session master classes meet for five consecutive days at 10 am and feature well-known professionals demonstrating their specialties. Weekend workshops, for both professional (continuing education) and nonprofessional cooks, cover a wide variety of topics and guest chef specialties. Classes meet on Friday from 6 to 9 pm and on Saturday and Sunday from 11 am to 2 pm. The school also sponsors cooking vacations, culinary tours, and a series of children's classes.

Specialties: Professional and nonprofessional courses covering a wide variety of culinary topics; classes for children.

Faculty: Director Peter Kump studied with James Beard and Simone Beck and served as president of the IACP. Regular faculty members, all Certified Culinary Professionals, are Katherine Alford, Gaynor Grant, Paul Grimes, Bianca Borges Henry, Anita Jacobson, Nicholas Malgieri, Rosa Ross, Richard Simpson, Allen Smith, and Michelle Tampakis. Guest faculty includes Anna Teresa Callen, Dolores Custer, Giuliano Hazan, Diana Kennedy, Shirley King, Jeffrey Loh, Ann Nurse, Rosa Ross, Jack Ubaldi, and Reggie Young.

Costs, Accommodations: Tuition for the 12-week Professional Program is $5,550 and the evening 20-week Professional Program is $4,750 (plus an additional $800 for those who attend the daily demonstrations). The 12-week Professional Pastry program is $5,550. A 10% deposit must accompany application with another 10% due 30 days prior to the first class and the balance due ten days prior. Tuition (deposit) is $500 ($200) for the five-session Master Classes and $225 to $240 ($100 to $125) for the Weekend Workshops. The five-session Techniques and Pastry courses range from $400 to $435 ($100 to $125) per course, depending upon the number taken. The daily demonstrations are $35 each, $150 for five, $360 for twelve. Credit card (VISA, MasterCard, American Express) reservations are accepted and deposits are transferable if written notice is received ten days prior to the first session. Housing and restaurant suggestions are provided to out-of-towners.

Location: In a brownstone on New York's Upper East Side.

Contact: Bill Grant, Director of Admissions, Peter Kump's New York Cooking School, 307 E. 92nd St., New York, NY 10128; (800) 522-4610 or (212) 410-4601.

SAPORE DI MARE
Wainscott, New York

June-September

Since 1991, this regional Italian restaurant has offered classes one to three times weekly during the summer. The demonstration (limit 15 students) sessions meet on Mondays, Wednesdays, and Fridays from 11 am to 2:30 pm and conclude with a meal of the dishes prepared. The emphasis is on using a minimum of ingredients and topics include appetizers, pasta, main courses, pizza, bread making, and desserts.

Specialties: Regional Italian.

Faculty: Restaurateur Pino Luongo, author of *A Tuscan in the Kitchen*, is owner of Sapore di Mare in the Hamptons and St. Barth's, French West Indies, and Le Madri and Coco Pazzo in New York. Instructors include chefs Marta Pulini, Tamara di Giorgio, and Ciro Verde of Le Madri, Mark Strausman of Coco Pazzo, and Pietro Marcato and Massimo Fiorillo of Sapore di Mare.

Costs: Nonrefundable tuition is $150 for one class, $400 for three classes and $1,500 for 12 classes.

Location: In the Hamptons, 90 miles from New York City.

Contact: Kristen Dell'Aguzzo, Director, Sapore di Mare Summer Cooking Classes, P.O. Box 1358 (Wainscott Stone Rd. & Montauk Hwy.), Wainscott, NY 11975; (516) 537-2764, Fax (516) 537-1828.

THE SEASONAL KITCHEN
Pittsford, New York

Year-round

Since 1980, Ginger and Dick Howell have offered approximately 26 weeks of demonstration classes annually. The two-hour sessions are scheduled mornings and evenings in the well-equipped country kitchen and feature easy-to-prepare recipes and specialties of this bed and breakfast establishment. Classes for men only, couples, and special groups are also offered from time to time.

Specialties: A variety of topics, including seasonal foods, regional cuisines, and menus for entertaining.

Faculty: Ginger and Dick Howell are members of the IACP.

Costs: Range from $25 to $28. Cancellations receive a 50% refund.

Location: Pittsford is a suburb of Rochester.

Contact: The Seasonal Kitchen, 610 W. Bloomfield Rd., Pittsford, NY 14534; (716) 624-3242.

THE WANDERING SPOON (page 202)

NORTH CAROLINA

COOKS & CONNOISSEURS COOKING SCHOOL
New Bern, North Carolina

February-July, September-October

Established in 1983, this gourmet cookware shop and school offers one to four-session demonstration/participation courses (limit 12 students) on a variety of topics, including Chinese, Italian, French, and regional American cuisines, seasonal and local chef specialties, popular cookbook recipes, and wine selection. The three-hour sessions are scheduled both mornings and evenings in the store's 200-square-foot teaching kitchen.

Specialties: A variety of topics; chef specialties; wine selection.

Faculty: Proprietor Candace H. Lynn, her assistant, K.A. McCarthy; and guest chefs and lecturers, including Keith Ball, Betty Gryb, and Priscilla Mitchell.

Costs: Range from $10 to $15 per session. Credit cards (MasterCard, VISA) are accepted and refunds are granted cancellations more than two days prior.

Location: Near Tryon Palace Restoration Complex and 30 miles from beaches.

Contact: Candace Lynn, Cooks & Connoisseurs Cooking School, 3310 Trent Rd., New Bern, NC 28560; (919) 633-2665.

COOK'S CORNER, LTD.
Greensboro, North Carolina

January-November

Established in 1983, this cookware store and school for nonprofessional cooks offers demonstration (limit 24 students) and participation (limit 10) classes in a variety of cuisines. Two to three-hour classes are scheduled twice weekly at 9:30 am or 6:30 pm in the teaching kitchen with overhead mirror.

Specialties: A variety of cuisines.

Costs: Range from $12 to $40, payable by credit card, with full refund granted cancellations at least 48 hours prior.

Location: A restored area of the city.

Contact: Cook's Corner, Ltd., 401 State St., Greensboro, NC 27405; (919) 272-2665.

THE STOCKED POT & CO.
Winston-Salem, North Carolina

Year-round

Established in 1980, this school offers about 30 classes (limit 34 students) each quarter in its well-equipped teaching kitchen with overhead mirror. Lunch and Learn demonstrations are scheduled weekdays, two-hour children's participation and family classes are offered on Saturdays, and other two to three-hour demonstrations meet weekday mornings or evenings. The school also offers private bridal shower cooking classes and operates a catering service.

Specialties: Include ethnic and regional cuisines, holiday and seasonal specialties, nutritional cooking; children's classes; wine appreciation.

Faculty: Owner/chef Donald C. McMillan, who also owns and operates Gisèle's Fine Foods Restaurant and Catering, Thea Cvijanovich, Tim Booras, and Linda Lapiejko. Guest teachers include Jacques Pépin, Hugh Carpenter, John Desmond, Nicholas Malgieri, Jane Freiman, and John Folse.

Costs: Lunch and Learn classes are $9 to $10; children's classes are $12.50 ($35 for three); other classes range from $16 to $23. Advance payment is required and refund is granted cancellations more than 48 hours prior to class.

Location: Reynolda Village, the former Richard Joshua Reynolds estate, is a collection of shops and restaurants housed in quaint buildings.

Contact: Nancy Barnes, The Stocked Pot & Co., 111-B Reynolda Village, Winston-Salem, NC 27106; (919) 722-3663.

OHIO

LA BELLE POMME
Columbus, Ohio

Year-round

Established in 1976, this school offers more than 40 one to three-hour morning and evening demonstrations (average 30 students) each quarter on a variety of topics. Facilities include a large overhead mirror, eight burners, and four ovens.

Specialties: Include techniques, entertaining menus, ethnic cuisines, guest chef specialities, wine tastings.

Faculty: School director Betty Rosbottom attended La Varenne and the Greenbrier Cooking School and is author of *Betty Rosbottom's Cooking School Cookbook*. Other instructors include 1988 U.S.A. Culinary Olympics team member Carolyn Claycomb, Tom and Peggy Turgeon, and ethnic cuisine specialists Marsha and Harry Allen. Guest chefs have included Bernard Clayton, Jr., Giuliano Bugialli, Perla Meyers, Bert Greene, and Sheila Lukins.

Costs: A one-hour class is $23.50 and a 2½ to 3-hour class is $28 to $34. Full refund, less $5, is granted cancellations at least 10 days prior.

Location: Lazarus Department Store in downtown Columbus.

Contact: La Belle Pomme at Lazarus, P.O. Box 16538, Columbus, OH 43216-4105; (614) 463-2665.

THE CLEVELAND RESTAURANT COOKING SCHOOL
Cleveland, Ohio

Year-round

Established in 1988, this school offers one and two-week basic classes, specialty classes, pastry classes, and one-day demonstrations. In 1993, the offerings will be expanded to include a six-month career program.

Faculty: Chef Parker Bosley, owner of Parker's Restaurant and Catering Company, and the restaurant staff.

Contact: Parker Bosley, Cleveland Restaurant Cooking School, 12031 Edgewater Dr., Cleveland, OH 44107; (216) 521-9322.

CREATIVE KITCHEN COOKING CLASSES
Cincinnati, Ohio
Year-round except August

Opened in 1986, this school offers 25 to 30 classes each quarter. The $2\frac{1}{2}$ to 3-hour demonstration (limit 30 students) and participation (limit 12) sessions are scheduled at 10:30 am and 5:30 pm in Lazarus Department Store's teaching kitchen, which has overhead mirrors and individual desks. A variety of topics are covered and guest chefs are sometimes featured. A noon-time gourmet class meets occasionally and a four-session basic techniques course is held yearly.

Specialties: Include ethnic and regional cuisines, seasonal menus, healthful cuisine, techniques, desserts.

Faculty: The 14-member faculty includes director Carol Tabone, who earned her Grand Diplome from La Varenne and attended the London Cordon Bleu, assistant JoAnne Shapiro, Kathleen Sweeney, Kathy Baker, Barbara Bond, John Bostick, Judy Burnstein, Toni Devena, Dara Dynnett, Marge Haller, Rita Heikenfeld, Mary McMahon, Glenn Rinsky, and Shirley Tenhouer. Guest chefs have included Giuliano Bugialli, Hugh Carpenter, Nicholas Malgieri, and Anne Willan.

Costs: Sessions range from $28 to $35, guest chef classes are $40 to $45, and gourmet classes are $16. Pre-payment is required and refund is granted cancellations more than five days prior. Credit card registrations accepted.

Location: The lower level of Lazarus Department Store.

Contact: Carol Tabone, Director, Creative Kitchen Cooking Classes, Lazarus, 699 Race St., Cincinnati, OH 45202; (513) 369-7911.

GOURMET CURIOSITIES, ETC.
Sylvania, Ohio
Spring and Fall

This cookware store has operated a creative cooking school since 1974 and offers five to seven 2-hour evening classes (limit 16 students) each month. A variety of topics are covered and all foods are sampled. Facilities occupy about 400 square feet and include a complete kitchen and overhead mirror.

Specialties: Include ethnic cuisines and holiday and seasonal specialties.

Faculty: The school's owners, Bruce and Geneva Williams, attended La Varenne, are members of the IACP, have served on consumer panels, and had recipes accepted for publication. Other instructors include local and area chefs.

Costs: Most classes are $20, those with wine tastings are $25; payment is due with registration. Full refund is granted those who cancel at least three days prior.

Location: The school is 11 miles from Toledo and 60 miles from Detroit.

Contact: Bruce C. Williams, Gourmet Curiosities, Etc., Starlite Plaza, 5700 Monroe St., Sylvania, OH 43560; (419) 882-2323.

THE LORETTA PAGANINI SCHOOL OF COOKING
Chesterland, Ohio

Year-round

This gourmet shop and school offers a variety of one to four-session demonstration (limit 25 students) and participation (limit 12) courses that are designed to build confidence, encourage creativity, and teach the techniques needed in a professional kitchen. The school's modern facilities, which are handicapped accessible, include a fully-equipped kitchen with gas ranges, ovens, and an overhead mirror. More than 100 different classes are offered each year, most scheduled in the evenings, with daytime classes on weekends. During sessions on international cuisines, students are taught by a native chef and learn about the country's costumes, culture, and foods. Basic technique classes cover professional bread and pastry making, garde manger, knife skills, and stocks and sauces. Couples classes and a Young Gourmet Series for children are also offered as well as trips to ethnic markets, organic farms, flour mills, and nurseries.

Specialties: A variety of topics, including Italian and other ethnic cuisines and basic techniques; children's classes.

Faculty: School director and owner Loretta Paganini was born in Bologna, Italy, where her mother is an accomplished chef. She serves as a culinary consultant for area restaurants and clubs and is a food writer for the local newspaper. Guest faculty includes local chefs, teachers, and food professionals, and visiting chefs. The school is affiliated with Lakeland Community College.

Costs: Individual classes range from $12 to $35, four-session series range from $75 to $125, children's classes are $15. One-week advance registration is required and refunds are granted cancellations at least 48 hours prior.

Location: Near major highways and approximately 25 miles east of Cleveland.

Contact: Loretta Paganini, The Loretta Paganini School of Cooking, Cambridge Square, 8613 Mayfield Rd., Chesterland, OH 44026; (216) 729-1110 *or* (216) 285-8832, Fax (216) 729-6435.

PAM'S KITCHEN
Springfield, Ohio

September-June

Since 1989, Pamela Peterson has offered demonstration (limit 15 students) and participation (limit 12) classes primarily for nonprofessional cooks and excursions to nearby markets, herb farms, and other sites of culinary interest. About 40 morning and evening three-hour classes are scheduled annually on a variety of topics in the new, professionally designed, 400-square-foot teaching kitchen, which has a demonstration island and five individual work areas.

Specialties: A variety of topics, including ethnic and regional cuisines, baking and pastry, party and entertaining menus, and healthful foods.

Faculty: Pamela W. Peterson, M.S., a Professional Member of the IACP, and guest restaurateurs, chefs, and home economists.

Costs: Fees range from $26 per class. A 50% nonrefundable deposit must accompany registration with balance due at class.

Location: Springfield is 25 miles from Dayton and 45 miles from Columbus.

Contact: Pamela W. Peterson, 1717 N. Fountain Blvd., Springfield, OH 45504; (513) 399-8755.

ZONA SPRAY COOKING SCHOOL
Hudson, Ohio

Year-round

Founded in 1969, this gourmet cookware shop and school offers approximately 30 to 35 demonstration classes (limit 38 students) and one or two participation classes each quarter, as well as eight to ten 5-day professional technique courses (limit 10) each year. The school also offers a two-session course on professional food writing and on running a catering business and provides job placement assistance to those who complete the professional techniques course. Five-day gastronomic bicycle tours, scheduled during the summer, feature discussions by wine experts, chefs, and food celebrities.

Demonstration classes, which meet for $2^1/2$ to 3-hours on week nights and some Saturday afternoons, fall into two categories: Basics I, which stresses fundamentals and Basics II, which emphasizes more difficult techniques. The Levels I and II professional technique participation programs are offered Monday through Friday from 10 am to 3 pm or two Thursday evenings from 6 to 10:30 pm and three Saturdays from 10 am to 4 pm. Those who complete Levels I and II are awarded a diploma and those who complete Level I and II plus an eight demonstration class series qualify for the special professional restaurant apprentice program, which provides the opportunity to work for two weeks in a restaurant, hotel kitchen, or catering kitchen.

Specialties: Include French techniques and cuisine, ethnic specialties, pastries and desserts, catering.

Faculty: Proprietor Zona Spray teaches many of the classes. Instructors and guest chefs have included Rick Bayless, Zachary Bruell, Shirley Corriher, John Desmond, Pamela Grosscup, Nicholas Malgieri, Lydie Marshall, and Dinah Schley. All faculty members are either Certified Culinary Professionals or Teachers by the IACP, members of the ACF, or professional chefs, caterers, or cookbook authors.

Costs: Classes range from $8 to $45, with most guest chef classes costing $35 to $45. Students who enroll in a series of three classes save $5 to $15. Tuition for the Levels I and II professional programs is $385 each and gastronomic wine tours are $750 each. Advance registration is required and refund is granted cancellations more than 48 hours prior to class. Credit card (VISA, MasterCard) registrations accepted.

Location: In historic Western Reserve, 20 miles south of Cleveland and 15 miles east of Akron.

Contact: Zona Spray Cooking School, 140 N. Main, Hudson, OH 44236; (216) 650-1665 *or* (216) 656-2665.

OKLAHOMA

COOKING SCHOOL OF TULSA
Tulsa, Oklahoma

Year-round

Founded in 1991, this school offers 10 to 12 demonstration (limit 12 students) and participation (limit 6) classes monthly in a fully-equipped home kitchen. Classes are usually scheduled from 6 to 8:30 pm weekdays and conclude with a complete meal. Titles have included French Bistro Cooking, Outdoor Grilling, Homemade Gourmet Pizza, and Cooking with Wine.

Specialties: A variety of topics, including techniques, entertaining menus, ethnic cuisines, guest chefs; wine tastings.

Faculty: Classes are taught by the proprietor, Keith Lindenberg, and local chefs and nutritionists.

Costs: Range from $20 to $35 per class.

Location: South Tulsa.

Contact: Cooking School of Tulsa, 8710 S. College Pl., Tulsa, OK 74137; (918) 298-7110.

GOURMET GADGETRE, LTD.
Lawton, Oklahoma

January-June, October-November

Established in 1980, this cookware store offers three-hour evening demonstrations (limit 20 students) in breadmaking, candy making, and ethnic cuisines.

Specialties: Mexican, Italian, and Oriental cuisines; candy and breadmaking.

Faculty: Restaurateurs Hazel Wong and Patty Quarles; June Harris, a Certified Culinary Professional by the IACP.

Costs: $15 per class. Cancellations more than 48 hours prior receive refund.

Contact: Gourmet Gadgetre, Ltd., 1105 Ferris, Lawton, OK 73507; (405) 248-1837.

OREGON

WESTERN CULINARY INSTITUTE
Portland, Oregon

Year-round

Established in 1983, this school offers a 12-month Culinary Arts Diploma Program consisting of 42 weeks of school instruction and a six-week internship in a school-approved quality foodservice operation — a total of 1,486 hours. The curriculum is based on the classical principles of Escoffier with emphasis on modern technique and trends. The 18 courses cover basic skills and techniques, purchasing and cost control, butchering, human relations, kitchen management, international cuisine, nutrition, dining room procedures, wines, soups, stocks, sauces, garde manger, buffet, baking and pastries, and à la carte kitchen. Students are taught in up-to-date, well-equipped kitchens and receive practical experience in the school's restaurant, which is open to the public for lunch and dinner. Classes are 80% participation with an average of 15 to 20 students to one chef/instructor. New classes begin every six weeks. The school is accredited by the Accrediting Commissions of the ACFEI and CCA (NATTS) and offers employment advice and placement assistance throughout the careers of its graduates. Approximately 85% of applicants are accepted and 98.5% of graduates obtain employment within 90 days.

Specialties: A 12-month Diploma Program for those aspiring to a culinary career.

Faculty: The 17-member teaching faculty consists of individuals with international experience and training, many of whom have won culinary awards.

Costs, Accommodations: Tuition is $11,495 for the Diploma Program. A $25 nonrefundable fee is required with application. After acceptance, a $100 enrollment fee is required to accompany the enrollment agreement. Arrangements for financial aid and payment of tuition must be made on or before entering class. The housing director assists in locating lodging.

Location: Near Portland State University in the middle of the University District in downtown Portland, convenient to public transportation.

Contact: Admissions Dept., Western Culinary Institute, 1316 S.W. 13th Ave., Portland, OR 97201; (800) 666-0312 *or* (503) 223-2245.

PENNSYLVANIA

CHARLOTTE ANN ALBERTSON'S COOKING SCHOOL
Philadelphia and Haverford, Pennsylvania and Naples, Florida

September-June

Founded in 1973, this school offers classes for nonprofessional cooks from September through June at Assouline & Ting, Philadelphia, and some evening classes in Bryn Mawr, Pennsylvania. From December through March morning classes are held at What's Cookin'? in Naples, Florida. Both the Philadelphia, and Naples shops have a teaching kitchen with overhead mirror. Most of the three or four classes each month are two-hour demonstrations (limit 15 to 25 students), scheduled at 10 am or 6 pm, with an occasional hands-on class. These cover a variety of topics. Other programs include three master classes devoted to the science of food and solutions to cooking problems; a men's participation class; culinary tours of local markets and restaurants in Philadelphia and Maryland; and Parties in the Kitchen cooking classes for children's birthdays. Customized spouse programs are available for conventions and organizations.

Specialties: Include ethnic cuisines, holiday menus, garnishing, herbs, the science of food and cooking.

Faculty: Well-known local chefs teach most of the Philadelphia classes. Charlotte Ann Albertson, a charter member and Certified Teacher of the IACP and member of the AIWF, teaches all of the Florida classes and directs the Philadelphia School. She has studied at La Varenne and Le Cordon Bleu in Paris and has worked in the American Embassy and fine hotels in Switzerland and restaurant kitchens in Italy. Ann-Michelle, Peter, and Mary-Kristin Albertson direct the children's parties. Other faculty members include food scientist and biochemist Shirley Corriher and executive chefs.

Costs: Tuition, payable in advance, ranges from $30 to $50. Credit is granted cancellations unless teacher is a guest chef.

Location: Assouline & Ting is located in downtown Philadelphia. Bryn Mawr is a 10-minute train ride away. What's Cookin'? is at the Coastland Mall in Naples, a resort community on Florida's southwest Gulf Coast.

Contact: Charlotte Ann Albertson's Cooking School, P.O. Box 27, Wynnewood, PA 19096; (215) 649-9290.

THE COOK'S CORNER, INC.
Yardley, Pennsylvania
Year-round

Established in 1986, this gourmet cookware store and cooking school offers 12 to 15 two-hour demonstration classes (limit 35 students) each season, usually week nights. Facilities include a fully-equipped demonstration kitchen with an overhead mirror.

Specialties: Include ethnic and regional cuisines, guest chef specialties, baking, wine appreciation.

Faculty: Owner/director is Catherine Rowan. Guest chefs have included cookbook authors Ann Clark, Madeleine Kamman, Nicholas Malgieri, Stephen Schmidt, and Thelma Snyder.

Costs: Range from $25 to $45. Nonrefundable payment in full must accompany registration.

Location: Yardley is 45 minutes from Philadelphia, five minutes from Trenton.

Contact: The Cook's Corner, 90 W. Afton Ave., Yardley, PA 19067; (215) 493-9093.

THE HOTEL HERSHEY THEME WEEKENDS
Hershey, Pennsylvania
January and February

The Hotel Hershey in central Pennsylvania offers its guests a variety of theme weekends each spring, including a Cooking School Weekend in late January and a Chocolate Lovers Extravaganza in mid-February. The Cooking School Weekend begins with a Friday evening get-acquainted social and concludes after Sunday morning breakfast. Saturday morning and afternoon classes cover such topics as cake decorating, cold salad presentations, basic hors d'oeuvres, and the preparation of elementary sauces, salad dressings, and desserts. A wine tasting and social seminar is held in the evening. The Chocolate Lovers Extravaganza features hands-on workshops for adults and children, demonstrations, games such as Let's Make a Chocolate Deal and Chocolate Trivia, chocolate movies, a gallery of chocolate creations, trolley tours of Chocolatetown, U.S.A., and a chocolate dessert contest. The program, which begins at noon Friday and concludes Monday morning, features cocoa stenciling and chocolate decoration workshops for adults and chocolate dipping and modeling workshops for children.

Specialties: Chocolate; cooking basics.

Faculty: The culinary staff of The Hotel Hershey.

Costs, Accommodations: Rates begin at $94 ($113) per person per night for the Cooking School Weekend (Chocolate Lovers Extravaganza), which includes double occupancy deluxe lodging, daily breakfasts and dinners, and all events. The Hotel Hershey, built in 1933 as Milton Hershey's dream hotel and modeled after his favorite Mediterranean resorts, has a Four Diamond rating from the American Automobile Association and was designated one of 50 Favorite Family Resorts in America by *Family Circle Magazine.*

Location, Facilities: Hershey is accessible by car via Interstates 81, 78, and 83, and the Pennsylvania Turnpike. Complimentary transportation is provided hotel guests from Harrisburg International Airport and the Amtrak station in Harrisburg. Hotel facilities include an indoor pool, whirlpool, saunas, and exercise room. Sledding and tobogganing are available as well as cross-country skiing on the hotel's golf course.

Contact: The Hotel Hershey, P.O. Box 400, Hershey, PA 17033; (800) 437-7439 *or* (717) 533-2171.

JACQUALIN ET CIE CUISINIÉRE
Lahaska, Pennsylvania

Year-round

This gourmet cookware shop, catering business, and school for nonprofessionals, founded in 1978, offers 25 to 30 different three to four-hour classes (limit 10 students), full-day breadmaking workshops (limit 6) each quarter, day trips to Philadelphia and New York outdoor markets and gourmet food emporiums, and gastronomic tours in France. The classes, which are mostly demonstration with participation encouraged, are held in the school's French country kitchen at either 10 am or 7 pm and conclude with a lunch or dinner of the recipes prepared. The focus is primarily on French and Italian cuisines but includes other topics.

Specialties: French and Italian cuisines, breadmaking, desserts, gourmet tours.

Faculty: Jacqualin Giles, the school proprietor and cooking instructor, who studied in France and Italy; her daughter and partner Christine Hutkin.

Costs: Range from $35 to $45, the breadmaking workshop is $65. Full tuition must accompany reservation. No refunds.

Location: In picturesque Bucks County, an hour from Philadelphia.

Contact: Jacqualin Giles *or* Christine G. Hutkin, Jacqualin et Cie Cuisiniére, P.O. Box 303, Route 202, Lahaska, PA 18931; (215) 794-7316, Fax (215) 794-7693.

JANE CITRON
Pittsburgh, Pennsylvania

Year-round except summer

Since 1978, Jane Citron has taught cooking and conducted culinary tours to Europe and the Far East. The three-hour sessions are held in her newly designed home kitchen and adjoining eating area and are scheduled both at 10 am and 6:30 pm. Approximately eight to ten classes are offered each quarter, except summer, emphasizing proper techniques and creative dishes. Students are limited to 10 when a complete menu is prepared and served, 12 when just the kitchen is used. Most classes are demonstration, with the exception of breadmaking, pasta, and others that require hands-on participation. Culinary trips planned for 1993 include the Napa Valley and San Francisco in May and Provence, the French Riviera, Lyon, and Paris in September.

Specialties: Topics include ethnic and regional cuisines, menus for entertaining, individual foods, and breadmaking.

Faculty: Jane Citron has studied with Julie Dannenbaum, Marcella Hazan, Madeleine Kamman, Jacques Pepin, and Roger Vergé and writes a monthly food column for *Pittsburgh Magazine*.

Costs: Classes range from $40 to $50 and advance payment is required.

Location: The Murdoch Farms section of Pittsburgh.

Contact: Jane Citron, 1314 Squirrel Hill Ave., Pittsburgh, PA 15217; (412) 621-0311.

THE KITCHEN SHOPPE AND COOKING SCHOOL
Carlisle, Pennsylvania

September-May

Suzanne Hoffman founded this retail store and cooking school in 1975 and offers approximately 15 to 20 classes for adults and children each quarter. Most adult classes are demonstrations (limit 20 to 30 students) that cover a variety of topics. Master classes are conducted by well-known guest chefs and culinary day trips to New York, Washington, and Philadelphia are scheduled from time to time. Classes are two to three hours in length and are usually held at 6 pm for adults and at 10 am for children, ages 8 to 13.

Specialties: A variety of topics, including entertaining menus, ethnic cuisines, guest chef specialties; children's classes.

Faculty: Proprietor and instructor Suzanne Hoffman is a Certified Member of the IACP. Other teachers are head cooking instructor Sherry Ball and Kevin Fisher. Guest chefs have included Giuliano Bugialli, Julia Child, Karen Lee, Nick Malgieri, Marlene Sorosky, Martha Stewart, Chef Tell, and Martin Yan.

Costs: Adult classes range from $20 to $30, master classes are $50, children's classes are $15, and day trips are approximately $125. Full payment must accompany reservation and credit card (VISA/MasterCard) registrations are accepted. Cancellations more than 48 hours prior to class receive class credit.

Location: Carlisle is just west of Pennsylvania Dutch Country, a 20-minute drive from Harrisburg and 2¹/₂ hours from Philadelphia.

Contact: Tracee Clepper *or* Suzanne Hoffman, The Kitchen Shoppe, 101 Shady Lane, Carlisle, PA 17013; (717) 243-0906, Fax (717) 245-0606.

THE PENNSYLVANIA INSTITUTE OF CULINARY ARTS
Pittsburgh, Pennsylvania

Year-round

This private institution, accredited by the CCA (NATTS) and ACFEI, was founded in 1986 to provide quality technical and practical culinary education to those desiring a career in the hospitality and foodservice industry. The 16-month program, leading to an Associate Degree in Specialized Technology, begins six times each year (January, February, May, June, September, October) and is divided into four semesters that include a 16-week paid externship during the fourth semester. Graduates are prepared for entry-level positions as cooks and chef trainees. Students also have the opportunity to participate in a study tour of Paris with classes at La Varenne, the Ritz-Escoffier, and Le Cordon Bleu; visits to cheese factories, bakeries, and wineries; hotel inspections; and sightseeing excursions. On-campus facilities include a bakeshop and kitchens for skill development; stocks, soups, and sauces; meat and poultry; seafood; garde manger; and classical and international cuisines. The school also houses a library, a commercial storeroom, and several lecture/demonstration and multi-purpose rooms. Career placement assistance is available to students, graduates, and alumni and the placement rate is 100% of all available graduates since the school's inception.

Students attend classes 25 to 30 hours per week on one of six class time schedules. Kitchen laboratory sessions average 18 participants and lecture classes average 35. Courses include culinary skill development; safety and sanitation; nutrition; stock, soup, and sauce preparation; storeroom procedures; wine and mixology; meat and poultry processing and cookery; foodservice math and communication; food and beverage management; charcuterie; seafood processing and cookery; breads and desserts; employment and interviewing techniques; menu planning; human relations; garde manger; and advanced international and classical cookery. Total enrollment is 550 full-time students.

Specialties: Full-time 16-month professional program leading to an Associate Degree in Specialized Technology.

Faculty: The faculty of 21 certified chefs, maitres d'hotel, and educators is supervised by Certified Master Chef Dieter Kiessling, winner of several awards, including a Gold Medal in the International Culinary Olympics..

Costs, Accommodations: Tuition is $3,500 for each of the first three semesters, $3,200 for the fourth semester. A $50 fee, which must accompany application, is refundable until the applicant has been accepted. Applicants must have a high school diploma or equivalent and foodservice experience is desirable. Refunds are granted on a semester basis and range from a full refund less $350 for withdrawal during the first seven calendar days to no refund after 50% of the semester has elapsed. Financial aid is available for those who qualify. A housing director assists students with school-sponsored and off-campus housing.

Location: The school is in downtown Pittsburgh.

Contact: Pennsylvania Institute of Culinary Arts, 717 Liberty Ave., Pittsburgh, PA 15222; (800) 432-2433 *or* (412) 566-2433.

RANIA'S TO GO
Pittsburgh, Pennsylvania
Year-round

This catering service, gourmet shop, and cooking school, opened in 1985, offers more than 40 demonstration classes (limit 25 students) each year. Most classes are scheduled from 7 to 9 pm and cover a variety of topics.

Specialties: Include ethnic/regional cuisines, holiday foods, appetizers, desserts.

Faculty: In addition to school proprietor Rania, instructors include chefs Michael Barbato, Bill Hunt, Joe Nolan, Red Raynor, Kelly Stapleton, and John Vennare.

Costs: Tuition is $25 for each class, $70 for three. No refunds are granted.

Contact: Rania's To Go, 100 Central Square, Pittsburgh, PA 15228; (412) 531-2222.

THE RESTAURANT SCHOOL
Philadelphia, Pennsylvania
Year-round

This professional school, founded in 1974, offers twelve-month programs beginning every six months in Restaurant Management, Chef Training, Hospitality Management, and Pastry Chef Training. Each curriculum is specifically designed for the fine dining restaurant or fine hotel business and combines intensive classroom training (lecture, demonstration, participation) with practical experience (research projects, field trips, apprenticeships). Facilities include four classroom kitchens, two 100-seat demonstration kitchens with overhead mirror, a 100-seat wine tasting room with bar, a pastry shop, and a restaurant. Each program has a student to teacher ratio of 25 to 1 and includes a seven-day culinary tour of France or Disney/Bahamas. The school has a placement service and offers financial aid to those who qualify. Approximately 90% of applicants are accepted and 96% of graduates obtain employment.

The Restaurant Management program consists of 2,220 clock-hours of instruction covering business and management, culinary arts, dining room service, bar management, and wine, with emphasis on marketing, computer technology, human resources, and business law. Students rotate through various positions in the kitchen and dining room of the open-to-the public restaurant of the Restaurant School. The Chef Training program consists of 2,220 clock-hours that combine classroom instruction in the culinary arts with an apprenticeship. Courses include culinary arts, business management, dining room service, wines, career development, and nutrition. Students complete 1,080 hours of apprenticeship in an approved area restaurant. The Hospitality Management program consists of 2,220 clock-hours of instruction covering business and management, culinary arts, sales, marketing, communication, meeting planning, hotel management, wines, computer technology, human resources, and cultural communication classes. Students rotate through various positions in a restaurant and hotel during their 540 hours of apprenticeship. The Pastry Chef Training program consists of 2,220 clock-hours of instruction that concentrate on skills enabling the graduate to run a full-service bakery. Courses include basic culinary skills, baking skills, science of baking, business management, and career development. Students produce the inventory for the school's open-to-the-public European-style pastry shop.

Specialties: Professional programs in Restaurant Management, Chef Training, Hospitality Management, and Pastry Chef Training.

Faculty: The school's 16-member faculty of seasoned professionals has many years of experience in the restaurant, foodservice, and hotel industry.

Costs: The $14,000 cost of each program includes the seven-day culinary trip to France or Disney/Bahamas. Application must be accompanied by a $50 application fee which is refunded if student is not accepted. Students who withdraw five days or more after signing the enrollment agreement are refunded all monies except application fee and $100 of the registration fee. Students who withdraw after the first week but within 25% of the first three-month semester forfeit $637.50 tuition; withdrawals after 25% but before 50% of the first semester forfeit $1,325 tuition; withdrawals after 50% of the first semester forfeit full semester tuition. A similar policy applies to the remaining three semesters.

Location: University City in Philadelphia.

Contact: Director of Admissions, The Restaurant School, 4207 Walnut St., Philadelphia, PA 19104; (215) 222-4200.

PUERTO RICO

KITCHENS OF THE WORLD COOKING SCHOOL
Kitchen World, Inc.
San Juan, Puerto Rico

Year-round

Established in 1991, this kitchen and tableware store and nonvocational school offers demonstration and participation classes (limit 30 students) on a variety of topics, including Puerto Rican and international cuisines, guest chef specialties, and wine selection. Classes are held in a 500-square-foot teaching kitchen with four work stations. Three-hour classes for adults are scheduled mornings, evenings, and Saturdays from August through May; two-hour classes for children are scheduled on Friday afternoons from January through May and October and November; and three-week young people's cooking camps, during June and July, consist of two three-hour classes per week.

Specialties: A variety of topics, including Puerto Rican and international cuisines; classes for children.

Faculty: Proprietor Asela M. Crumley, Jesus Ramiro of Ramiro's Restaurant, José Luis Diaz de Villegos, caterers Jackeline Kleis and Carmen Luisa Pons, food consultants Susan Fairbank and Carole Kotkin, and guest chef Jacques Pepin.

Costs: Range from $25 to $50 per class; $135 for summer camps plus $15 enrollment fee. Prepayment is required and refunds are granted cancellations at least two days prior to class. Credit cards accepted.

Location: Garden Hills Plaza, a new suburban shopping center in Guaynabo, four miles from San Juan.

Contact: Asela Crumley, Proprietor, Kitchen World, Inc., P.O. Box 362040, San Juan, PR 00936-2040; (809) 783-7802 or (809) 782-5850.

RHODE ISLAND

JOHNSON & WALES UNIVERSITY
COLLEGE OF CULINARY ARTS
Providence, Rhode Island; Charleston, South Carolina; Norfolk, Virginia; North Miami, Florida

Year-round

This private, nonprofit, career-oriented educational institution established its College of Culinary Arts in 1973 and the International Baking & Pastry Institute in 1982 and offers a one-year Certificate program in Culinary Arts (at Norfolk campus), two-year programs leading to the Associate in Applied Science degree in Culinary Arts (at Providence, Charleston, Norfolk, and North Miami campuses), and Baking & Pastry Arts (Providence and Charleston), and a two-year Associate in Science degree program in Food & Beverage Management (both years at Providence and Charleston; first year at Norfolk, second year at Providence). Students who receive the Associate in Applied Science degree can enroll in the Bachelor of Science degree programs in Culinary Arts, Food Service Management, or Food Marketing (Providence and Charleston). All of the University's campuses offer modern teaching facilities.

Each year is divided into three 11-week trimesters (beginning March, September, and November) during which the more than 2,500 students attend laboratory and theory classes and gain practical experience. School is usually in session four days a week (Monday through Thursday), five hours a day, and students are assigned to morning, afternoon, or evening classes, allowing them to obtain part-time employment. A variety of summer programs are offered to those who wish to explore a culinary career as well as professionals who want to learn new skills.

The two-year Culinary Arts program is designed for the student who desires a position as a trained chef, sous (second) chef, or maitre d'hotel. For two trimesters of the freshman year and one of the sophomore, culinary arts students are divided into groups of 20 for laboratory classes. First-year laboratories emphasize basic cooking and baking methods and dining room procedures; second-year laboratories cover advanced techniques and classical and international cuisines. One trimester each year is devoted to food service and management classes (40 students maximum) that cover foodservice math, nutrition, communication skills, sanitation, cost control and purchasing, and menu and facilities planning. For one trimester of the sophomore year, students serve the public and gain practical experience through the Culinary Arts Practicum (at the Johnson & Wales Airport Hotel, J. Wales Seafood & Pasta restaurant, the Johnson & Wales Hospitality Center, the Johnson & Wales Inn, and Audrey's Grille) or apply for a Selective Career Co-op, a paid, full-time assignment at a recognized facility such as Caesar's Lake Tahoe in Reno, Nevada; The Rainbow Room in New York City; or the Grand Traverse Resort in Traverse City, Michigan. A select group of second-year students spend this trimester in a student exchange program with a culinary school in Paris or the Cork Regional Technical College or Dublin College of Catering in Ireland. Top graduates are invited to continue study at the University for one year as Teaching Assistants and a few assistants are invited to remain a second year as teaching fellows.

The two-year Baking & Pastry Arts program is designed for the student who desires a position as a baker or pastry chef. Students attend hands-on laboratory (maximum 18) classes for two trimesters each year and one trimester per year is devoted to baking and pastry arts studies in the classroom (maximum 40). First year laboratories concentrate on basic ingredients and production techniques for breads, rolls, folded doughs, batters, cakes, pies, creams, and desserts; second year laboratories cover French pastries and classical desserts, including petit fours, cake decoration and calligraphy, sugar and chocolate work, pralines and candies, showpieces, and specialty items. Classroom studies focus on foodservice math, sanitation and management, baking and pastry chemistry, purchasing and cost control, facilities planning, marketing, and merchandising.

The Bachelor of Science degree program in Food Service Management, for those who aspire to a managerial position such as food and beverage director, banquet manager, or executive chef, provides hands-on training in food preparation and service with specialized courses in business management. Students recommended by the department chairperson may apply for a one-trimester Selective Career Co-op in lieu of three academic courses.

Five-day summer programs in the Culinary Arts and Baking & Pastry Arts are designed for both professional foodservice personnel and serious cooks. Each course consists of morning and afternoon classes, Monday through Friday. One afternoon a week is devoted to such special demonstrations as tableside cooking, vegetable and fruit carving, canapés, marzipan molding, and cake decorating. Culinary Arts programs include special courses in Professional Catering, Classical French Cuisine, American Regional Cuisine, Italian Cuisine, and Nutritional Cuisine. Baking & Pastry Arts programs include Basic Breads, Hotel/Restaurant Baking, Classical Pastry, and basic and advanced courses in Cake Preparation & Decorating. Other summer programs include a Professional Bartending/TIPS Certification class and career exploration courses for high school students. Certificates of Course Completion are awarded to summer program students on the last day of class.

Specialties: Two-year career programs in culinary/baking and pastry arts, food and beverage management; four-year baccalaureate program in culinary arts, foodservice management, and food marketing; summer courses in culinary/baking and pastry arts for cooks of all levels; two and four-year programs in business, hospitality, and technology.

Faculty: The University's 140 full-time faculty members are oriented toward instruction rather than research and many are chosen for their professional experience in business, culinary arts, hospitality services, and technology. The College of Culinary Arts annually honors outstanding chefs who present lectures and demonstrations. Past Distinguished Visiting Chefs include Louis Szathmary, Madeleine Kamman, Roger Vergé, Keith Keogh, John Folse, Benno Eigenmann, Gustav Ernst Mauler, and Andrea Hellrigl.

Costs, Accommodations: Annual tuition and fees for the 1992-93 culinary/baking and pastry arts programs are $11,238 for commuters, $15,120 for students housed in the University's residence halls. A variety of payment options are available. A nonrefundable $25 application fee must accompany application and a nonrefundable reservation deposit of $100 for commuter students or $200 for residents is required on acceptance. Graduation from high school or equivalent credentials are required and some foodservice-related experience is desirable.

About 84% of applicants are admitted to the undergraduate programs and 100% to the professional programs. In the past, approximately 85% of the University's students have received financial assistance. The Office of Career Development maintains an active on-campus recruitment schedule and the most recent graduating class had a 98% job placement rate.

Tuition for the summer programs for professionals is a per-course charge determined each academic year. Payment in full must accompany registration two weeks prior to the course. A 10% discount is offered for multiple courses.

Location: The University offers a variety of academic, athletic, and social activities. Its urban location enables students to take advantage of the Providence Civic Center, Performing Arts Center, Trinity Square Repertory Company, and other cultural and recreational facilities. Providence is one hour from Boston and Cape Cod and three hours from New York City. The Charleston campus is in the Port City Center of East Bay Street. The Norfolk campus is in the Westgate Center of the Norfolk Commerce Park. The Florida campus is on 127th St., near Biscayne Blvd. in North Miami.

Contact: Mark Burke, Director of Enrollment Management, Johnson & Wales University, 8 Abbott Park Place, Providence, RI 02903; (800) 343-2565 *or* (401) 456-1000.

SAKONNET MASTER CHEFS SERIES
Little Compton, Rhode Island

September-June

Sakonnet Vineyards, founded in 1975, began offering classes in food and wine in 1980. The program now features one-day demonstration/participation classes (limit 12 students) taught by a well-known chef. Approximately ten classes are offered annually, each beginning at 10 am and concluding with an evening banquet of the foods prepared, accompanied by wines selected by Sakonnet's winemaker in consultation with the chef. Kitchen facilities include a large main work table and counter space which serves as individual work areas.

Specialties: Well-known chefs teach their specialties.

Faculty: Chefs change each year. Previous chef-instructors included Johanne Killeen and George Germon, owner-chefs of Al Forno Restaurant in Providence; Maureen Pothier, executive chef of the Bluepoint Oyster Bar and Restaurant; Jasper White, owner-chef of Jasper's in Boston; Nancy Verde Barr, backstage chef to Julia Child; and Todd English, owner-chef of Olives in Boston.

Costs: Each session is $175, all inclusive; banquet-only $50. A nonrefundable $100 deposit must accompany reservation with balance due prior to session. Accommodations in Little Compton can be arranged.

Location: Sakonnet Vineyards comprises 50 acres planted with Chardonnay, Pinot Noir, Vidal, and others. Little Compton is 30 minutes from the Massachusetts towns of New Bedford and Fall River, 40 minutes from Providence and 75 minutes from Boston.

Contact: Sakonnet Vineyards, P.O. Box 197, Little Compton, RI 02837; (401) 635-8486.

SOUTH CAROLINA

IN GOOD TASTE
Charleston, South Carolina
Year-round

This gourmet shop and school, founded in 1983, offers a variety of demonstration and participation classes and guest chef sessions, each limited to 12 students per instructor. The four to five monthly classes that are offered each month meet from 6:30 to 8:30 pm in the well-equipped teaching kitchen. A series of Back to Basics foundation classes demonstrates techniques, equipment, and presentation. The school also offers five different four-class wine series. Of special interest to visitors is a class in Low Country Cuisine, featuring vegetable and seafood recipes of the region, which can be arranged for private groups to include bed and breakfast and tours of the area's historical and culinary attractions. Classes for children ages 5 to 7 and 8 to 12 are taught on Saturday mornings and teenager classes are offered Thursday evenings in the summer.

Specialties: Include ethnic and regional cuisines, basic techniques, breadmaking, appetizers, desserts; wine appreciation; classes for children.

Faculty: School owner Jacki Boyd, chefs Ruth and Scott Fales, Roland Gilg, and Andrew Hoxie, Oriental cook Dr. Alan Martin, Cajun cook Mary Wichmann, and cooking instructors Donna Florio and Celia Strong. Guest instructors included Madeleine Kamman.

Costs: Most classes for adults are $22, wine appreciation classes are $45 per series, and classes for children and teens are $12. Credit card reservations are accepted and refunds are granted cancellations more than 72 hours prior to class.

Contact: Jacki Boyd, In Good Taste, 1124 Sam Rittenberg Blvd., Charleston, SC 29407; (803) 763-5597.

JOHNSON & WALES UNIVERSITY (page 111)

TENNESSEE

CLASSIC GOURMET COOKING SCHOOL
Nashville, Tennessee
Year-round except summer and December

Opened since 1983, this gourmet cookstore and school offers about seven different demonstration (limit 20 students) and participation (limit 8) classes for adults and one or two participation classes for children most months. Sessions range from two to three hours and are scheduled at 5:30 pm for adults and at 9:30 am on Saturdays for children. Classes are held in a teaching kitchen with overhead mirror and cover a variety of topics. Two area medical centers also hold cooking classes in the school kitchen. Group classes and children's birthday parties can be arranged.

Specialties: Include ethnic cuisines, holiday foods, wine selection, and guest chef specialties; children's classes.

Faculty: Owner/Chef Hilda Pope, Mary Clarke, and Janet Flanagan serve as regular faculty members. Guest chefs include Tom Allen, David Hart, Anita Hartel, Debra Paquette, and Robert Siegal.

Costs: Tuition is $18 for children's classes, $28 for adult demonstrations, and $45 for adult participation classes. Credit card registration is accepted and full payment must accompany reservation. Refunds are granted cancellations more than 48 hours prior to class.

Location: Nearby attractions include Opryland, The Hermitage, Belle Meade Mansion, and Cumberland Museum.

Contact: Hilda Pope, Classic Gourmet Cooking School, Paddock Place, 73 White Bridge Rd., Nashville, TN 37205; (615) 352-5837.

CULINARY CLASSICS COOKING SCHOOL
Nashville, Tennessee
Year-round

Founded in 1963, this school offers three-session lecture-demonstration courses that cover a variety of ethnic cuisines. The facility, located in Gloria Olson's home, seats 12 students in a Florida room that opens onto a kitchen and cookbook library. Three-hour sessions, held once weekly in the morning and once monthly in the evening, conclude with a meal. Students are taught culinary techniques, the art of presentation, economy, creative substitution, how to buy and use food and equipment, historical information, and the relationship of dishes throughout the world. Culinary tours are planned from time to time.

Specialties: Ethnic cuisines: French nouvelle, California contemporary, Italian, East meets West, Middle Eastern, Latin American, African.

Faculty: School owner, instructor, and world traveler Gloria Olson is a Certified Charter Member of the IACP, a chef rotisseur member of Chaine des Rotisseurs, and author of *Culinary Classics*. She also serves as a consultant on menu planning, international travel, and kitchen design.

Costs: Each three-session course is $60; evening classes are $25 each; consultations are $25 per hour. Refunds are granted cancellations at least 48 hours prior to class.

Location: In Nashville's Belle Meade and Forrest Hills area.

Contact: Gloria Olson, Culinary Classics Cooking School, 1145 Balbade Dr., Nashville, TN 37215; (615) 665-0893.

MEMPHIS CULINARY ACADEMY
Memphis, Tennessee
Year-round

Founded in 1984, this mid-South school devoted exclusively to the culinary arts offers basic, intermediate, and advanced professional courses and specialized evening demonstration courses for the nonprofessional cook and operates two fine restaurants staffed by students under supervision of professional chefs. Special seminars in pastry, garde manger, and kitchen management are also offered.

The basic professional course, a ten-week (350 hour) program limited to 12 students, consists of 40 hours of classic instruction devoted to French and European pastry work with the remaining time covering basic culinary skills. Techniques, illustrated with over 500 recipes, are stressed throughout the course and the graduation reception features students' preparations. The 15-week intermediate and advanced courses are held at either of the two restaurant teaching kitchens. The intermediate course includes five weeks at each of the three kitchen stations (boiler, sauté, and pantry) and a weekly Certified Sanitation class. Upon acceptance to the advanced program, the student is assigned to the school's other restaurant for a 15-week period that includes rotation through the kitchen stations, bakery and pastry shop, and the ACF-approved nutrition course. Students successfully completing the entire 40-week program are awarded the Grand Diploma. The four-session evening demonstration courses focus on one specialty, such as southern Louisiana classic cuisine or cooking of the American Southwest.

Specialties: Ten and fifteen-week professional courses; regional American cooking; classic and nouvelle cuisine, French and European pastries.

Faculty: Director Joseph Carey, CEC, has worked as an executive chef and culinary arts instructor since 1971 and is a Certified Culinary Professional (IACP). Elaine Wallace-Carey, also a member of the ACF, is a professionally trained pastry chef. All members of the teaching staff have training in classic cuisine and extensive restaurant and/or hotel experience.

Costs: Fee for the 350-hour basic professional course is $2,950. A $150 nonrefundable deposit is required and the $2,800 balance may be paid two weeks prior to class or in two installments, two weeks prior to and midway through the course. Total cost of the Grande Diplome program is $3,550. Intermediate and advanced courses are $300 each and four-session evening course is $75.

Contact: Joseph Carey or Elaine Wallace-Carey, Memphis Culinary Academy, 1252 Peabody Ave., Memphis, TN 38104; (901) 722-8892.

TEXAS

BLANCO RIVER COOKING SCHOOL
Wimberley, Texas

January-June, September-November

Established in 1989 by Leslie McGrath, this school offers more than 50 demonstration (limit 20 students) and participation (limit 15) classes annually in a variety of international and regional cuisines. Three to four-hour sessions are scheduled on Saturday and Sunday afternoons in the 575-square-foot kitchen of Ms. McGrath's 450-acre ranch.

Specialties: International and regional cuisines, including French, Italian, Vietnamese, Chinese, Thai, and Indian; guest chef specialties.

Faculty: Restaurant chefs and cookbook authors, including Bruce Auden and Guiliano Bugialli.

Costs: Range from $50 to $85, payable within five days of registration, no less than two weeks prior. No refunds.

Location: The ranch is 35 miles from Austin and 40 miles from San Antonio.

Contact: Blanco River Cooking School, Rte 4, Box 1745, Wimberley, TX 78676; (512) 847-2583.

LA BONNE CUISINE SCHOOL
Austin, Texas

Year-round

Established in 1973 by Ann Clark, this school for cooking enthusiasts offers more than 80 participation classes (limit 12 students) in four different programs: four-hour Wednesday evening Dinner Classes feature French, Italian, and ethnic cuisines; six-hour Saturday Basic Skills classes focus on French, Italian, and quick cuisines, seafood, and entertaining; a Weekend Seminar on Easy, Healthful Cuisine — 10 Meals to Change Your Life — runs from Friday evening to Sunday afternoon; and a week-long catering seminar is scheduled in January and August. Sessions are taught in Ms. Clark's well-equipped country home kitchen. She also hosts small groups of French-speaking Europeans on culinary tours of the Texas Hill Country.

Specialties: Quick and healthful food, seafood, French and Italian, basic skills.

Faculty: IACP-Certified proprietor/instructor and chef Ann Clark spent six years in France, is author of the forthcoming *Quick Cuisine*, and is a kitchen design consultant.

Costs: Dinner classes $55; basic skills classes $90; weekend seminar $250; one-week catering seminar $550.

Location: Ten miles west of Austin, in the Hill Country.

Contact: Ann Clark, La Bonne Cuisine, 100 Congress Ave., Ste. 2000, Austin, TX 78701; (512) 469-6319, Fax (512) 469-6306.

LE CHEF COLLEGE OF HOSPITALITY CAREERS
Austin, Texas

Year-round

This nonprofit institution, founded in 1985, approved by the ACFEI, and accredited through the Southern Association of Colleges and Schools, offers an Associate of Applied Science Degree in Culinary Arts and Food and Beverage Management, a one-year full-time culinary program, and a six-month Food and Beverage Management course. Short courses and seminars for those aspiring to a career in the culinary, food and beverage management, and nutritional arts are also offered. Facilities include a lab, two classrooms, food storage room, and student lounge. The school maintains a job placement service. About 60% of applicants are accepted and 97% of graduates obtain employment.

The 72 credit-hour A.A.S. program and the 1,720-hour full-time culinary arts course both enroll 20 students in each of three classes with one or more instructors in each class. Classes meet five hours daily, five days a week, at different times to accommodate students' schedules. The A.A.S. degree program covers all subjects taught within the one-year full-time culinary arts course and the six-month food and beverage management course in addition to general education coursework involving algebra, English, public speaking, psychology, and personal computing. The culinary program covers the kitchen; sanitation and safety; pre-preparation; cooking methods; recipes and measurements; building flavor, body, and texture; soups; sauces; vegetables, rice, and pasta; fish, poultry, and meat cookery; breakfast and brunch; pantry production and garde manger; baking and desserts; production and control; and planning and presenting the meal. The Food and Beverage Management Course, which currently enrolls 15 with one to two instructors, is 600 hours in length and meets five hours daily, five days a week. Short courses include tableside cookery (9 hours), food service nutrition (30 hours), food service supervision (30 hours), management by menu (12 hours), Bartending/Advanced Bartending, (25 hours each), waiter/waitress training (9 hours).

Specialties: Associate of Applied Science Degree program, one-year full-time culinary arts course, six-month food and beverage management course.

Faculty: Instructors must have a level of certification with the ACF. School founder and president of the college Ronald F. Boston, C.D.M., C.F.B.E., was 1987-1988 Texas Chef of the Year and has chef, management, and culinary instructor experience. Other instructors are Certified Executive Chefs James A. Alverson and Bud Wheeler and Certified Working Chefs David E. Steffen and Thomas Ciapi.

Costs: Tuition is approximately $16,000 for the A.A.S. Degree program, $10,500 for the one-year full-time culinary program, and $4,390 for the Food and Beverage Management course. Short courses range from $95 to $200. Applicants must have a high school diploma or equivalent and submit a $50 nonrefundable registration fee and complete pre-entrance testing and a personal interview. Financial aid is available. Withdrawals during the first week or one-tenth of the course, whichever is less, receive a 90% refund of remaining tuition; refund is prorated thereafter. If the student withdraws after expiration of the 72-hour cancellation privilege, the school may retain $100 of the tuition and fees prior to the above refund.

Location: In north central Austin, convenient to transportation, shopping, and lakes, and within a 30-minute drive of the Texas Hill Country.

Contact: Le Chef College of Hospitality Careers, 6020 Dillard Circle, Austin, TX 78752; (512) 323-2511.

CUISINE CONCEPTS
Fort Worth, Texas

September-November and January-May

Founded in 1979, this school offers five or six demonstration (limit 24 students) and participation courses (limit 10). A different two to four-session course is featured every other month and may be offered two or three times in the school's specially designed home kitchen with overhead mirror. Sessions meet from 6:30 to 9:30 pm and include a full meal and wine, served on a unique table setting. Facilities include a seven-foot teaching kitchen and overhead mirror.

Specialties: A variety of topics, including regional and ethnic cuisines, menus for entertaining, and nutritional cookery.

Faculty: School proprietor Renie Steves, a Certified Culinary Professional of the

IACP, was co-owner of The French Apron for 11 years. She has studied with Madeleine Kamman, James Beard, Julia Child, Gaston Lenôtre, and Marcella and Victor Hazan. Guest chefs include Jacques Pépin, Stephan Pyles, Diana Kennedy, Nick Malgieri, and Lori and David Holben of Dallas' Riviera Restaurant.

Costs: Range from $120 for a two-session course to $350 for three sessions. A 50% deposit must accompany application with balance due 10 days prior to class. Cancellations more than 10 days prior receive a refund.

Location: In the west side of Ft. Worth, near the Kimbell Museum.

Contact: Renie Steves, Cuisine Concepts, 1406 Thomas Pl., Ft. Worth, TX 76107-2432; (817) 732-4758, Fax (817) 732-3247.

CUISINE INTERNATIONAL
Texas, Massachusetts, Italy, England, France

Year-round

Cuisine International represents cooking schools and culinary tours in Europe and the U.S. Programs in Italy include Badia Coltibuono with Lorenza de Medici (page 210), Villa Mozart (page 224), the Luna Convento Hotel with Enrico Franzese (page 213), and Venetian Cooking in a Venetian Palace (page 224); in England they include Le Manoir aux Quat' Saisons with Raymond Blanc (page 176) outside of Oxford; and in the U.S. they include The Summer House on Nantucket Island with Charles François Salliou (page 62). Culinary tours of varying length and description are scheduled to Italy, France, and England.

Specialties: Italian and French cuisines.

Faculty: Owner Judy Terrell is a Certified Culinary Professional of the IACP, a food stylist for the *Dallas Morning News*, and runs a catering business. She studied at Le Cordon Bleu in London, Badia a Coltibuono in Italy, and L'Academie de Cuisine in Maryland.

Contact: Judy Terrell, 7707 Willow Vine Ct., Ste. 219, Dallas, TX 75230; (214) 373-1161, Fax (214) 373-1162.

DOLORES SNYDER HAUTE CUISINE
Irving, Texas

January-May, September-November

Since 1976, Dolores Snyder has taught one to three-session demonstration (limit 16 students) and participation (limit 10) courses in French, American, and Chinese cuisine, seafood cookery, and the art of English tea. Her teaching emphasizes the techniques and organization of food preparation. Approximately 12 to 15 courses are offered annually with each session running three hours and scheduled at 10 am, 1 pm, or 6:30 pm. Single-session English tea classes cover the three sequential tea courses — sandwiches, crumpets and scones, and pastries — as well as the preparation and service of the beverage itself. Guest chef classes are also featured from time to time. Classes are conducted in a 320-square-foot teaching kitchen with six work areas.

Specialties: English tea; French, American, and Chinese cuisine; seafood.

Faculty: Dolores Snyder received a B.S. in Home Economics from the University of Texas and attended La Varenne, the Cordon Bleu, the Ritz-Escoffier Ecole d'Cuisine, and the Hong Kong Gas & Electric Cooking Schools. She studied with Simone Beck, Giuliano Bugialli, Julia Child, Jacques Pépin, Robert Linxe, and Lucy Lo and is a second level Certified Culinary Professional of the IACP.

Costs: Range from $30 to $100 per class and full payment reserves a space. Cancellations at least seven days prior receive full refund.

Location: The school is in Irving, six miles from Dallas.

Contact: Dolores Snyder, P.O. Box 140071, Irving, TX 75014-0071; (214) 717-4189.

NATURAL FOOD LIFESTYLE
Houston, Texas

September-July

This school offers 30 to 40 one and two-session courses each year in low-calorie, low-fat cooking with natural foods that contain no dairy or sugar. The $2^1/_2$-hour evening sessions cover such topics as guest chef specialties, ethnic recipes, raw foods cuisine, baking with whole grains, tofu dishes, and sauces, gravies, and salad dressings. Courses for children, ages 5 to 12, are also offered as well as market tours and lectures on natural remedies and a variety of diets. Personal instruction is available.

Specialties: Vegetarian and macrobiotic cuisines.

Faculty: Marian Bell, nutritional counselor, has taught for more than 15 years. Guest instructors include Chef Carl of Moveable Feast.

Costs: Classes range from $20 to $28; cancellations receive a full refund.

Contact: Natural Food Lifestyle, 4418 Wood Valley, Houston, TX 77096; (713) 523-0171.

RICE EPICUREAN MARKETS COOKING SCHOOL
Houston, Texas

Year-round

Established in 1990, this school offers approximately 200 demonstration (limit 32 students) and participation (limit 12) classes a year on a variety of topics, including ethnic and regional cuisines, seasonal foods, healthful recipes, and guest chef specialties. The two-hour sessions are scheduled mornings and evenings in the school's 1,100-square-foot classroom with overhead mirror. Classes for young adults and children are also offered.

Specialties: A variety of topics; classes for children.

Faculty: Local chefs, including Robert McGrath; IACP members Dorothy Huang, Mimi Kerr, and Terry Thompson; and nationally known chefs.

Costs: Most classes are $20 to $35. Payment is required with registration and refund is granted cancellations at least 72 hours prior. Credit cards accepted.

Location: On a major road in a fine residential area of Houston.

Contact: Peg Lee, Director, The Cooking School, Rice Epicurean Markets, 6425 San Felipe, Houston, TX 77057; (713) 789-6233, Fax (713) 781-4710.

SAY HI
Austin, Texas

Year-round

Since 1978, Pat Teepatiganond has taught Thai and Chinese cooking privately at a local church and at West Lake and West Wood High School Food Lab, which has overhead mirrors. All are one-session demonstration classes (limit 12 students) that meet from 6:30 to 9 pm on a weekday. Private at-home cooking lessons can be arranged.

Specialties: Chinese and Thai cuisines.

Faculty: Pat Teepatiganond is Chinese, born in Thailand. She is a consultant to Oriental restaurants and operates a catering service.

Costs: Classes are $20. Payment is required at least two weeks prior to class and refund is granted cancellations more than two days prior.

Location: Local church, high school, and instructor's home.

Contact: Say Hi, 5249 Burnet Rd., Austin, TX 78756; (512) 453-1411.

VERMONT

CULINARY MAGIC COOKING SEMINARS
The Governor's Inn
Ludlow, Vermont

June-August

Since 1992, innkeeper and chef Deedy Marble has conducted vacation seminars for nonprofessional cooks (limit 16) in the kitchen of The Governor's Inn. The two and three-day programs offered each spring, summer, and fall emphasize fresh, healthful ingredients and such Inn specialties as Nightingale's Nest, Poached Chicken with Salmon Force Meat, and Apricot Victorian. The two-day seminar, which runs from Friday afternoon until Sunday noon, features a Saturday morning cooking class followed by lunch and tour of a local winery. The three-day seminar, which runs from Sunday afternoon to Wednesday noon, features two morning cooking classes followed by lunch, a winery tour, visits to a cheese factory and maple sugar shack, and a tour to New England's largest antique collaborative.

Specialties: Healthy gourmet.

Faculty: The Governor's Inn, rated four-stars by Mobil Travel Guide, was twice judged one of the nation's *Ten Best Inns*. Deedy Marble, innkeeper and chef since 1982, studied with Madeleine Kamman, Lorenza de Medici, and Roger Verge. She and her husband, Charlie, have received 12 national culinary awards and placed fifth in the World Chef Competition.

Costs: Cost is $630 ($937) double, $507 ($727) single for the two-day (three-day) seminar, which includes private room and bath, arrival dinner, breakfasts and lunches, and all planned activities. A 50% deposit is required and full refund less 10% fee is granted cancellations at least 20 days prior to arrival.

Location: Ludlow, surrounded by lakes in the Okemo Valley, is 132 miles from Hartford Airport, 135 miles from Boston, and 230 miles from New York. Nearby attractions and activities include golfing, summer theater, historical sites, and antique shops.

Contact: Chef Deedy Marble, Culinary Magic Cooking Seminars, The Governor's Inn, Ludlow, VT 05149; (800) 468-3766 *or* (802) 228-8830.

FARMHOUSE 'ROUND THE BEND
Grafton, Vermont

November-August

This three-bedroom bed & breakfast establishment began offering weekend and five-day cooking vacation courses in 1991. Morning demonstration/participation classes, held in the country kitchen and limited to six students, emphasize the scientific aspects of various cuisines as well as quality, efficiency of preparation, and presentation. Afternoon activities include visits to farms, markets, and wineries.

Specialties: A variety of cuisines, stressing the hows and whys of cooking.

Faculty: Chef, caterer, and proprietor Thomas F. Chiffriller, Jr., is a graduate of the University of Vermont and author of *Successful Restaurant Operation, The Butternut Tree Cookbook,* and *Woodstock Presents.* He established The Butternut Tree Restaurant in Woodstock and taught at the Culinary Institute of America and the New England Culinary Institute.

Costs, Accommodations: Cost of weekend (five-day) course is $250 double, $325 single ($650, $750), which includes continental breakfasts and lunches (one dinner for five-day course). Queen and twin-bedded rooms are available.

Location: The Farmhouse, which was built in 1844 and is decorated with period antiques, is a five-minute walk from the village of Grafton, a two-and-a-half hour drive from Boston, and five hours from New York City.

Contact: T. F. Chiffriller, Jr., Farmhouse 'Round the Bend, P.O. Box 57, Grafton, VT 05146; (802) 843-2515.

NEW ENGLAND CULINARY INSTITUTE
Montpelier and Essex Junction, Vermont

Year-round

The curriculum of the New England Culinary Institute is designed to give qualified students a broad range of culinary skills and the experience necessary to begin a successful career in the food service industry. Founded in 1980 and accredited by the CCA (NATTS), the Institute offers a two-year Associates degree. A two-year Service and Management program is scheduled to begin in 1993.

The program admits students in May, September, November, and March and emphasizes small classes, hands-on training in restaurant settings, and paid internships in fine food service establishments throughout the country. Approximately 25% of applicants are accepted and 100% of graduates obtain employment. The term consists of a 24-week residency in the classrooms and restaurants of each campus, followed by an internship of at least 700 hours (18 to 20 weeks), selected to conform to the student's skills, interests, and geographic preferences. After successfully completing first year requirements, students then return for an additional residency period, followed by a second internship appropriate to career goals. More than 70% of the second internships develop into permanent positions and the placement rate for graduates is 100%. Approximately 224 students are admitted each year (56 per term), divided into groups of seven who work together all term and rotate through three-week blocks of study. Students spend 75% of their class time in the Institute's production kitchens preparing food for the public. Facilities in Montpelier include Tubbs Restaurant (gourmet cuisine), Elm Street Cafe (American cuisine), La Brioche (production bakeshop), and a catering and banquet department. Essex facilities include Butler's Restaurant (formal dining) and Birch Tree Cafe (innovative American), as well as a catering, banquet and bakery department. The remaining class time is devoted to such subjects as cooking theory, food and wine history, wine and beverage management, meat fabrication, tableservice, service management, and purchasing. Students in each program are also required to devote at least 45 hours to a structured physical fitness plan and complete a notebook detailing their experiences and progress during their internships.

Specialties: Two-year professional courses (Associate in Occupational Studies degree in Culinary Arts); two-year Service & Management program.

Faculty: The 32 faculty members, headed by Executive Chef Robert Barral, are selected on the basis of their experience and ability to teach. The Institute has a 19-member administrative staff and has also established three advisory boards: Educational, Business, and Food.

Costs, Accommodations: The annual $16,175 comprehensive fee includes room, board, and uniforms. Additional costs include a nonrefundable $25 application fee, a $200 dormitory security deposit, $225 for books, and $225 for equipment. A $100 enrollment deposit is due within 30 days of acceptance, the first tuition payment of $4,800 is due 75 days prior to registration, and the final payment of $11,275 is due at registration. Enrollment deposit is refundable within three days of signing enrollment agreement, nonrefundable thereafter. Students who withdraw during the first week forfeit an additional $200 of tuition; withdrawals from the second through fifth weeks but before the sixth weeks forfeit 25% of tuition, withdrawals from the sixth through twelfth weeks forfeit 50% of tuition, withdrawals from the twelfth through eighteenth weeks forfeit 75% of tuition, no refunds thereafter. Applicants must have a high school diploma or equivalent. Advanced placement second year students must take a written and practical examination, which costs $50 at the school, $100 elsewhere. A variety of sources of financial aid are available. The school provides dormitory facilities and the use of Wedgewood, a health club center located in nearby Berlin.

Location: The Montpelier campus is situated in Vermont's ski country and is 3 hours from Boston, 2½ hours from Montreal, and 7 hours from New York City. The Essex Junction Campus, located at The Inn at Essex, a country hotel that opened in 1989, is 40 minutes north of Montpelier near Burlington.

Contact: Admissions Department, New England Culinary Institute, RR #1, Box 1255, Dept. S, Montpelier, VT, 05602; (802) 223-6324.

VIRGINIA

CHANNEL BASS INN
Chincoteague, Virginia

January-May, September-November

James S. Hanretta, innkeeper and chef of the Channel Bass Inn since 1972, offers three-day master cooking classes for cooks of all levels. Check-in is Sunday night, demonstration/participation classes are conducted Monday and Tuesday from 10 am to 2 pm in the Inn's working restaurant kitchen, and Wednesday morning is devoted to a two-hour general review and discussion session. Each session is limited to three participants or two couples, who may prepare sauces, paella, vegetable dishes and the chef's specialties. Students are provided with a binder of recipes. The program includes three continental breakfasts, two brunches of the foods prepared, two dinners, and lodging in the Inn's best rooms.

Specialties: Sauces, soufflés, vegetables, seafood, desserts, chef specialties.

Faculty: Jim Hanretta, a master chef for 20 years, teaches the sessions.

Costs, Accommodations: The $850 fee covers classes, meals, and lodging at the Inn. A $425 deposit must accompany registration with balance due on arrival. Those who cancel more than two weeks prior to class receive a full refund and cancellations within two weeks receive class credit.

Location: The Mobil four-star rated Channel Bass Inn is a 100-year-old three story frame house with ten guest rooms located on the Delmarva Peninsula. The Chincoteague Wildlife Refuge and Assateague Seashore are nearby.

Contact: James S. Hanretta, Innkeeper and Chef, The Channel Bass Inn, Chincoteague Island, VA 23336; (804) 336-6148.

DOLORES KOSTELNI COOKING SCHOOL
Roanoke, Virginia

September-November

This school offers demonstration and participation classes on request.

Specialties: Italian, French, American, and Chinese cuisines.

Faculty: School owner and teacher Dolores Kostelni studied at the Cordon Bleu, Anne Byrd's Cookery School, and The Greenbrier Cooking School.

Costs: Each class is limited to 15 students who pay $25 each.

Location: At Christ Episcopal Church or Ms. Kostelni's home kitchen.

Contact: Dolores Kostelni Cooking School, Rte. 4, P.O. Box 251, Turtle Brooke, Lexington, VA 24450; (703) 261-2304.

EXQUISITE WORLD OF CHOCOLATES (page 147)

HELEN WORTH'S CULINARY INSTRUCTION
Charlottesville (Ivy), Virginia
Year-round

Helen Worth offers private one-on-one demonstration/participation lessons that cover essential skills; the practical concerns of marketing, cooking equipment, and kitchen efficiency; and the aesthetics of cooking, including table refinements and wine appreciation. Her "Reasons-Behind-the Recipes" method emphasizes the important principles of cooking and encourages creativity. The lesson, held in a fully-equipped kitchen , ends with a meal of the foods prepared.

Specialties: Student selects from Ms. Worth's original recipes and modernized international classics.

Faculty: Helen Worth is the author of *Hostess Without Help* and *Cooking Without Recipes* and creator of Brown-Quick, a seasoning and browning aid. In 1940, she founded The Helen Worth Cooking School in Cleveland and subsequently established her school in New York City and now in Ivy, Virginia. She initiated a food and wine appreciation course at Columbia University and also taught it at Charlottesville's University of Virginia.

Costs: The cost of each lesson is $75 per hour (or any part thereof). Food costs are additional. A $25 nonrefundable deposit must accompany registration.

Location: Ivy, a suburb of Charlottesville, is near Richmond.

Contact: Helen Worth, 1701 Owensville Rd., Charlottesville (Ivy), VA 22901-8825; (804) 296-4380.

JOHNSON & WALES UNIVERSITY (page 111)

JUDY HARRIS' COOKING SCHOOL
Alexandria, Virginia
September-June

Founded in 1978, this school offers more than 80 three-hour classes a year on a variety of topics. Participation (limit 12 students) and demonstration (limit 18) classes are taught in a large, well-equipped kitchen. Students utilize a culinary herb garden and vegetable plot and usually dine on a complete dinner at the end of class.

Specialties: Include ethnic cuisines, food processor, baking, techniques, holiday and dinner parties, wholesome cooking.

Faculty: Most classes are taught by Judy Harris, an IACP-Certified Culinary Professional who has studied French regional cuisine in Paris. Some classes are taught by well-known restaurant chefs and cookbook authors.

Costs: Range from $28 to $42. Full refund is granted cancellations at least 72 hours prior to class.

Location: Five miles from Old Town, Alexandria, and 10 miles from Washington, D.C.

Contact: Judy Harris, 2402 Nordok Place, Alexandria, Virginia 22306; (703) 768-3767.

WORLD OF CUISINE
Alexandria, Virginia

September-June

Marcia Fox has operated this school since 1984 and has been a cooking teacher since 1970. She offers three to four 3-hour participation classes (limit eight to ten students) per week in her home teaching kitchen. Classes are scheduled at 10 am and 6:30 pm and each session begins with a discussion and demonstration after which students prepare the menu. Emphasis is on technique and creativity, using written recipes as guidelines. Classes for couples and private sessions are also offered, as well as a course in pairing wine and food.

Specialties: Include ethnic and regional cuisines, seasonal and holiday menus, hors d'oeuvres, breadmaking, fish dishes, and nutritional cookery.

Faculty: Marcia Fox ran a catering company and taught for 15 years in Denver. She is on the teaching staff of L'Academie de Cuisine and is a Certified Cooking Professional by the IACP.

Costs: Range from $50 to $60 and full amount must accompany reservation. Cancellations more than seven days prior receive a refund or credit.

Location: The school is a 15-minute drive from downtown Washington.

Contact: Marcia Fox, World of Cuisine, 5833 Colfax Ave., Alexandria, VA 22311; (703) 998-3079.

WASHINGTON

BON VIVANT SCHOOL OF COOKING
Seattle, Washington

Year-round

Established in 1977 by Louise Hasson, this school offers two 9-session certificate courses, two 4-session certificate courses, and over 150 three-hour individual selections. The mostly demonstration classes (limit 20 students) cover a variety of topics, including seasonal, regional, and international cuisines. The 9-session courses are Mastering the Basics, which covers fundamental techniques, and Foundations of Fine Cuisine, which emphasizes French technique. The 4-session courses are The Complete Bread Course and Pastry Techniques. Classes are from 10:30 am to 2 pm and from 7 to 10 pm. Graduates of the certificate courses are eligible to participate in the Assistant Program, which offers the opportunity to assist instructors.

Specialties: Basics, international and regional cuisines, seasonal specialties and special events menus; Pike Market tours.

Faculty: Director Louise Hasson has a B.A. in education and 20 years of teaching and catering experience and is a member of the IACP. She studied at the London Cordon Bleu, Badia a Coltibuono in Tuscany, and with touring chefs. Other instructors include Northwest area chefs and teachers.

Costs: Tuition is $295 for 12 classes and $275 for an additional 12 classes. Enrollment in a 20-class certificate program is $469. Payment may be made by credit card and/or in two or three installments. No refunds.

Location: Classes are held in private homes in Seattle and suburban areas. One class per month is held in Tacoma and Mt. Vernon. Students who are members of the program and who volunteer their homes receive a free class.

Contact: Louise Hasson, Bon Vivant School of Cooking, 4925 N.E. 86th, Seattle, WA 98115; (206) 525-7537.

CLARK COLLEGE CULINARY ARTS PROGRAM
Vancouver, Washington
Year-round

At its present location since 1958, this community college offers one and two-year programs in baking, cooking, and management for those aspiring to a culinary career. The culinary arts facility was remodeled and modernized in 1980 and operates like a large hotel kitchen. Students gain practical experience by making all of the food products sold in the campus food operations and working on a variety of evening functions, including the Oregon Chefs Society Annual Christmas Meeting, Clark's Annual Dinner of the Year fundraising event, and the Drama Department's Dinner Theatre productions. The school was named the Number One culinary program in the state of Washington by the National Restaurant Association in 1984 and 1988.

The one and two-year baking programs are set up like a commercial retail bakery. Students spend one day a week learning baking theory, merchandising, and bake shop management. The rest of the week is spent in the baking lab producing products for the school's retail store. Classes are from 8 am to 1:30 pm, Monday through Thursday. Those in the first year program receive practical work experience in baking fundamentals through the preparation of donuts, Danish pastries, breads, rolls, cookies, cakes, and a variety of sweet rolls. The second-year baking students may select from several course offerings to specialize in their area of interest: Gourmet Cake & Pastry Production, Dessert Preparation & Pastry Art, Frozen Bake-off, Back to Basics (refresher of a first-year station), Cake Decorating, Experimental Baking Lab, Retail Sales/Merchandising, Cooperative Work Experience, Oven Operation, and Retail Bakery Management. The program accepts twenty students and has a student to teacher ratio of 5 to 1. A Certificate of Completion is awarded those who complete the baking program; a Certificate of Proficiency is earned by those who complete the bakery management program; additional academic courses may be taken to earn an Associate in Applied Science degree in Baking. Graduates are employed in retail bakeries, specialty bake shops, in-store bakeries, restaurants, hotels, and country clubs.

The cooking and restaurant management programs are set up like a hotel kitchen. The cooking students have an hour of theory classes each morning and spend the remainder of the day in the kitchen, where they rotate through ten stations during a ten-week quarter. Students progress to a different station each week: salads and cold buffets, meat cutting, soups and sauces, main courses, vegetables and starches, table service, a la carte kitchen operations, breakfast cooking, and delicatessen and catering. Specialized afternoon classes are offered in: advanced meat cutting, ice carving, advanced garde manger, wine appreciation, cake decorating, advanced soups and sauces, and pastillage. Those who complete the cooking program earn a Certificate of Proficiency in Cooking and may enter the second-year restaurant management program, in which the students run a station of the kitchen. The management program consists of three 10-week quarters. Students spend one hour daily in a theory class covering management principles and five weeks on each management lab station, planning the menu, costing items, preparing requisitions, and supervising cooking students. Instruction covers purchasing, receiving, issuing, cost control, resumé writing, security, menu design and planning, employee interviewing, psychology, bookkeeping, computers, and inventory control. Students are also involved in the storeroom operations, including purchasing, receiving, and managing inventory. The cooking program accepts 30 students, typically 50% return for the management program, and the student to teacher ratio is 5:1. Additional academic courses may be taken to earn an Associate in Applied Science degree in Restaurant Management. Graduates can seek employment in all phases of the hospitality industry, including restaurants, country clubs, hotels, hospitals, and retirement centers. Advanced placement credit is awarded for prior culinary arts schooling and/or work experience.

Specialties: Professional one and two-year programs in baking, cooking, and restaurant management.

Faculty: Baking program instructors are Certified Master Baker, Culinary Educator, Executive Pastry Chef Ryan de Ruyter, Jean Williams, Katharine Ellis, and Jeannie Burden. Cooking program instructors are Certified Executive Chef, Culinary Educator/American Academy of Chefs Larry Mains, Certified Culinary Educator/American Academy of Chefs George Akau, Sharon Sharp, Glenn Lakin, Joan Brown, Kaye Shattuck, John Suguitan, and Charles Charvat.

Costs: The cost per quarter for each program is $458 ($1,373 per year) and the two-year program is $2,745; out-of-state tuition is $1,400 per quarter. Most Oregon residents qualify for lower in-state tuition fees. Credit card registration (MasterCard, VISA) is accepted. Applicants are admitted on a first-come, first-served basis during any quarter. The college has an ongoing job placement center; financial aid is available and department scholarships are available during the summer quarter. About 80% of applicants are accepted and 95% of graduates obtain employment.

Location: Vancouver is located minutes from Portland, Oregon.

Contact: Larry Mains, Clark College, 1800 E. McLoughlin Blvd., Vancouver, WA 98663-3598; (206) 699-0143.

EVERYDAY GOURMET SCHOOL OF COOKING
Seattle, Washington

Year-round

Founded in 1988 by Beverly Gruber, this school offers an 18-session participation Comprehensive Basics Certificate Course, a 10-week Basic Pastry Certificate Course, a 6-week Kitchen Survival Skills for Beginners Course, and one to five-session courses on a variety of topics. Day and evening three-hour demonstrations emphasize an understanding of how foods interact. They are held in Ms. Gruber's newly remodeled kitchen, which accommodates 20 students for demonstrations and 12 for participation sessions. The certificate course meets once a week and examines the practices and techniques involved in fine food preparation, including stocks, soups, and sauces, egg and meat cookery, fish and shellfish, vegetable and starches, desserts, pastries, breadmaking, and baking. Multi-session courses, guest chefs, and single classes cover a variety of topics. The Northwest Experience, a one-week intensive that includes cooking classes, visits to markets, and other Seattle culinary attractions is planned and group tours can be arranged. An apprentice/assistant program is available to serious students.

Specialties: A variety of topics, including a basic cooking and pastry series, ethnic and regional cuisines, holiday and seasonal menus, and beginner skills.

Faculty: Beverly Gruber is a cum laude graduate of Madeleine Kamman's two-year professional cooking school, a Certified Teacher by the IACP, and has taught professionally for more than ten years. The school is endorsed by the IACP.

Costs: Courses are $30 to $35 per session. A $50 nonrefundable deposit is required for the certificate course, with balance due 15 days prior to first class. Other courses require a $35 refundable deposit (full payment for single classes) with balance due 15 days prior. No refunds within 15 days of class.

Location: The school is in north Seattle.

Contact: Beverly Gruber, Director, Everyday Gourmet School of Cooking, 5053 NE 178th St., Seattle, WA 98155; (206) 363-1602 (phone and fax).

FLAVORS OF MEXICO (page 226)

LE GOURMAND RESTAURANT
Seattle, Washington

Year-round

This school, established in 1988, offers lecture demonstration classes (limit 20 students) in French techniques and Northwest cuisine from 2:30 to 5:30 pm the third Sunday of every month. Sessions are conducted in the restaurant's kitchen.

Specialties: French and Northwest regional cuisine.

Faculty: All classes are taught by Le Gourmand Chef Bruce Naftaly.

Costs: The $25 fee must accompany reservation. Full refund is granted cancellations at least one week prior to class.

Location: Near Seattle's Ballard District.

Contact: Le Gourmand Restaurant, 425 N.W. Market St., Seattle, WA 98107; (206) 784-3463.

KITCHEN/KITCHEN COOKING SCHOOL
Bellevue, Washington

Year-round

This school, established in 1983 in the rear of the Kitchen/Kitchen Store, offers approximately 100 demonstration classes (limit 22 students) and occasional specialized participation classes (limit 8) throughout the year. Most classes are scheduled twice a week from 6 to 8:30 pm and cover a variety of topics.

Specialties: Include ethnic and regional cuisines, entertaining ideas and menus, baking, herb cooking, seafood preparation.

Faculty: Includes Italian specialist Bonita Atkins, herb specialist Bill Kraut, and such well-known local teachers as Sharon Button, Carol Foster, Suzanne Hunter, and Mary Jane Landau. Cookbook authors and guest chefs from the Northwest region are also featured.

Costs: Evening demonstration classes are $20 and specialized participation classes are $32. Tuition is due with registration and major credit cards are accepted. Refund is granted cancellations more than seven days prior to class.

Location: Bellevue, east of Lake Washington, is 10 miles from Seattle.

Contact: Donna Lundquist, Kitchen/Kitchen Cooking School, 242 Bellevue Sq., Bellevue, WA 98004; (206) 451-9507.

PACIFIC NORTHWEST FIELD SEMINARS
Washington

June

This self-supporting nonprofit program, sponsored by the Northwest Interpretive Association in cooperation with the U.S. National Park Service, U.S. Forest Service, and other agencies, offers more than 50 weekend workshops a year devoted to art and nature, astronomy, birds, ecology, geology, natural history, nature writing, photography, and cooking. "Life Along the Oregon Trail", a two-day seminar, is an introduction to some of the skills and crafts practiced along the Trail. The first day, Native American Beadwork of the Northwest, is devoted to making a bead work project. During the second day, Oregon Trail Pioneer Cooking, students learn the early settlers' cooking techniques, including how to start a fire with flint and steel, how to churn butter and bake bread, and how to use a Dutch oven over a campfire. One college credit is available from Seattle Pacific University and Portland State University. Clock-hour credits are available for Washington teachers.

Specialties: Cooking methods of American pioneers.

Faculty: More than 40 naturalists and other professionals.

Costs: Fee, due four weeks prior to seminar, is $45 plus $20 for beads and food used in class. Credit cards (VISA, MasterCard, American Express) accepted. Participants make their own arrangements for food and lodging.

Location: Near Washington's southeast border.

Contact: Field Seminar Coordinator, Pacific Northwest Field Seminars, 83 S. King St., Ste. 212, Seattle, WA 98104; (206) 553-2636.

UWAJIMAYA COOKING SCHOOL
Bellevue, Washington

Year-round

This retail store and school, founded in 1928, offers one to three-session demonstration (limit 30 students) and participation (limit 12) courses. Most courses are devoted to Asian and Far Eastern cuisines. Students may register for an individual session in some courses.

Specialties: Far Eastern cuisines emphasizing Thai and including Chinese, Japanese, Korean, and Vietnamese; macrobiotic and low fat cookery.

Faculty: Includes cookbook authors and guest chefs.

Costs: Range from about $20 for a single session to $60 for a three-session course. Refund is granted those who cancel more than one week before class.

Contact: Director, Uwajimaya Cooking School, 15555 N.E. 24th, Bellevue, WA 98007; (206) 747-9012/525-6510, Fax (206) 525-6970.

WEST VIRGINIA

LA VARENNE AT THE GREENBRIER
White Sulphur Springs, West Virginia

March, April, May

In 1991, The Greenbrier — which created the first resort cooking school in 1978 — joined Anne Willan, president of La Varenne, to introduce La Varenne at The Greenbrier. Eight Sunday evening to Friday afternoon sessions, each limited to 60 cooks of all levels, are offered from late February through early May. The sessions begin with a Sunday evening reception and Monday through Friday mornings, from 9 am to noon, are devoted to classes taught by Anne Willan and other cooking teacher guests, featuring a variety of cuisines. Ingredient selection and equipment use are discussed, with an emphasis on fundamental French technique and how it applies to other cooking styles. Each afternoon, from 1 to 2:30, members of The Greenbrier culinary staff and guests conduct classes that focus on American cuisine, including such topics as regional specialties and low-fat menus. Late afternoons are free for students to avail themselves of the resort's facilities and six-course dinners are served in the Main Dining Room, where special tables are reserved. On Tuesday evening, a specialty restaurant dinner prepared by a celebrity guest chef is served and Thursday evening features The Greenbrier's Gold Service Dinner for students and guests. The session concludes following Friday morning class, during which students are presented with a La Varenne at The Greenbrier cooking school certificate and gift. The Greenbrier also offers a two-year Culinary Apprenticeship Program for accomplished professional chefs.

Specialties: French technique and recipes, contemporary American cuisine.

Faculty: Sessions are taught by Anne Willan, president and founder of La Varenne in France, a noted food columnist, and author of more than a dozen cookbooks, including *La Varenne Pratique*. Some sessions are taught by invited cooking teachers and special afternoon programs are presented by members of The Greenbrier's culinary staff and celebrity American restaurant chefs.

Costs, Accommodations: Tuition for each session includes lodging for five nights, daily breakfast and dinner, and hotel amenities (indoor swimming, afternoon tea and concerts, evening movies, live music and dancing, complimentary golf, tennis, and a visit to The Greenbrier Spa). A $175 ($275) deposit secures a reservation in February/March (April/May). Full refund is granted those who cancel more than seven days prior.

Location: The resort is located just off Interstate 64, a 15-minute drive from the Greenbrier Valley Airport in Lewisburg. Air taxi is available from Roanoke and Charleston and there is also convenient Amtrak service.

Contact: Cooking School Coordinator, La Varenne at The Greenbrier, White Sulphur Springs, WV 24986; (800) 624-6070 *or* (304) 536-1110.

WISCONSIN

CREATIVE CUISINE — KAREN MAIHOFER
Milwaukee, Wisconsin

April-December

This school, founded in 1977, offers several three-hour demonstration classes (limit 16 students) per week. Sessions are held at 9:30 am and 6:15 pm and include a complete meal of the foods prepared. Private demonstrations and programs for organizations and groups can be arranged. Each fall and spring, Karen Maihofer sponsors Seasonal Food Fare exhibits, one devoted to Holiday Foods and the other to Spring Foods. These Saturday demonstrations are limited to 75 students.

Specialties: Ethnic cuisines, food processor and microwave, entertaining.

Faculty: Food consultant and teacher Karen Maihofer is a Certified Member of the IACP, studied with Julia Child, James Beard, Perla Myers, Abby Mandel and Guiliano Bugialli, hosts a radio show, and is author of *Appetizers for All Occasions*, *Holiday Cuisine*, and *Salads and Muffins*.

Costs: Fees range from $20 to $25 per class. No refunds unless place can be filled.

Location: Fifteen minutes north of downtown Milwaukee.

Contact: Karen Maihofer, Creative Cuisine, P.O. Box 17664, Milwaukee, Wisconsin 53217; (414) 352-0975.

ECOLE DE CUISINE
Mequon, Wisconsin

Year-round

Established in 1988, this school and kitchenware store with a French bakery and French ovens offers more than 100 demonstration (limit 45 students) and participation (limit 10) courses a year and an annual food tour of Paris. The four participation courses, which are based on instructional methods of Paris schools and designed to be taken consecutively, are Basic, Intermediate, and Advanced Cuisine (eight sessions each) and Diploma (four sessions). The five-hour sessions are scheduled once weekly, mornings and evenings, and include a full meal of the foods prepared. One-session $2\frac{1}{2}$-hour demonstration courses, scheduled mornings and evenings, cover a variety of topics, including appetizers, vegetables, main courses, desserts, seasonal foods, and guest chef specialties. The school's 1,400-square-foot teaching kitchen has four ovens, three cooktops, and an overhead mirror. Some courses are offered as condensed one-week programs that include lodging to accommodate out-of-town students.

Specialties: French cuisine and topics, including guest chef specialties.

Faculty: Jill Prescott, school owner, and Barbara Graham have studied in Paris at Le Cordon Bleu, Ecole de Gastronomie Francaise Ritz-Escoffier, and La Varenne. Guest faculty includes well-known culinary personalities Giuliano Bugialli, Julia Child, Richard Grausman, Robert Linxe, Jacques Pepin, Anne Willan, and Michelin-star restaurant chefs from France.

Costs: The eight-session Cuisine courses are $650 each and the Diploma course is $400. Demonstration sessions are $20 and guest chef sessions range from $35 to $150. Payment is required in advance and no refunds are granted. One-week programs, which include hotel accommodations and some meals, are $1,250. Credit cards (VISA, MasterCard) accepted.

Location: Twelve miles from downtown Milwaukee.

Contact: Jill Prescott, Ecole de Cuisine, 10050 N. Port Washington Rd., Mequon, WI 53092; (414) 241-8066, Fax (414) 241-1060.

THE POSTILION SCHOOL OF CULINARY ART
Fond du Lac, Wisconsin

Year-round

This school for professional and serious nonprofessional cooks was founded in 1951 by Madame Liane Kuony in her Victorian home, which has a specially constructed professional kitchen with individual work areas. The school, which is accredited by the state of Wisconsin, offers a complete course consisting of four 100-hour sessions: two weeks basic, two weeks advanced, two weeks menu planning, and two weeks cost accounting. A two-week catering/carry-out course is optional. Courses in professional pastry making are offered in early spring and late fall and consist of three sessions: beginner, intermediate, and advanced, which also includes sugar, chocolate, and marzipan work. A certificate of attendance is granted after each session and a diploma is awarded upon satisfactory completion of the full course. Each course is limited to 12 students and classes begin at 9:30 am and continue through the evening dinner each weekday. Optional Saturday classes are devoted to such topics as dissecting a whole side of meat, sausage making, or ice creams, sorbets, and bombes. Class begins after breakfast with an informal lecture by Mme. Kuony about theories, techniques, and methods of preparation. The rest of the day is devoted to participation under Mme. Kuony's guidance. Special emphasis is on classic technique, economy, professionalism, and building a chef larder, and the pitfalls of various cooking methods.

Specialties: Classic French and international cuisine.

Faculty: Mme. Kuony was educated in Belgium, France, and Switzerland. Her restaurant, Postilion, is open by appointment and is known for its French cuisine.

Costs, Accommodations: Each two-week segment is $1,400, which includes all materials and three meals a day, and students must begin with the basic class, regardless of their level of experience. A nonrefundable $100 registration fee and a $200 tuition deposit is required prior to class, with balance due the date of entry. Class dates are announced at the beginning of the year. Inexpensive lodging is available at nearby motels. Prior to enrollment, in the absence of a personal interview for admission, Mme. Kuony telephones prospective students to determine their objectives and answer their inquiries.

Location: On the south side of Fond du Lac at the southern tip of Lake Winnebago, about an hour's drive from Milwaukee and 120 miles from Chicago.

Contact: Mme. Liane Kuony, The Postilion School of Culinary Art, 220 Old Pioneer Rd., Fond du Lac, WI 54935; (414) 922-4170.

ASIA

EXPLORING THE KITCHENS OF ASIA WITH JOYCE JUE
InnerAsia Expeditions
Hong Kong, Bangkok, Singapore, Malaysia, Indonesia

September-October or April-May

Established in 1981, InnerAsia Expeditions specializes in exotic destinations in Asia and the Pacific, with emphasis on culture/education, wildlife/natural history, and/or walking/trekking. Exploring the Kitchens of Asia, an annual 15-day tour limited to 20 participants, features cooking demonstrations at the Mandarin Oriental Hotel in Hong Kong and the Oriental Hotel in Bangkok, a dim sum class, lectures and demonstrations of traditional Thai recipes, and a private cooking lesson in the home of Singaporean food writer and teacher Violet Oon. Other activities include visits to country markets and the Kodari experimental farm in Hong Kong, dining at restaurants noted for their cuisine, shopping excursions, and sightseeing. A three-day extension to Bali features a kitchen tour and lecture on Indonesian cooking by Chef Genn of Amandari's restaurant.

Specialties: Asian cuisine.

Faculty: Joyce Jue, Asian food editor for the *San Francisco Chronicle*, is a frequent traveller to Asia and served as a consultant to the Mandarin Oriental Hotel Cooking School. She is author of *Wok and Stir Fry Cooking* and *Asian Appetizers*.

Costs, Accommodations: To be determined. Credit cards (VISA, MasterCard, American Express) accepted.

Location: The itinerary includes five days in Hong Kong, with a trip to Macau, four days in Bangkok, three days in Singapore, and a three-day Bali extension.

Contact: InnerAsia Expeditions, 2627 Lombard St., San Francisco, CA 94123; (800) 777-8183 *or* (415) 922-0448, Fax (415) 346-5535.

WHAT'S COOKING (page 44)

AUSTRALIA

ACCOUTREMENT COOKING SCHOOL
Sydney, New South Wales, Australia

April-October

Established in 1976, this school offers culinary tours and approximately 100 sessions a year on a variety of topics, including Thai, Japanese, Italian, French, Middle Eastern, and Indian cuisine, as well as seafood, salads, desserts, and guest chef specialties. The one to three-session courses are scheduled from 10:30 am to 1 pm or 6:30 to 9 pm and are mostly demonstrations (limit 30 students) with some participation (limit 12). Classes are held in the school's open planned kitchen with overhead mirror. Culinary tours visit cooking schools in the U.S., Thailand, and Italy.

Specialties: A variety of topics, including ethnic and international cuisines and guest chef specialties.

Faculty: Proprietor Susan Jenkins trained at Ecole Lenôtre France and worked with many chefs. Most classes are taught by prominent Australian chefs, including Damien Pignolet, Mogens Bay Esbensen, Mark Armstrong, Maggie Beer, Gai Bilson, Stephanie Alexander, and Marieke Brugman. A few classes each year are taught by chefs from abroad, including Samsern (Bangkok), Joanne Weir (U.S.), and Diane Seed (Rome).

Costs: Cost is A$55 per session. No refunds but a substitute may be sent.

Location: Sydney, which offers many cultural and recreational attractions.

Contact: Accoutrement, 611 Military Rd., Mosman, Sydney, NSW, Australia; (61) 2 969 1031.

AUSTRALIAN GAS COOKING SCHOOL
North Sydney, New South Wales, Australia
February-November

This school offers evening courses and all-day Saturday workshops on a variety of topics. In the Creative Cooking Series (limit 20 students), participants begin each weekly class with a demonstration, then prepare the recipes under the instructors' guidance, and conclude the session with a meal of the foods prepared. Chefs For All Seasons consists of demonstrations by well-known New South Wales hotel and restaurant chefs. Specialized workshops, offered on Saturdays from 10 am to 4 pm, concentrate on such specific themes as pasta, chocolate and confectionery, and Japanese cuisine. Hosted Tours include visits to wine growing regions and fish and produce markets and fine dining at specialty restaurants. The school's large kitchen is equipped with modern gas appliances.

Specialties: Include ethnic cuisines, menus for special occasions, breads and pastries, and vegetarian cookery.

Faculty: Head of School Jan Boon, author of two gas cooking recipe books and columns for magazines and newspapers, has 29 years of experience in the food field. Other faculty members are qualified cooking instructors. Guest chefs are from Australia and abroad.

Costs: Range from A$35 to A$360 and full tuition must accompany application. Credit cards (VISA, MasterCard, BankCard) accepted. No refunds.

Contact: The Australian Gas Cooking School, AGL Centre, Corner Pacific Hwy. & Walker St., N. Sydney, NSW 2060, Australia; (61) 2 922 8608/8400.

BEVERLEY SUTHERLAND SMITH COOKING SCHOOL
Mt. Waverley, Victoria, Australia

February, April-June, August, October-December

Established in 1967, this school offers one and three-session demonstration courses (limit 30 students). The three-hour sessions are held weekly mornings or evenings in the mirrored teaching kitchen, which looks out on an herb garden.

Specialties: Instructor and guest chef specialties, ethnic and regional dishes.

Faculty: Beverley Sutherland Smith, a Grand Dame Chaine des Rotisseurs and member of the IACP, has contributed to such publications as *Epicurean* and *Gourmet* and is author of 13 books, including *Gourmet Gifts, The Complete Beverley Sutherland Cookbook,* and *A Taste in Time,* winner of the Australian Gold Book award. She is food writer for *The Age* and *The Weekly Times* newspapers, has a weekly TV program, and is food consultant to David Jones Australia.

Costs: Begin at A$39.

Location: Mt. Waverley, a suburb of Melbourne, is approximately 12 miles from the City Centre.

Contact: Beverley Sutherland Smith, 29 Regent St., Mt. Waverley, Vic. 3149, Australia; (61) 3 802 5544.

CALEULA SCHOOL OF COOKING AND ETIQUETTE
Dural, Sydney, New South Wales, Australia

March-May, October-November

Established in 1990, this school offers one and three-session demonstration courses for adults (limit 20 students), one-session participation courses for children (limit 6 to 12), and one-session etiquette courses for teenagers. All adult courses are scheduled mornings and evenings, with each session lasting three hours. The three-session course covers English and French cuisines with an Australian flair; a three-session course is also devoted to advanced techniques. One-session courses include Maximum Effect/Minimum Effort, Dinner in the Dordogne, and Christmas Entertaining. Three-hour holiday courses for children cover basic cooking skills, holiday cake decorating, and other topics. Private etiquette classes are available. The home with its new 405-square-foot kitchen, which has an overhead mirror and seats 20, was recipient of the Master Builders of New South Wales 1991 Excellence in Workmanship Award and was featured in a number of Australian magazines.

Specialties: English, French, and Australian.

Faculty: Mrs. Judith A. White T.T.C.D.A., Fellow Principal, taught home economics in Sydney schools for 20 years, is a former lecturer at Larnook College in Melbourne, and is a nutritionist who has appeared on ABC television. Pamela Melocco, Fellow Principal and Chairman of King and Amy O'Malley Home Economics Scholarship Assessment Panel, N.S.W., teaches etiquette.

Costs: Adult course cost (deposit) is A$50 (A$30) for one session, A$55 (A$30) for one-session Christmas Entertaining course; A$120 (A$50) for three sessions; children's session cost is A$40 to A$45 (full amount); etiquette sessions are A$40 (full amount). Balance is due two weeks prior to course.

Location: In Round Corner, Dural, on the northwest outskirts of Sydney.

Contact: Mrs. Pamela J. Melocco, Co-Principal, Caleula School of Cooking and Etiquette, Caleula, 627 Old Northern Rd., Dural, NSW 2158, Australia; (61) 2 651 3378, Fax (61) 2 651 2934.

CARRINGTON HOUSE RESTAURANT AND COOKING SCHOOL
Newcastle, New South Wales, Australia

March-October

Established in 1985, this school offers one and two-session demonstration (limit 50 students) and participation (limit 10) classes approximately eight to ten times per year. The three to four-hour sessions are held mornings and evenings in the restaurant kitchen and adjacent classroom with overhead mirror. Topics include Australian and guest chef specialties, holiday menus, and low fat cookery. Shopping excursions in Newcastle and Sydney are also scheduled.

Specialties: International guest chef and Australian specialties.

Faculty: Chef-proprietor and radio food commentator Barry Meiklejohn has more than 15 years international culinary experience.

Costs: A$45 to A$70 per class, payable by cash or credit card. Full refund is granted for cancellations.

Contact: Barry Meiklejohn, Proprietor, Carrington House Restaurant and Cooking School, 130 Young St., Carrington, Newcastle, NSW 2294, Australia; (61) 4 961 3564.

COUNCIL OF ADULT EDUCATION
Melbourne, Victoria, Australia

Year-round

This educational organization offers hundreds of on-going classes, short courses, workshops, and travel programs on a wide range of topics, including food and wine, art, crafts, photography, performing arts, recreation, personal development, history, writing, languages, literature, and nature. Most of the more than 70 cookery and catering and programs offered during the year are demonstration two to six-session courses and full-day classes. Topics include international cuisines, microwave, bread making, vegetarian cookery, appetizers, desserts, and menus for diabetics and the elderly. Other programs include a three-day Do It Yourself Catering workshop, a five-day So You Want to Be A Caterer? course, and three and four-session courses in basic and intermediate wine appreciation.

Specialties: A wide variety of topics, including vegetarian cookery, international cuisines, and catering; wine appreciation.

Faculty: Cooking instructors and guest chefs.

Costs: Nonrefundable tuition ranges from A$20 to A$40 per session for multi-session courses and from A$45 to A$70 for a full-day class. The catering programs are A$160 for the three-day course, A$250 for the five-day course. Discounts are granted seniors and pensioners. Credit cards accepted.

Contact: Council of Adult Education, 256 Flinders, St., Melbourne 3000, VIC, Australia; (61) 3 652 0611, Fax (61) 3 654 6759.

CROWS NEST COLLEGE OF TAFE
Crows Nest, New South Wales, Australia

February-November

This vocational school provides a variety of courses for those pursuing a career in catering and/or nutrition management. The Small Business Catering Division offers seven Certificate courses for students who want to manage or be employed by a coffee shop, restaurant, catering business, or motel. Courses that can be completed in one semester (18 weeks from February to June or July to November) are Business Catering Assisting (459 hours), Health Food Industry (306 hours), Practical Food Skills (243 hours), Cake Decorating (270 hours), Patisserie (324 hours), and Food Specialty Markets (306 hours). The 810-hour Business Catering Operations Advanced Certificate Course can be completed in one year, full time. Enrollment is in February and July and instruction covers food preparation, menu design, catering, nutrition, wine and food service, marketing, and management.

Specialties: Catering and nutrition management.

Faculty: Specialist teachers.

Costs: Tuition for the year is A$130.

Contact: Crows Nest College of TAFE, Rodborough Ave., Crows Nest, NSW 2065, Australia; (61) 2 965 4411/4432.

LA CUCINA
Paddington, Sydney, New South Wales, Australia

This school offers three-session demonstration courses (limit 12 students) in Italian and French cuisines. The three-hour classes are scheduled at 10 am and 7 pm in the school's kitchen, which is equipped with overhead mirrors.

Specialties: French and Italian cuisines.

Faculty: Margaret Agostini studied in Italy for four years.

Costs: A three-session course is A$150. Full refund is granted cancellation at least two weeks prior.

Location: Paddington is two-and-a-half kilometers from Sydney.

Contact: La Cucina, 28 Queen Rd., Paddington, Sydney, NSW, Australia; (61) 2 332 1037.

DAVID EGAN COOKING SCHOOL
Cottesloe, Perth, Australia

Year-round

Established in 1991, this school offers seven-session demonstration courses (limit eight students) in vegetarian cookery. The 80-minute sessions cover Chinese, Indian, Italian, French, Mexican, and Australian cuisines as well as eggless cakes and desserts. Facilities include a 750-square-foot room with overhead mirror and individual work spaces.

Specialties: Vegetarian cookery.

Faculty: A cook and chef since 1968, David Egan has worked in London, France, Switzerland, and as a chef at the Southern Cross Intercontinental Hotel in

Melbourne and the Sheraton Perth Hotel, and is an associate member of the Catering Institute of Australia.

Costs: A$140 for seven sessions includes a small meal of the foods prepared. A videotape of the seven lessons is A$38, payable by bank draft in Australian funds.

Contact: David Egan, P.O. Box 435, Applecross, 6153, Western Australia; (61) 9 337 9514.

DIANA MARSLAND COOKING
Armadale, Victoria, Australia

Year-round except January

Established in 1981, this school offers 20 to 30 different one to five-session demonstration (limit 30 students) and participation (limit 10) courses and two or three culinary tours each year. Classes are scheduled at 10:30 am and 7:30 pm weekdays in a large kitchen with overhead mirror. Topics include fish cookery, basics, bread making, ethnic cuisines, entertaining and seasonal menus, appetizers, and desserts. Trips in 1993 visit Tasmania and England and Ireland. Children's classes and guest chef practical workshops are also offered.

Specialties: A variety of topics; guest chef specialties.

Faculty: Director Diana Marsland studied at the Cordon Bleu and Leith's School of Food and Wine in London. Guest chefs include Greg Brown, Gay Glover, Josephine Ive, Jessie Lewis, Aaron Maree, Pierre Stinzy, and Spencer Whiteley.

Costs: Most courses range from A$40 to A$50 per weekly session. Payment must be received two weeks prior to session. No refunds or transfers.

Location: A residential suburb of Melbourne, near public transportation.

Contact: Diana Marsland, 24 Barkly Ave., Armadale, 3143, Australia; (61) 3 509 3971 (phone or fax).

ELISE PASCOE COOKING SCHOOL
Darling Point, New South Wales, Australia

February-Easter, June-August, October-November

Established in 1975, this school offers demonstration courses (limit 25 students) in Italian, Mediterranean, and Modern Australian cuisines and an annual Australian culinary tour. Courses are scheduled six times a year and each course consists of three three-hour evening sessions with an occasional focus on a special subject or theme.

Specialties: Italian, Mediterranean and Modern Australian cuisines.

Faculty: Elise Pascoe is the food writer for *The Sydney Morning Herald*, hosts a weekly show on national television, and is author of three books. She trained at Le Cordon Bleu and La Varenne in Paris and with Angelo Paracucchi in Ameglia, Italy, and has been a guest instructor at schools in England, Italy, Munich, Rome, Vancouver, and the United States.

Costs: A$150 per course, payable in advance. Credit cards (VISA, MasterCard, BANKCARD) accepted.

Location: Sydney's eastern suburbs, six minutes from the city. The annual tour visits Queensland, the Sunshine Coast and Darling Downs, and Adelaide in South Australia.

Contact: Elise Pascoe, Managing Director, Elise Pascoe Marketing, 1/44 Darling Point Rd., Darling Point, NSW, 2027, Australia; (61) 2 363 0406, Fax (61) 2 363 3122.

ELIZABETH CHONG COOKING SCHOOL AND GOURMET TOURS
Melbourne, Victoria, Australia

Year-round

This school, established in 1961, offers year-round demonstration/participation courses (limit 30 students) in Chinese cuisine and an annual culinary tour. Courses meet for two to five $2^1/2$-hour sessions, once weekly at 10:30 am and 7:30 pm. Teaching facilities include an overhead mirror and individual work areas. China gourmet tours are planned from time to time .

Specialties: Various aspects of Chinese cuisine, including etiquette, customs, tradition, and current and new directions.

Faculty: School founder and principal teacher Elizabeth Chong is the author of four books and a food writer for magazines and newspapers. Her assistant, Margaret Fildes, has been trained by Elizabeth Chong.

Costs: Range from A$100 to A$150. A A$30 nonrefundable (but transferable) deposit must accompany registration with balance due two weeks prior to first session. American Express card accepted.

Location: The school is centrally located near public transportation.

Contact: Elizabeth Chong Cooking School, 68 Hawthorn Grove, Hawthorn, Melbourne, Vic. 3122, Australia; (61) 3 819 3666, Fax (61) 3 818 1870.

THE FRENCH KITCHEN
Armadale, Victoria, Australia

Year-round

Established in 1969, this school offers five-session courses and a five-day intensive in classic French cuisine, one to four-session courses in a variety of specialties, and children's courses in January and July. All classes are demonstration (limit 20 to 25 students), except the intensive and children's courses, which have a participation component (limit 10 adults, 20 children). Sessions are taught in the school's French country-style kitchen, which has an island bench, overhead mirror, and large seating area.

The five-session classical courses are offered about six times a year, with menus changing according to the season. Classes, which feature the preparation of an appetizer, main course, and dessert, are scheduled once weekly at 10 am and 8 pm. Approximately ten courses on individual specialties are offered during the year and there is a guest chef on the last Monday of every month. The five-day intensive, scheduled in May and October, is designed to illustrate many of the techniques of French cuisine. The program includes five demonstration sessions, one participation session, a tutored wine tasting, and a dinner at Stephanie's Restaurant; the more advanced intensive class is held in conjunction with Melbourne's Paul Bocuse Restaurant. Courses for children ages 9 to 12 and 13 and over are scheduled over a three-day period.

Specialties: French classic and regional cuisines, guest chef cuisines, single subjects such as fish, desserts, ice creams, cakes and pastries, low cholesterol foods; classes for children.

Faculty: School director and head instructor Diane Holuigue studied at Le Cordon Bleu in Paris and London, Ecole Lenôtre, and with Simca Beck, Paul Bocuse, Giuliano Bugialli, Julia Child, and Roger Vergé. A Certified Professional of the IACP, she is former food editor of *Home Beautiful* and *Epicurean* magazines, currently food editor of *The Australia Newspaper* and its weekly magazine, and author of *The French Kitchen, The Best of Home Beautiful* and *Master Class.* Senior teacher Huguette Quennoy studied at Ecole Lenôtre.

Costs: Five-session courses are A$195, the specialty courses range from A$35 for one session to A$150 for four sessions, the five-day intensive is A$595, and the children's courses are A$60. Application must be accompanied by A$25 nonrefundable deposit (A$50 for the intensive), with balance due three weeks prior to first session.

Location: In Armadale, a residential suburb of Melbourne, near public transportation, fine shopping, and public gardens.

Contact: The French Kitchen, 3 Avondale Rd., Armadale, Vic. 3143, Australia; (61) 3 509 3638, Fax (61) 3 500 9650.

GRETTA ANNA SCHOOL OF COOKING
Sydney, Australia

Year-round

Established in 1958, this school offers demonstration courses (limit 50 students) in French, Continental, and Italian cuisine. Three-session courses are scheduled one day or evening per week for three weeks and four-session live-in courses are conducted on four consecutive days each March. Facilities include a lecture room, commercial kitchen, shop, and herb garden.

Specialties: French, Continental, and Italian cuisine; low fat cookery.

Faculty: Gretta Anna Teplitzky studied at the Cordon Bleu cooking schools in London and Paris, has worked in Michelin three-star restaurants in France, writes cookbooks and articles for food magazines, and has appeared on TV and radio.

Costs: Each three-hour lesson is A$41.

Location: Three-session courses are conducted at the school, which is situated in a Sydney suburb. Four-session courses are held in the country, where meals and lodging are provided at a nominal additional cost.

Contact: Gretta Anna School of Cooking, 67 Clissold Rd., Wahroonga 2076, Sydney, Australia; (61) 2 487 2425.

HARRY'S CHINESE COOKING CLASSES
Bright-le-Sands, Sydney, New South Wales, Australia

February-December

Established in 1977, this school offers the following three demonstration courses (limit 30 students) on a rotating basis: Thai, Basic Chinese, and Advanced Chinese cuisine. Each course consists of eight or nine once-weekly, two-hour, afternoon or evening sessions. Instruction is provided in rented halls with kitchen facilities. Hands-on and special classes can be arranged.

Specialties: Chinese and Thai cuisines.

Faculty: A third generation chef, Harry Quay has more than 30 years experience.

Costs: Approximately A$20 per session, payable at class.

Location: Various Sydney suburbs and Wollongang, NSW.

Contact: Harry Quay, Proprietor, Harry's Chinese Cooking Classes, 47 Bruce St., Brighton-le-Sands, Sydney, NSW 2216, Australia; (61) 2 567 6353.

HOWQUA-DALE GOURMET RETREAT
Mansfield, Victoria, Australia

March-June, September-October

Howqua-Dale Gourmet Retreat, established as a small country house-hotel in 1977 with a cooking school added in 1983, offers a four-day and weekend cooking course once during each quarter and three or four Australian celebrity chef two-day programs each year. These demonstration and participation courses for up to 12 nonprofessional cooks involve preparation and presentation of complete meals with contemporary themes, emphasizing fresh local foods. The day begins with breakfast, followed by class that includes lunch. A full course dinner features the day's preparations. Menus are designed around the season with a strong orientation toward mastery and refinement of techniques and presentation of sauces, fish and seafood, meats, vegetables, and desserts.

Specialties: A variety of contemporary dishes with the emphasis on fresh, local ingredients and seasonal foods; wine selection.

Faculty: Co-owner Marieke Brugman, a noted food writer and cooking demonstrator, conducts the classes. Her partner, Sarah Stegley, acts as hostess and instructs students in wine selection, with emphasis on Australian wines.

Costs, Accommodations: All-inclusive fee is approximately A$550 for the weekend course and A$1,100 for the four-day course. The celebrity chef two-day course is A$600, all inclusive.

Location: The retreat is situated on a 40-acre estate on the Howqua River where it adjoins Lake Eildon, 18 miles from Mansfield, a country town 128 miles northeast of Melbourne. Recreational activities include swimming, fishing, tennis, boating, water-skiing, and horseback riding. The ski fields of Mt. Buller are a 40-minute drive.

Contact: Marieke Brugman or Sarah Stegley, Howqua Dale Gourmet Retreat, Howqua River Rd., P.O. Box 379, Mansfield, Vic. 3722, Australia; (61) 5 777 3503, Fax (61) 5 777 3896.

JAPANESE COOKING CLASSES
Frenchs Forest, New South Wales, Australia
February-November

Established in 1986, this school offers both demonstration (limit 12 students) and participation (limit 6) courses in basic to advanced techniques of Japanese cooking, including sashimi, sushi, tempura, and garnishes. The one to five-session courses are scheduled for 2 to 2½ hours once weekly, mornings and evenings, and each course is offered up to five times a year. Classes, which conclude with a serving of the foods prepared, are held in a 350-square-foot facility with three cooking and work areas.

Specialties: Japanese cuisine.

Faculty: Proprietor Jane Arakawa, a graduate of Sydney University, trained with Japanese chefs and holds a catering and food skills certificate.

Costs: A$30 to A$50 per session, payable in advance.

Location: A 15 to 20 minute drive north of Sydney's central business district.

Contact: Mrs. Jane Arakawa, Japanese Cooking Classes, 19 Garner Ave., Frenchs Forest, NSW 2086, Australia; (61) 2 451 4058.

THE JOHN OXLEY COOKERY SCHOOL
Gas Corporation of Queensland
Milton, Queensland, Australia
Year-round except January

Established in 1950 and upgraded in 1982 and 1989, this school offers demonstration (limit 60 students) and participation (limit 16) courses that cover a variety of topics utilizing gas cookery, including Australian and Asian cuisines, vegetarian recipes, regional foods, cakes and pastries, seasonal dishes, and guest chef specialties. Facilities include an auditorium with overhead mirror for demonstrations and individual work areas with two-person cooking bays for practical classes. The 2½ to 3-hour sessions are scheduled both mornings and evenings for most courses and several one to four-session courses are held each month. The Blue Ribbon Cookery Class, a six-month, 18-session course, covers poultry and game, meat, vegetables, pastry and cakes, fish and seafood, yeast cookery, and finishing techniques. Interstate and/or overseas Visiting Chefs Classes (limit 45 students) are held four to five times a year and the Restaurant Class (limit 40) features a local chef class followed by lunch or dinner at the chef's restaurant. Children's classes are offered during school holidays.

Specialties: Guest chef specialties, international cuisines; children's classes.

Faculty: Trained home economists Joanne Capper and Carol Weeks work with Cookery School Head Barbara Harman.

Costs: Ranges from A$15 to A$30 per session, A$35 to A$75 for visiting chef classes; Restaurant Class is A$85. Payment is due one week prior to course.

Location: Five minutes from Brisbane in the John Oxley Centre.

Contact: The John Oxley Cookery School, Gas Corp. of Queensland, John Oxley Centre, 339 Coronation Dr., Milton, Queensland, 4064, Australia; (61) 7 858 0444, Fax (61) 7 368 1513.

KISETSU JAPANESE COOKING COURSES
Waitara, Sydney, New South Wales, Australia

February-November

Established in 1987, this school offers basic and advanced demonstration/ participation courses (limit 8 students) and a cookery club for students who have completed both courses. The eight-session basic course, held mornings and evenings three times a year, consists of three-hour weekly sessions devoted to such topics as teriyaki, sashimi, sushi, tempura, one-pot cooking, Japanese vegetables, and noodles. The advanced course is held once a year. All sessions conclude with a complete meal.

Specialties: Japanese cuisine.

Faculty: Margaret Ubukata.

Costs: A$280 per course, payable at first lesson.

Contact: Margaret Ubukata, 43 Edgeworth David Ave., Waitara, Sydney, NSW 2077, Australia; (61) 2 476 2537.

LINDA QUO COOKERY SCHOOL
Booragoon, Western Australia

Year-round

Founded in Malaysia in 1961, this school was incorporated in Western Australia in 1978. While instruction is suited to all levels, the emphasis is on professional training and private individual and group lessons. Courses meet for three or five 3-hour sessions, scheduled once weekly or daily. Chinese cooking courses cover a variety of basic dishes and popular dishes from North, Central, and South China. Privately arranged lessons cover Peking Duck, Chinese roasting, Malaysian Satay, and a one-week intensive course for non-residents (certificate of completion awarded) is also available.

Specialties: Chinese and other Far Eastern cuisines and Hawkers' Food.

Faculty: Director and Principal Linda Quo trained in Malaysia, Singapore, Thailand, Hong Kong, Formosa, China, the U.S., and Europe. She is author/ publisher of *Recipes by Linda Quo* and *Asean Cookbook* and was chief Asian food lecturer at the School of Hotel and Catering, Mara Institute of Technology.

Costs: Fees are A$400 for the week-long intensive, A$80 for a three-session course, and A$30 for a single session. No refunds.

Location: In Booragoon, near the Garden City Shopping Centre.

Contact: Linda Quo Cookery School, P.O. Box 279, Applecross 6153, Western Australia; (61) 9 330 4660.

A LITTLE COOKING CLASS
St. Peters, South Australia

Year-round except January and August

Established in 1989 in a renovated 80-year-old butcher shop, this school offers two or three four-session participation courses per month for 20 cooks of all levels.

The three-hour morning and evening sessions cover a variety of topics, including easy entertaining, microwave, and low-calorie, low-cholesterol recipes.

Specialties: Easy-to-prepare and healthful foods; microwave techniques.

Faculty: Self-taught cook Prue Little also performs in amateur theatre.

Costs: A$90 per course.

Location: Inner suburb of Adelaide.

Contact: Prue Little, 87, Sixth Ave., St. Peters, 5069, S. Australia; (61) 8 363 0526.

MA CUISINE COOKING SCHOOL
Cottesloe, Australia

Year-round

Established in 1982, this school offers one to three-session demonstration (limit 35 students) and participation (limit 12) courses in French, Italian, Southeast Asian, American, and modern Australian cuisines. About 65 evening courses are offered annually, with each class ranging from 2^1/$_2$ to 3 hours in length. Sessions are held in the school's teaching kitchen, with an overhead mirror and individual work areas. International culinary tours are also offered.

Specialties: International cuisines; single subjects such as fish, desserts, yeast cookery, low cholesterol; guest chef specialties.

Faculty: School director is Beverly Sprague, a member of the IACP. Classes are taught by prominent Western Australian chefs and specialty teachers, as well as Australian and international chefs.

Costs: Per-session cost ranges from A$28 to A$55; series classes range from A$56 to A$135. Full payment reserves a space. No refunds but replacement may be sent.

Location: The beach-side suburb of Perth, Western Australia's capitol.

Contact: Ma Cuisine Cooking School, Suite 17, Napoleon Close, 12 Napoleon St., Cottesloe 6011, Perth, Australia; (61) 9 384 0378/3860, Fax (61) 9 384 5790.

MARCEA WEBER'S COOKING SCHOOL
New South Wales, Australia

February-November

Since 1979, Marcea Weber has taught four to six-session demonstration/ participation (limit 15 students) courses with themes that change each year. The 2^1/$_2$-hour sessions are scheduled once weekly in the mornings and evenings and cover a variety of health-related topics. Classes are held in the open plan home kitchen, which has wooden bench space for 10 students to work simultaneously. Future plans include a larger facility and weekend retreats in cooking and lifestyle.

Specialties: Include macrobiotic cooking, wholefoods, Japanese cuisine, low fat and low salt cuisine, cooking for health and vitality, and children.

Faculty: Marcea Weber studied with macrobiotic cooking authority Aveline

Kushi for seven years and with Lima Oshawa for one year. She is author of *The Australian and New Zealand Book of Wholemeals*, *The Sweet Life*, *Naturally Sweet and Sugar Free*, *Macrobiotics and Beyond*, and a book on natural health and healing for children.

Costs: The cost of each session is A$24, which includes a shared meal. A 50% nonrefundable deposit must accompany booking.

Location: An hour's drive from Sydney, in the Blue Mountains, which has bush walking tracks and sightseeing.

Contact: Marcea Weber, 56 St. George's Crescent, Faulconbridge, NSW 2776, Australia; (61) 4 751 1680.

NATURAL FOODS VEGETARIAN COOKING SCHOOL
Better Living Seminars
Sydney, New South Wales, Australia
May and November

Established in 1987, this school offers two five-session demonstration programs (limit 36 students) each year. The two-hour sessions meet once weekly and cover nutrition and the preparation of fruits, vegetables, and wholegrains.

Specialties: Vegetarian cookery.

Faculty: Certified cooking demonstrator Myrna Fenn.

Costs: A$60.

Location: S.D.A. Community Centre, 7 Kingsway, Dee Why, Sydney.

Contact: Myrna Fenn, Cooking School Coordinator, Natural Foods Vegetarian Cooking School, Better Living Seminars, 20/21 Rangers Rd., Cremorne, Sydney, NSW 2090, Australia; (61) 2 953 7175.

SYDNEY SEAFOOD SCHOOL
Fish Marketing Authority
Pyrmont, New South Wales, Australia
Year-round except January

Established in 1989, this school offers more than 50 two to four-session demonstration (limit 66 students) and participation (limit 48) courses a year. The two-hour sessions, scheduled both mornings and evenings, cover the various aspects of seafood cookery, guest chef specialties, and advanced techniques. Facilities include a practical kitchen and demonstration auditorium with tiered seating and overhead mirror. A four-hour hands-on sushi and sashimi class (limit 20) is offered each quarter.

Specialties: Seafood.

Faculty: Qualified home economists and guest chefs, including Tony Bilson (Fine Bouche), Serge Dansereau (Kables), and Hideo Dekura.

Costs: Nonrefundable tuition, payable in advance, ranges from A$30 to A$110 per course; credit cards (VISA, MasterCard) accepted.

Location: Pyrmont is in Sydney's central business district. The School, which is wheelchair accessible, is in the Sydney Fish Market, a new complex that incorporates the Fish Marketing Authority, fish auction hall, fish retail outlets, a sushi bar, and other food and drink establishments. Early morning tours of the market, fish auction, sashimi bay, and fileting area are available.

Contact: Bettina Jenkins, Manager, Sydney Seafood School, Fish Marketing Authority, Blackwattle Bay, Pyrmont, NSW 2009, Australia; (61) 2 660 1611, Fax (61) 2 552 1661.

VICTORIA'S KITCHEN OF CREATIVE COOKING
Mt. Hawthorn, Western Australia

February-September

Established in 1981, this school offers 12 to 15 one and two-session demonstration courses a year. The schedule is from 7 to 9 pm and topics include international cuisines, entertaining and holiday menus, vegetarian cookery, microwave, beef cuts, and poultry and seafood preparation. Instruction covers buying, cooking, and storing, with emphasis on cost saving.

Specialties: A variety of topics.

Faculty: Victoria Blackadder was named *Australian Women's Weekly* Best Cook in Australia in 1981, began a radio program the same year, and established a catering business in 1986. She is author of *Victoria's Kitchen*, has written for newpapers and food magazines, and serves as a consultant to food photographers and the hospitality industry.

Costs: Range from A$14 to A$20 per session, payable in advance; 10% discount for four sessions or more.

Location: The Home Base Exhibition Centre Auditorium, at the corner of Salvado Road and Harborne Street in Subiaco, 10 minutes from Perth city center.

Contact: Victoria Blackadder, Victoria's Kitchen, P.O. Box 278, Mt. Hawthorn 6016, Western Australia; (61) 9 443 2266.

BERMUDA

EXQUISITE WORLD OF CHOCOLATES
Invitation to Travel
Bermuda

June

This four-day cruise on the Queen Elizabeth 2 features presentations/demonstrations of chocolates and desserts.

Faculty: Richard Howland, chairman of Charbonnel et Walker, Chocolatier by Appointment to Her Majesty The Queen, and François M. Dionot, founder of L'Academie de Cuisine.

Costs, Accommodations: Cost ranges from $975 to $1,304, which includes double occupancy stateroom and all on-board meals and entertainment.

Location: Bermuda, roundtrip New York City.

Contact: Mary Callan Charlesworth, President, Invitation to Travel, Inc., P.O. Box 31, Upperville, VA 22176; (703) 592-3755.

CANADA

ACADEMIE DE CUISINE ENR.
Dollard des Ormeaux, Quebec, Canada

May, June, September-January

Established in 1972, this school offers one to seven-session demonstration courses (limit 12 students) in Italian, Spanish, and French cuisines. The two-hour sessions meet weekly at 7 pm in the school's 500-square-foot kitchen with overhead mirror. A tour of Quebec province and Saturday classes for children are also offered.

Specialties: Italian, Spanish, and French cuisines.

Faculty: Manager of Les Pates Pastamore, Inc., Mario Novati received his training in Venice, Italy, and at the Lewis Hotel Training School in Washington, D.C. He has published three cookbooks and hosted a weekly television cooking series in Ottawa and Montreal.

Costs: Approximately C$40 per lesson, payable in advance. Cancellations more than 48 hours prior to class receive full refund.

Location: Ten miles from Montreal.

Contact: Chef Mario Novati, Academie de Cuisine, Les Pates Pastamore, Inc., 60 Paddington Pl., Dollard des Ormeaux, QB, H9G 2S4, Canada; (514) 696-6110.

BENKRIS SCHOOL OF CULINARY ARTS
Calgary, Alberta, Canada

September-June

Founded in 1979, this gourmet cookware store and school offers 100 to 150 demonstration (limit 25 students) and participation classes a year on a variety of topics. Most classes are scheduled from 11 am to 1:30 pm, 1 to 3:30 pm, or 6:30 to 9:30 pm in the school's well-equipped, mirrored kitchen.

Specialties: Include ethnic and regional cuisines, wine and food harmonies, hors d'oeuvres, desserts, soups.

Faculty: Includes school director Lorna Hurst, assistant director Carole Martin, caterer Dee Hobsbawn-Smith, J. Webb Wine Merchants, and more than 20 local chefs and caterers. Guest instructors include Hugh Carpenter, Deborah Madison, Caren McSherry-Valagao, Perla Meyers, and Joanne Weir.

Costs: Range from C$30 to C$100 per class. Credit card registrations accepted. Student volunteers who assist the chef in exchange for tuition are required for every class. Cancellations more than 48 hours prior to class receive a credit.

Location: In the historic Kensington area, approximately 90 miles east of the Canadian Rocky Mountain resorts at Banff, Lake Louise, and Emerald Lake.

Contact: Benkris School of Culinary Arts, 120-10th St. N.W., Calgary, AB, T2N 1V3, Canada; (403) 283-9399, Fax (403) 270-2820.

BETTY'S KITCHEN
Ottawa, Ontario, Canada

Year-round

Founded in 1978, Betty's Kitchen offers more than 50 demonstration (limit 25 students) and participation (limit 20) cooking classes during each six-month period. About half the classes specialize in microwave and convection oven cookery, one-quarter cover a variety of topics, and the remaining are guest teacher workshops. Other classes cover a variety of topics and guest faculty specialties. Most classes are one session, two or four hours in length, and the others range from one to four sessions. Classes are scheduled at 7 pm weekdays and Saturday mornings and afternoons in the school's teaching kitchen with overhead mirror. The school also offers children's classes, private group lessons, and free seminars.

Specialties: Microwave and convection oven cookery as well as breadmaking, cake decorating, food processor cuisine; children's classes.

Faculty: Classes are taught by home economist Connie McCalla and cookbook authors are often featured.

Costs: Classes taught by the school faculty range from C$20 for a single two-hour session to C$80 for four sessions. Guest instructor two-hour classes range from C$20 to C$30. Registration must be accompanied by full payment. Credit cards (Mastercard, VISA) accepted. Refunds are granted cancellations more than 48 hours prior.

Location: Classes are taught in the in-store classroom at Betty's Kitchen, Bleeker Mall, 1400 Clyde Ave., in Ottawa.

Contact: Betty Shields, Betty's Kitchen, Ltd., Greenbank Square Shopping Center, 250 Greenbank Rd., Nepean, ON, K2H 8X4, Canada; (613) 829-0214.

THE BONNIE STERN SCHOOL OF COOKING
Toronto, Ontario, Canada

Year-round

Founded in 1973, this school offers a variety of one to six-session cooking and wine courses, Saturday workshops, and guest chef classes. Demonstration courses (maximum 30 students) are scheduled from 7 to 10 pm. Saturday workshops, from 10:30 am to 3 pm, cover a variety of topics.

Specialties: Include ethnic and regional cuisines, holiday menus, guest chefs.

Faculty: School proprietor Bonnie Stern has studied with Simone Beck, Marcella Hazan, Jacques Pépin, Julie Dannenbaum, Nina Simonds, Giuliano Bugialli, and Madeleine Kamman and is the author of six cookbooks, including *At My Table* and *Bonnie Stern's Appetizer Cookbook.*

Costs: Range from C$134 for two sessions to C$268 for a six-session course; Saturday workshops are C$100 and guest chef classes are C$134 each, C$482 for a series of four.

Contact: The Bonnie Stern School of Cooking, 6 Erskine Ave., Toronto, ON, M4P 1Y2, Canada; (416) 484-4810, Fax (416) 484-4820.

CAREN'S COOKING SCHOOL
North Vancouver, British Columbia, Canada

September-May

Founded by Caren McSherry-Valagao in 1978, this school offers up to 12 classes monthly as well as an annual culinary tour. The mostly demonstration sessions are limited to 32 students and scheduled from 7 to 10 pm week nights. Participation classes for young people are held on Saturdays and port and wine workshops are also available. Facilities include a full-sized overhead mirror, large butcher block demonstration table, and eight gas burners. Each class has a full-table sit-down meal complete with linen and china service.

Specialties: Include ethnic and regional Northwest cuisine, seasonal and holiday foods, hors d'oeuvres, port and wine tasting, buffet catering, and guest chef specialties; classes for youngsters.

Faculty: Caren McSherry-Valagao trained at the Cordon Bleu, the CIA, and The Oriental in Bangkok and is a Certified Cooking Professional of the IACP. She has studied with Giuliano Bugialli, Julia Child, Jacques Pépin, and Paul Prudhomme, and contributed food articles to publications. Guest chefs have included John Ash, Giuliano Bugialli, Jane Butel, and Hugh Carpenter.

Costs: Tuition ranges from C$40 to C$75 per class. Credit cards (VISA, MasterCard) accepted.

Location: In the North Shore area, near Beaver and Prospect Roads.

Contact: Cindy Burridge, Caren's Cooking School, 1856 Pandora St., Vancouver, BC, V5L 1M5, Canada; (604) 255-5119, Fax (604) 253-1331.

CHLOE FOX VEGETARIAN COOKING
Montreal, Quebec, Canada

February-June, October-November

Established in 1985, this school offers four-session demonstration courses (limit 12 students) in vegetarian cuisine. The two-hour sessions, which are scheduled mornings and evenings in Ms. Fox's large home kitchen, cover tofu, grains, and ethnic specialties.

Specialties: Vegetarian cuisine.

Faculty: Chloe Fox, owner of Chloe's Kitchen, and her son, Joshua.

Costs: C$100 per course, payable in advance. No refunds.

Location: Montreal's West End.

Contact: Chloe Fox, Owner, Chloe's Kitchen, 2009 Ward St., Ville St. Laurent, QB, H4M 1T3, Canada; (514) 744-2675.

COOKING WITH SUSAN LEE
London, Ontario, Canada

January-March, May-July, September-November

Established in 1988, this school offers three-hour demonstration/participation (limit 12 students) in the large family kitchen of a North London home. Lessons are scheduled on Wednesday and Saturday mornings and Thursday evenings and topics include seasonal foods, ethnic and regional cuisines, entertaining menus. Private lessons can be arranged.

Specialties: A variety of topics.

Faculty: Home economist and food writer Susan Lee and local chefs.

Costs: Classes are C$35 each. Two-day notice is required for refund.

Contact: Cooking with Susan Lee, 1011, Wellington St., London, ON, N6A 3T5, Canada; (519) 439-1423.

THE COOKING WORKSHOP
Maria Pace & Associates
Toronto, Ontario, Canada
Fall, winter, spring

Established in 1985, this school offers one-day (usually Sunday) demonstration/participation workshops (limit 12 students) that are designed to teach techniques not easily learned from recipe books. Approximately 14 different workshops are offered in four major areas: Italian cuisine (including pasta and sauces, fish and seafood, regional dinners, wine tasting, and pizza, foccacia, & calzone), bread (including rye & bagels, classic bread, baguettes, and holiday breads), pastry (including croissants, strudel, and puff pastry), and foundations (soups and stocks, basic sauces and dressings). Sessions, which conclude with a meal of the foods prepared, are scheduled from 10 am to 3:30 pm in a large kitchen. Food, wine, and culture tours to Italy are also offered from time to time.

Specialties: Italian cuisine, bread, pastry, soups and stocks, wine tasting.

Faculty: Maria Pace has taught cooking since 1981 in various Toronto locations, including the Columbus Centre, the Network for Learning, and Boards of Education. She has taught on CTV's "What's Cooking", served as a restaurant consultant, and was coordinator for the Great Cooks cooking forum. Professional baker Paula Bambrick trained at George Brown College and worked at Dufflet Pastries for six years. Doris Eisen specializes in developing recipes for specialty breads and pastries for the home cook.

Costs: Range from C$65 to C$75. Advance nonrefundable payment is required.

Location: Three blocks west of Bathurst Street in Toronto's "Little Italy" and also at Dufflet Pastries (787 Queen St. West).

Contact: The Cooking Workshop, M. Pace & Associates, 33 Clinton St., Toronto, ON, M6J 2N9, Canada; (416) 588-1954.

LE CORDON BLEU PARIS COOKING SCHOOL
Ottawa, Ontario, Canada
Year-round

The only Le Cordon Bleu school in North America has been owned and operated since 1988 by Le Cordon Bleu-Paris (page 151). Its modernized facilities include a classroom and a fully equipped kitchen with individual work spaces for 12 students. The school offers three of Le Cordon Bleu's five Classic Cycle courses leading to the Grand Diplôme: Level I (Basic) Cuisine, Level II (Intermediate) Cuisine, and Level I (Basic) Pastry. Students who successfully complete each course and its examination receive a certificate and are eligible to take the Level III (Advanced) Cuisine and Level II (Advanced) Pastry courses at Le Cordon Bleu in Paris, where they can obtain Le Grand Diplôme.

No experience is required for Level I courses, which must be completed before proceeding further. Cuisine and Pastry curricula may be taken simultaneously, in which case the Classic Cycle can be completed in nine months, or consecutively, which takes twelve to fifteen months. Instruction is through demonstration followed by a 2^1/$_2$-hour practical class, concluding with a tasting. Day and evening sessions are available as well as intensive sessions tailored to the student's schedule. One-day, one-week, two-week, and one-month short courses are also offered. Demonstrations are open to the public.

Specialties: Classical French cuisine.

Faculty: Gérard L. Breissan is the director. Instructors, all professional chefs qualified by Le Cordon Bleu in Paris, include Philippe Guiet, Jean Claude Terrettaz, and pastry chef Michel Denis.

Costs: Tuition is C$3,250 for Level I Cuisine, C$3,550 for Level II Cuisine, and C$2,800 for Level I Pastry. A C$450 deposit must accompany registration with balance due four weeks prior to first class. Cancellations more than two weeks prior receive a C$400 refund. Of those who apply 95% are accepted and 70% obtain employment within the first year. Demonstrations are C$25 for individuals, C$15 per person for groups of eight or more.

Location: In Ottawa's Chateau Royale Professional Building.

Contact: Gérard L. Breissan, Le Cordon Bleu Paris Cooking School, 1390 Prince of Wales Dr., #400, Ottawa, ON, K2C 3N6, Canada; (613) 224-8603/8656, Fax (613) 224-9966.

DUBRULLE FRENCH CULINARY SCHOOL
Vancouver, British Columbia, Canada

Year-round

Established in 1982 and certified by the Ministry of Labour under the Private Trade Schools Act, this privately-owned cooking school offers a 17-week Pre-Employment Culinary Training Program for individuals desiring a culinary career. Approximately 70% of applicants are accepted and 90 to 95% of graduates obtain employment. Three programs, each identical in content and limited to 24 students, begin annually in January, April, and August. Classes are scheduled from Monday through Friday with one program from 8:30 am to 2:30 pm and the other program from 2 to 8 pm. Instruction is 80% practical and 20% theoretical and cooking methods are based on classic French techniques that are adapted to the contemporary North American market. The program is designed to develop technique and method and covers stocks, soups, sauces, garde manger, salads, vegetables, deep frying, broiling, buffets, charcuterie, butchery, bread making, doughs, pastries, desserts, fish and seafood, poultry and game, wine appreciation, and education. Theoretical examinations are given at the end of each eight-week term and practical work evaluation is on-going on a daily basis. A diploma is awarded graduates. There is accreditation given for this training towards the B.C. Apprenticeship program. The modern 6,000-square-foot, three-level facility has two training kitchen-classrooms equipped with nine full stations, a baking station, two demonstration stations, and a dining area. A theatre-style demonstration lecture room seats 30.

Specialties: A 17-week career program focused on classic French cuisine. The school also offers programs in Hospitality Management Training, Restaurant Management, and Professional Bartending.

Faculty: European-trained chefs who are bilingual in English and French.

Costs, Accommodations: The course fee is C$5,550. A C$500 deposit, applicable to the third term, secures a place. Fees are due in three interest-free installments — C$1,850, C$1,850, C$1,350 — at the beginning of each term. Deposit refunds are in accordance with the Ministry of Advanced Education regulations and are granted written withdrawals at least 30 days prior to the first term. Student loans are available and job placement assistance is provided.

Location: One block from a main intersection, Broadway and Granville, and accessible by public transportation from the Lower Mainland.

Contact: Dubrulle French Culinary School, 1522 W. 8th Ave., Vancouver, BC, V6J 4R8, Canada; (800) 667-7288 (in BC) *or* (604) 738-3155, Fax (604) 738-3205.

GEORGE BROWN COLLEGE
OF APPLIED ARTS AND TECHNOLOGY
Toronto, Ontario, Canada

Year-round

George Brown, one of Canada's largest colleges, offers diploma (more than one year) and certificate (one year or less) programs in downtown Toronto. Established in 1965, the School of Hospitality offers 20 full-time programs to approximately 1,750 career aspirants and 30 part-time programs to approximately 3,000 cooking enthusiasts and hospitality career-oriented individuals. Full-time programs meet five days per week; most part-time programs meet from 6 to 9 or 10 pm, once weekly for ten weeks; demonstration/participation classes are scheduled between 7 am and 11 pm. Facilities include 12 laboratories with 24 individual work stations. All demonstration areas have overhead mirrors.

Full-time culinary courses include Culinary Management (two years), Pre-Employment Chef Training (one year), General Food Preparation — Basic and Advanced (20 weeks each), Chinese Cooking — Basic and Advanced (eight weeks each), and Baking Techniques (one year). The Culinary Management diploma course begins in September and provides training in food preparation, cooking, and presentation to international standards. Graduates, who complete two 6-week periods of supervised work under Ontario chefs, are qualified for jobs as chef de partie or sous chef and eligible, after two years work, to take the professional certification examination for Journeyman Cook. They also may enroll in the post-diploma third year specialization courses: Culinary Arts — Italian (18 weeks in Canada, 15 weeks in Italy), Food Service Supervisor (one year), Patissier Certification (30 weeks part-time), and Chinese Cuisine. Pre-Employment Chef Training (begins in September and January) and the General

Food Preparation certificate courses (begin every 20 weeks) include food theory classes covering products and presentation, demonstrations by experienced chefs, and hands-on preparation of dishes served in the college's cafeterias and Plumer's Dining Room, an open-to-the-public student training restaurant. Graduates qualify for a variety of positions in the food service industry. The Chinese Cooking certificate courses teach the food preparation, kitchen supervising, and theoretical methods to meet the needs of various styles of Chinese cuisine and prepare students for a position in a Chinese restaurant. The Baking Techniques certificate course is divided into eight-week skill sections that cover breads, pastries, cakes, and decorating, and prepare students to be apprentice bakers.

Approximately 16 part-time courses are offered each semester, including Small Quantity Food, Vegetarian Cooking, Chinese Cuisine, Baking, Cake Decorating, Sausage Making, and Junior Gourmet. Students receive a certificate of competence on completion of a course and a certificate in Haute Cuisine for completion of five courses. A professional certified Sommelier program is also available. The school provides trades updating courses tuition-free to Toronto employees of hotels and restaurants.

Specialties: One to two-year career programs in culinary arts; third year specialty courses in Italian and Chinese cuisines; part-time career and avocational courses in vegetarian and Chinese cuisines, baking, and cake decorating; wine appreciation; cooking classes for youngsters.

Faculty: The 80 culinary and hospitality management faculty members are professors and most chef professors hold a Master Chef, Master Pâtissier, or Chef de Cuisine Certification. All have a minimum of five years industry experience and have served as a Senior Managerial or Executive Chef in a recognized facility.

Costs, Accommodations: Resident (nonresident) tuition for most diploma programs is C$1,031 (C$7,289) for 32 weeks. Resident (nonresident) tuition for certificate programs is $C23.90 (C$198) per week. Senior citizen resident tuition is C$50 per academic year for a full-time program, C$15 for funded part-time program (non-funded pay full fee). VISA accepted. For full-time programs, a full refund less C$50 for resident, C$416 for nonresident, is granted up to two weeks after start of program. For part-time programs, a maximum charge of C$15 is assessed for withdrawal or transfer prior to the third class. Minimum requirement for admission to a diploma program is an Ontario Secondary School Diploma, an Ontario Secondary School Graduation Diploma, or an equivalent diploma from within North America. Minimum requirement for admission to a certificate program is Ontario Grade 10 or North American equivalent, Ontario Basic Training for Skills Development Level III, Academic Upgrading III, or an Ontario Certificate of Education. Canadian citizens or Permanent Residents may be eligible for financial assistance under the terms of the Ontario Student Assistance Program. The college's job placement offices are successful in finding employment for 95% to 97% of graduates. Accommodations are not provided but the housing service maintains a daily listing of local lodging. A furnished room averages C$75 to C$125 per week.

Location: The School of Hospitality, a newly constructed four-story facility completed in 1987, is situated at 300 Adelaide St. E., at the college's St. James campus, which is named for a nearby cathedral. The campus has a library and gymnasium for varsity and intramural sports and recreational programs.

Contact: Information Services, George Brown College, P.O. Box 1015, Station B, Toronto, ON, M5T 2T9, Canada; (800) 263-8995 *or* (416) 867-2225, Fax (416) 867-2501.

GREAT COOKS
Toronto, Ontario, Canada

January-May, September-December

Established in 1989, this school offers approximately 65 demonstration classes (limit 21 students) annually. Topics range from appetizers to desserts and some classes include wine tasting. Classes are scheduled from 6:30 to 9:30 pm in the school's 600-square-foot teaching kitchen with overhead mirrors. Daytime classes are also available.

Specialties: Guest chef specialties, international and regional cuisines, menus for entertaining, pasta, desserts, vegetarian meals; wine tasting.

Faculty: More than 30 Toronto chefs, including Joe Bersani, Massimo Capra, Michael Carlevale, Jean Pierre Challet, Eunice Champlain, Greg Couillard, Allison Cumming, Donna Dooher, Renèe Foote, Jamie Kennedy, Martin Kouprie, Arpi Magyar, Lucia and Roberto Martella, Mark McEwen, Dale Nichols, Steven Potovsky, and Dufflet Rosenberg, school director and owner of Dufflet Pastries.

Costs: Fee is C$65 per class; C$75 for classes that include wine tasting. A 10% discount is granted those who register for three classes or more. Credit cards (VISA) accepted. No refunds.

Location: Downtown Toronto.

Contact: Great Cooks, 787 Queen St. West, Toronto, ON, M6J 1G1, Canada; (416) 594-0388.

HOLLYHOCK FARM
Cortes Island, British Columbia, Canada

May-November

Established in 1983, Hollyhock offers more than 70 workshops annually in the practical, creative, spiritual, and healing arts. Topics include drawing, painting, basketry, papermaking, drum-making, ceramics, photography, and cooking. West Coast Cooking, a four-day workshop limited to 20 to 40 participants, focuses on preparation and open-pit style cooking of seafood and fresh produce. Other activities include morning yoga, meditation, and birdwalks, evening owling expeditions, star talks, and rowing tours.

Faculty: Includes cook, teacher, and author James Barber.

Costs, Accommodations: Workshop cost, which includes dormitory-style or semi-private lodging and meals, is C$545. A C$100 deposit is required with balance due on arrival. Cancellations more than three weeks prior receive a C$65 refund or credit.

Location: Cortes Island is about 100 miles north of Vancouver.

Contact: Hollyhock, Box 127, Manson's Landing, Cortes Island, BC, V0P 1K0, Canada; (604) 935-6465.

McCALL'S SCHOOL OF CAKE DECORATION, INC.
Etobicoke, Ontario, Canada
September-May

Founded in 1976, this school offers cake decorating, baking, and chocolate participation workshops for nonprofessionals and five and ten-day full-time courses for professional cooks. Evening (6:30 to 9:30) and Saturday morning (9:30 to 12:30) workshops cover various aspects of entertaining and include petit fours, cheese fours, tea for two, and croissants. All day Saturday workshops (9:30 to 4:30) cover such topics as strudel, coffee cake, torten, and bread. A series of four weekly three-hour classes (limit 10 students) in cake decorating is scheduled weeknights and Saturday mornings and a course in Australian rolled fondant is offered those with decorating experience. Students may sign up for individual weeknight or Saturday workshops on such specialties as roses, writing (cake inscriptions), gingerbread houses, marzipan figures, and flowers and borders. Two and three-hour evening classes, demonstrations, and workshops in chocolate feature such delicacies as truffles, liqueur chocolates, Easter eggs and bunnies, and chocolate gifts. The School's 1,000 square feet of teaching space include overhead mirrors and two 20-seat classrooms.

The professional courses (limit 10) in baking, commercial cake decorating (ten days each), and Swiss chocolate techniques (five days) meet from 9 am to 4 pm and emphasize techniques needed in a small restaurant, caterer, bakery, or chocolate shop. Baking and chocolate course students receive a Certificate of Participation. Thosed who complete the commercial cake decorating course and additional part-time workshops receive a Master Decorator's Certificate at the Intermediate or Advanced Level.

Specialties: Baking, chocolate, and cake decorating for professionals and nonprofessionals.

Faculty: Includes school director Nick McCall, Klara Johnston, and Kay Wong.

Costs: Nonprofessional fees: three-hour workshops C$45 to C$55, six-hour baking workshops C$90, four-session cake decorating classes C$130 to C$160. Professional courses range from C$480 (Swiss chocolate techniques) to C$700 (baking and commercial cake decorating). A 50% deposit is requested upon registration with balance due the first day of class. Full refund less 10% of total cost is granted those who cancel at least one week prior to class. Deposit is forfeited for cancellations less than one week prior. Credit cards (VISA, MasterCard) accepted.

Location: In Etobicoke, a western subdivision of Toronto, on a subway line close to major highways.

Contact: McCall's School of Cake Decoration, Inc., 3810 Bloor St. W. Etobicoke, ON, M9B 6C2, Canada; (416) 231-8040, Fax (416) 231-9956.

NATURAL FOODS COOKING CLASSES
Montreal, Quebec, Canada
September-June

Established in 1989, this school offers one, five, and seven-session demonstration (limit 12 students) and participation (limit 5) courses devoted to vegetarian and fish cookery. One-session courses usually run from 10 am to 4:30 pm, longer courses meet once weekly from 6:30 to 9 pm. Classes are held in a 200-square-foot well-equipped kitchen and topics include soups, whole grains, beans, land and sea vegetables, condiments, and dairy-free desserts.

Specialties: Vegetarian cookery.

Faculty: Bonnie Jean Tees served as head cook at the Macrobiotic Institute of Switzerland and studied at the Natural Gourmet Institute in New York.

Costs: C$75 for a one-day session, C$140 for five sessions, C$195 for seven sessions. A 50% refundable deposit is required with balance due at class.

Contact: Bonnie Tees, Natural Foods Cooking Classes, 6962 Somerled, Montreal, QB, H4V 1V5, Canada; (514) 482-1508.

NEELAM KUMAR'S NORTH INDIAN CUISINE
Kirkland, Quebec, Canada
January, April, September

Established in 1984, this school offers four eight-session participation courses (limit eight students) per year in vegetarian and non-vegetarian Indian cuisine. Students can attend the three-hour weekly sessions either mornings or evenings. Classes are held in a 140-square-foot kitchen with three work areas.

Specialties: The food of North India.

Faculty: Neelam Kumar has a university degree in home science and prepared Indian foods at a social club for two years.

Costs: C$90 for vegetarian, C$100 for non-vegetarian.

Location: Kirkland is a western suburb of Montreal.

Contact: Mrs. Neelam Kumar, 6 Daudelin, Kirkland, QB, H9J 1L8, Canada; (514) 697-4029.

STRATFORD CHEFS SCHOOL
Stratford, Ontario, Canada
Year-round

Established in 1983, this private, nonprofit institute offers a three-year full-time apprenticeship program leading to a diploma and Province of Ontario accreditation as Journeyman upon passing provincial exam. Enrollment each November is limited to 65 students — about 25% of applicants — who are selected on the basis of aptitude and commitment. The curriculum includes gastronomy, nutrition, food styling, and wine appreciation, as well as kitchen management, menu preparation, and food costing. Second-year students research, prepare, and serve theme menus in simulated restaurant settings. A job placement service is available and 100% of graduates obtain employment.

Specialties: Three-year apprenticeship program.

Faculty: Directors are restaurateurs Eleanor Kane of The Old Prune and James Morris of Rundles. The 14-member faculty is made up of chefs, pastry chefs, restaurateurs, restaurant managers, and other experienced food professionals.

Guest instructors have included Michael Bonacini, Rafaelo Ferrari, Marcella Hazan, Jamie Kennedy, Chris Klugman, Susur Lee, Chris McDonald, Mark McEwan, and Jean-Georges Vongerichten.

Costs: Annual tuition is C$500 for Ontario residents, C$4,800 for others. Financial aid and scholarships are available; externships can be arranged.

Location: Stratford, about 90 minutes from Toronto, has the closest airport.

Contact: Stratford Chefs School, 150 Huron St., Stratford, ON, N5A 5S8, Canada; (519) 271-1414, Fax (519) 271-5679.

CHINA

CHINA ADVOCATES
Beijing, China
Fall

This private cultural organization, established in 1987 to help Americans study in China, offers a variety of in-depth programs in culture, crafts, language, medicine, and culinary arts. The four-week program in Chinese cuisine, hosted by the China International Exchange Center and limited to ten participants, is conducted at the Beijing Culinary School, which trains cooks for China's fine restaurants. One week is devoted to each of the following regional styles: Sichuan-Hunan, Guangdong (Cantonese), Shandong, and Beijing Royal Cooking. Those unable to stay four weeks can enroll for two or three weeks. Four-hour Monday through Friday morning classes consist of a short lecture, a demonstration, and a participation session. Each student has an individual work area with chopping block and stove space. Saturday is reserved for an all-day excursion and Sundays are free. Other activities may include demonstrations by noted Beijing chefs, tours of leading restaurant kitchens, and lectures on Chinese culture and Taiji study. An optional 11-day China tour follows the program.

Specialties: Chinese regional cuisine.

Faculty: The professional staff of the Beijing Culinary School.

Costs, Accommodations: Cost of $2,775 includes transportation from San Francisco and double occupancy lodging. A $400 deposit must accompany application with balance due 75 days prior to program. Cancellation penalty ranges from $200 (more than 75 days prior) to 40% of program cost plus airline cancellation charges (less than 15 days prior). Students are lodged at the Academy of Traditional Chinese Medicine, a 30-minute drive from the School. Meals are available in the Academy's private cafeteria.

Contact: China Advocates, 1635 Irving St., San Francisco, CA 94122; (800) 333-6474 *or* (415) 665-4505.

CZECHOSLOVAKIA

GOURMET AMERICAS (page 227)

ENGLAND

AGA WORKSHOP
Penn, Buckinghamshire, England

Year-round except August and December

Mary Berry conducts one and two-day AGA demonstration workshops (limit 18 students) twice monthly in the kitchen of Watercroft, her Queen Anne home. The emphasis is on getting the most out of the AGA cooker, including how to use the roasting oven for grilling and frying, saving fuel and time, utilizing fresh herbs and vegetables, entertaining and holiday cookery, and specialized AGA equipment. Sessions run from 10 am to 4 pm on Tuesdays and Wednesdays.

Specialties: AGA cookery.

Faculty: Mary Berry studied at the Paris Cordon Bleu and the Bath College of Home Economics and has a City and Guilds teaching qualification. Author of 20 cookery books, she was cookery editor of *Ideal Home Magazine*, is a contributor to *Family Circle*, and has a television program.

Costs, Accommodations: Cost of a one-day (two-day) workshop is £68.15 (£129.25), which includes lunch and VAT. Payment with booking is required and cancellations more than four weeks prior to workshop receive full refund. Thereafter refund only if space can be filled. A list of nearby bed and breakfasts is provided.

Location: Watercroft, situated on three acres of informal garden, pond, and wildflower meadow, is 29 miles from London. It's accessible by mainline railway from London Marylebone to Beaconsfield, 3 1/2 miles south.

Contact: Mary Berry, AGA Workshop, Watercroft, Church Rd., Penn, Buckinghamshire, HP10 8NX, England; (44) 49481 6535 (phone or fax).

BONNE BOUCHE SCHOOL OF COOKERY
Devon, England

Year-round

Established in 1987, this residential cooking school offers an intensive four-week Professional Foundation Course for those planning a culinary career and shorter special theme courses for cooks of all levels. A variety of European, ethnic and international cuisines are taught. Classes, which focus on hands-on work, are limited to six students and are conducted in the specially designed kitchen of a 16th century converted Devon longhouse. Additional demonstration and lecture facilities have been added in a restored old barn alongside. The Professional Foundation Course, offered at various times throughout the year, covers traditional French, English, vegetarian, and other cuisines, with emphasis on practical and creative skills as well as taste, presentation, and healthful eating. In addition to basic and advanced techniques, topics include menu planning, matching wine with food, portion and cost control, and flower arrangment. Students also share in the early morning bread making and evening dinner preparation, working individually and as members of small teams. The course concludes with a private reception prepared by the students for their guests. Those who satisfactorily complete the course receive a certificate of competence and may utilize the school's "hot-line" telephone service. Assistance is also available to find employment in the UK and overseas. The school also offers courses in Basic Food Hygiene and Catering Business Management with Personal Presentational Skills for people in or about to enter the catering industry.

Five-day special theme courses, scheduled at various times, begin on Sunday or Friday evenings. Students include cooking enthusiasts and professionals seeking to refresh their skills and students' special needs can be accommodated. Weekend and mid-week courses and leisure breaks, scheduled six to eight times a year, begin with dinner the first day and end the third day after lunch. Based on the same themes, students decide how much they wish to participate. Day classes (residence available for out-of-towners) for larger groups are offered from time to time and focus on a variety of topics, including boning and stuffing meats and poultry, the cuisines of several Far-Eastern countries, and fish and sauce cookery. The demonstration-oriented sessions, which include lunch, begin at 10 am and end at 3:30 pm. Tailor-made classes can be organized for special groups.

Specialties: Four-week comprehensive Professional Foundation Course, traditional French Provincial cooking, new and traditional English cuisine, East and West European regional cooking, healthy eating, cooking with sauces, fish cookery, food hygiene, and business management.

Faculty: Proprietor Anne Nicholls has taught professionally since 1985. She has run a catering firm, acted as a consultant, and completed the full Thai cookery course at Bangkok's Oriental Hotel. Master chef Sonia Stevenson, founder of The Horn of Plenty, specializes in sauce and fish cookery. Gerald Nicholls, former partner in charge of the UK and European management consulting division of a major international CPA firm, leads the business management course.

Costs, Accommodations: Cost (in 1992), which includes lodging and all other items, is £1,199 for the Professional Foundation Course, from £310 for the short courses, and £210 for the weekends. Day classes are £22. Accommodations are provided in single and twin-bedded rooms with private baths at Bonne Bouche, which has three-crown status from the English Tourist Board.

Location: The school, which has herb and vegetable gardens on the grounds, is centrally situated in the West Country, 10 to 15 miles from the university and cathedral city of Exeter and two hours by train from London. Nearby locales include Bath, Plymouth, Dartmoor, Exmoor, and the Somerset Levels and Quantock Hills. Attractions include historic buildings, gardens, fishing, golf, riding, and bird watching. Well-known hotels and restaurants are nearby.

Contact: Bonne Bouche School of Cookery, Lower Beers House, Brithem Bottom, Cullompton, Devon, EX15 1NB, England; (44) 884 32257.

CAKE ICING COURSE
Dunnington, York, England

Year-round

Since 1985, Audrée Massey has offered four-day courses (limit 4 students) that combine three days of demonstrations and practical work in sugarpaste icing with one day free for sightseeing in York and the surrounding countryside. The course covers basic to advanced techniques, including leaves and flowers, sprays and bouquets, and fine fingering work. Instructional sessions are scheduled from 9 am until 4 pm at The Icing Parlour, where students are provided with individual work areas and all necessary equipment.

Specialties: Sugarpaste icing.

Faculty: Organizer and instructor Audrée Massey is a qualified home economics teacher and learned sugarpaste icing in Australia.

Costs: The £250 cost includes all meals and accommodations. A nonrefundable £50 deposit must accompany reservation with balance due on arrival. Lodging and meals are provided at a comfortable Yorkshire farmhouse.

Location: The Roman walled city of York, located three miles away, offers historic sites, stately homes, fine shops, and many attractions.

Contact: Audrée Massey, The Icing Parlour, Chippings, Greenside, Dunnington, York, YO1 5NJ, England; (44) 904 489474.

CAROLINE HOLMES — HERBS
Bury St. Edmunds, Suffolk, England

Year-round

Since 1983, Caroline Holmes has taught demonstration (limit 16 students) courses that focus on growing, maintaining, and using herbs. Her one-day courses —Create and Maintain a Herb Garden and Cook's Secrets — begin at 9:30 am with an introductory walk through the herb garden at Denham End Farm, include a lunch of herb bread, cheese, salad, and sorbet, and conclude at 3:30 pm. Create and Maintain a Herb Garden covers such growing techniques as hedging, ground cover, design, and shapes. Students are taught how to plant herbs in the ground and in pots ands how to maintain, propagate, and increase stock. Cook's Secrets features discussions of fines herbes, bouquet garni, spices, and the uses of herbs in salads, sauces, and sorbets. A two-day course, Planning Your Own Herb Garden, covers the history of herbs; fragrant, medicinal, and cooking herbs; planting, maintenance, and propagation; and preservation techniques. Specialist herb and salad cookery courses with accommodation can be arranged for groups of 10 to 40. A one-week guided tour to France studies French influences in garden and kitchen history.

Specialties: Growing and using herbs.

Faculty: Caroline Holmes holds a Certificate in Gourmet Cookery and City and Guilds Horticulture. She works with more than half a dozen centers, including the Museum of Garden History (London), Hintlesham Hall (Ipswich), and Suffolk County Council.

Costs, Accommodations: The one-day course fee is £20, payable in advance. One-day Cordon Vert and Gourmet Gardening courses begin at £30 per day. Accommodation costs begin at £20 per night.

Location: Denham End Farm is 25 miles from Cambridge, 7 miles from historic Bury St. Edmunds, and 10 miles from Lavenham. The Museum of Garden History is next to Lambeth Place, London, and Hintlesham Hall is 7 miles from Ipswich.

Contact: Caroline Holmes, Denham End Farm, Denham, Suffolk, IP29 5EE, England; (44) 284 810653.

CATHERINE BLAKELEY'S COOKERY COURSES
Newport, Shropshire, England

Year-round

This school, established in 1987, offers weekend and mid-week residential courses and evening and day-long nonresidential courses on a variety of topics. Students are provided with individual work areas in the large kitchen of Arlington House, a large Victorian home. The residential courses cover such topics as beginner basics, game cookery, new English cookery, cooking with herbs, and holiday and entertaining menus. They extend over a weekend (Friday evening to Sunday afternoon) or midweek (Monday evening to Friday morning) and include demonstrations and practical work. Sessions are scheduled for three hours in the morning and two hours in the afternoon. The nonresidential courses, devoted to special occasion dishes, are offered as either demonstration (limit 12 students) or practical (limit 6) classes. Each are scheduled for a full day (10:15 am to 3:30 pm) or an evening (7:30 to 10 pm).

Specialties: Include English cookery, game cookery, menus for festive occasions, and Aga cookery.

Faculty: Catherine Blakeley is a professional Home Economist with a first class diploma from Edinburgh College of Domestic Science. She has taught cookery for more than 25 years.

Costs, Accommodations: The residential course fees, which include meals and lodging in Arlington House, are £125 for the weekend course, £225 for the midweek course. A £25 deposit must accompany booking, with balance due on arrival. The one-day course is £25 demonstration, which includes lunch with wine; evening session is £10 demonstration. Full fee is payable with booking for nonresidential courses.

Location: The market town of Newport is situated in the tourist county of Shropshire. Nearby places of interest include Shrewsbury, Bridgnorth, Ironbridge Gorge Museum, Hodnet Hall Garden, Eccleshall Castle, Ludlow, Church Stretton, and The Long Mynd.

Contact: Catherine Blakeley's Cookery Courses, Arlington House, Station Rd., Newport, Shropshire, TF10 7EN, England; (44) 952 812852.

CLOS DU ROY AT BOX HOUSE
Box, Wiltshire, England

January-July, September-November

Since 1989, Philippe Roy has conducted three-day demonstration (limit 10 studets) and participation (limit 6) courses in the kitchen of the Clos du Roy restaurant in the Box House country house hotel. Instruction is from 9 am to 6 pm daily and covers French regional, traditional, classic, and modern cuisines. Box House, a Georgian mansion, has a heated swimming pool and seven acres of pastures and gardens, where much of the restaurant's produce is grown.

Specialties: French cuisine.

Faculty: Philippe Roy is chef patron of the Clos du Roy.

Costs, Accommodations: Cost is £390, which includes double occupancy individually designed room and private bath, meals, and VAT. Full payment is required and refund is granted for cancellations more than one month prior.

Location: In England's West Country, 15 minutes from Bath and less than two hours from London. Train station pickup can be arranged.

Contact: Philippe Roy, Clos du Roy, Box House, Box, Wiltshire, SN14 9NR, England; (44) 225 74447, Fax (44) 225 743971.

COOKERY AND ACTIVITY HOLIDAYS
Young Cooks of Great Britain
West Sussex, England

August

Established in 1983 to encourage young people to learn more about food, the Young Cooks Club offers five-day cooking and activity vacations twice during August, each limited to 20 boys and girls, ages 11 to 16. The program features daily demonstrations and supervised practice as well as a restaurant tour, competitions, swimming, tennis, and organized sports. Culinary topics covered include bread, casseroles, roasts, stir-fry, fish, sauces, meringue, and pastries.

Specialties: A variety of topics for young cooks.

Faculty: Food writers Sophie Grigson and Janet Laurence.

Costs, Accommodations: Cost of £265 includes meals, dormitory lodging, planned activities, and lunch for one guest the last day of class. Application must be accompanied by a £50 deposit, refundable only if space can be filled.

Location: Lavant House, Chichester.

Contact: Anna Best/Peta Brown, Young Cooks of Britain, 2 Terminus Rd., Chichester, W. Sussex, P019 2DR, England; (44) 243 779239, Fax (44) 243 784241.

COOKERY AT THE GRANGE
Whatley, Frome, Somerset, England

Year-round

Founded in 1981, this school offers four and six-week courses and several two to four-day short courses, each limited to 16 participants. The four-week Basics to Bearnaise course takes the student through the methods and principles of cookery covered in a basic Cordon Bleu course. The program consists of four weeks of daily six-hour practical sessions, from Monday morning to Friday afternoon, with emphasis on recipe reading, stressing omissions and substitutions, shortcuts, lessons in pastry and bread baking, and the most used methods for sauces, soups, meat, fish, fowl, vegetables, salads, fruits, and desserts. Dishes from all over the world are tried, particularly "everyday French", and each day's work is coordinated in method and principle to other applications. Most days are spent in hands-on practical work with continuous personal instruction and at least one teacher is in the kitchen from 9 am to 9 pm each day. Outings or talks on relevant topics, guest nights, and weekend arrangements are also offered. In addition to a certificate, students completing this course may also receive a letter of recommendation to further their culinary careers. The six-week To Bearnaise and Beyond course consists of the standard Basics to Bearnaise course plus two more weeks to provide students with additional cooking and individual menu planning experience. Students take charge of the kitchen and prepare menus with emphasis on French and Italian regional cooking. Students may elect to attend the final two-week segment as a self-contained course (Beyond Bearnaise). Thursday evenings usually include a wine-tasting and a certificate is presented at the end of all courses.

Specialties: Four and six-week courses for aspiring professionals; short courses for cooking enthusiasts. All courses emphasize French and Italian cuisine.

Faculty: Jane Croswell-Jones and her teaching staff.

Costs, Accommodations: Cost for Basics to Bearnaise, including meals and double occupancy housing, is £1,190 to £1,250; Beyond Bearnaise is £660; To Bearnaise and Beyond is £1,738 for the six weeks; short courses range from £180 to £325. A £120 deposit is required for the four or six-week course, £60/£75 for the short courses. Students are lodged at The Grange in two double bedrooms and at a nearby cottage in Nunney. Single supplement is £30 (£15 for weekends). Fees are subject to VAT. Deposit is payable with enrollment and is refunded only if not accepted. Balance is payable six weeks in advance and is returnable subject to deduction of enrollment fee if written cancellation is received more than six weeks prior. Nonresident students are expected to stay for dinner each evening.

Location: The Grange, situated in a vineyard with its own herb garden in rural England, is 15 miles from Bath, 90 minutes from London by train, and 40 minutes from Bristol. Nearby attractions include Longleat, about 10 minutes away, the gardens at Stourhead, Glastonbury, Wells, Cheddar, and Sherborne. Southampton is an hour's drive to the south.

Contact: Jane Croswell-Jones, Cookery at The Grange, The Grange, Whatley Vineyard, Whatley, Frome, Somerset, BA11 3LA, England; (44) 373 836579.

COOKING AT VERITY
Commonwood, Kings Langley, England

February-June, September-November

Since 1985, Eileen Follows has conducted demonstration classes (limit 10 students) in her 300-year-old country home, which has a demonstration area and overhead mirror. The whole day classes feature a two-hour morning session, a 90-minute afternoon session, and a three-course lunch.

Specialties: British, French, and Italian cuisines.

Faculty: Eileen Follows and guest demonstrators.

Costs, Accommodations: Class fee is £30, which includes lunch. Lodging is available in the nearby village.

Location: Seventeen miles from London, a 30-minute train ride to Rickmansworth.

Contact: Mrs. Eileen Follows, Cooking at Verity, Verity, Commonwood, Kings Langley, Hertfordshire, WD4 9BA, England; (44) 923 263104. Fax (44) 442 833868.

LE CORDON BLEU
London, England
Year-round

Founded in 1933 and acquired by Le Cordon Bleu-Paris (page 186) in 1990, this school for professional and nonprofessional cooks offers a variety of day and evening courses in classic French cuisine. The Classic Cycle, designed for those who wish to pursue a culinary career or desire a comprehensive course of study, consists of Introduction to Classic Cuisine, Advanced Classic Cuisine, and Introductory and Advanced Pâtisserie, each 11-week certificate courses beginning in January, April, July, and October. Programs for cooks of all levels include the two-day to one-week intensive and specialized courses and the five-session evening demonstrations and practicals. Demonstrations, limited to 70 students, last three hours and practical classes, limited to 12, last 2½ hours. Facilities, completely refurbished in 1991, occupy four floors and include four professionally-equipped cuisine kitchens; individual chilled work surfaces, stoves, and refrigerators; a specially designed pâtisserie and boulangerie room; sous-vide (vacuum-packed cuisine) equipment and Aga cooker (popular in English country homes); and two demonstration classrooms with overhead mirrors and videos.

Introduction to Classic Cuisine, the foundation course in the Classic Cycle, covers knife skills, preparation of vegetables, and techniques for cooking fish, meat, poultry, and stocks and sauces. Daytime sessions begin at 9 am, 1:30 pm, or 4:30 pm, Mondays through Fridays, for all courses in the Classic Cycle; evening courses, which run for 33 weeks, begin in January, April, and October and meet from 6:30 to 9:30 pm, Mondays and Thursdays. Pâtisserie, scheduled to be taken concurrent with the Introduction course, provides instruction in such French pastries as pâte brisée, pâte sable, pâte sucrée and pâte feuilletée, genoise, meringue, and a variety of fillings and finishes. Advanced Classic Cuisine, for those who've completed the Introduction course, includes recipes for elaborate first courses, clarification in consomme and aspic, fish and shellfish dishes, the boning and preparation of fish, meat, and poultry, regional cuisine, and the preparation of vegetables, fruits, garnishes, sorbets and ice creams, and other desserts. Advanced Pâtisserie covers savoury and sweet petit fours, chocolates, sorbets, complex recipes, and croqembouche with pulled sugar. The Introduction and Advanced Cuisine courses consist of 33 demonstrations and 33 practical classes; the Introductory and Advanced Pâtisserie courses consist of 22 demonstrations and 22 practicals. Classic Cycle evening training courses, available every term, include the Primary Food Hygiene Certificate Course (five Wednesdays from 7:30 to 9:30 pm), The Marriage of Food and Wine (five Wednesdays from 7:30 to 9:30 pm), and Wines from Around the World (five Tuesdays from 7 to 9 pm). Students who satisfactorily complete Introduction to Classic Cuisine, Advanced Classic Cuisine, and Introductory and Advanced Pâtisserie, are awarded the Cuisine and Pâtisserie Diploma, which enables them to further their studies at Le Cordon Bleu in Paris, where they can take Cuisine Superieure and qualify for the Grand Diplôme. Stagieres (working scholarships) in leading hotel and restaurant kitchens are available to top students.

Intensive and specialized courses, scheduled at 9 am, 1:30 pm, or 4:30 pm, include A Taste of Cordon Bleu (one-week), French Regional Cuisine (five days), Fish and Shellfish (four days), Game and Poultry (five days), Boulangerie (three and four-day courses), Pâtisserie (three and five-day courses), Festive Buffets (five days), Cocktail Savouries (three days), Petits Fours (three days), Chocolates and Confectionery (three days), Charcuterie (five days), Smoked Foods and Accompaniments (four days), Sous-vide Cooking (four days), and Cooking with an AGA Cooker (two-day workshop).

Evening demonstrations and practicals (five demonstrations and five practical sessions given over ten evenings, from 6:30 to 9 pm), for cooks of all levels, are Entertaining with Ease (begins January, April, and October) and French Regional Cuisine (January and October). Evening demonstrations by guest chefs and culinary experts are scheduled about a half dozen times a term.

Specialties: Classic French cuisine.

Faculty: The school is run by directors Lesley Gray, Sarah Nops, and Susan Eckstein. The culinary staff consists of three French and two British master chefs, all bilingual teachers from Michelin-starred and other fine establishments. Chef exchanges with Le Cordon Bleu in Paris are also planned.

Costs, Accommodations: Classic Cycle course tuition (nonrefundable deposit) is £1,993 for Introduction to Classic Cuisine, £1,495 (£75) for Introductory Pâtisserie, £2,195 (£110) for Advanced Classic Cuisine, £1,645 (£90) for Advanced Pâtisserie, £65 for Primary Food Hygiene, £195 for The Marriage of Food and Wine, and £275 for Wines from Around the World. Intensive and specialized course tuition is £320 for the one-week A Taste of Cordon Bleu; £300 for the one-week and £180 for the three-day Patisserie; £300 each for French Regional Cuisine, Game and Poultry, Festive Buffets, and Charcuterie; £250 each for Fish and Shellfish; £240 for the four-day and £180 for the three-day Boulangerie; £240 each for Smoked Foods and Sous-vide; £180 each for Cocktail Savouries, Petits Fours, and Chocolates and Confectionery; £60 for the two-day AGA. Evening demonstrations and practicals are £240 for each ten-session course, £25 per guest chef demonstration. Classic Cycle course deposits must accompany application and balance is due six weeks prior to course. Full fees for short courses must accompany application and are refundable, less 10% (50%), for written cancellations received at least four weeks (less than four weeks) prior. All fees include 17$^{1}/_{2}$% VAT and are payable in sterling unless other arrangements are made. A limited number of working scholarships are available.

Location: In London's West End, close to the shopping areas of Oxford and Bond streets with easy access via bus and tube.

Contact: Le Cordon Bleu, 114 Marylebone Lane, London, W1M 6HH, England: (44) 71 935 3503, Fax (44) 71 935 7621.

LA CUISINE IMAGINAIRE COOKERY SCHOOL
London, England

Year-round

Established in 1989, this vegetarian cooking school offers a variety of one-day courses for cooks of all levels and three-day certificate courses for the more serious cook or chef. Approximately 30 one and three-day courses are scheduled weekdays and Saturdays each year, all limited to 12 students. Classes are held above the Books for Cooks bookstore and the day runs from 10:30 am to 1 pm and 2:30 to 4:30 with a buffet lunch of the dishes prepared. One-day course topics include Great Family Meals, Meals in a Moment, Dinner Party Cooking, French for Fun, and Cuisine Imaginaire (gourmet vegetarian cookery). The three certificate courses — Foundation, Progressive, and Advanced — cover beginning to advanced recipes and techniques, nutritional considerations, deep-freezing and pressure cooking, international dishes, and yeast and pastry cookery. Private instruction is available.

Specialties: Vegetarian cuisine.

Faculty: Director and instructor Roselyne Masselin is a food writer, cookbook author, qualified home economist, and owner of Catering Imaginaire. She was principal tutor at the Vegetarian Society UK for seven years.

Costs: Fee is £49.50 per day, which includes lunch and VAT. Full payment is required with registration and cancellations receive a course credit.

Location: Books for Cooks bookstore in Central London, near the Ladbroke Grove and Notting Hill Gate tube stations.

Contact: La Cuisine Imaginaire Cookery School, 18 Belmont Ct., Belmont Hill, St. Albans, Hertfordshire, AL1 1RB, England; (44) 727 837643, Fax (44) 727 47646.

DIANA MARSLAND COOKING (page 139)

THE EARNLEY CONCOURSE
Chichester, Sussex, England
Year-round

This residential center for courses and conferences was established in 1975 by the Earnley Trust, Ltd., an educational charity founded in 1951. Approximately 15 two-day (Friday evening to Sunday afternoon) demonstration and participation courses are offered annually on such topics as Indian cookery, cooking for health, advanced techniques, and special occasion dishes. Courses are taught in the center's fully equipped kitchen workshop, which has a demonstration area, dining area, and working space for up to 12 students.

Specialties: A variety of topics, including ethnic cuisines, menus for entertaining, healthy eating.

Faculty: Instructors include Savita Burke, Deh-Ta Hsiung, Steven Page, and Mary Whiting.

Costs, Accommodations: Each two-day course is priced from £122, which includes lodging, meals, and 17$\frac{1}{2}$% VAT. Nonresident tuition is £85, which includes coffee, lunch, afternoon tea, and VAT. The cost of ingredients is additional. A £33 deposit (£20 for nonresidents) must accompany application, with balance due 28 days prior. Cancellations more than 28 days prior receive 50% deposit refund; thereafter full deposit is forfeited.

Location: The center is situated in a rural setting in West Sussex, six miles south of Chichester. Facilities include lecture rooms, a conference hall, arts and crafts studios, fully-equipped computer room, heated pool, squash court, and gardens.

Contact: The Earnley Concourse, Earnley, Chichester, Sussex, PO20 7JL, England; (44) 243 670392, Fax (44) 243 670832.

EASTBOURNE COLLEGE OF FOOD AND FASHION
Eastbourne, England

January-July, September-December

Established in 1907 and recognized as efficient by the British Accreditation Council, this school offers one-year and ten-week courses for girls in Cordon Bleu cookery and catering. Participation classes, scheduled from 9 am to 4 pm, Monday through Friday, and limited to 12 students, are conducted in the school's seven specially-equipped teaching kitchens.

The one-year course, which commences in September and January, consists of two twelve-week terms — the Foundation Course — followed by an eleven-week term of specialized study. A one-week half-term break separates each term. During the Foundation Course students are divided into groups according to level of experience and study basic cookery, catering, dress and fashion, typing, home and consumer studies, flower arranging, child care, and first aid. During the third term, they study cordon bleu cookery, catering, or advanced dress and tailoring. Students in the catering course operate the College's open-to-the-public teaching restaurant, Rannie's Restaurant. Evening lectures are offered on specific topics and a four-lecture wine course is followed by an examination for a wine diploma. The Eastbourne College of Food and Fashion Diploma is awarded those who successfully complete the course and examinations.

The ten-week Intensive Cookery Certificate Course, which begins in January, April, and September, emphasizes French and English cuisine with a range of international dishes. Students are taught the planning, cooking, and the serving of menus for entertaining, dinner parties, and larger scale buffets, as well as flower arranging, table decor, cake artistry, carving, garnish, decoration, and wine appreciation. A certificate in wine and Intensive Cookery Certificate are granted those who pass the examinations. The ten-week Advanced Cordon Bleu Diploma, which begins in January and includes an optional visit to Paris during Easter vacation, is open to those with the Cordon Bleu Diploma or equivalent experience. One day each week is devoted to the study of famous chefs and various cooking styles; advanced techniques and preparations with unusual foods; advanced patisserie, baking, confectionery, and cake decoration; and workshops on such topics as pulled sugar work, microwave cookery, wine appreciation and restaurant presentation. Students spend three days working in a fine restaurant and visit markets, hotel and restaurant kitchens, company directors' dining rooms, and food preparation companies. The Paris trip includes visits to cookery and cheese shops, markets, and a well-known bakery, a wine tasting at Academie du Vin, and a demonstration at the Ritz Escoffier Cookery School.

Specialties: One-year and ten-week courses in Cordon Bleu, English, and international cookery.

Faculty: Principal Janet E. Jenion, recipient of the La Varenne Advanced Certificate, is assisted by a staff of qualified specialist teachers.

Costs, Accommodations: The costs are £2,750 (£2,000 nonresident) per term for the one year course, £2,990 (£2,200) for the Intensive Cookery Certificate Course, and £3,000 (£2,500) for the Advanced Cordon Bleu Diploma. A £50 nonrefundable registration fee must accompany application. For students in the United Kingdom the tuition for each term must be received by the College at least seven days prior to the start of term and full refund is granted only if cancellation is received four months prior. For overseas students, the full nonrefundable tuition must be paid four months prior to term. The College provides residential accommodations and assists in finding employment.

Location: The College is situated in the seaside town of Eastbourne, an 80-minute drive from London.

Contact: Eastbourne College of Food and Fashion, 1 Silverdale Rd., Eastbourne BN20 7AA, England; (44) 323 30851.

FARTHINGHOE COOKERY SCHOOL
Brackley, Northamptonshire, England
March-May, September-November

This retail wine merchant and cooking school, operated by Simon and Nicola Cox in their Old Rectory home since 1975, offers one-day cookery demonstrations (limit 63 students). About 10 to 15 sessions are scheduled half-yearly in a specially designed demonstration hall. Two or three sessions are often scheduled on consecutive days to accommodate out-of-towners. Each session is held from 10 am to 4 pm and includes a morning and afternoon demonstration and a three-course lunch with wine. A variety of topics are covered, including 18th century specialties, entertaining menus, and microwave cookery. Special days on flowers and other subjects are scheduled occasionally.

Specialties: Include ethnic cuisines, entertaining menus, freezer and microwave cookery, guest chef specialties; wine tastings.

Faculty: Former *Sunday Times* Cook of Britain Nicola Cox is author of five cookbooks, including *Good Food from Farthinghoe, Country Cooking from Farthinghoe,* and *Good Housekeeping Creative Food Processor Cookery.* Master of Wine Simon Cox presents the wine tastings.

Costs, Accommodations: Most sessions are approximately £31.95. Full payment must accompany registration. A list of recommended local bed and breakfasts, ranging from £13 to £24 per night, per person, is provided.

Location: In rural south Northamptonshire, near Oxford, Stratford, the Cotswolds, and two hours from London via the Banbury line.

Contact: Simon Cox, Director, Farthinghoe Fine Wine & Food, The Old Rectory, Farthinghoe, Brackley, Northamptonshire NN13 5NZ, England; (44) 295 710018, Fax (44) 295 711495.

FOOD IN FRANCE (page 193)

FRANCES KITCHIN COOKING COURSES
Curry Rivel, Langport, Somerset, England
January-October

Since 1987, Frances Kitchin has conducted a three-day Cooking and Candlelit Dinners course, a half-day Day Out-Cooking course, and special courses tailor-made for small groups. These demonstration courses (limit 12 students) are held in her home, Stoney Mead, and cover a variety of cuisines, including Cordon Bleu and traditional English specialties. The three-day course features two morning two-hour classes, after which guests are free until dinner. The Day Out-Cooking course is a morning class with lunch. Sessions are held in the large kitchen.

Specialties: Cordon Bleu, Italian, Indian, and traditional English cuisines.

Faculty: Frances Kitchin, a qualified home economist and chef who has lectured at Strode College for 21 years, is a freelance writer and author of two cookbooks.

Costs, Accommodations: The price of Cooking and Candlelit Dinners ranges from £220 (single room with shared bath) to £250 (double occupancy room with private bath), which includes breakfasts and dinners. A nonrefundable £50 deposit must accompany reservation. The Day Out course is £15, including lunch.

Location: Stoney Mead, a country house in the village of Curry Rivel, is situated 12 miles from Taunton, which is on the railway line from Paddington (London), and 14 miles from Yeovil, which is on the railway line from Waterloo (London). Bath, Bristol, Exeter, and Glastonbury are within an hour's drive.

Contact: Frances Kitchin, Stoney Mead, Curry Rivel, Langport, Somerset, TA10 0HW, England; (44) 458 251203.

THE HEXHAM SCHOOL OF COOKERY
Hexham, Northumberland, England

Year-round

This school, founded in 1986 by Della Marian, offers a 10 or 12-session participation course (limit 6 students), From Basic Techniques to Gourmet Cooking, and two 1-day demonstration courses (limit 8), Cooking With Herbs and Vegetarian Cookery Covering New Ways With Vegetables. All courses are scheduled on request in the up-to-date professional kitchen of the FoodCraft catering firm, with individual work areas for every two students.

Specialties: Cordon Bleu and classic French cuisine, vegetables and herbs.

Faculty: Della Marian trained at the Tante Marie School of Cookery in Surrey and joined two other chefs to run the kitchen of Knights' Farm Restaurant in Berkshire. She began her catering business, FoodCraft, in 1976.

Costs: Tuition for the 10 and 12-session courses ranges from is £165 to £250 plus the cost of ingredients; one-day courses range from £25 to £30.

Location: The school is situated near Hexham, Northumberland, which borders Scotland and is near the major city of northeast England, Newcastle-Upon-Tyne, with direct air and rail transportation to London.

Contact: Della Marian, The Hexham School of Cookery, Pig Hall, Walwick Grange, Humshaugh, Northumberland, NE46 4BH, England; (44) 434 681652.

JILL PROBERT'S COOKERY DEMONSTRATION COURSES
Chester, Cheshire, England

February-March and October-November

Since 1983, Jill Probert has taught intermediate and advanced courses for home cooks (limit 14) in her 17th century farmhouse kitchen. The six-session courses meet for two hours once weekly — Wednesday or Thursday mornings or afternoons — and emphasize dinner party/freezer cookery. Each session features the preparation of a main course and dessert. Other topics, such as using a food processor to make bread, rolls, and mayonnaise, are covered, if time allows. Home-made biscuits and a hot beverage are served at each session and the courses conclude with a holiday lunch.

Specialties: Dinner parties, freezer cookery.

Faculty: Jill Probert, a magazine and newspaper food editor, is a member of the Guild of Food Writers and the Institute of Home Economics. She also addresses food photography seminars.

Costs: Each six-session course is £34.

Location: On the Welsh border, two miles from Chester.

Contact: Jill Probert, Bretton Hall, Chester, Cheshire, CH4 ODF, England; (44) 244 660209.

KEN LO'S MEMORIES OF CHINA
CHINESE COOKERY SCHOOL
London, England

Year-round

This school offers several four to ten-session morning and evening demonstration courses (limit 18 students) on various aspects of Chinese cuisine. Students may enroll in individual 1 1/2 to 2 hour sessions on a space available basis. The teacher demonstrates all items and steps required to make a dish or complete meal, acquainting pupils with Chinese ingredients, the importance of timing and heat control, cutting and slicing techniques, blending of textures, colors, and shapes, and menu creation. The demonstration may be followed by a full-scale meal, with prepared dishes supplemented by additional courses from Mr. Lo's Memories of China restaurant. Courses for professional chefs are also available.

Specialties: Far Eastern cuisines.

Faculty: Broadcaster and TV personality Kenneth Lo, author of 36 books on Chinese cooking, Chef Kam-Po But of the Memories of China restaurant, cookbook author Terry Tan, and Mr. Deh-Ta Hsiung.

Costs: Fee for the complete course ranges from £75 (four sessions) to £165 (ten sessions). Individual sessions range from £15 to £23. A deposit of £15 is required with application. Refunds are granted those who cancel more than two days prior.

Location: In the basement beneath Mr. Lo's Chinese grocery shop, an extension of his Memories of China restaurant.

Contact: Memories of China Cookery School, Ken Lo's Kitchen, 14 Eccleston St., London, SW1, England; (44) 71 730 4276/7734.

LEITH'S SCHOOL OF FOOD AND WINE
London, England

Year-round

Founded in 1975, Leith's School, associated with Leith's Good Food catering firm and Leith's Restaurant, offers a variety of one, two, and four-week French/

English-style cooking courses, one-week specialty courses, five and ten-week evening sessions, Saturday morning demonstrations, and a wine program for both the beginner and advanced nonprofessional. For the student seeking a career, the school offers a one-year diploma consisting of three 10 to 11 week certificate courses, a 10-session restaurant management course, and an advanced certificate course in wine. Approximately 90% of applicants are admitted and 90% of graduates obtain employment. With the exception of the Saturday demonstrations and the evening participation classes, all courses are half demonstration and half participation. In the participation classes, there are 16 students and 2 teachers. The school is nonresidential but assists students in obtaining lodging.

In July, a four-week Intensive beginner's course and in September, a four-week Intensive advanced course are scheduled and students may also enroll for only the first or last two weeks of either course. These follow the same format as the 10 and 11-week professional courses but are more concentrated. Students are accepted on their own assessment of ability and it is suggested that program suitability be discussed with the faculty. A beginner menu might be *carbonnade de boeuf*, artichokes vinaigrette, and chocolate profiteroles. Advanced course menu could include spinach timbales with tomato sauce, *pot au feu de la mer*, and *feuilletteé des poires tièdes*. A certificate of attendance is awarded and references are given on request.

A four-day entertaining course is scheduled in January and March. Students are divided into beginner and advanced classes and cook all day, stopping only for lunch to eat the meal they have prepared. Subjects covered during these intensive courses might include family fare, cooking for the freezer, Italian dishes, and breadmaking. In June, a five-day Specialty course is offered, 9:45 am to 4:30 pm, Monday through Friday, which might feature Chinese food, health food, or vegetarian cooking. The Evening Cookery School features a series of ten 2-hour participation lessons on Tuesday or Thursday evenings at 6:30, from October to June, for the beginner and the advanced host or hostess-cum-cook. Assisted by teachers, the 16 students prepare menus such as *poulet vallée d'Auge*, saffron pilaf, green fruit salad with ginger syllabub (beginner) and Italian seafood salad, veal escalopes with sweetbreads, and turned mangoes (advanced). The week-long participation Healthy Cooking Course, based on a low fat, low sugar diet, covers a broad range of styles, including Indian, Mexican, and vegetarian cuisines. From January to July, Saturday morning demonstrations of a six or seven-course meal are scheduled from 9:30 to 1:00. In February, the five-session Certificate in Wine course and in October, the 10-session Advanced Certificate in Wine course commence on Monday evenings at 6:30. During these two-hour classes, students learn how to taste, decipher the label, match wines with food, serve, store and consider all of the principal wine styles in the world. Specialty wine courses are also offered.

The Beginner's, Intermediate, and Advanced Certificate in Food and Wine courses are designed for the serious or aspiring professional cook. Classes are scheduled from 9:45 am to 4:30 pm, Monday through Friday. Basic cookery methods are practiced and three-course meals are cooked most days in the 10-week Beginners' course, which includes lectures on hygiene, nutrition, party planning, and wine and may include a menu of crème Vichysoisse and English roast pheasant. Students must pass an interview to qualify for the eleven-week

Intermediate course, which is suited to the experienced cook with no previous formal training. Butchery, preserving, and pressure cooking are taught and recipes may include *coquilles St. Jacques* and lemon soufflé. The 11-week Advanced course, for accomplished cooks, covers such techniques as boned poultry dishes, seafood and fish dishes, aspics, French breads, and cake decorating. Menus may feature such specialties as *mousseline de brochet* and fillet of duck breast. The courses run consecutively, from October through June, and successful completion of all three leads to Leith's Diploma in Food in Wine. Restaurant management, a 10-session evening course offered in April, is designed for the student desiring to set up on his/her own and covers design, planning, legal, marketing, and management.

Specialties: Professional and nonprofessional courses in a variety of cuisines; wine selection; restaurant management.

Faculty: Prue Leith, school founder, began her catering business in 1962 and opened Leith's Restaurant seven years later. She has written cookbooks and articles and appeared on TV and radio. The principals are Caroline Waldegrave, writer and former head cook of Leith's Good Food caterers, and Fiona Burrell.

Costs: All prices include 17½% VAT. July and September intensive courses (add charge of £6 for course literature): four-week beginners' £995 (deposit £99), advanced £1,060 (deposit £100); two-week beginners' £500 (deposit £50), advanced £530 (deposit £53). Entertaining courses: one-week beginners' £255, advanced £280. Evening Cookery School: ten-lesson course (beginner) £245, ten-lesson course (advanced) £255. Saturday morning demonstrations £30 each. Restaurant management course £245. Certificate in Wine course £180; Advanced Certificate in Wine course £300. Beginner's Certificate in Food and Wine £2,270 (deposit £100), Intermediate Certificate in Food and Wine £2,470 (deposit £100), Advanced Certificate in Food and Wine £2,710 (deposit £100), Leith's Diploma in Food and Wine (all three courses) £5,980 (deposit £200), Credential Certificate in Food and Wine (intermediate and advanced terms) £4,645 (deposit £150). Compulsory extras not included in the above: wine examination fees, utensils, literature, and trips, which cost approximately £156.

Location: In Kensington, the center of London, on the corner of Kensington Garden, and well serviced by buses and by underground station.

Contact. Caroline Waldegrave *or* Fiona Burrell, Principal, Leith's School of Food and Wine, 21 St. Alban's Grove, London, W8 5BP, England; (44) 71 229 0177.

LOAVES AND FISHES COOKSCHOOL AND BOOKSHOP
Marlborough, Wiltshire, England

Year-round

Established in 1992, this school offers morning and afternoon two-hour demonstrations (limit 10 to 12 students) and full-day participation courses that emphasize compassion in farming utilizing naturally-grown produce, hormone-free meats, and free-range poultry. Topics include field and garden vegetarian cookery, bread making, fish and seafood, game, and a variety of international cuisines. Classes are held in two 100-square-foot kitchens equipped with gas and electric appliances designed for home use. Demonstrations are scheduled at 10 am and 2 pm; participation courses meet from 10 am to 4:30 pm over one to four consecutive days. Classes for children, ages 4 to 12, are held from 10 to 11:30 am the first and third Saturdays of the month.

Specialties: Recipes using naturally grown and chemically free foods.

Faculty: Former restaurateurs Nikki Kedge and Angela Rawson, whose great aunt founded the Tante Marie School of Cookery, are authors of three cookbooks.

Costs, Accommodations: Demonstrations are £8; participation courses are £42 per day (students can enroll for one or more days); children's classes are £4. A 10% deposit is required with balance due at class. A list of nearby lodging is provided and reduced rates are available at the Castle and Ball Hotel.

Location: Marlborough's west end, a one-hour drive from London on M-4.

Contact: Nikki Kedge, Loaves & Fishes Cookschool, 76 High St., Marlborough, Wiltshire, SN8 1HF, England; (44) 672 516716 (day), (44) 672 513737 (eve.).

THE MANOR SCHOOL OF FINE CUISINE
Widmerpool, Nottinghamshire, England
Year-round

Established in 1988, this school offers weekend, five-day, and four-week courses, each limited to 12 students. The foundation for all cuisine taught is Cordon Bleu, encompassing classic and modern English cooking. Other European cuisines are also featured as well as advanced courses in vegetarian and game cookery, pastries, fish, and desserts. In addition to producing the recipes, students are taught raw ingredient selection, food storage and hygiene, kitchen management, table etiquette, and the selection and handling of wines. Each student receives a syllabus, glossary, and file of recipes. The Manor, a newly refurbished 17th century coaching inn, provides individual work stations, a modern demonstration area with overhead mirror, a combination of traditional and modern appliances, a library of cookbooks and cooking videos, and a large dining room.

The Gourmet Weekends and AGA Weekends are offered about six times a year and begin with a three-course luncheon followed by a demonstration of the five-course evening meal. Following afternoon tea, participants prepare the meal and dine on it, accompanied by appropriate wines. Those who stay overnight are served breakfast Sunday morning and then observe the demonstration of the luncheon dishes, which they prepare and eat. The five-day and four-week residential and nonresidential courses meet daily, Monday through Friday, from 9:30 am to 5:30 pm, followed by supper at 7:30. The daily schedule is divided equally between demonstrations and practical work and includes breakfast, a three-course lunch, afternoon tea, and a four to five-course dinner with fine wines. Five-day courses include the beginners' Foundation Course, offered about five times a year, and six Entertaining Courses, each offered two or three times a year. The four-week Certificate Course, designed for those embarking on a culinary career, is offered five times a year. Approximately 90% of applicants are accepted and essentially all graduates obtain employment if desired. The course covers basic methods as well as more advanced practical and creative skills, with emphasis on Cordon Bleu cuisine and professional technique.

Specialties: Cordon Bleu cuisine, vegetarian, game cookery, menus for holidays.

Faculty: Principal Claire Gentinetta earned the Cordon Bleu Diploma, served as head chef of noted restaurants, and is a member of the Cookery and Food Association, Craft Guild of Chefs, and Chefs and Cooks Circle.

Costs, Accommodations: Tuition (inclusive of VAT) is £207 (£230 resident) for the Foundation Course, £230 (£253 resident) for the Entertaining Courses, £874 (£989 resident) for the Certificate Course, and £120 for the full residential gourmet and AGA week-ends. A nonrefundable 10% deposit must accompany enrollment, with balance due six weeks prior to course. Full refund, less 10% deposit, is granted cancellations at least six weeks prior; 40% of fee is refunded thereafter. Resident students are housed in The Manor.

Location: The Manor, once a hunting lodge for the Quorn, is situated in the County of Nottinghamshire, nine miles from Nottingham City Centre. Nearby attractions include Belvoir Castle, Burleigh House, and Chatsworth.

Contact: The Manor School of Fine Cuisine, Old Melton Rd, Widmerpool, Nottinghamshire NG12 5QL, England; (44) 949 81371.

MILLER HOWE COOKERY COURSES
Windermere, English Lakes, England

Spring and Fall

This country hotel and school, founded in 1971 by John Tovey, offers residential five-day courses, each limited to 15 students who arrive after tea on Sunday and depart after lunch on Thursday. Tovey demonstrates his specialties during $2^{1}/_{2}$-hour morning and afternoon sessions in the main restaurant kitchen and after dinner, teacher and students discuss the meal and the day. The emphasis is on fresh ingredients and topics include starters, main courses, sweets, tea accompaniments, and sauces and garnishes. During the starters class, students are taught the Cordon Bleu Method for preparing *paté brisé* and a variety of fillings. Other starters demonstrated are Miller Howe cheese and herb paté with hot spiced cob and variations of tarragon cream and cream soups. Main courses include breast of chicken stuffed with mushrooms and puree of parsnips with ginger and pine kernels. The sweets class is devoted to the mastery of farmhouse pastry, as well as basic almond meringue and choux pastry. Tea accompaniments include wholemeal bread, farmhouse scones, and Marsala cake.

Specialties: Appetizers, main dishes, desserts, garnishes, tea accompaniments.

Faculty: Miller Howe chef-proprietor John Tovey, a graduate of the Cordon Bleu School, cookbook author, and TV chef, teaches the classes.

Costs, Accommodations: The all-inclusive cost is £400 (includes $17^{1}/_{2}$% VAT) plus a $12^{1}/_{2}$% surcharge for staff gratuities. Refund for cancellation only if space is filled. Miller Howe, an Edwardian country house, has three lounges, a new Victorian conservatory overlooking the lake, and 13 centrally-heated private bedrooms. Credit cards accepted.

Location: In The Lakes district above Lake Windermere near the Langdale Pikes and accessible to London by train.

Contact: John J. Tovey, Chef Patron, Miller Howe, Windermere, The English Lakes, Cumbria, LA23 1EY, England; (44) 96 62 2536.

LA PETITE CUISINE (page 196)

RAYMOND BLANC'S LE PETIT BLANC ECOLE DE CUISINE
Great Milton, Oxford, England

October-April

Established in 1991 at Le Manoir aux Quat' Saisons, this five-day cooking vacation school runs from Sunday afternoon to Friday morning and features four full days of instruction in contemporary French cuisine. Beginner (intermediate) courses are held a dozen (8 to 10) times a year and limited to eight participants, who have individual work areas in Le Manoir's restaurant kitchen. Intermediate courses are open only to those who complete the beginners' week. Daily classes run from 8:30 or 9 am to 5:30 pm and cover hot and cold appetizers, fish and vegetables, meat and vegetables, and pastries. A working lunch and afternoon tea are served each day, dinners are taken at Le Manoir and the program ends with a champagne reception and Raymond Blanc's eight-course Menu Gourmand.

Specialties: Contemporary French cuisine.

Faculty: Prominent chef Raymond Blanc owns and operates Le Manoir. Sessions are taught by head chef Clive Fretwell.

Costs: Course cost is £975 (£875 during most of December and January) and includes lodging at Le Manoir, all meals, service, and VAT. Lodging is free for non-cooking guests. A £150 deposit is required with balance due four weeks prior to course. No refunds unless space can be filled.

Location: The 15th century Cotswold manor house Le Manoir aux Quat' Saisons is credited with the highest classification of Relais & Châteaux. It's situated seven miles from Oxford and 40 miles from London.

Contact: Le Petit Blanc, Ecole de Cuisine, Blanc Restaurants Ltd., Church Rd., Great Milton, Oxford, OX44 7PD, England; (44) 844 278881, Fax (44) 844 278847. U.S. Contact: Judy Terrell, Cuisine International, 7707 Willow Vine Ct. #219, Dallas, TX 75230; (214) 373-1161, Fax (214) 373-1162.

SONIA STEVENSON
London and other locations in England

Year-round

Master chef Sonia Stevenson does consultancy work and conducts $2^1/2$ to 4-day participation courses (limit six to eight students) that focus on sauces and fish cookery. The Sauce Course explores techniques for making sauces that are cream, oil, butter, brown, and shellfish-based, as well as sweet sauces and stocks. Students begin the course by ruining a sauce in order to explore the nature of the ingredients. The Fish Course covers methods for handling, preparing, and cooking many types of fish.

Specialties: Sauce and fish cookery.

Faculty: Founder of The Horn of Plenty Restaurant near Tavistock, Devon, Sonia Stevenson is a Master Chef of Great Britain.

Costs: The $2^1/2$-day course fee is £195, which includes two lunches.

Location: Venues include Glasgow, Inverness, Warwick, London, and Somerset.

Contact: Sonia Stevenson, 7 Lynn Ct., Mitcham Lane, Streatham, London, SW16 6LL, England; (44) 81 677 1172.

SQUIRES KITCHEN SUGARCRAFT SCHOOL
OF CAKE DECORATING
Farnham, Surrey, England

Year-round

Established in 1987, this cake decorating school and manufacturer/distributor of equipment and edibles offers more than a dozen demonstration (limit 45) and participation (limit 14) courses each month for beginning through advanced students. Most courses range from one to four full-day sessions, held on consecutive days. One-day intensive demonstrations touch on all the major cake decorating, sugarcraft, and chocolate skills. Other beginner courses include Writing in Icing, Sugar Flowers, Brush Embroidery, and Chocolate Work. Intermediate topics include Wiring and Stencilling Skills, Wild Flowers, Lace and Filigree, and Piped Decorations. Advanced and exhibition standard courses include Advanced Florals, Pastillage Wedding Tops, Exhibition Standard Royal Icing, and Creative Stencil Work. One-hour morning demonstrations, on a variety of beginner topics, are scheduled two or three Saturdays per month. Squires Kitchen also provides custom demonstrations for groups of up to 40 participants and holds its annual Sugarcraft Exhibition in March.

Specialties: Cake decorating, sugarcraft, chocolate.

Faculty: Senior tutor Peggy Green, resident tutor Pat Trunkfield, and ten visiting instructors, many of whom have authored books on their subjects and have exhibited nationally and internationally.

Costs, Accommodations: One-day demonstrations for beginners are £17.50, including light lunch; other courses range from £25 to £35 per day. VAT is included. Lodging information is provided.

Location: Approximately 30 miles from London, a 40-minute train ride.

Contact: Squires Kitchen Sugarcraft, Squires House, 3, Waverley Lane, Farnham, Surrey, GU9 8BB, England; (44) 252 711749/734309, Fax (44) 252 714714.

TANTE MARIE SCHOOL OF COOKERY
Woking, Surrey, England

Year-round

Founded in 1954 by Iris Syrett, the noted cookery writer, and named after the legendary French cook, this cookery school is one of the oldest and largest in the United Kingdom, teaching 96 students each term with 24 staff members. The school offers two Cordon Bleu Diploma courses for career cooks and a 12-week Cordon Bleu Certificate course, three to five-day practical courses, and one-day demonstrations for nonprofessionals who wish to increase their expertise. Class hours are from 9:30 am to 4:30 pm, Monday through Friday, with participation classes limited to 12 students and demonstrations to 24. The school has five modern teaching kitchens with at least six cookers in each. Theory classes are conducted in the lecture room and demonstrations are held in the mirrored theatre, which contains a fully-equipped kitchen. Virtually 100% of applicants are accepted (the only limitation being a lack of fluency in English or a severe physical disability) and all students obtain employment if desired.

The Diploma course, open to all those over the age of 16 who wish to pursue a culinary career, begins in late September and consists of three 12-week terms. Students begin with instruction in basic skills and progress to learning about labor-saving appliances. The course covers traditional British cookery and the entire spectrum of French cuisine, including the preparation and cooking of meat, eggs, fish, poultry, vegetables, stocks, and sauces, as well as hors d'oeuvres, canapés, aspic, pastries, gâteaux, icings and chocolates, and desserts. Flower arranging, food presentation, preparing a meal on a small budget, and practical business skills are also taught. Weekly lectures cover nutrition, microwave cookery, deep-freezing, cooking for invalids, menu planning, wine, and cheese. Well-known TV cookery demonstrators are invited to lecture on their specialties and local tradesmen bring their supplies and demonstrate their skills. A four-day seminar conducted by an internationally known Master of Wine prepares students for the Wine Certificate examination. Homework is assigned throughout the course with a written project during the first two terms. The intermediate and final examinations, held in the spring and summer terms, consist of a two-hour theory paper and six-hour practical. The Intensive Diploma Course, designed for those with previous experience, begins in January and May and consists of two 12-week terms. The course includes all the practical and theoretical elements of the Diploma course, but assumes that students have previously learned basic techniques. Students who successfully complete either course are awarded the Tante Marie Diploma and those who fail receive a certificate of attendance.

The 12-week Certificate course for home cooks, beginning each January and September, covers manual techniques and menus that are selected to provide participants with a balanced repertoire of recipes. The course includes weekly lectures on cooking theory, hygiene, menu planning, and costing and a one-day talk on wine selection. Those who successfully complete a three-hour practical exam and one-hour theory paper are awarded a Tante Marie Certificate. Three to five-day short participation courses on such topics as entertaining, cake icing, freezer cooking, and wine appreciation are held throughout the year. One-day demonstrations, scheduled during term recess in April and September, center around a special theme, such as dinner parties, weddings, microwave cookery, or flower arranging. Morning coffee and lunch with wine and tea are served and the food prepared in the demonstrations is raffled at the end of the day. Private group demonstrations can also be arranged.

Specialties: Career and home cookery courses featuring British and French cuisine and a variety of topics.

Faculty: The school, which is accredited by the British Accreditation Council for Independent Further and Higher Education and Endorsed by the IACP, is owned and administered by John Childs, a Chartered Accountant who teaches the business management classes, and his wife Beryl, Tante Marie's top student of 1980. All staff members are qualified to work in state schools and many have held catering positions. All teachers must have undergone teacher training.

Costs, Accommodations: Diploma course (three terms) £1,950/term; Intensive Diploma course (two terms) £2,300/term; Certificate course £2,400; fees include uniform and equipment (set of knives, school recipe book). A nonrefundable deposit of 10% of one term's fee is payable at the time of enrollment. The first term's fee is due four weeks prior to course for U.K. residents, six weeks prior for residents outside the U.K. Those who cancel less than six weeks before the start of term forfeit the term fee. The school assists students in finding local lodging and operates an international employment register for graduates.

Location: Near the center of Woking, a small country town approximately 25 minutes by train from London. The university town of Guildford and the Surrey countryside are nearby.

Contact: Tante Marie School of Cookery Limited, Woodham House, Carlton Rd., Woking, Surrey, GU21 4HF, England; (44) 483 726957.

TASTE OF TUSCANY (page 223)

TASTING ITALY (page 223)

TRAVEL CONCEPTS (page 182)

TURNAROUND COOKS
London, England

October to mid-August

Established in 1992, this Italian cookery school offers one-day courses daily and five-day courses once a month in the demonstration kitchen of Books for Cooks, a bookstore devoted to food and drink. The daily schedule runs from 10 am to 4:30 pm and demonstration (participation) courses are limited to 14 (6) students, who are taught the techniques to create modern interpretations of classic Italian and Mediterranean cuisines. Six to ten recipes are prepared and served for lunch. Emphasis is on vegetarian cookery, influenced by the spicy flavors of Thai, Caribbean and Ethiopian dishes, with classes in chocolate, pasta, bread making, fish cookery, and Italian regional desserts also offered. The school regularly schedules meetings and discussions on the art of cooking with noted chefs and cookbook authors.

Specialties: Modern Italian, Mediterranean, and vegetarian cuisines; pasta and bread making; fish cookery.

Faculty: School founder and instructor Carla Tomasi graduated from Prue Leith's Diploma course, was employed by Antonio Carluccio at his Neal Street restaurant, and was chef-owner of Frith's restaurant in London's SoHo. Guests include Alastair Little, chef-owner of Alastair Little, and Anna del Conte, author of *Gastronomy of Italy* and *Entertaining alla Italiana*.

Costs, Accommodations: Cost is £55 per day, which includes tea and coffee on arrival and lunch. Payment in £ Sterling only; no refunds. Lodging for out-of-towners is available.

Location: In West Kensington at Books for Cooks, 4 Blenheim Crescent, London W11. Nearest tube stations are Notting Hill Gate (Central Line) and Ladbroke Grove (Metropolitan Line).

Contact: Carla Tomasi, Turnaround Cooks, 73 Clare Ct., Judd St., London, WC1H 9QW, England; (44) 71 278 2659 *or* Lucinda Anta Von Dörgicse, 37a Cologne Rd., London, SW11 2AH, England; (44) 71 585 0315. Contact Books for Cooks for lodging information.

THE VEGETARIAN SOCIETY OF THE UNITED KINGDOM
Altrincham, Cheshire, England

Year-round

The Vegetarian Society UK, a registered charity and membership organization, offers a wide variety of demonstration (limit 14) and participation (limit 12) courses for both vegetarian cooking enthusiasts and professionals. Non-vegetarians are welcome. Courses have been scheduled year-round since 1982, when Sarah Brown began offering them, based on her BBC-TV series, "Vegetarian Kitchen". The cuisine taught is vegetarian, utilizing wholefood ingredients and no meat, fish, fowl, or animal by-products; however, the use of milk, free range eggs, and vegetarian cheeses is permitted. The school offers four one-week Foundation Courses that lead to the Cordon Vert Diploma, weekend courses on a variety of topics, one-day demonstration classes, and special courses for caterers leading to the Professional Cordon Vert Diploma. Membership in the Society is open to all. Benefits include a subscription to *The Vegetarian*, voting privileges, and the opportunity to participate in sponsored events.

The four Foundation Courses must be taken in sequence. Foundation 1, an in-depth introduction to vegetarian cookery, covers legumes and grains; the use of flavorings, herbs, spices, and shoyu; nuts and seeds; and techniques for preparing bread, pastries, and sauces. Foundation 2, designed to expand the culinary repertoire, covers Oriental (tofu, stir-fry, sweet and sour sauces), Mexican (tortillas and refritos), Indian (samosas, dhal, chutney), and Russian (buckwheat roast, beetroot soup) cuisines and techniques for preparing hot-water crust pastry, agar for jellies, and carob as a substitute for cocoa. Foundation 3 covers Greek (olive paté, lentil moussaka), Italian (gnocchi, lasagna, caponata), French (onion soup, roulade), and Middle Eastern (stuffed peppers, nut-and-garlic sauce) cuisines and techniques for making flaky choux pastry, rye breads, and yogurt ice cream. Foundation 4 continues to explore different techniques, ingredients, and cookery styles and covers Indonesian, Thai, Japanese, and California cuisines; the last part of the course consists of preparing a dinner party for two invited guests and one fellow student, and completing a written project and a short answer "exam" paper. These three elements and the continuous assessment contribute to the overall grading of Pass, Merit, or Distinction. The Foundation Courses are scheduled from 9 am until late afternoon or early evening, from Monday through Friday. The Society confers the Cordon Vert Diploma on students who complete all four courses and an written project.

Weekend courses, which begin with Friday dinner and end at 4:30 pm on Sunday, include Italian Vegetarian Cookery, Cuisine Vitesse (quick meals), Absolute Beginner, Learning to Demonstrate (for students who wish to teach), and So You Want to Open Your own Vegetarian Restaurant (for individuals who want to start a business). One-day classes, scheduled from 10 am until 4:30 pm, feature such topics as introductory vegetarian cookery, quick main courses, international themes, dinner party menus, Italian cookery, and Christmas recipes.

Specialties: Lacto-vegetarian and wholefood cookery.

Faculty: Tutors include Ursula Ferrigno, Rosalind Binham, Mary Scott Morgan.

Costs, Accommodations: Tuition ranges from £235 nonresident (£295 resident) for Foundation Courses 1 to 3 to £260 (£320) for Foundation 4. Resident tuition includes full board and lodging in twin-bedded rooms in the school's Lodge. Weekend course tuition ranges from £140 (£170) to £160 (£190). A nonrefundable £60 deposit must accompany booking with nonrefundable balance due five weeks prior to course. Nonrefundable tuition for the one-day classes and evening courses is £45 to £50, which must accompany booking. Payment in sterling, international money order, or credit cards (Access, VISA) accepted. Tuition grants can be applied for if students are under age 25 and are vegetarian. Society membership dues range from £10 per year (£180 life) for seniors and full time students to £16 per year (£250 life) for full members (those who pledge to abstain from consuming animal flesh) and associate members (those who are not full time practitioners of vegetarianism). Junior memberships are £4 per year.

Location: The school is situated ten miles south of Manchester in Altrincham, Cheshire, a 900-year-old market town. The town of Chester and historic attractions are nearby and Manchester airport is a 15-minute drive.

Contact: Rosemary Stewardson, The Cookery School Secretary, The Vegetarian Society UK, Parkdale, Dunham Rd., Altrincham, Cheshire, WA14 4QG, England; (44) 61 928 0793.

WOODNUTT'S SCHOOL OF CAKE DECORATING
Hove, East Sussex, England
Year-round

Established in 1980, this school offers a variety of cake decorating demonstrations, workshops, and courses for beginners to professionals. Sessions are conducted in the classroom and fully equipped teaching area with overhead mirror. Demonstrations (limit 30 students) are held on request and participation workshops (limit 14) are held from 10 am to 4:30 pm on an occasional basis. Topics include chocolate, smocking, novelty figure piping, crimping and embossing, and bas-relief. Three-day introductory, intermediate, and advanced courses cover cake decorating, sugarpaste icing (Australian style), royal icing, and sugar flowers. Courses meet from 9:30 am until 4 pm on three consecutive weekdays.

Specialties: Tuition to international competition standard, sugar pulling and blowing by visiting teachers.

Faculty: Woodnutt's co-owner (with husband Stuart) and principal instructor Elaine MacGregor is author of *All Colour Cake Decorating Course, Wedding Cakes, Quick to Decorate Cakes*, and a series of videos on cake decorating techniques. Other teachers include professional cake decorators Diana Beeson and Pauline Giles.

Costs, Accommodations: Demonstrations are £3.50, one-day workshops are £27.50 to £33, three-day courses range from £77 to £95, and a five-day course with a visiting teacher is £150. A nonrefundable deposit of £25 must accompany booking with remainder due four weeks prior to course. MasterCard/VISA accepted.

Location: Approximately one hour by train from central London. This resort area is known for its countryside and Regency-style architecture.

Contact: Woodnutt's, 97 Church Rd., Hove, East Sussex, BN3 2BA, England; (44) 273 205353, Fax (44) 273 207104.

EUROPE

THE ANNEMARIE VICTORY ORGANIZATION, INC.
Locations throughout Europe

Since 1978, Annemarie Victory has conducted and represented deluxe culinary tours to locations that include Italy, France, Switzerland, Portugal, Spain, Belgium, Austria, Germany, and Great Britain.

Specialties: Deluxe culinary travel programs.

Faculty: Austrian-born Annemarie Victory studied at the Sorbonne, attended the hotel school in Zurich, and has traveled extensively throughout the world. She has been specializing in luxury travel for more than 25 years.

Costs, Accommodations: The price for each program is approximately $4,000 per week, double occupancy. A $500 deposit is required to confirm reservation.

Contact: The Annemarie Victory Organization, Inc., 136 E. 64th St., New York, NY 10021; (212) 486-0353.

KAY PASTORIUS SCHOOL OF CUISINE (page 13)

NELL BENEDICT COOKING CLASSES (page 64)

TRAVEL CONCEPTS
France, Italy, England, Ireland, Switzerland

Year-round

This travel organization, founded in 1982, specializes in customized European culinary and wine tours for groups. Titles of programs emphasizing cooking classes include The Château Country Cooking School (page 184), Badia A Coltibuono (page 210), Champagne and Cuisine With Mrs. Charles Heidsieck, The English Experience, An Irish Gourmet Experience, and The Swiss Gourmet Experience. Champagne and Cuisine With Mrs. Charles Heidsieck, a nine-day culinary adventure limited to 15 participants, spends four days in the Champagne Region under the guidance of Mrs. Heidsieck and three days in Paris. The program includes demonstrations by Michelin-starred chefs Gerard Boyer and Jean-Pierre Lallement, champagne tastings, and gourmet meals. The English Experience, an eight-day gastronomic program limited to ten participants, features demonstrations by well-known English chefs Raymond Blanc, Stanley Mathews, and Brian Turner. Visits to an ale brewery, a vineyard, a cheese shop and dairy are also scheduled. An Irish Gourmet Experience, a nine-day gourmet program, includes a two-day stay at Ballymaloe House (page 205) with a cooking demonstration. Other activities include the Kinsale Gourmet Festival, visits to Youghal, Ballycotton, the Dingle Peninsula, and the Ring of Kerry. The Swiss Gourmet Experience, a ten-day program, features a visit to the Swiss Hotel School in

Lucerne with a demonstration by Marianne Kaltenbach. Excursions to Gstaad, Berne, Interlaken, and Brienz are also scheduled.

Specialties: Culinary and wine travel programs.

Costs: Group rates are dependent upon the time of year and the number of participants. Some programs may be able to accommodate individuals who are not members of the group.

Location: Tours visit the Loire Valley, northern France, northern Burgundy, northern Italy, England, Ireland, and Switzerland.

Contact: Dr. Patricia A. McNally, Director, Travel Concepts, 62 Commonwealth Ave., #3, Boston, MA 02116; (617) 266-8450, Fax (617) 267-2477.

FRANCE

ANDRÉ DAGUIN HOTEL DE FRANCE
Auch en Gascogne, France

October-April

Established in 1985, this school offers three-day to two-week demonstration/ participation courses (limit 6 students). Students work with staff in the hotel's restaurant kitchen, where they are taught the regional cuisine of Gascony and the hotel specialty — duck and its many preparations, such as foie gras and confit de canard. The three and five-day courses feature two and three days of classes, respectively, scheduled from 9 am to 3 pm and from 6 to 10 pm. Additional activities include a tour of the Armagnac region with visits to wine cellars, a foie gras duck farm, and an outdoor farmer's market.

Specialties: The cuisine of Gascony.

Faculty: Instructors include J. François Leclerc, under the supervision of Chef André Daguin, hotel proprietor and author of *Foies Gras and Other Good Foods from Gascony*.

Costs, Accommodations: The fee, which includes meals and lodging at the hotel, is approximately 2,850 FF for three days; rates for longer stays are available upon request. A 25% deposit must accompany reservation with balance due three weeks prior to course. No refunds less than eight days prior. Credit cards (MasterCard, VISA, American Express) accepted.

Location: The hotel is situated in city center.

Contact: André Daguin, Hotel de France, Place de la Libération, 32000 Auch en Gascogne, France; (33) 62 05 00 44, Fax (33) 62 05 88 44.

LES CASSEROLES DU MIDI
Avignon, France

September-June

Established in 1992 in the large kitchen of a private home, this school offers one-week participation classes that feature daily five-hour classes in Provençal cuisine. Sessions are scheduled weekly, usually beginning on Monday, and are limited to four to six participants. The day begins with a trip to the market in

Avignon, where students learn how to select the best produce, which will determine the menu for the day. Under supervision, each student is responsible for preparing one dish from beginning to end. Excursions to nearby sites are planned in the afternoons.

Specialties: The cuisine of Provence.

Faculty: Italian-born Olga Manguin was owner/chef of Les Nattes in Avignon.

Costs: The daily rate of 1,000 FF includes all meals, excursions, and double occupancy lodging in the four-bedroom, three-bath home of Olga Manguin and her husband, distiller Henri Manguin.

Contact: Mme. Olga Manguin, Les Casseroles du Midi, La Barthelasse, 84000, Avignon, France; (33) 90 82 62 29, Fax (33) 90 82 94 49.

THE CHÂTEAU COUNTRY COOKING SCHOOL
Montbazon-en-Touraine, France
March-April and October-November

Since 1986, Denise Olivereau-Capron and her son, Xavier, have hosted six-day participation courses (limit 15 participants) at Le Domaine de la Tortinière, their 19th century manor-house château in the Loire Valley. The courses in French regional cuisine, which begin on Sunday evening and conclude the following Saturday morning, feature four morning classes in the château's newly renovated restaurant kitchen, afternoon excursions, and a day in Tours, the capital of the Touraine and home of one of France's largest flower markets. Instruction covers first courses, fish, meats, sauces, and desserts. Visits are scheduled to the historic châteaux of the region, a goat cheese farm, the market town of Chinon, and the caves of Vouvray, where comparative wine tastings are held. Participants dine at L'Orangerie (the château restaurant), with the owners of a private château, and at fine area restaurants.

Specialties: French regional cuisine.

Faculty: Chef Edouard Wehrlin of L'Orangerie.

Costs, Accommodations: The course fee of 14,000 FF single, 13,500 FF double, includes lodging at the château, three meals daily, wine tastings, and scheduled tours and excursions.

Location: Touraine, the château country, is in the Loire Valley, near Tours.

Contact: Mme. Denise Olivereau-Capron, Le Domaine de la Tortinière, 37250 Montbazon-en-Touraine, France; (33) 47 26 00 19, Fax (33) 47 65 95 70 or Sara Monick, The Cookery, 4215 Poplar Dr., Minneapolis, MN 55422; (612) 374-2444, Fax (612) 333-3554.

CHÂTEAU DE SAUSSIGNAC COOKING SCHOOL
Saussignac, France
May-October

Founded in 1984 by Fred and Joan Montanye in their private château, this school offers maximum participation courses of one week or more. Sessions are held in the 17th century château's large, modern kitchen, equipped with an overhead demonstration mirror, marble-topped pastry center, and time-saving appliances. Each week's attendance is limited to 11 resident students, who are taught a variety of dishes based on beef, lamb, pork, fish, game, poultry, fresh fruits and vegetables, and cheese, and such skills as sautéing, making sauces, pastries, and doughs, folding, reducing, boning, deglazing, and caramelizing. Two to three meals are prepared and dined on daily, accompanied by appropriate wines, with emphasis on working within a time schedule. Breakfast preparation takes approximately 45 minutes, lunch an hour, and dinner 2½ hours. Students learn specific techniques that extend to a wide range of preparations as well as how to recognize and avoid problems. Individual requests are accommodated when possible. The students also visit farmers' markets, wineries, and local fêtes and are escorted on trips to the Dordogne region, including châteaux, Bastide towns, picnics, and a pre-historic Cro-Magnon cave. During the week, at least three restaurant trips are scheduled: a country inn and Michelin-starred restaurants. When a guest stays for a number of consecutive weeks, menus and excursions are planned to avoid duplication.

Specialties: Classical, provincial, and nouvelle French cuisine with the emphasis on produce of the Perigord region.

Faculty: Joan and Fred Montanye have attended Le Cordon Bleu and La Varenne in Paris, the Oxford Chef's Seminars at Oxford University, and Tsuji, professional chef's school in Osaka. Joan, a home economist with a master's degree in management, is a retired college professor and family therapist. Fred, a retired architect who designed kitchens from a cook's perspective, has taught cooking classes for 15 years.

Costs, Accommodations: The one-week (Saturday afternoon to Saturday after breakfast) fee, which includes all meals, lodging, wine, and planned restaurants and excursions, ranges from $2,200 to $2,450 per person, double occupancy, $2,375 to $2,525 single. Noncooking guests pay the same fee; no extras for tipping or service. All bedrooms have modern heating systems and private baths. The full amount must accompany reservation and the cancellation charge is $50 for those who cancel more than 112 days prior and ranges from 25% of fee 84 to 111 days prior to 75% of fee within 30 days of course.

Location: Saussignac is located 58 miles from Bordeaux International Airport and ten miles from the Bergerac airport, which has commuter flights connecting with Paris. Several daily TGV connect the Paris train station, Gare Montparnesse, with Bordeaux and Ste. Foy la Grande, five miles away, where students are met.

Contact: Joan Rye Montanye, 24240 Saussignac, France; (33) 53 27 80 78, Fax (33) 53 57 33 30.

COOKING AT THE ABBEY
Hostellerie Abbaye de Sainte Croix
Salon-de-Provence, France

November

Since 1987, this resort has offered one or two demonstration/participation courses (limit 12 students) in Provençal cooking and wine selection in November and customized courses for groups of eight or more year-round except July.

Classes meet in the restaurant kitchen for three or four hours each afternoon and other activities include trips to Aix-en-Provence, Avignon, nearby wineries, and the caves of Chateauneuf du Pape.

Specialties: Provencal cuisine.

Faculty: Chef P. Morel of the Abbaye's Michelin one-star restaurant.

Costs, Accommodations: Cost ranges from 3,000 FF to 9,000 FF, depending on length of stay, and includes meals, accommodations, and all planned activities.

Location: The Abbaye, a member of Relais & Chateaux, is two miles from Salon, 20 miles northeast of the nearest airport, 20 miles west of Aix-en-Provence, and 35 miles south of Avignon.

Contact: Cooking at the Abbey, Hostellerie Abbaye de Sainte Croix, Rte. du Val de Cuech, 13300 Salon-de-Provence, France; (33) 90 56 24 55, Fax (33) 90 56 31 12.

LE CORDON BLEU
Paris, France

Year-round

Founded in 1895, this school for professional and nonprofessional cooks offers a variety of courses in classic French cuisine. The Classic Cycle, designed for those who wish to pursue a culinary career or desire a comprehensive course of study, consists of three levels of cuisine and two levels of pastry instruction, each 11-week certificate courses beginning the first week of January, April, July, and October. The Intensive Sessions, designed for professionals and amateurs with a limited amount of time, consist of four and five-day single topic workshops scheduled primarily between the terms of the Classic Cycle. Hands-on classes for children are held on Wednesday afternoons. The teaching method is through demonstrations followed by practical classes (limit 12 students) in which each student prepares one of the dishes demonstrated by the chef. The $2^{1}/_{2}$ to 3-hour demonstrations, scheduled weekdays at 9 am and 1:30 pm and Thursdays at 4:30 pm, are open to the public and translated into English. Facilities include seven practical classrooms with individual work areas consisting of a refrigerated marble work surface, four-burner stove, oven and refrigerator; and two demonstration/lecture theatres equipped with modern appliances, professional cuisine and pastry ovens, overhead mirrors, and video monitors. Certain areas are devoted to pastry, breadbaking, and sous-vide (vacuum-packed cuisine), for which specialized appliances are provided. An indoor garden is designed as a student recreation area. Le Cordon Bleu also has schools in London (page 165), Tokyo, and Canada (page 151), and representatives in Australia, Hong Kong, Singapore, and Taiwan.

Basic Cuisine introduces techniques for preparing meat, fish, poultry, classic sauces, bisques, consommes, mousses, vegetable garnishes and doughs; Intermediate Cuisine covers menus from traditional, regional, and contemporary French cooking; and Superior Cuisine emphasizes time management and the execution, presentation, and decoration of French haute cuisine. Each course consists of 18 to 20 hours of instruction a week in three demonstrations, three practical classes, and one optional demonstration/lecture each Thursday at 4:30 pm. Basic Pastry

covers sweet pastry, short pastry, puff pastry, croissant dough, brioche, meringues, genoise, choix pastry, and sponge cake; Advanced Pastry covers more
complex preparations and decoration. Each course consists of 10 to 12 hours of
instruction a week in two demonstrations and two practical classes. Basic Cuisine
must be completed first and the other cuisine and pastry courses can then be taken
either simultaneously or sequentially. If taken simultaneously, the Classic Cycle
can be completed in nine months. Students who satisfactorily complete the three
cuisine (two pastry) courses, which each conclude with a practical exam, are
awarded the Cuisine (Pastry) Diploma. Those who complete all five receive the
Grand Diplôme. Approximately 60 Gourmet Cuisine Workshops each year cover
such topics as regional cuisine, traditional cuisine, bistro cuisine, fish and
crustaceans, holiday menus, sous-vide cuisine, classic desserts, and bread baking.
Wine classes and Paris market tours are also offered.

Specialties: Classic French cuisine.

Faculty: Full-time faculty includes master chefs who have won national and
international competitions and have practiced in Michelin-starred restaurants.
Guest chefs and culinary experts conduct the demonstrations/lectures.

Costs, Accommodations: Tuition (deposit) is 28,940 FF to 31,940 FF (9,500 FF)
for cuisine courses; 23,940 FF and 24,940 FF (7,500 FF) for the basic and the
advanced pastry courses; and 750 FF to 4,400 FF for one to five-day Intensive
Sessions. Deposit is required at least two months prior to course and balance is
due at least one month prior. Discounts are available to those who enroll in more
than one course and/or pay the balance at least two months prior. An insurance
payment of 50 FF must accompany registration and course material fee, payable
on arrival, is 1,800 FF to 1,950 FF (270 FF) for Classic Cycle (Gourmet
Workshops) courses. Cancellations received more than six (three) weeks prior to
the Classic Cycle (Gourmet Workshops) courses forfeit 1,500 FF. A work/study
program is available to a limited number of students in the Classic Cycle and top
students have the opportunity to train in well-known restaurants and catering
firms. A list of recommended hotels is provided on request.

Location: A central residential area of Paris in the 15th arrondissement (Metro
Vaugirard).

Contact: Le Cordon Bleu, 8, rue Leon Delhomme, 75015 Paris, France; (33) 1
48 56 06 06, Fax (33) 1 48 56 03 96.

THE COUNTRY KITCHENS OF GASCONY
Gascony, France

August-July, September-October

Since 1987, Kate and Patrick Ratliffe have conducted culinary tours to the
Southwest of France. The eight-day tours, held once a month and open to 15
participants, are primarily an in-depth introduction to the regional cuisine of
Gascony as demonstrated by Kate Ratliffe aboard the luxury canal barge Julia
Hoyt and in the restaurant kitchens of Andre Daquin's Hotel de France, Maria-
Claude Gracia's A La Belle Gasconne, and Michel Trama's L'Aubergade. In
addition, participants visit farmhouse kitchens of local cooks, markets, foie gras
farms, and wine and Armagnac cellars.

Specialties: Southwest French country cooking, Gascon specialties.

Faculty: Kate Ratliffe, who serves as chef aboard the canal barge she and her husband charter; well-known chefs of the region.

Costs: Land cost is $1,985 per person, which includes lodging, breakfasts, eight meals, and all planned activities. Participants are lodged at Le Prince Noir, once a 17th century convent, in the 12th century village of Serignac Sur Garonne.

Location: The Duchy of Gascony is in an area of southwestern France midway between Bordeaux and Toulouse. Participants are met in Bordeaux or Agen, which is accessible by train from Paris.

Contact: Kate Ratliffe, The Country Kitchens of Gascony, 5 Ledgewood Way, #6, Peabody, MA 01960; (800) 852-2625 *or* (508) 535-5738.

CUISINIERES DU MONDE
Chavagnac, France

Year-round

Daniele Delpeuch conducts one and two-week participation courses year-round and Foie Gras and Truffles Weekends during the winter at the 16th-century stone farmhouse that has been in her family for generations. The one and two-week courses (limit seven students) feature six-hour daily classes that cover traditional French cooking and conclude with a four-course meal. Other activities include visits to the market, neighboring farms, a well-known baker, and a 17th century walnut oil mill. During the first week, the two-day La Borderie Diploma Course focuses on geese and ducks, including the preparation of foie gras and confit and a trip to a foie gras farm. Those enrolled in the two-week course explore French gastronomy more thoroughly and visit the region's prehistoric caves on the intervening Sunday.

Specialties: Cuisine Bourgeoise, foie gras and confit, truffles.

Faculty: Daniele Delpeuch contributed to the *Time-Life Great Meals in Minutes* series, served as guest lecturer at La Varenne, conducted workshops throughout the U.S and for the annual meeting of the IACP, and was private chef to French president M. François Mitterrand. She currently tours as a cooking teacher and acts as a restaurant consultant.

Costs, Accommodations: Cost, which includes meals, lodging at the farmhouse, and all planned activities, is approximately $2,000 per week.

Location: In the Perigord region near the town of Sarlat.

Contact: Daniele Mazet-Delpeuch, Cuisinieres du Monde, la Borderie, 24120 Chavagnac, France; (33) 53 51 00 24, Fax (33) 53 50 53 71.

ECOLE DES ARTS CULINAIRES ET DE LA L'HOTELLERIE
Lyon-Ecully, France

Year-round

Conceived in 1985 by Jack Lang, France's Minister of Culture, and opened in 1990 as a joint venture of the French government and the private sector, this school offers two 23-week professional programs in culinary arts/restaurant operations and hotel management from October through April and four three-week summer programs in French cuisine for those pursuing a career. Approximately 85% of applicants are accepted and 95% of graduates obtain employment. The school is in the restored 19th century Château de Vivier and modern extension, a $3-million teaching complex that contains 16 seminar rooms, 4 training kitchens, lecture hall, library, oenology lab, wine cellar, and central, pastry, and cold kitchens.

The Culinary Arts/Restaurant Operations professional program, Cuisine and Culture, consists of 25 courses that cover food purchasing and preparation, introduction to pastry, basic cooking techniques, food and wine tasting, nutrition, menu planning, beverage service, and business aspects. Enrollment is limited to 100 students (student to teacher ratio 10 to 1), who are awarded the Paul Bocuse Diploma on graduation. The summer Culinary Arts program, which runs from May to August, consists of four increasingly advanced three-week (85-hour) modules (limit 36 students) that are taken in sequence, unless applicant can demonstrate prior knowledge and/or experience. Module I, The Basics of French Cuisine, covers preliminary food preparation, basic techniques for cuisine and pastry, and restaurant dining service; Module II, Discovering French Gastronomy, covers client service, basic wine selection, classic French pastries and cuisine, sensory analysis, and menu composition; Module III, Advanced French Culinary Arts, covers professional table service, in-depth wine study, advanced cuisine and pastry, and decorative accompaniments; Module IV, France's Culinary Heritage, covers tableware selection, famous French chef recipes, ceremonial pastries, decorative displays, French wine production, study of the characteristics of fine French restaurants, and menu development. The last three modules feature demonstrations by Michelin-starred restaurant chefs. Students who complete all four receive a Paul Bocuse certificate. All courses are either taught in English or offer simultaneous translation from French.

Specialties: Professional and nonpfessional programs in French culinary arts and restaurant and hotel management.

Faculty: In addition to a seven-member board of directors, headed by Paul Bocuse, the eight-member permanent teaching faculty of accomplished chefs includes Alaine Berne, Bernard Esnault, Alain Le Cossec, Jean-François Orcel, and Pascal Queyrel. Guest lecturers are all professionals.

Costs, Accommodations: Tuition for each 23-week program is 55,000 FF. Application must be accompanied by a $75 nonrefundable fee and $1,000 is due on acceptance. At least 80% of tuition is due prior to course. Single (double) student residence room is $300 ($400) per month; full board is $240 per month. Each three-week summer module costs 15,000 FF, which includes meals, student residence housing, and planned activities.

Location: Situated in a 17-acre wooded park, the school is in the Lyon-Ecully university and research zone, ten minutes from downtown Lyon, two hours from the Alps, and three hours from the Mediterranean.

Contact: A.C.R.C. Corporation, 37 W. 57th St., Ste. 703, New York, NY 10019; (212) 980-5139, Fax (212) 980-6944.

ECOLE DE GASTRONOMIE FRANÇAISE RITZ-ESCOFFIER
Paris, France

Year-round

This year-round school, founded in 1988 in the Hotel Ritz and named for its first chef, Auguste Escoffier, offers a variety of courses in cooking, bread and pastry making, and wine and table service for cooking enthusiasts and aspiring and established professionals. The school occupies approximately 2,000 square feet and includes a main kitchen, a pastry kitchen, a conference room, and changing rooms. The workspace was designed to be attractive as well as functional and has stainless steel work surfaces and an adjustable mirror over the demonstration table. Courses include the one to six-week César Ritz Diploma Course, the one to ten-week Pastry Diploma Course, and the advanced level 12-week Ritz-Escoffier Diploma Course. The school also offers three one-week December holiday courses the week before Christmas as well as custom-designed programs for groups throughout the year. During the summer months, the school offers special short-term courses (French Regional Cooking, Fish Cookery, Escoffier Today, Wine in Food, and Parisian Brasserie and Bistro French Cooking). All courses are taught in both French and English and written recipes in both languages and in Japanese are provided.

Each week of the César Ritz Diploma Course consists of four participation classes (maximum 10 students), four demonstration classes, and one theory class — a total of 28 class hours. Two of the participation classes are devoted to cooking, followed by a meal of the dishes prepared, and the remaining two focus on pastry. Each week features different techniques and recipes. During a six-week period, four theory classes concentrate on wine study and the other two are bread and cheese tastings or a floral decoration class. Students who complete one to five weeks receive the César Ritz Certificate and those who take the full six-week course and pass a practical exam are awarded the César Ritz Diploma. Each week of the Pastry Diploma Course is devoted to a specific area of bread or pastry making and consists of five afternoon participation classes (maximum eight students) — a total of 25 class hours. The ten weekly topics are pastry doughs, cakes and entremets, petits fours, chocolate and confectionery, individual cakes and pastries, breads, holiday cakes and sugar work, catering, desserts: plate presentations, and all about chocolate. Students take their confections home after each session. Students who complete one to five weeks receive the Pastry Certificate and those who take a minimum of six of the ten weeks and pass a practical exam are awarded the Pastry Diploma. Students who receive this diploma may apply for an internship in the Hotel Ritz's main pastry kitchen. Candidates for the Ritz-Escoffier Diploma Course must have the César Ritz Diploma or equivalent experience and enroll for the full 12 weeks. Each week consists of five participation classes (maximum 10 students), three demonstration classes, and one theory class — a total of 32 class hours. Three of the participation classes are devoted to cooking and two focus on pastry. The theory classes include six sessions of wine study, three sessions of table service, one session of floral decoration, and a bartending class. During the final week, the classes consist of three practical exams, one theory exam, and four sessions of buffet preparation for the Diploma reception. Those who pass the exams are awarded the Ritz-Escoffier Diploma. Courses begin in January, April, June, and September. Students enrolled in this Diploma Course are invited to apply for internships in the kitchen of the Espadon, the Michelin-rated two-star Hotel Ritz restaurant.

Demonstration Classes in cooking and pastry, part of the diploma courses, feature two to three dishes and tastings of the foods prepared. These sessions, which are open to the public, are held Monday through Thursday from 3 to 5:30 pm. Those planning a visit to Paris can write for the monthly Gastronomy Program, which lists the menu for each class. Certificates can be provided to those who attend. During the December holiday season, the Ecole offers three festive courses. The Ritz-Escoffier Christmas Course features a week of meals based on traditional French Christmas and New Year's dishes and wines selected from the Ritz cellars. In addition to the practical cooking and pastry making classes, activities include wine tastings, a cheese, bread, and wine tasting, a flower arranging class, and a gala Belle-Epoque dinner. The Holiday Entertaining Certificate Course, which concludes with a buffet prepared by the participants, features ideas for intimate dining and buffet entertaining and emphasizes dishes that can be prepared in advance and served with ease. The five-day All About Wine: Treasures from the Ritz Cellars Course includes wine and food pairing meals at the Espadin restaurant, wine tastings, and a day trip to Champagne.

Specialties: Certificate and Diploma courses in French cooking and pastry-making for cooking enthusiasts and aspiring and professional chefs; demonstrations of French cuisine and pâtisserie; wine selection and table service.

Faculty: School director Gregory Usher served as director of Le Cordon Bleu de Paris and La Varenne and was awarded the Mérite Agricole by the French government in 1989. The three full-time instructors, Chef de Cuisine Christian Guillut, Chef Pâtissier Bruno Neveu, and Chef de Cusisine Vincent Lange have a total of 60 years of professional experience. Ritz Executive Chef Guy Legay was awarded the Légion d'Honneur and elected a Meilleur Ouvrier de France; Master Baker Bernard Burban teaches the bread courses and is one of only two Meilleur Ouvrier bakers in Paris; Restaurant Manager Georges Lepré is the consultant on table service; Chief Sommelier Jean-Michel Deluc and Pascal Normand teach the wine courses; Jean Mauny, the hotel's chief florist, is the floral consultant.

Costs, Accommodations: César Ritz Diploma Course is 5,550 FF per week, the Pastry Diploma Course is 4,900 FF per week, the Ritz-Escoffier Diploma Course is 68,400 FF, the Demonstration Classes are 220 FF per class, and the Ritz-Escoffier Christmas Course is 8,000 FF. Summer courses range from 5,750 FF to 7,000 FF per week. The school provides a list of nearby lodging and low-season rates at the Hôtel Ritz are available for attendees. Upon receiving applications with preferred dates and course(s), the school, if it accepts the student, sends an enrollment form. A 25% deposit must accompany enrollment with the balance due four weeks prior to course. Written cancellations at least four weeks prior forfeit 500 FF; no refunds thereafter. Reservations for daily Demonstration Classes must be made by noon the day of class; payment is due before class begins.

Location: The school is located in the center of Paris, close to three main subway entrances and most major department stores.

Contact: Gregory Usher, Directeur, Ecole de Gastronomie Française Ritz-Escoffier, 15, Place Vendome, 75001 Paris, France; (33) 1 42 60 38 30, Fax (33) 1 40 15 07 65; (800) 966-5758 (in U.S.A.).

ECOLE LENOTRE FRANCE
Plaisir, France

Year-round

This school for culinary professionals who wish to improve their technique was founded in 1971 as the first gastronomic training and improvement school in France. It offers approximately forty courses in bakery, pastry, chocolate and candy, ice cream and sherbet, ice carving, sugar decoration, catering and buffets, holiday specialties, and meat, fish, and game dressing. Based on the school's motto, "To learn the most in a least amount of time", sessions last five days with 7½ hours of class daily. The five or six courses offered each week, taught in French and English and limited to 12 students per instructor, are 90% participation so that students can practice the recipes they learn. The school has many classrooms, each with carefully selected equipment.

Specialties: French cuisine, French bread, cakes, puddings, ice-creams, sweets.

Faculty: The school was founded by Gaston Lenôtre and is managed by Marcel Derrien, "Meilleur Ouvrier de France" and master in confectionery. All instructors are qualified professionals.

Costs, Accommodations: Tuition is 7,830 FF for confectionery, breadmaking, ice cream, and chocolates, and 8,240 FF for cuisine. Tuition must accompany application to confirm reservation. The school can reserve accommodations in one of Plaisir's hotels for about 250 FF per night.

Location: Approximately 30 miles from Paris and six miles from Versailles.

Contact: Marcel Derrien, Director, Ecole Lenôtre, 40, Rue Pierre-Curie, 78372, Plaisir Cedex, France; (33) 1 30 81 46 34, Fax (33) 1 30 55 14 88.

ESPACE FRIAND ECOLE DE GASTRONOMIE
Sevres, France

Year-round

Established in 1992, this school offers courses in baking, pastries, confectionery, icing, cake decoration, oenology, cheeses, art of the table, and entertaining menus for the home cook. Two, three, and five-day practical and theoretical courses (limit 6 to 12 students) are scheduled weekly in the school's five new fully-equipped lecture theaters. Classes meet Monday through Friday, from 9 am to noon and 1:30 to 4:30 pm with instruction in French, English, Japanese, Korean, and German. The five-day Prestige course, offered each week, consists of three days of classes and two days touring patisseries, confectioners, wine and cheese shops, and Paris and Versailles tourist attractions. The three-day Tradition Boulangerie course, held at the Moulin Le Comte in Chartres, covers a variety of breads and Viennese pastries and features a visit to the Viron flour mill. Participants receive the "Certificat d'Honneur" on completion of course.

Specialties: Bread and pastries, confectionery, cake decoration, wine selection, cheeses, table setting, party dishes.

Faculty: Chairman and Managing Director Serge Fribault spent 20 years in Japan, where he taught patisserie and managed 15 bakery/confectionery/catering shops. His staff consists of well-known restaurant chefs and instructors.

Costs: Course fees, which include lunches, range from 5,000 FF to 9,500 FF; Prestige course, which includes three lunches, one dinner, six nights' lodging, and most activities, is 15,000 FF to 17,000 FF; Tradition Boulangerie, which includes three lunches and two nights' lodging at the Grand Hôtel Monarque in Chartres, is 8,500 FF. A 50% deposit, of which 25% is nonrefundable, is required; nonrefundable balance is due four weeks prior to course. A 350 FF fee is assessed for insurance and supplies. Credit cards accepted.

Location: Espace Friand is situated on the western outskirts of Paris in a fine office development, La Cristallerie, and opposite the Sèvres porcelain factory.

Contact: Espace Friand, 2, Ave. de la Cristallerie, 92310 Sèvres, France; (33) 46 23 17 17, Fax (33) 46 23 18 70.

FOOD IN FRANCE
Gourgé, France

March-June, September-October

Since 1990, Food in France has offered one-week participation courses in French Cookery, French Wine & Food, and Patisserie and Sugar Craft. Six weekly courses are held between May and July and seven courses are held in September and October, each limited to seven participants whose individual preferences are accommodated. French Cookery focuses on regional cuisines, including those of Provence, Normandy, Brittany, Burgundy, Languedoc, and Ile de France. Days are free until 3 pm, when a three-hour class is scheduled to prepare the four-course evening meal. French Wine & Food combines wine appreciation and cookery, with a different wine-producing region covered each day. Patisserie and Sugar Craft consists of nine two-hour sessions devoted to continental gateaux and torten, patisserie, petit fours, sweetmeats, icing, and professional decoration. Since 1992, Food in France has also offered one-week courses in quilting, embroidery, drawing, and other art and craft topics.

Specialties: French regional cuisines, wine appreciation, pâtisserie, sugar craft.

Faculty: Pat Cove has taught a variety of cookery courses in Adult and Further Education colleges for the Inner London Education Authority and has specialized in French regional cuisines at Morley College in London; David Normand-Harris holds the advanced diploma of the Wine and Spirit Education Trust; Janet Glazier is a course director and lecturer in food studies at West Kent College, Tonbridge, England, and studied with Susan and Ewald Notter of Zurich.

Costs, Accommodations: Cost, which includes full board and lodging, is £275 per course, 20% less for nonparticipant guests (10% reduction for all bookings prior to March). A 10% nonrefundable deposit is required with balance due four weeks prior to arrival. Courses and lodging are at Les Belles Etoiles, two adjoining houses in the center of the village.

Location: Gourge, a rural village in the Deux Sevres, is 125 miles north of Bordeaux and 185 miles southwest of Paris.

Contact: Pat Cove, 14 Thorpewood Ave., London, SE26 4BX, England; (44) 81 699 3437.

HOLIDAYS IN THE SUN IN THE SOUTH OF FRANCE
Gordes, France

Spring, fall, and the first week in December

Since 1980, Sylvie Lallemand has conducted classes in Provencale specialties at her country home, Les Mégalithes, near Avignon. Her one-week participation courses begin and end on Saturday and are limited to six cooks of all levels. The daily schedule includes morning market visits, where students learn how to select poultry, fish, and produce, and cooking classes starting at 3 pm. Instruction in English, French, and German covers the preparation of meats, vegetables, salads, terrines, bread, appetizers, jams, and jellies. The December week is devoted to preparing traditional Christmas dishes. Available recreational activities include horseback and bicycle riding, shopping at handicraft boutiques, and visits to museums and historic sites.

Specialties: The cooking of Provence.

Faculty: Sylvie Lallemand, president/founder of the Association des amis de la cuisine et des traditions provençales, learned to cook from her mother and grandmother and studied with Roger Vergé at l'Ecole du Moulin de Mougins.

Costs, Accommodations: The one-week course is 2,700 FF, which includes private room and bath at Les Mégalithes, use of pool, and meals.

Location: Gordes is near Avignon, which is accessible by train from Paris and Marseilles, the nearest airport, and is a 3½-hour drive from Nice.

Contact: Sylvie Lallemand, Les Mégalithes, 84220 Gordes, France; (33) 90 72 23 41.

JANE CITRON (page 106)

PARIS EN CUISINE
France

Year-round

Founded in 1975 by Robert Noah, Paris en Cuisine provides cooking classes, courses, and tours throughout Paris and the French provinces with activities guided and translated into English by Robert Noah or a member of his staff. Programs for cooks of all levels of ability include Paris day trips to markets, restaurants, bakeries, and cheese shops; a five-day gastronomic tour of Paris and several three to six-day regional courses; and a nine-month professional course and four one-week courses at the Centre de Formation Technologique Ferrandi. Robert Noah also offers a restaurant and hotel reservation service and publishes a bi-monthly gastronomic newsletter.

Day trips are scheduled every Tuesday, Wednesday, and Thursday (except August and December) and by request. The trip to Rungis, the largest market in the world, is offered every Tuesday from 5:30 to 9 am and includes six of the food pavilions, breakfast in one of the cafes, and transportation to and from Paris. A Paris restaurant class is arranged every Wednesday and includes three courses, recipes, and a tasting. Three restaurant kitchens are visited during a walking tour each Thursday. The history of the restaurant and its organization are explained and the dining rooms are viewed. Additional day trips arranged by request include a trip to purveyors of bread, cheese, and wine, with samplings of each; classes with such pastry chefs as Denis Ruffel and Paul Bugat; afternoon classes in French bread making with explanation and demonstration; and wine classes that cover wine making, wine service, and the tasting of six wines. Wine regions to be studied can be selected by the group.

The five-day gastronomic Paris tours are held twice a year (May and July) and limited to eight participants, who dine in three well-known restaurants, one of which has the Michelin three-star rating. The program includes a demonstration in a restaurant kitchen and a demonstration class at the Ecole Ritz Escoffier, a tour of restaurant supply stores, a chocolate tasting, and the day trip activities listed above. Robert Noah can also arrange for individualized tours and cooking instruction in two and three-star restaurants. The regional classes, each scheduled once or twice a year, include meals, lodging, transportation during the program, planned activities, and gratuities. A special regional trip to Normandy includes encounters with the region's finest producers of cheese, cider, Calvados, and cooking classes with two top local chefs. Private group visits to any region of France, including classes with experienced chefs, can be arranged.

The nine-month (1,200 hour) professional program at one of France's nationally accredited hotel/restaurant schools, Centre de Formation Technologique Ferrandi, provides instruction in English in all aspects of French cuisine, restaurant service, and cheeses, by a specialized staff in professional teaching kitchens. Also scheduled are visits to museums, Rungis market, fine Paris restaurants, and three days in the Bordeaux region visiting wine châteaux. At the end of the course students take the exams for the Certificat d'Aptitude Professionel (C.A.P.).

Specialties: French cuisine.

Faculty: Robert Noah has worked in the kitchens and dining rooms of restaurants all over France, including Les Anges and the three-star L'Archestrate and the wine shop of Lucien Legrand. He is originally from St. Louis, Missouri, where he managed a wine store and worked as a chef. Classes are taught by the chefs of each restaurant hosting the course, with translation by Robert Noah.

Costs, Accommodations: Per person fees for day trips and regional classes are dependent on the total enrollment in each program. The Tuesday Rungis trip is 425 FF for five or more; the Wednesday restaurant demonstration is 350 FF; the Thursday walking tour is 250 FF for three or more; day trips by request range from 325 to 775 FF; the Normandy trip is 9,300 FF; the nine-month professional course is 79,000 FF. A nonrefundable deposit of 200 FF is required for day trips, 2,000 FF for regional classes, and balance is billed when program is filled and rate is determined. A nonrefundable deposit of 1,000 FF is required for the five-day gastronomic tour and balance is billed 60 days prior to tour. Full refund (less deposit) is granted those whose written cancellation reaches Paris en Cuisine no less than 45 days prior to program, two-thirds refund thereafter.

Location: Day trips visit Paris restaurants and culinary attractions; regional classes vary each year. The Centre de Formation Technologique Ferrandi is centrally located in Paris, two blocks from Montparnasse.

Contact: Robert Noah, Paris en Cuisine, 49 rue de Richelieu, 75001 Paris, France; (33) 1 42 61 35 23.

LA PETITE CUISINE
Morzine, France and Berkshire, England
February-December

Lyn Hall teaches one-week vacation courses at Chalet Gueret in the French Alps from late June to September and conducts two and five-day courses at Michel Roux's Waterside Inn in Berkshire during spring and fall.

The one-week course (limit eight participants), La Petite Cuisine in the Savoie, features five days of four-hour morning participation classes, where students prepare lunch and dinner, and four afternoon excursions, which may include a dairy, bakery, vineyard, market, mountain farm, and local restaurants. Visits to Yvoire, Annecy and Chamonix are also planned. Lessons, held in the chalet's modern kitchen, emphasize classic and modern technique and cover Italian and Swiss regional cookery and both haute and provincial French cuisine.

Two-day intensives and five-day courses (limit four), La Petite Cuisine at the Waterside Inn, are held in Michel Roux's personal kitchen, where he develops recipes for his Michelin three-star Relais Gourmand restaurant. Lessons cover French haute cuisine, modern French and British cuisines, sauces, and advanced pastry. Professional intensives are also scheduled and students who wish to pursue a career are assisted in finding a suitable setting for further training.

Specialties: French, Italian, and Swiss classical and provincial cuisines; modern British cuisine; sauces and pastry; professional courses.

Faculty: Pastry chef Lyn Hall has diplomas in wine and butchery and won a gold medal in the Culinary Olympics of 1988. She began her cooking school in 1980, was a food consultant from 1986 to 1990, and then returned to teaching.

Costs, Acommodations: One-week course in the Savoie is £850, which includes double occupancy room with private bath in the chalet (single supplement £350), all meals, and all planned excursions. Five-day courses at the Waterside Inn range from £588. Students can stay at the Inn or at special rates at nearby hotels.

Location: Chalet Gueret, a fully renovated 18th century farmhouse situated in high pastureland near Morzine, is a 90-minute drive from Geneva. The Waterside Inn, on the River Thames, is a 45-minute drive west of London on M4.

Contact: Lyn Hall, La Petite Cuisine, 21 Queen's Gate Terr., London, SW7 5PR, England; (44) 372 470457, Fax (44) 372 469891.

PRINCESS ERE 2001
Paris, France
Year-round

Founded in 1977, this school offers a variety of participation courses in French cuisine. Classes are small (maximum six) and emphasis is on preparation methods simplified to today's busy lifestyle. Students learn how to organize their time in the kitchen and make full use of appliances. The classes may be taught in French, English, or Spanish. The Intensive Course, scheduled six hours daily, Monday through Friday, runs from October through July. Students prepare a complete meal, planned according to the season, and dine on it at the conclusion of class. A typical menu might feature a fish and vegetable terrine, country style roast of lamb, and strawberrry bavaroise for dessert. L'Art de Vivre, the essence of entertaining in the French style, emphasizes the blending of table arrangements, menu variations, French culture, and museum visits. The Summer Session — a one-week class open six weeks during August and September— is held in Normandy. Classes are scheduled mornings and afternoons, Mondays through Fridays. A new participation course, sponsored by the Hotel Plaza Athénée, focuses on entertaining at home and features menus created by Chef de Cuisine Gérard Sallé. Special classes can also be arranged.

Specialties: French cuisine emphasizing at-home entertaining.

Faculty: Marie-Blanche de Broglie, the school's founder and director, is a Certified Member of the IACP, holds a Grand Diplôme from the Cordon Bleu of Paris and is author of *The Cuisine of Normandy.*

Costs, Accommodations: Intensive Course: one week 5,000 FF; two weeks 9,000 FF. One week sessions: 3,000 FF each. Summer session: 12,000 FF per week (includes three meals daily, Monday through Friday, and double occupancy twin-bedded room with bath); 7,000 FF per week (no lodging). Payments should be made in full. Refunds, less 15%, are granted for cancellations less than 30 days before start of class and no refunds are made once the class or series has begun. All reimbursements are in French francs.

Location: The school is in the large kitchen of Marie-Blanche's apartment in Paris, located near la Tour Eiffel. Summer sessions are held in Normandy with lodging provided in an 18th-century estate home about15 miles from Rouen and 100 miles from Paris. Sightseeing trips are scheduled to Rouen, Deauville, Honfleur, Fecamp and other locations.

Contact: Marie-Blanche de Broglie, Director, Princess ERE 2001 Ecole de Cuisine, 18, Ave. de la Motte-Picquet, 75007 Paris, France; (33) 1 45 51 36 34, Fax (33) 1 63 67 38 68.

SARA MONICK CULINARY TOURS
The South of France, Bordeaux and San Francisco

Sara Monick, a cooking instructor since 1977, has conducted culinary tours in the U.S. and Europe since 1986. Each tour is limited to 12 participants and features demonstration and participation classes conducted by local and guest chefs, visits to cultural sites, and dining at fine restaurants. The Food and Wine of San Francisco, a spring tour, includes two days in wine country, cooking classes, tours of the city's ethnic neighborhoods, wine tastings, garden visits, and dining at a variety of fine local restaurants. The Food and Wine of the South of France, a 12-day October tour, features five days of participation at the "Cooking in Provence" program in the Haut Var, including lessons, wine and olive oil tastings, and excursions to Moustier and the Grand Canyon du Verdon and six days of excursions to Arles, Aix en Provence, Les Baux, and Nice. Other fall destinations include The Food and Wine of Bordeaux, an insider's look at the cuisine and wines of this region. Customized small group tours to Italy and France can be arranged.

Specialties: Such cuisines as French, Italian, and American regional.

Faculty: Sara Monick, a Certified Member of the IACP, owns The Cookery, a Minneapolis-based cooking school. She studied in France with Madeleine Kamman and a variety of chefs in the Loire and southern region, and in the U.S.

with Jacques Pépin, Nicholas Malgieri, Paula Wolfert, and Giuliano Bugialli. Culinary tour classes are taught by local and guest chefs and teachers.

Costs, Accommodations: Costs, which include double occupancy lodging, several meals, and all scheduled activities, are approximately $2,000 to $4,000 for each tour. A $500 deposit must accompany reservation. Cancellation penalty ranges from $50 (more than 60 days prior to departure) to $500 (less than 45 days prior). No refunds within seven days.

Contact: Sara S. Monick, The Cookery, 4215 Poplar Dr., Minneapolis, MN 55422; (612) 374-2444 *or* (612) 333-1440, Fax (612) 333-3554.

TRADITIONAL FAMILY COOKING IN THE QUERCY
Les Vignes de Brassac, France

May-September

The Agence de Voyages Midi-Pyrenees, established in 1978, offers two participation courses: a five-day family cooking course and a weekend or two-day course in which students prepare goose foie gras and confit goose to take home with them. The five-day course (limit six students), offered from May to October, features daily cooking lessons from 9 am to 1 pm. The class is followed by lunch of the foods prepared and afternoons are free for such activities as swimming, vineyard visits, and tours of medieval villages and the basilica of Moissac. During the two-day Cooking Goose Foie Gras and Confit on a Farm course (limit eight), offered from November to February, participants learn with one of five farm ladies how to prepare goose delicacies. The program includes two morning cooking sessions and two lunches at the farm with the family.

Specialties: French country cooking; goose foie gras and confit.

Faculty: Accomplished French farm cooks.

Costs, Accommodations: The five-day course, which includes lodging, breakfast, and lunches, is 2,230 FF double (700 FF single supplement) for lodging in a 17th-century manor house without dinner, 3,045 FF (420 FF) in a two-star hotel with dinner, and 3,980 FF (1,200 FF) in a three-star hotel with dinner. The two-day session, which includes lunches, one night in a two-star hotel, breakfast, and dinner, is 725 FF (70 FF) plus 150 FF for the goose and 420 FF for foie gras. A 25% deposit must accompany registration with the balance due 45 days prior to arrival. Those who cancel more than 30 days prior to course are charged 100 FF, cancellations less than 30 days and more than seven days prior are charged 50% of total cost. No refunds thereafter.

Location: The farms are located in southwest France and can be accessed by car from Montauban, a five- hour train ride from Paris, or Agen, about a two-hour plane ride from Orly Airport.

Contact: Andre Pochat, Agence de Voyages Midi-Pyrenees, Vignes, Brassac, 82190 Bourg-de-Visa, France; (33) 63 94 24 30.

TRAVEL CONCEPTS (page 182)

LE TROU RESTAURANT AND COOKING SCHOOL (page 22)

TWO BORDELAIS
Bordeaux, France

May-July, September

Jean-Pierre and Denise Moullé conduct six-day culinary vacations that include hands-on instruction in classic and regional French cuisine. Five programs are offered each summer, limited to eight participants, who attend classes in the professional private kitchen of the Château La Louvière, an 18th century monument belonging to Mrs. Moullé's family. The programs feature three cooking classes; visits to markets in Castillon, Bordeaux, and Branne; private tours of wine cellars in St. Emilion, Médoc, and Graves; lunch and lecture by Jean D'Alos, owner of a Bordeaux cheese shop; tours of well-known châteaux, including Pichon Lalande, Margaux, and Mouton; dinners in Michelin-starred restaurants; and a trip to the seaside resort of Arcachon with picnic aboard a fisherman's boat and excursion to the oyster beds.

Specialties: French classic and regional cuisine.

Faculty: Jean-Pierre Moullé graduated from Ecole Hotelière in Toulouse and served as chef at Chez Panisse in Berkeley from 1975 to 1983. He was Food and Beverage Director at the Hotel Meridien in San Francisco and now teaches and consults for restaurants and still cooks at Chez Panisse two or three nights a week. Denise Moullé's family owns several châteaux in Bordeaux. A native of Bordeaux, she opened two wine shops in California's Bay Area and now markets her family's wines in the U.S.

Costs, Accommodations: Cost is $2,500 (single supplement $200), which includes all meals, planned excursions, and first class room and private bath at the modern Château Mouchac. An $800 deposit is required with balance due 75 days prior to arrival. Cancellation penalty ranges from $150 (more than 75 days prior) to 25% of total (30 to 75 days prior); no refund thereafter.

Location: France's Bordeaux region.

Contact: Jean-Pierre Moullé, Two Bordelais, P.O. Box 8191, Berkeley, CA 94707; (415) 848-8741, Fax (415) 845-3100.

VACANCES CUISINE COOKING IN PROVENCE
Entrecasteaux, Provence, France

December-February, April-October

Established in 1990 by Anthony and Sarah Beerbohm, this four to seven-day program is individually designed to meet the requirements of culinary tour leaders and groups of at least 10 cooks of all levels. Culinary activities can include instruction at farmhouse, wine domaine, château, and/or restaurant kitchens, where Provençal home cooks and guest chefs demonstrate traditional French country recipes. Topics include fresh vegetables, fish, chicken, olive oil, herbs of the region, and garlic, with emphasis on easy-to-prepare, healthful meals. Food-related excursions can include comparative olive oil tastings at a 17th century olive mill, wine tastings and gourmet meals at private Côte de Provence wine estates and restaurants, and buying trips to open-air street markets. Guided visits can also be scheduled to the Château of Entrecasteaux, the Abbey of Le Thoronet, the Museum of Arts and Popular Traditions, the Gorge and Grand Canyon of Verdon, and the pottery and terracotta tile workshops of Moustiers Ste.-Marie and Salernes. Special programs are available during the black truffle season in January/February and the olive oil harvest in December.

Specialties: Provençal and French country cuisine, wine appreciation, and cultural trips for tour leaders and groups.

Faculty: Kitchen designer and experienced cook Sarah Beerbohm directs the program and translates into English for the home cooks and chefs who teach. Anthony Beerbohm, who owns a wine business, conducts the wine tastings and arranges customized wine appreciation holidays.

Costs, Accommodations: According to needs of group.

Location: The Côte de Provence wine-producing region in the Centre-Var region, 45 miles east of Aix-en-Provence, 35 miles north of St. Tropez and 35 miles northwest of Cannes. Tennis, horseback riding, golf, and fishing, are available locally and Nice and Marseille International Airports are a 75-minute drive.

Contact: Sarah Beerbohm, Domaine du Grand Jas, 83570 Entrecasteaux, Provence, France; (33) 94 04 49 77, Fax (33) 94 04 48 02 *or* Sara S. Monick, The Cookery, 4215 Poplar Dr., Minneapolis, MN 55422; (612) 374-2444, Fax (612) 333-3554.

LA VARENNE
Château du Feÿ
Burgundy, France
May-November

La Varenne, established in Paris in 1975, offers one-week programs for cooking and wine enthusiasts and a five-week course for experienced culinary professionals at the 17th-century Château du Feÿ, a registered historic monument owned by La Varenne founder Anne Willan. All programs are limited to 14 participants and are held in the château's custom-built teaching kitchen.

The one-week Summer Series, which runs weekly from July through August, features a different specialty and a variety of chef-instructors each week, with five half-day participation classes, three demonstrations, a wine tasting, excursions to Joigny and Chablis, and a concluding dinner at a fine country restaurant. Weekly specialties include bistro cooking, entertaining menus, contemporary French, French pastry, and three courses in French regional cuisine: Burgundy and Alsace, Provence and Gascony, and Brittany and Pèrigord. Students work in groups of two or three on each day's menu, using fresh ingredients and practicing several techniques. A few places are available for those who desire a five-week intensive immersion in French cuisine and pastry and/or who wish to qualify for the Intensive Professional Program. Such students follow five different course themes, work extra time on evenings and weekends with the teaching chefs, and take practical and written exams to earn La Varenne's Intermediate Diploma.

The one-week Grand Luxe Gastronomic Course and the Wines and Food of Burgundy Program, scheduled five or six times in the early summer and fall, are hosted by Anne and her husband Mark Cherniavsky. The Gastronomic Course includes four practical classes in regional specialties, a master chef demonstration, three wine tastings, visits with a cheese producer and artisan baker, a balloon trip with champagne, and four excursions highlighted by a vineyard visit in Chablis and dining at two of France's top restaurants: Côte St. Jacques in Joigny and L'Espérance in Vèzelay. The Wines and Food of Burgundy course is similar but devotes more to the exploration of wine making and visits to prominent vintners.

The five-week Intensive Professional Program is designed for career professionals from a wide range of food fields. It is scheduled three times a year and features 40 hours of demonstrations and practical classes each week, special events such as wine and cheese tastings, and eight days of culinary excursions to Burgundy, Champagne, Lyonnais, and Paris. The first week focuses on the La Varenne method (techniques of classic French cuisine) and instruction covers sautes, braises, souffles, omelets, crepes, sauces, and knife skills. The second week is devoted to the La Varenne method for pastries, biscuit and genoise cakes, meringue, nut doughs, almond paste and fondants, and the use in cooking of wine and spirits. The third week covers fish and vegetables, table settings and service, and carving techniques. The fourth week's theme is contemporary French cooking and the fifth week features advanced pastries, chocolate, hors d'oeuvre, aspic, and molded desserts. Culinary excursions include the weekly market in Joigny, vineyards and wineries in Chablis, Beaune, Beaujolais, and Champagne, food shops and open markets in Paris, the Rungis wholesale market, delicatessens in Lyon, a goat cheese producer and foie gras farm in Burgundy, and visits to fine restaurants culminating in a graduation dinner at the Côte St. Jacques in Joigny.

Specialties: Classic French cuisine and pastry.

Faculty: The programs are directed by Anne Willan, whose recent books include *La France Gastronomique, Great Cooks and Their Recipes,* and the how-to series, *Look and Cook.* About two-thirds of the curriculum is taught by La Varenne's cuisine and pastry chefs, the remainder by visiting chefs from well known restaurants in Paris and Burgundy. English translation is provided.

Costs, Accommodations: One-week program fees, which include transportation to and from Paris, full board, shared twin lodging with private bath or shower at the château, and all planned activities and excursions, are $2,250 for a Summer Series course and $2,995 for a Grand Luxe program. Single supplement is $400 and a reduced rate is available for stays of more than one week. Full payment must accompany enrollment. Cancellation penalty ranges from $100 (more than 90 days prior to course) to $250 (30 to 90 days prior); no refund thereafter. Intensive Professional Program fee is $10,750, which includes all of the above as well as copies of Anne Willan's *La Varenne Pratique* and La Varenne's *Basic Recipe Book.* Applicants, who must be at least 19 years old, are required to submit a resume and will be questioned on their training and background. About 65% of those who apply are accepted. A $1,000 nonrefundable deposit within 15 days of acceptance secures a space and balance is due 60 days prior to course. Cancellation penalty ranges from $100 (more than 90 days prior) to $1,000 (30 to 60 days prior); no refund thereafter.

Location: The 100-acre Château property, 90 minutes south of Paris, includes woodland, a walled garden supplying fruit and vegetables in season, a tennis court, an extensive cookbook library, and an outdoor swimming pool in season.

Contact: La Varenne, P.O. Box 25574, Washington, DC 20007; (800) 537-6486 *or* (202) 337-0073, Fax (703) 823-5438. In France: La Varenne, Château du Feÿ, 89300 Villecien, France; (33) 86 63 18 34, Fax (33) 86 63 01 33.

GREECE

P. K. SHELDON CULINARY TOURS (page 18)

THE WANDERING SPOON
Greece and Portugal
Spring and fall

Lucille Haley Schechter started this cooking school series, which is conducted in Mediterranean villas, in 1983. The one-week program is limited to eight to ten participants and emphasizes participation along with demonstrations and discussions of local and international cooking techniques. Students attend classes and/ or reside in villas in Greece and Portugal where they are taught ethnic and continental cuisines during five daily three-hour sessions. Graduation dinner is arranged in a fine restaurant and excursions are planned to marketplaces, vineyards, and cultural centers. Ms. Schechter also tailors programs for private groups.

Specialties: Portugese, Greek, and other ethnic cuisines.

Faculty: Former *Harper's Bazaar* magazine editor Lucille Haley Schechter is co-author of the *The International Menu Diabetic Cookbook* and is a Professional Member of the James Beard Foundation.

Costs, Accommodations: The price of each one-week session, excluding airfare, is $1,990, double occupancy. Students often are housed in deluxe Mediterranean hotels with swimming pools.

Location: Include Crete, Corfu, Santorini, and the Algarve.

Contact: Lucille Haley Schechter, The Wandering Spoon, 340 E. 57th St., New York, NY 10022; (212) 751-4532, Fax (212) 753-1714.

HONG KONG

CHOPSTICKS COOKING CENTRE
Kowloon, Hong Kong
Year-round

This school, founded in 1971, offers a variety of one to two-hour demonstration and participation courses in Chinese cuisine. Professional courses include a four-week intensive, eight-week intensive, 13-week professional course, and a 17-week teachers training course. Tourist programs range from a single-session demonstration to a one-week course. Visitors can also enroll in a single session of a dozen four to twenty-four session courses on specific topics as well as a six-session summer course for children. Private group classes and four-session courses in banquet dishes, vegetable carving, wedding cake, piping, and ingredients are available by special arrangement. Classes are conducted in the school's modern teaching kitchen.

The professional four-week intensive course is offered at the beginner and advanced level and begins the first Monday of every month except January, February, July, and August. The eight-week basic-to-intermediate intensive begins the first Monday of March, April, May, September, October, and November. The 13-week basic-to-advanced professional course begins the first Monday of March, April, September, and October. The 17-week teachers training course, which commences the first Monday of March and September, is the professional course plus four weeks of practical training. Students learn 4 to 20 Chinese roasts, 16 to 36 dim sum, 5 to 20 breads, 9 to 30 cakes and pastries, and 30 to 100 other Chinese dishes during each course.

The single-session tourist program features the preparation of two dim sum, two Chinese roasts, or two other Chinese dishes. The half-day Chinese cookery course, held from 3 to 9 pm, includes a market and kitchen visit, demonstration of three dishes, and a 12-course banquet dinner. The one-day course includes a demonstration of four to eight dishes selected by the students. The two-day moon cake course and bean curd course are specially arranged. The one-week tourist course includes a market visit and demonstration of four dim sum, four roasts, and 18 other Chinese dishes. Courses are limited to 25 students. Demonstration (limit 20 students) courses on individual topics range from 4 to 24 sessions and cover regional dishes (Pekingese, Sichuan, Cantonese), basic roasts, basic cakes and pastries, and basic Western dishes. Participation (limit 12) courses range from 4 to 16 sessions and include basic, intermediate, and advanced dim sum, advanced roasts, advanced cake and pastries, and professional breadmaking.

Specialties: Regional cuisines, dim sum, roasts, breads, cakes and pastries.

Faculty: School director, Cecilia J. Au-yang, and her staff.

Costs, Accommodations: The four-week intensive ranges from about $1,700 (basic) to $2,000 (advanced); the eight-week intensive is $2,500; the 13-week professional course is $3,500; and the 17-week teachers training course is $4,000. The tourist classes range from $30 for a demonstration to $80 for a half-day to $500 for the one-week course. Individual courses range from $120 for a four-session course ($40 per session) covering 8 simple Chinese roasts to $1,200 for a 24-session course ($50 per session) covering 48 restaurant dishes. Accommodations for full-time students are available at private hostels for $40 to $60 per day, $200 to $350 per week, or $600 to $1,000 per month. Arrangements should be made at least one month in advance, accompanied by half the tuition. The balance is due on arrival in Hong Kong. No refunds are granted.

Location: In Kowloon next to St. Rose of Lima College, near Mongkok Railway Station, a ten-minute ride to Jade Market and a ten-minute walk to Food Market.

Contact: Cecilia J. Au-yang, Director, Chopsticks Cooking Centre, 108 Boundary Street, Ground Floor, Kowloon, Hong Kong, *or* P.O. Box 73515, Kowloon Central Post Office, Hong Kong; (852) 3368433 *or* 3390454.

ELEGANCE SCHOOL OF CULINARY ART
Hong Kong
Year-round

Established in 1984, this school offers demonstration and participation courses (limit 20 students) in Chinese, Japanese, and Western-style cuisines and a pastry certificate in bread, cake, and chocolate making. More than 100 courses are scheduled annually, during evenings, weekdays, and all-day on weekends, in the

1,000-square-foot, 20-seat facility. Each specialty is taught on the beginner, intermediate, and advanced levels and consists of four to seven three-hour sessions. The school also offers customized classes for groups of 10 or more and culinary tours of Hong Kong, Macau, and southeast China.

Specialties: Eastern and Western cuisines, bread, pastries, chocolate.

Faculty: Principal Sylvia Lai, hotel chefs, technical school instructors. The school is a member of the IACP.

Costs: $30 per session.

Location: Central Hong Kong.

Contact: Sylvia Lai, 1/F, Flat A5, Bayview Mansion, 21 Moreton Terr., Causeway Bay, Hong Kong; (852) 5 890 7278.

IRELAND

ALIX GARDNER'S COOKERY SCHOOL
Dublin, Ireland

Year-round

Established in 1978, this school offers a 12-week certificate course primarily for those pursuing a culinary career, a one-week leisure learning course, two 10-session evening courses, demonstration classes, and gourmet tours. Instruction in cordon bleu-style cookery, modern cuisine, and Irish cooking is by both demonstration (limit 45 students) and participation (limit 16). The school's modern facilities include video and slide projection equipment, two demonstration rooms with overhead mirrors, and a practical room with 16 individual work areas.

The 12-week certificate course, which begins in September, January, and April, runs from 9 am to 5 pm, Monday through Friday (450 hours). Training is provided in the theoretical and practical aspects of modern and traditional cookery with the first half of the course spent learning the basic principles of Escoffier and the second half devoted to such advanced techniques as boning chicken, preparing aspic, making meringue baskets, and decorating cakes. During the morning students produce a three-course meal; afternoons are reserved for demonstrations and lectures on hygiene, marketing, quantity cooking, catering, budgeting, freezing, menu-planning, and wine appreciation. Practical work experience in restaurants and catering is arranged. The term concludes with written and practical examinations, including an optional exam by the Wine & Spirit Education Trust, and successful students are awarded a diploma and assisted in finding jobs.

The one-week leisure learning course consists of 15 hours of classroom instruction and visits to cheese makers, organic farms, fishing ports, and other places of culinary interest. The two 10-session evening participation courses meet weekly from 6:30 pm to 9 pm. Intermediate Syllabus I covers such topics as fish preparation, meringues, roulades, cold buffets, and the use of yeast; Intermediate Syllabus II covers puff pastry, game, Hollandaise sauce, phyllo pastry, and boning techniques. Demonstration classes, taught by the school faculty and guest chefs, cover such topics as dinner party menus, ethnic cuisines, healthful foods, wine appreciation, and microwave cookery. The gourmet tours feature dining at Ireland's fine restaurants and a demonstration of traditional Irish cooking.

Specialties: Classical cordon bleu cooking, modern cuisine, Irish cooking.

Faculty: School proprietor and main instructor Alix Gardner received the London Cordon Bleu School diploma, the Prue Leith School of Food & Wine Certificate, and the Wine Information Board Teacher's Certificate. She is a member of the IACP, Eurotoque (association of chefs), and the Institute of Master Chefs. Assistant teachers are Ruth Wallace, who received the Cordon Bleu diploma, and Mary O'Sullivan, who received the Tante Marie diploma.

Costs, Accommodations: Costs range from IR £2,000 for the certificate course (non-residential) to IR £1,250 for the leisure learning course (residential). A series of evening demonstrations is IR £85. A 20% deposit reserves a space with balance payable the first day of class. Fees are payable by check, bank draft, or American Express and full refund is granted cancellations at least 14 days prior to course. Students in the certificate course are assisted in finding accommodations.

Location: The school is situated in central Dublin, a ten-minute walk from the downtown shopping area.

Contact: Alix Gardner's Cookery School, Kensington Hall, Grove Park, Lr. Rathmines Rd., Rathmines, Dublin 6, Ireland; (353) 1 96 00 45.

BALLYMALOE COOKERY SCHOOL
Shanagarry, Midleton, County Cork, Ireland
April-September, December and January

Ballymaloe House, a late Georgian manor built around a medieval tower, has been one of Ireland's foremost restaurants and hotels since it opened, in 1964. Its founder, Myrtle Allen, and her daughter-in-law, Darina, collaborate in running the Ballymaloe Cookery School, founded in 1983 and located two miles away in the courtyard of Kinoith, a regency farmhouse. The school features traditional Irish and French classical cookery and international cuisine. Facilities include a fully-equipped, specially designed kitchen with gas and electric cookers, an overhead mirror in the demonstration area, as well as orchards and vegetable and herb gardens that supply much of the fresh produce. Courses, geared to students of all levels of experience, include a 12-week Certificate Course (44 students maximum) twice yearly, in January and September; and one-day to one-week courses on a variety of topics.

Short courses of varying lengths and subject matter are offered from April to July and in mid-December. Most of these courses are hands-on, limited to 44 participants, and consist of an afternoon demonstration followed the next morning by a practical session where students cook lunch applying the principles they have learned. A limited number of demonstration-only programs (75 students maximum) are offered, such as the one-day Christmas Cooking, the one-day Barbecue Course, the week-end Entertaining Course, and the Ballymaloe Buffet Course. Other classes are devoted to such specific topics as cakes and biscuits, game cookery, vegetarian, and seafood, and a one-week introductory course is also offered. Each year a well-known international chef is invited as guest instructor.

Specialties: Dishes from the small and great houses of Ireland, Ballymaloe House specialties, French and international cuisine.

Faculty: Classes are taught by School Principal Darina Allen and her brother,

Rory O'Connell, both of whom trained in the Ballymaloe House restaurant kitchen. Darina Allen is a Certified Teacher and Food Professional by the IACP. Guest chefs include Marcella Hazan, Madhur Jaffrey, and Anne Willan.

Costs, Accommodations: The 12-week Certificate Course is IR £3,175, one-day courses are IR £75, weekend courses are IR £215 to IR £240, and one-week courses are IR £298 to IR £315. Students enrolled in the 12-week course live in cottages adjoining the school and may assist in the Ballymaloe House restaurant kitchen a couple of nights each week. Students may stay in the self-catering cottages, at Ballymaloe House, or in local accommodations (housing charges are in addition to the course fee for the 12-week and short courses). A 25% nonrefundable deposit (personal checks in foreign funds and credit cards are accepted) for short courses and 10% for the Certificate Course are required. Balance is due no less than four weeks prior to course. Written cancellations more than six weeks prior are refunded the balance.

Location: The school is located one mile from the sea, outside the village of Shanagarry, County Cork, in the south of Ireland a 2½-hour drive from Shannon Airport, a one-hour drive from Cork Airport, and a 4½-hour drive from Dublin Airport. The Fota House and Arboretum are 15 miles away and the Waterford Crystal Factory is approximately 70 miles away. The school can arrange for pick-up at airports and train stations.

Contact: Darina Allen, The Ballymaloe Cookery School, Shanagarry, County Cork, Midleton, Ireland; (353) 21 646785, Fax (353) 21 646909.

THE COOKERY CENTRE OF IRELAND
Dalkey, Ireland

September-April

This school offers a full-time 12-week Certificate Course beginning each September and January, six-session evening participation courses, and six-session evening demonstration courses. The Busy Bee Summer School of Cooking, a hands-on program for 11 to 16-year-olds, is held every two weeks from mid-June to mid-August. Classes are conducted in the school's new, specially-designed facilities. Essentially 100% of applicants are admitted and 100% of graduates obtain employment.

The Certificate Course consists of 12 weeks of instruction, from Monday through Friday (10 am to 4 pm). Designed for those who desire a comprehensive program or who are pursuing a career, the course emphasizes basic and advanced cordon bleu cookery along with such subjects as food preservation, menu planning, wine appreciation, and flower arranging. Mornings are devoted to the preparation of a four-course meal, which is then served for lunch, and afternoons feature lectures, discussions, and a demonstration of the following day's menu. Twice weekly classical cookery lectures and visits to meat manufacturers, a fish smoking house, bakeries, and hotel kitchens are also scheduled. After six weeks, students spend one day a week during the next four weeks in work experience at a Dublin-area restaurant or hotel kitchen. A certificate is awarded those who successfully complete examinations in theory and practical work.

Specialties: Twelve-week Certificate Course and evening courses in cordon bleu cookery.

Faculty: The school is under the supervision of Mrs. Bee Mannix-Walsh, D.Sc.I., Cordon Bleu (London). An experienced teacher of home economics and City & Guilds (London) chef, she has prepared and presented food for magazines and television commercials.

Costs: The course fees are IR£2,250 for the 12-week Certificate Course, IR£130 for the six-week participation course, and IR£80 for the six-week demonstration course; two-week non-residential summer course for youngsters is IR£100 A nonrefundable deposit of 10% of the course fee must accompany application with balance due on first day of class.

Location: The school is centrally situated in Dalkey, close to the DART and the No. 8 bus terminal.

Contact: The Cookery Centre of Ireland, 2A St. Patrick's Ave., Dalkey, Co. Dublin, Ireland; (353) 1 2858728, Fax (353) 1 2857823.

DIANA MARSLAND COOKING (page 139)

EUROPEAN EDUCATIONAL CENTRE (EEC)
THE PARK HOTEL
Virginia, County Cavan, Ireland
Year-round

Baltimore International Culinary College (page 55) administers the European Educational Centre, which offers year-round programs for cooking enthusiasts and hospitality professionals. All programs employ advanced level instruction incorporating methods developed by the City and Guilds of London. One, two, three, and six-week Short-Course and Skills Maintenance elective programs cover Epicurean Baking and Pastry Skills and Epicurean Cooking Skills. Professionals affiliated with the ACF may apply programs as credit toward certification.

One, two, three, and six-week programs start on the same day and are offered at least once a month. The Monday through Friday classes consist of six hours of daily lectures, demonstrations, and participation sessions (limit 20 students). Continental breakfast, lunch, and a dinner of the day's preparations are provided. Epicurean Cooking Skills, based on Auguste Escoffier's methodology, covers menu planning, recipe costing, and the order of work. Recipes may include borscht, quail with gooseberry sauce, Duchess potatoes, baked apple in pastry, and sauce Anglaise. Epicurean Baking and Pastry Skills introduces theories and skills for preparing European pastries and breads. Students create yeast-raised doughs, delicate pastries, sauces, puddings, cakes, and such individual projects as decorative work with marzipan, pastillage, and other techniques.

Specialties: International cooking, baking, pastry skills for cooking enthusiasts and hospitality professionals.

Faculty: European-trained professional chefs with credentials from the London City and Guilds.

Costs, Accommodations: Program fee, which includes double occupancy lodging, shuttle service, and three meals per class day, is $1,125 for a one-week course, $1,900 for a two-week course, $2,475 for a three-week course, and $4,800 for the six-week course (Epicurean Cooking Skills and Epicurean Baking & Pastry

Skills). A $472.50 per week fee for nonparticipant guest covers three meals per class day and accommodations. Single supplement surcharge (private bedroom in shared cottage) is $70 per week. A nonrefundable $100 deposit must accompany application with balance due at least six weeks prior to departure. Written cancellations received at least six weeks prior receive full refund of balance, less the $100 tuition deposit. Students are lodged in shared two-bedroom cottages at Bective Court, adjacent to the lecture/demonstration classroom wing. Private rooms, subject to the single occupancy surcharge, are available.

Location: Built in the 18th century as a summer residence for the Marquis of Headfort and converted to a resort hotel in the 1930s, this 58-acre country estate is located on the shores of Lough Ramor, an hour's drive from Dublin. The complex adjoins the 900-acre National Forest and offers a nine-hole golf course, tennis courts, fishing, and boating. Nearby attractions include Kells, birthplace of St. Columbanus; Loughcrew, known for its prehistoric hieroglyphics; Tara, seat of the ancient High Kings of Ireland; and Quilca House and Stella's Bower, where Jonathan Swift wrote *Gulliver's Travels*.

Contact: Baltimore International Culinary College, 25 S. Calvert St., Baltimore, MD 21202; (800) 624-9926 *or* (410) 752-4710, ext. 209.

P. K. SHELDON CULINARY TOURS (page 18)

TRAVEL CONCEPTS   (page 182)

ISRAEL

TNUVA, TRAINING CENTER FOR FOOD CULTURE
Tel-Aviv, Israel
Year-round except August

Tnuva, the largest food distributing company in Israel, established its training center for food culture in 1973 and offers classes that teach both adults and children how to prepare food inexpensively and efficiently. More than 20,000 individuals enroll annually and classes for adults are taught year-round except July, which is reserved for children's classes, and August, when the school is closed. Sessions taught in English can be arranged for groups of 25 persons or more. Topics include Russian, Middle Eastern, Moroccan, Italian, and Chinese cuisines, as well as microwave, vegetarian, and nutritional cookery.

Specialties: Middle Eastern and Chinese cuisines, microwave, baking.

Faculty: School director Tova Aran and a teaching staff of food writers, home economics instructors, restaurant chefs, pastry chefs, and caterers.

Costs: Classes for English-speaking groups are about 35 Shekels per person.

Location: In the heart of Tel-Aviv.

Contact: Tova Aran, Tnuva, Training Center for Food Culture, 47 Ben-Gurion Blvd., Tel-Aviv, Israel; (972) 3 5243 157/8, Fax 972 3 5230 055.

ITALY

ADA PARASILITI COOKING SCHOOL
Milan, Italy

September-June

This school, established in 1969, offers demonstration (limit 15) and participation (limit 8) courses that emphasize Italian and international cuisines. The
number of sessions varies from course to course, with each session scheduled from
2 or 3 pm until 4:30 or 5 pm. Classes are held in an apartment used exclusively
for the school. The kitchen has an overhead mirror and ample work space.

Specialties: Italian and international cuisines.

Faculty: Ada Parasiliti is an Accredited Teacher with the IACP.

Costs: The cost of each lesson ranges from $60 to $100.

Location: The school is situated in the historical center of Milan.

Contact: Ada Parasiliti, L'Angolo-Scuola di Cucina, Via Ponte Vetero 13, 20121
Milan, Italy; (39) 2 876398.

L'AMORE DI CUCINA ITALIANA
Inland Services, Inc.
Pomino, Tuscany, Italy

April-May, September-October

This one-week program, first held in 1992 and scheduled six times a year,
features hands-on cooking instruction in Italian regional and Tuscan cuisine as
well as shopping expeditions and winery visits. Five classes (limit 14 students),
three hours each, alternate mornings and afternoons in the kitchen of the Locanda
di Praticino and are followed by a meal of the foods prepared. Emphasis is on
preparation, presentation, and historical aspects of cooking. Other activities
include visits to an outdoor market and one of Italy's fine wineries; a trip to
producers of cheese and olive oil; shopping at a well-known clothing manufacturer and ceramic, porcelain, and silk factories; museum and castle tours; a
concert, opera, or ballet performance in Florence; and dining at fine restaurants.

Specialties: Tuscan and regional Italian cuisines.

Faculty: Cristina Blasi and Gabriella Mari, who own a cooking school in Florence
and are authors of a book relating to the cooking of ancient Rome; wine and olive
oil experts.

Costs: Land cost is $2,450 ($2,250 for non-cook guest), which includes meals,
double occupancy lodging ($300 single supplement) at the historic Locanda di
Praticino, and all planned activities. A $400 deposit is required with balance due
30 days prior to departure. Cancellations more than 60 days prior forfeit $100; no
refund thereafter.

Location: Pomino, near Michelangelo's birthplace, is approximately a half-hour
drive from Florence.

Contact: l'Amore di Cucina Italiana, Inland Services, Inc., 630 Third Ave., New
York, NY 10017; (212) 687-9898.

ANNA TERESA CALLEN ITALIAN COOKING SCHOOL (page 74)

BADIA A COLTIBUONO
Siena, Italy

May, June, September, October

Founded in 1985 by Lorenza de' Medici, "The Villa Table" is a five-session demonstration/participation course in regional Italian cooking. Twelve courses (limit 14 students) are scheduled annually at Badia a Coltibuono (the Abbey of the Good Harvest), an 11th century villa on a 2,000-acre estate. During the week, mornings begin with a three to four-hour cooking class conducted by Signora de' Medici in her large teaching kitchen, followed by a five-course lunch of the morning's preparation. Students are taught a simple, elegant, and organized approach to cooking and entertaining. Fresh salad greens, vegetables, and herbs from the large kitchen garden are used in the lessons, as are Coltibuono's other products, especially its extra virgin olive oil. The estate is primarily a winery and appropriate vintages are tasted and discussed. In the afternoons, participants visit local producers of meats, cheese, breads and pastries, and tour Siena and other Tuscany attractions. The first and last nights' dinners are held in Badia's dining room and on the other evenings participants are invited to dine at private villas and castles as her guests.

Specialties: Regional Italian cooking emphasizing the Tuscan area.

Faculty: Lorenza de' Medici, who owns the villa and lives there during the summer with her husband and four children, teaches all classes. She has written several cookbooks as well as a series of 12 practical cooking manuals.

Costs, Accommodations: The all-inclusive (except airfare) fee is $4,200 single occupancy, $3,600 double. Participants are houseguests at Badia a Coltibuono and stay in the private guestrooms, overlooking the villa's gardens. The rooms have been redecorated and most are single with full modern bathrooms.

Location: On a hill in Tuscany, overlooking more than 2,000 acres of woods, olive groves, vineyards, and farmhouses. The library contains books on wine, cooking, and art and a swimming pool and sauna are available to guests. The estate is approximately 20 miles north of Siena and 40 miles south of Florence.

Contact: Lorenza de' Medici, Badia a Coltibuono, 53013 Gaiole in Chianti (Siena) Italy; Fax (39) 577 749235 *or* The Villa Table, c/o Judy Terrell, 7707 Willow Vine Ct., #219, Dallas, TX 75230; (214) 373-1161, Fax (214) 373-1162.

BED AND BREAKFAST IN TUSCANY
FOOD AND WINE APPRECIATION PROGRAM
Montevettolini, Italy

May, October, November

Since 1985, restaurateur and caterer Lucia Ana Luhan has offered one-week and mini-courses in Italian cuisine and wine at her family farm (also operated as a bed and breakfast) in Italy. The week-long demonstration/participation courses (limit 8 to 10 students), which are scheduled three or four times a year, are taught by Ms. Luhan with demonstrations by visiting chefs. The week includes five days of morning (9:30 am to noon) classes, with afternoons reserved for shopping in local markets and touring local attractions. The mini-courses are devoted to such topics as olive oil, pastas, and pizza. In October, students have the opportunity to pick grapes for the home production of Chianti wine; those who visit in November pick olives and make olive oil. Class slide lectures cover such topics as making Parmesan cheese, pasta, and balsamic vinegar. Sessions are conducted in the farm's kitchen, which has individual work areas.

Specialties: Italian cuisine.

Faculty: Lucia Luhan completed her studies for a master's degree in public relations from Boston University and studied in Europe, Mexico, and South America. She is proprietor of What's Cooking? in Newport Beach and Luciana's Ristorante in Dana Point.

Costs, Accommodations: The $1,540 fee includes lodging and most meals, from 4 pm on the first day to noon on the seventh day. If rooms are available, those who wish to extend their stay pay the regular bed and breakfast daily rate of $100 single, $130 double occupancy.

Location: The farm is situated in the wine country of central Italy, a five-minute drive from the spa town of Montecatini Terme, less than 30 minutes from Florence, Pisa, Pescia, Viareggio, Vinci, and about 90 minutes from Siena and the Italian Riviera.

Contact: Food and Wine Appreciation Program, B & B in Tuscany, 24312 Del Prado, Dana Point, CA 92629; (714) 661-6500. In Italy (39) 572 628 817.

CHIANTI IN TUSCANY — ITALIAN COOKERY AND WINE
Chianti, Tuscany, Italy
March-October

Since 1986, Countesses Paola and Simonetta Bevilacqua de'Mari have conducted one-week courses in northern and southern Italian cookery, Italian language, and painting at their home, Podere Le Rose. Courses run continuously from spring through fall and cookery courses are taught in English the third week of each month. Classes are held from 9:30 am to 2 pm, Monday through Friday, and consist of both demonstration (limit 20 students) and participation (limit 8) sessions followed by a lunch of the foods prepared. Instruction covers home-style and light Italian cuisine with emphasis on fresh ingredients and easy-to-make recipes, including pasta, gnocchi, focaccia, risottos, bruschettas, vegetables, cakes, and biscotti. Other activities include a wine selection lesson, shopping at a local market, and a visit to a Chianti Classico winery.

Specialties: Northern and southern Italian cooking.

Faculty: Simonetta and Paola Bevilacqua de'Mari di Altamura learned from their mother, Contessa Maria Giulia di Bevilacqua, and worked with Italian restaurant chefs. Alvaro Luddi, formerly a chef in a well-known Tuscan restaurant, and guest chefs also instruct and wine lessons are given by father Luigi de'Mari. The school is accredited by the Italian Ministry of Foreign Affairs.

Costs, Accommodations: Cost of five days of cooking classes is 410,000 Lira. Saturday-Saturday lodging at Podere Le Rose ranges from 210,000 Lira to

350,000 Lira (280,000 Lira to 490,000 Lira) for a shared room without (with) breakfast and from 1,540,000 Lira to 1,820,000 Lira for a shared hotel room with breakfast. Single rooms are available. Complete package cost of 1,450,000 Lira includes classes, lodging, full board, ground transportation, and planned excursions. A 30 percent deposit is required and full refund, less expenses, is granted written cancellations received at least 30 days prior to course.

Location: The 13th century Podere Le Rose, a restored Italian farmhouse, is in Poggio S. Polo, Gaiole, half an hour from Siena and an hour from Florence.

Contact: Simonetta de'Mari di Altamura, Chianti in Tuscany, Centro Pontevecchio, Podere Le Rose, Poggio S. Polo 2, 53013 Lecchi - Gaiole, Italy; (39) 577 746152 *or* (39) 55 294511, Fax (39) 55 2396887.

COOKHAMPTON (page 77)

COUNT TASCA'S COOKERY COURSES AT REGALEALI
Palermo, Sicily, Italy

April, May, November

Marchesa Anna Tasca Lanza, the daughter of Count Tasca d'Almerita, offers five-day demonstration/participation courses (limit 12 students) in Sicilian family cooking in her ancestral family home, Regaleali. The courses are scheduled from Monday afternoon through Saturday morning during April, May, and November, with other dates (exclusive of the summer months) available for private group bookings. Mornings are devoted to cooking instruction and afternoons include visits to archeological sites and programs on the estate's agricultural enterprises, which include the production of Regaleali wines, ricotta cheese, and breads.

Specialties: Sicilian family cooking.

Faculty: Mario Lo Menzo, the family chef, as well as other local or guest chefs.

Costs: The $2,000 cost includes all meals and lodging at Regaleali.

Location: The Regaleali estate is located near Palermo, in the center of Sicily.

Contact: Marchesa Anna Tasca Lanza, Viale Principessa Giovanna, 9, 90149 Palermo (Mondello), Italy; (39) 91 450727, Fax (39) 921 542783.

LA CUCINA AL FOCOLARE
Fattoria Degli Usignoli
Reggello, Tuscany, Italy

February-April, October-November

The 15th-century Fattoria Degli Usignoli conducts one-week culinary vacations that feature hands-on instruction in the villa's converted wine cellar, wine tastings, and tours. A dozen programs a year are offered, each limited to 16 to 20 participants, who attend five 4-hour classes followed by a five-course meal. The emphasis is on Tuscan specialties, including antipasti, pasta, pizza prepared in wood-fired ovens, grill and rotisserie dishes, desserts, and a variety of breads. Afternoons are devoted to teaching tours of outdoor markets, visits to museums and artist's studios, and sightseeing in nearby towns, including Florence. The week concludes with a graduation dinner.

Specialties: Tuscan cuisine and breads.

Faculty: The chefs of The Ristorante Fattoria Degli Usignoli.

Costs: Cost is $2,400 ($1,950, $1,800, $1,550), which includes single (double, triple, quadruple) occupancy apartment with private kitchen at Fattoria Degli Usignoli, all meals, all planned activities, and transportation to and from the airport in Rome. A $400 deposit is required with balance due 45 days prior to departure. Cancellations more than 45 days prior forfeit $100, penalty thereafter is $400.

Location: The Fattoria, which was built by the friars of Vallombrosa and produces its own Chianti and extra virgin olive oil, is situated on 55 acres overlooking the Valdarno Valley, approximately 8 miles south of Florence. Amenities include tennis courts, equestrian stables, a pool, and vineyards.

Contact: Peggy Markel, La Cucina al Focolare, Box 646, Boulder, CO 80306-0646; (800) 988-2851, Fax (303) 440-8598.

CUCINA TOSCANA
Florence, Italy
Year-round

Established in 1983, this travel service custom tailors gastronomic excursions in Italy for groups that range from 2 to 25. The one day to one month trips, which can be scheduled at any time of the year, combine private food and wine tastings with other interests of the group, including antique hunting and garden visits. Cooking demonstrations are held in restaurant kitchens.

Specialties: Italian cuisine.

Faculty: Proprietor Faith Heller Willinger has studied Italian cooking for 15 years and is author of *Eating in Italy: A Traveler's Guide to the Gastronomic Pleasures of Northern Italy.*

Costs: Rates begin at $250 per day plus expenses for up to three people. Group day rates, which include meals and transportation, start at $150 per person. Rates for longer trips are lower.

Location: A truffle trip in Piemonte is scheduled each winter, Tuscan day trips are offered frequently, and other trips have visited Venice and Sicily.

Contact: Faith Heller Willinger, Cucina Toscana, Via Della Chiesa, 7, 50125 Florence, Italy; (39) 55 2337014 (phone and fax).

ENRICO FRANZESE'S COOKING CLASSES
Amalfi, Italy
January-March

Established in 1991, this one-week culinary vacation features five three-hour morning demonstrations, daily lunches of the foods prepared, three afternoon guided excursions along the coast, and an afternoon and evening in Sorrento. Classes are held in the Luna Convento Hotel's Saracen Tower, which once guarded the Amalfi harbour.

Specialties: Regional Italian cuisine.

Faculty: Enrico Franzese trained at the Cipriani in Venice and the Hassler in Rome. He won the 1990 Parma Ham Chef's Competition in Bologna and appears on Italian television. He is assisted by British cooking teacher Jennifer Aston.

Costs, Accommodations: Cost of the Sunday evening to Saturday morning program is approximately $1,600, which includes breakfasts, all but one lunch, and two dinners, planned excursions, transportation from/to Sorrento, and first class double occupancy lodging and private bath at the Luna Convento Hotel, a restored 13th century convent situated a short walk from town.

Location: Amalfi, an historic fishing village and resort area on Italy's west coast, is about 150 miles south of Rome and 40 miles south of Naples. In-town attractions include a 9th century cathedral and the Cloister of Paradise, which contains ancient marble and mosaics. Within a 30-mile radius are the excavations of Pompeii, the Greek temples at Paestum, and the ruins on the Isle of Capri.

Contact: Judy Terrell, 7707 Willow Vine Ct., #219, Dallas, TX 75230; (214) 373-1161, Fax (214) 373-1162.

GIULIANO BUGIALLI'S COOKING IN FLORENCE
Florence, Italy

May, July, September, October, December

This cooking school was founded in 1973 to combine cooking instruction with an immersion in the life and culture of Italy. Week-long participation programs, limited to 20 students, are taught by Giuliano Bugialli in his professional kitchen. Recipes and activities vary with each program so that individuals can sign up for two consecutive programs without repetition. Mr. Bugialli also teaches in New York (page 86).

The week-long programs begin on Sunday with dinner at a noted Florentine restaurant and feature five 4-hour morning participation classes followed by a full lunch with appropriate wines. Each daily class begins with a discourse on the dishes to be prepared and discussion of the previous night's menu. Students select the dishes they want to prepare from the day's roster of recipes, which includes everyday and special occasion courses. The selection always includes pasta, antipasti, breads, pastries, main dishes, vegetables, and seasonal specialties. Other events may include a guided tour through the central market, sightseeing, a country excursion, a truffle search, or a trip to Lucca, Siena, or one of the hill towns of Tuscany. Evenings are devoted to dinner at an elegant restaurant or rustic tratorria with specially selected menus. Students are awarded diplomas at the final gala dinner. The Christmas in Florence program features four cooking classes followed by lunch and wines. Recipes include winter and traditional holiday dishes and students are invited to assist in preparing the special holiday dinner. The group attends Christmas eve midnight mass, dines on a traditional late supper, and celebrates Christmas with a feast at Giuliano's home. Each year Giuliano conducts a tour to a certain part of Italy. The ten-day fall tour includes sightseeing and dining on local specialties.

Specialties: Italian cuisine.

Faculty: Giuliano Bugialli is author of *The Fine Art of Italian Cooking*, Tastemaker-award winners *Giuliano Bugialli's Classic Techniques of Italian*

Cooking and *Giuliano Bugialli's Foods of Italy*, and *Bugialli on Pasta*. He was honored with the Caterina di Medici award and the Ponte Vecchio award. Other faculty includes Henry Weinberg, who conducts art and sightseeing tours, and Lella Bugialli. A full kitchen crew provides assistance.

Costs, Accommodations: The week-long (Sunday evening to Sunday morning) and Christmas program fee is approximately $3,000 ($2,300 for non-cook guest), which includes three meals daily (one free evening excluded), planned excursions, and first class double occupancy accommodations (single room supplement $400) for seven nights in the Hotel Augustus. All programs require a $450 deposit, which includes a $50 nonrefundable registration fee with balance due 90 days prior. Full refund, less $50 fee, is granted those who cancel prior to the payment due date; no refunds thereafter.

Location: The hotel and school are situated in the center of Florence. The Hotel Augustus is located in a small piazza near the Arno and Ponte Vecchio, a short walk from cafes, shops, and museums.

Contact: Giuliano Bugialli's Cooking in Florence, P.O. Box 1650, Canal St. Station, New York, NY 10013; (212) 966-5325.

GRITTI PALACE COOKING COURSES
Venice, Italy

July

This five-day course, begun in 1974, is offered four or five times during each summer. Demonstration classes (limit 16 to 18 students) are conducted at the hotel each morning, Monday through Friday, in a specially equipped room with overhead mirrors. The instructor explores a precise theme that is closely connected with his or her professional activity and usually has a regional or other specialty bias. Representative titles include Mantuan Cooking From Refined to Traditional, The Great Tuscan Cuisine, and Milanese Cooking of Porta Cicca. The Gritti Palace sommelier presents and discusses two wines at every lesson and guest lecturers are scheduled from time to time. At noon, students sample the foods prepared, usually a full Italian lunch.

Specialties: Italian cuisine.

Faculty: Course director is writer, journalist, and cooking history expert Massimo Alberini, an Italian consultant for Time-Life International who has published 25 books, including *Storia del pranzo all' Italiana* and *Paste e Pizza*. Other faculty members are well-known guest chefs and culinary experts.

Costs, Accommodations: The five-day course fee is 450,000 Lira, which includes food, wine, and taxes. Participants receive a 20% discount on their room rate at the Gritti Palace.

Location: The deluxe Hotel Gritti Palace was once the palace of Doge Andrea Gritti in the 15th century. It is located 10 minutes from swimming pools, beaches, and tennis courts.

Contact: Gritti Palace Cooking Courses, Hotel Gritti Palace, Campo S.M. del Giglio, 2467, 30124 Venice, Italy; (39) 41 794611 *or* Cigahotels, 745 Fifth Ave., Suite 1201, New York, NY 10151-0007; (800) 221-2340 *or* (212) 935-9540.

ITALIAN COUNTRY COOKING CLASSES
WITH DIANA FOLONARI
Positano, Italy

May-June, September-October

Since 1980, Diana Folonari has taught one-week participation (limit 12 students) courses in Italian cuisine at her home. Recipes include veal, fish, and chicken dishes as well as vegetables, pasta, and fruits. Students meet from 9:30 am to 2 pm on Saturday, Sunday, Monday, Thursday and Friday, and prepare and dine on a multi-course meal. Tuesday is free for swimming and sightseeing. On Wednesday evening the class prepares homemade pizza and country dishes for cooks and their guests. A farewell dinner is held at the San Pietro Hotel.

Specialties: Italian cuisine.

Faculty: Diana and Vic Folonari.

Costs, Accommodations: The fee for the cooking classes is $1,500; cost of eight nights at the Villa Franca Hotel (other hotels available on request) is $462 per person; one-way transfer from Naples is $100. A $300 deposit must accompany enrollment with balance due 60 days prior to course. Those who cancel more than 60 days prior receive a full refund less $100.

Location: The Folonari home is located on a cliff overlooking the Mediterranean at Via del Canovaccio 10. Positano is accessible by train and limousine from airports in Rome and Naples.

Contact: E & M Associates, 211 E. 43rd St., New York, NY 10017; (800) 223-9832 *or* (212) 599-8280.

ITALIAN CUISINE IN FLORENCE
Florence, Italy

Year-round

Founded in 1983, this school offers four and five-day participation courses (limit eight students) that emphasize methods used in the Italian tradition complemented by historical and cultural anecdotes. The three to four-hour morning lessons are held in Masha Innocenti's large apartment kitchen, which overlooks her herb garden. Menus are usually four to five courses and feature seasonal fruits and vegetables. Gourmet I, a series of five daily four-hour lessons, concentrates on the characteristics of regional and classic Italian cuisine. Gourmet II, a series of five daily four-hour lessons, emphasizes the more sophisticated New Italian Cuisine with many recipes taken from the northern regions. Extra time is spent learning presentation and decorating techniques for various foods. Italian Desserts, a series of four daily three-hour sessions, is designed to acquaint the student with the many varieties of Italian first dishes and desserts. Preparations vary with the seasons and include cookies, pastries, tartes, and puddings. Each lesson is followed by lunch with an appropriate wine. Throughout the year a special Combination Week is offered, dedicated to all three courses in reduced form: two days of regional, two days of nouvelle Italian, and one day devoted to Italian desserts. Students have free time in the afternoons and evenings to visit Florence and the surrounding areas.

Specialties: Italian regional cuisine, pasticceria, desserts.

Faculty: Masha Innocenti, a Certified Teacher and Certified Culinary Professional of the IACP, holds a diploma from Scuola di Arte Culinaria Cordon Bleu
and is a member of the Associazione Italiana Sommeliers and the Commanderie
des Cordons Bleus de France.

Costs, Accommodations: Gourmet I 980,000 Lira; Gourmet II 980,000 Lira;
Italian Desserts course 700,000 Lira; Combination Week 980,000 Lira. Reduced
rates are available for more than one course. Arrival should be planned for the
Sunday prior to the first class and hotel information may be obtained from the
school. A nonrefundable 30% deposit is required; balance is due six weeks prior
to program. Payments should be made by bank check in Italian currency and no
personal checks are accepted.

Location: The school is located a short distance from the center of Florence.

Contact: Mrs. Masha Innocenti, Italian Cuisine in Florence, Via Trieste 1,
Florence, 50139, Italy; (39) 55 480041 (phone and fax). For information write to:
Mr. William Grossi, RDI, Ancramdale, NY 12503; (518) 329-1141.

JEAN BRADY COOKING SCHOOL (page 11)

KAY PASTORIUS SCHOOL OF CUISINE (page 13)

MANGIA: THE ART OF EATING AND COOKING ITALIAN
Florence, Italy

September-July

Since 1988, Cordon Bleu-trained cook Judy Witts has taught Italian-Tuscan
cooking "Rustica" in her Florentine apartment, which overlooks the central
market. Four-hour single session demonstration/participation classes, offered
year-round except August, are limited to ten students of all levels. One-week
classes, held in summer and fall, include a tour of the wine country. Three-day
sessions are also available.

Specialties: Italian regional cuisine.

Faculty: Judy Witts, a member of the IACP, received training in pastry at the
Stanford Court Hotel in San Francisco.

Contact: Judy Witts, Mangia, Via Taddea, 31, 50123 Florence, Italy; Phone or
Fax (39) 55 29 25 78.

MARIA BATTAGLIA — LA CUCINA ITALIANA, INC.
Milan, Verona, Sicily, Tentino-Alto Adige, Italy

Spring and fall

This school, which opened in the U.S. and Italy in 1981, offers one-week
regional Italian cooking courses in Milan, Verona, Sicily, and Tentino-Alto
Adige. Each course features four demonstration/participation three-hour classes
conducted in modern, fully-equipped kitchens. All classes conclude with a meal
of the recipes prepared, served with appropriate wines. The Milan course

emphasizes fall seasonal recipes representative of northern, central, and southern Italy. Other activities include visits to specialty food and wine shops, shopping at fish and produce markets, a truffle hunt in the Piedmont region, dining in fine restaurants and rustic trattorias, and trips to observe the making of cheese, wine, and pastry. The Verona course, which emphasizes fall regional specialties, features demonstrations of gnocchi, pastry, and pasta, as well as excursions to an antique rice mill and Trentino-Alto Adige for demonstrations of cheese and salami. Participants dine in family-owned restaurants and the Twelve Apostles Restaurant with chef-owner Giorgio Gioco. The Sicily course features spring recipes and demonstrations of marzipan, cannoli, ice cream, and Sicilian pastries. Visits include the fishing docks, vineyards, and markets. The Trentino Alto-Adige course features spring dishes, a trip to Merano and Trento, vineyard visits, and sausage and pastry demonstrations.

Specialties: Italian regional cooking with wine seminars.

Faculty: Maria Battaglia studied Italian cooking in Bologna, Florence, Messina, Sardinia, and Milan, where she lived for several years. She has been a recipe consultant and spokesperson for Contadina Foods and was awarded the Diploma Di Merito by the Federazione Italiana Cuochi in Milan and Verona. She is certified by the IACP and is a member of Les Dames d'Escoffier International.

Costs: Enrollment fee, which does not include transportation to and from Italy, is $4,150 ($3,950 for non-cook) for the Milan course and $3,200 ($3,000) for the other courses. A $300 deposit is required with $50 nonrefundable and the remaining $250 refundable more than eight weeks prior to course. Accommodations are provided at the centrally located four-star Palace Hotel in Milan, the three-star Villa Quaranta 17th century villa just outside Verona, the three-star Villa Sant'Andrea in Taormina, Sicily, and the three-star Stella d'Alpi in Trento.

Location: Milan, Verona, Sicily, and Trentino-Alto Adige, Italy.

Contact: Maria Battaglia, La Cucina Italiana, Inc., One Prudential Plaza, Ste. 1945, 130 E. Randolph Dr., Chicago, IL 60601; (312) 819-4121, Fax (312) 819-4113.

MASTER CLASSES IN VENICE
WITH MARCELLA AND VICTOR HAZAN
Venice , Italy

April-July, September-October

This five-day participation Master Class, scheduled once a month and limited to six students, follows a wide-ranging, loosely structured format, focusing on the fundamental techniques and improvisation of classic Italian cuisine. The first day is dedicated to a detailed visit to the Rialto market that concludes in a multi-course seafood banquet at one of Venice's best restaurants. Cooking class begins the following day and continues each morning for a total of five 5-hour sessions. During each class, Victor Hazan presents and discusses rare wines from their cellar.

Specialties: Italian breads and cuisine; Venetian specialties.

Faculty: Well-known Italian cook Marcella Hazan, author of *Marcella's Italian Kitchen* and other books.

Costs, Accommodations: Cost of the Master Class is $1,750 and reservations are accepted up to two years in advance. A $200 deposit is required, which becomes nonrefundable when class date is confirmed and accepted. Balance is due 120 days prior. Cancellations more than 45 days prior receive a 60% refund unless space can be filled.

Location: The Hazans' home atop a 16th century palazzo.

Contact: Susan Cox, Hazan Classics, P.O. Box 285, Circleville, NY 10919; (914) 692-7104, Fax (914) 692-2659.

MARY BETH CLARK — THE INTERNATIONAL COOKING SCHOOL OF ITALIAN FOOD AND WINE
Bologna, Italy and New York, New York
June, July, September, and October (Italy); year-round (New York)

Since 1987, Mary Beth Clark has offered a four or seven-day gastronomic course in La Cucina Italiana conducted at The International Cooking School Of Italian Food And Wine in Bologna. Each course is limited to 18 participants, combines cooking classes and excursions with dining at fine restaurants, and concludes with the preparation of a gala dinner where students are awarded certificates. During June, July, September, and October, four and seven-day courses are held in the modern, professional kitchen facilities. The four 5-hour participation sessions cover traditional, home style, and new light Italian cuisines with emphasis on fresh seasonal ingredients and easy-to-make recipes. Courses include: The Basics of Italian Cooking (seven days), Great Italian Classics, Wines and Truffles (four days). Each session features a discussion, demonstration, and hands-on preparation and concludes with a full meal and appropriate wines. A variety of other activities are scheduled during the program, including a walk through Bologna's food markets, an olive oil tasting and cheese class, a winery tour, visits to cheese manufacturers, and a one-day excursion to Venice. Students dine at specially selected restaurants, including a well-known farmhouse and trattoria. The course concludes with the preparation of a gala dinner where students receive certificates. Those in the October course participate in Italian classes and a wine and truffle festival with a special cooking class on preparing game and truffles, a private cooking class at La Frasca, and a private tour and tasting at Ca' del Bosco.

Mary Beth Clark also gives private cooking classes in New York. Instruction is designed to meet the student's needs and emphasizes technique and seasonal ingredients. Ingredient selection, storage, advance preparation, and menu design are covered.

Specialties: Regional Italian cuisines, regional Chinese cuisines, Indonesian cuisines, diet cooking, wine and champagne tastings.

Faculty: Mary Beth Clark is owner and managing director of The International Cooking School Of Italian Food And Wine and owner of International Food And Wine Consultants, Inc., a marketing and consulting firm for food manufacturers, retailers, and restaurants. She is chef-trained, has taught cooking since 1977, is co-author of *Immune Power Diet*, and is a Certified Food Writer, Certified Cooking Teacher, and Certified Culinary Professional. Other La Cucina Italiana instructors, all with at least 15 years' experience, include restaurant chef Emilio Volcan, pastry chef Fabio Minelli, and pasta specialists Adis Baroni and Dina Benini.

Costs, Accommodations: Fee is $2,650 ($2,150 for non-cooking guest) for the seven-day Bologna course and $1,950 ($1,700) for the four-day course, which includes planned activities, transportation during the program, most meals, and first class double occupancy (single supplement $455/seven-day, $310/four-day) modern hotel lodging. Airfare is not included. A $300 deposit is required to reserve a space with the balance due 45 days prior to trip. Penalty charge is $150 for cancellation 45 days or more prior to tour, $300 for cancellation 31 to 44 days prior, no refund thereafter. Full refund, less administrative fee, is granted if space is resold. Private or semi-private cooking classes or wine/champagne tastings in New York are $150 per 3-hour session, plus the cost of ingredients. A $50 deposit must accompany registration and refund is granted cancellations at least one week prior to class or a substitute may be sent.

Location: The hotel in Bologna is situated in the center of the city, convenient to shopping and dining and located 1½ hours from Florence, 2½ hours from Milan, and 4 hours from Rome. Private classes in New York are held in private homes.

Contact: Mary Beth Clark, The International Cooking School Of Italian Food And Wine, 300 E. 33 St., Suite 10J, New York, NY 10016; (212) 779-1921, Fax (212) 779-3248.

P. K. SHELDON CULINARY TOURS (page 18)

LA ROMITA SCHOOL OF ART, INC.
Terni, Italy

September

Founded as a painting school in 1966 in a 16th century monastery converted to modern quarters, La Romita began offering an annual two-week cooking school in the summer of 1989. The program, which features the regional foods of Umbria, is limited to 10 to 12 students per instructor and conducted in the kitchens of Restaurant Lu Somaru. Class sessions emphasize simplicity and quality and include introductory lectures, demonstrations, and hands-on preparation of a variety of dishes, including appetizers, pasta, fish, fowl, meat, vegetables, sauces, and pizzas. Field trips to wineries, pasta and pastry shops, and bakeries are scheduled as well as visits to trattorias to sample their specialties.

Specialties: Regional cuisine of Umbria.

Faculty: Instruction is provided by Rossana Rossetti, owner of Restaurant Lu Somaru, and her staff of chefs.

Costs, Accommodations: The $2,000 cooking school tuition includes ground transportation, double occupancy lodging, and most meals. A $300 deposit must accompany registration with balance due eight weeks prior to session. Written cancellations more than 30 days prior receive a full refund less $50; thereafter a 30% penalty is charged. Students are lodged in dormitory rooms in La Romita and meals are served on the open porch.

Location: Situated between Rome and Florence in the Umbrian mountainside above Terni, La Romita is a few miles from Spoleto, Orvieto, Perugia, Assisi, Bevagna, Viterbo, Todi, and Lake Piediluco.

Contact: La Romita School of Art, Inc., 1712 Old Town NW, Albuquerque, NM 87104; (505) 243-1924.

SARAH MONICK CULINARY TOURS (page 197)

SCUOLA DI ARTE CULINARIA CORDON BLEU
Florence, Italy
Year-round

Established in 1985 as a branch of the Italian Cordon Bleu School, this school offers three-session demonstration/participation courses in Italian cooking and six-session courses in Italian and Tuscan cooking. The three-hour sessions are scheduled weekly and limited to 12 students, who prepare a whole menu or work on a specific topic. Topics depend on the season and include Italian vegetable and fish dishes, pasta, pasta sauces, vegetable and bread soups, lasagna, risotto, and the history of Italian cooking. Instruction is given in Italian, French, or English and lunch or dinner follows the class. The school's other courses, taught in Italian, include International Cooking I (eight sessions) and II (ten sessions), Pastry (six sessions), and short courses in ice cream, chocolate, fish and seafood, baking, party menus, and other topics. A diploma is granted non-Italian students who complete six lessons and the Cordon Bleu Diploma is awarded students who complete both International Cooking courses and the Pastry course. The time schedule of classes for foreign students is flexible. Facilities include a kitchen-laboratory with modern equipment and demonstration area, a wine and food tasting room, and a library. Customized programs are available for groups and individuals.

Specialties: International, Italian, and Tuscan cuisines, pastry.

Faculty: Cristina Blasi and Gabriella Mari are Cordon Bleu teachers, wine tasters, and oil experts who emphasize the historical aspects of cooking. They have written a book about the cooking of ancient Rome, are members of the International Cordon Bleu Association, and are supervisors of a re-enactment of the banquet in honor of Maria De'Medici, held in October, 1600.

Costs: Tuition ranges from 80,000 Lira to 120,000 Lira; private lessons range from 120,000 Lira to 200,000 Lira. A 30% deposit is required with balance due at start of course. The school secretary can organize tours in and around Florence and help students find lodging.

Location: Central Florence, a two-minute walk from the Duomo.

Contact: Gabriella Mari, Director, Scuola di Arte Culinaria Cordon Bleu, Via di Mezzo, 55/r, 50121 Florence, Italy; ((39) 55 2345468, Fax (39) 55 280491.

SICILIAN COOKING ADVENTURE
Catania, Sicily, Italy
April and May

Marina Tudisco offers a nine-day, eight-night culinary travel program — Eat Italian at Least Once a Week — that features three 3-hour morning participation classes (limit 12 students), followed by a lunch of the foods prepared. Other activities include a trip up the slopes of the active volcano, Mt. Etna; a visit to Caltagirone, the ceramics center of Sicily; an afternoon excursion to Taormina; a full day archeological tour of Syracuse; sightseeing in Catania; and dinners at specialty restaurants. Mediterranean Cooking, an abbreviated course for English-speaking foreigners living in Italy, is also offered from time to time.

Specialties: Sicilian cuisine.

Faculty: Marina Tudisco has been director and instructor of the Cordon Bleu Culinary Arts School in Catania since 1978. She studied with Enrica Jarratt at the Cordon Bleu in Rome, is Accademico della Cucina Italiana e Commandeur des Cordons Bleus de France, and teaches Mediterranean cooking in North America.

Costs, Accommodations: The land price per person, double occupancy, is approximately $2,100 ($1,800 for non-participant); single supplement $350. A $300 deposit is required, which includes a $50 nonrefundable fee; balance is due 90 days prior. Full refund, less fee, is granted cancellations prior to payment due date; no refunds thereafter. All payments should be made by bank check in American currency; no personal checks accepted. Participants are lodged at the Grand Hotel Excelsior in Catania.

Location: The hotel and school are located in the center of the city.

Contact: Mr. Davide Ciancio, c/o Nicober Viaggi, Via Androne 43, 95100 Catania, Italy; (39) 95 312164, Fax (39) 95 327936.

THE TASTE OF ITALY
David Viaggi U.S.A.
Urio, Northern Italy

May-September

Since 1992, Italian tour specialist David Viaggi U.S.A. has offered eight-day programs that combine morning cooking and language instruction with afternoon sightseeing excursions. Programs run from Sunday to Sunday every other week and are limited to 10 participants of all levels. Each weekday morning, students receive four hours of instruction in Italian regional cuisines as well as Italian language lessons with emphasis on gourmet vocabulary. Classes are held in the dining room and kitchen of the Villa Sorriso and feature the preparation of a three-course gourmet meal, followed by a lunch of the dishes prepared. Afternoon activities include excursions to the lake areas of Como, Maggiore, Lugano, and Garda; boat tours of Lake Como and Lake Maggiore; and tours of nearby villas and palaces. Saturday is spent shopping and sightseeing in Milan and dinners are at fine restaurants in the lakes area.

Specialties: Italian regional cuisines.

Faculty: Giuliana Maggioni has studied at the Cordon Bleu, Alta Cucina Ipca, the FIE' in Alto Adige and is a pastry chef. Luisa Svandrlik has served as chef at two well-known restaurants in Milan and owns a catering company.

Costs: Land cost is $3,895, which includes double occupancy lodging at the Hotel Regina Olga in Cernobbio, most meals, and all planned activities. Single supplement is $250. A $900 deposit is required within seven days of reservation and balance is due 45 days prior to departure. Written cancellations more than 30 days prior receive full refund less $145 fee.

Location: The Villa Sorriso is in the village of Urio, on the hills overlooking Lake

Como in the Northern Italian Lake Region, five miles from Como and 30 miles from Milan.

Contact: David Viaggi U.S.A., 2162 Wisconsin Ave. N.W., Washington, DC 20007; (800) 243-0611 *or* (202) 333-2907.

A TASTE OF TUSCANY
Tuscany, Italy and Inverness-shire, Scotland
May and October

Since 1991, cookbook author Anna Del Conte and cooking instructor Betsy Newell have conducted one-week courses in regional Italian cuisine at the 4,000-acre Villa Arceno estate. The mostly demonstration courses are scheduled once or twice during the fall harvest and limited to 20 participants. Morning classes cover pasta, polenta, breads, stuffed vegetables, and wild game from the estate. Lunches relate to the morning's lesson and dinner is taken at local restaurants. Afternoon activities may include a trip to a cheesemaker, a tour of the estate's winery and the chianti estate at Castello Brolio, a half-day at Florence's central market, and exploration of artistic and gastronomic sites in Siena, Montepulciano, and Pienza. Non-cooking guests who do not attend classes can shoot pheasant, help harvest and tread the grsapes, ride horses or mountain bikes, play tennis, or swim. Beginning in May, 1993, Friday-Sunday cookery course are scheduled at Alvie House, a manor house in Inverness-shire, Scotland. Limited to eight participants, the classes feature hands-on pasta and bread making.

Specialties: Italian regional cuisine.

Faculty: Anna Del Conte, author of *Gastronomy of Italy, Italian Pantry,* and *A Casa,* and Betsy Newell, owner of a cookery school in London.

Costs: Cost is £1,300, which includes classes and double occupancy lodging at the Villa Arceno and all scheduled activities. Cost of the weekend program is £450 to £500.

Location: The 17th century Villa Arceno, in Chianti, Tuscany, was restored in 1825 and refurbished in 1991 as a luxury class hotel. Alvie House, a 10,500-acre estate, offers fishing, stalking, shooting, and walking.

Contact: Anna Del Conte, 93 Elm Bank Gardens, London, SW13 0NX, England; (44) 81 876 4509.

TASTING ITALY
Chianti, Tuscany, Italy
May and October

Chef Maddalena Bonino, caterer Sara Schwartz, and Tuscan food and wine expert Pia Scavia sponsor this series of one-week Italian cookery courses that are limited to 20 participants and hosted by well-known Italian chefs. Three or four courses are scheduled in May and October at La Chiara di Prumiano, which has a fully-equipped professional kitchen with traditional brick-built bread and pizza oven. Lessons cover pasta, bread making, fish selection and preparation, beef and game, vegetables and salads, and desserts. In addition to six half-day hands-on cooking classes led by the guest chef of the week, tasting sessions explore olive oils, Italian wines, local cheeses, wild mushrooms, and other Italian ingredients.

The program includes an excursion to Florence, Siena, or San Gimignano, and trips to nearby village food festivals. Optional visits to local markets, restaurants, historic churches, and other sites can be arranged. Cookery courses are also planned for other regions of Italy.

Specialties: Italian Tuscan cuisine.

Faculty: Head chefs of London's leading Italian restaurants: Maddalena Bonino from 192, Francesco Zanchetta from Riva, and Claudio Pecorari from Cibo.

Costs, Accommodations: Cost is £635, which includes double occupancy lodging, all meals, and excursion.

Location: La Chiara di Prumiano, a 17th century stone-built country hotel in Chianti's wine-producing region, is a half-hour drive from Florence, Siena, and San Gimignano. Facilities include a swimming pool, horseback riding, vegetable gardens, vineyards, olive groves, and golf nearby.

Contact: Tasting Italy, 5 Stockwell Ave., London, SW9 5SY, England; (44) 71 733 2974 (Maddalena Bonino) *or* (44) 71 627 0475 (Sara Schwartz).

VENETIAN COOKING IN A VENETIAN PALACE
Venice, Italy

January-December

Since 1984, Fulvia Sesani has taught traditional Venetian specialties and artistic cooking at her home in a 13th century Venetian palace. Participation classes (limit eight students) are scheduled on Tuesday and Friday mornings and include a visit to the Rialto market. Topics change each month as follows: special occasion dishes (January), cakes and desserts (February), first courses (March), luncheon menus (April), appetizers (May), main courses (October), dinner parties (November), and cooking for Christmas (December). Students are taught how to create such edible works of art as Christmas trees made of vegetables, landscapes and gowns made of sliced beef and veal, ice cream castles, and human figure bread sculptures. Classes are held in the palace's modern, fully-equipped kitchen and students dine on their preparations in the oval dining room.

Specialties: Traditional Venetian cooking, edible works of art.

Faculty: Fulvia Sesani, a former chemist, has attended more than 100 courses in many countries.

Costs: Classes are $120 each.

Location: The Palazzo Morosini is in the Santa Maria Formosa area of Venice.

Contact: Fulvia Sesani, Palazzo Morosini, Castello 6140, Venice, 30122, Italy; (39) 41 5228923. U.S. Contact: Judy Terrell, 7707 Willow Vine Ct., #219, Dallas, TX 75230; (214) 373-1161, Fax (214) 373-1162.

VILLA MOZART COOKING SCHOOL
Meran, Italy

February-July, September-November

This northern Italian resort, built in 1907 and renovated in 1979, offers monthly one-week cooking courses for groups of eight to ten students. Daily three-hour morning or afternoon participation classes cover Tyrolean and Italian specialties, hors d'oeuvres, pastries, dinner party menus, and personal recipes of the chef de cuisine. A complete meal of the foods prepared follows each class. Other activities include visits to gastronomy shops, fruit and vegetable markets, a winery, old city center, and the surrounding castles and valleys.

Specialties: Tyrolean and Italian specialties, entertaining menus.

Faculty: Mrs. Emmy, chef Raimund Frotscher, and sous-chef Armin Mairhofer.

Costs, Accommodations: Cost is $3,000, which includes meals, room with private bath, and all planned activities.

Location: A residential area of Merano, an officially designated spa in northern Italy near the Swiss and Austrian border in the South Tyrolean region of the Dolomite Alps. Hotel amenities include an indoor swimming pool, sauna, and solarium. Tennis, golf, horse racing, and horseback riding are nearby.

Contact: Judy Terrell, 7707 Willow Vine Ct., #219, Dallas, TX 75070; (214) 373-1161, Fax (214) 373-1162.

MEDITERREAN

THE CUISINE, WINES, AND CULTURE OF THE ISLANDS OF THE WESTERN MEDITERRANEAN
Classical Cruises
From Barcelona to Rome

July

This annual two-week cruise features two or three cooking lectures and demonstrations by a noted chef and wine lectures and tastings by an oenologist.

Specialties: The dishes of Spain, France, and Italy.

Faculty: Previous instructors include Jacques Pépin and David Rosengarten, editor-in-chief of *The Wine and Food Companion.*

Costs, Accommodations: Cost ranges from $3,625 to $4,775, which includes double occupancy stateroom, meals aboard ship, and all planned activities. A $1,000 deposit is required with balance due 90 days prior to departure. Cancellation penalty ranges from $100 (more than 90 days prior) to 10% of total cost (61 to 90 days prior).

Location: Ports of the Western Mediterranean.

Contact: Classical Cruises, 132 E. 70th St., New York, NY 10021; (800) 252-7745 *or* (212) 794-3200.

MEXICO

CULINARY JOURNEY WITH PATRICIA QUINTANA
Oaxaca and Huatulco, Mexico

February, March, and October

Cookbook author and chef Patricia Quintana conducts one-week tours that include demonstrations of Mexican cooking, meals in local restaurants, tours of archaeological sites, and visits to markets and homes of native Indians. Emphasis is on distinctive regional foods, such as breads, hand-ground chocolate, mole sauces, tamales, cheeses, tortillas, and salsas. The October tour is planned to coincide with the Day of the Dead festivities.

Specialties: Mexican cuisine.

Costs, Accommodations: Land cost is about $2,200, which includes meals, double occupancy lodging (single supplement $150), and planned activities.

Location: Oaxaca, Huatulco, and Veracruz.

Contact: Patricia Quintana, Reforma 1355, Mexico 11000, D.F.; (525) 5200714/ 5962626.

THE FLAVORS OF MEXICO
Culinary Adventures, Inc.
Veracruz, Oaxaca, Michoacan, and Puebla, Mexico
January and February

Since 1988, Marilyn Tausend has conducted 5 to 10-day culinary tours that feature classes by cookbook author Diana Kennedy and other specialists in Mexican cuisine. Classes and activities focus on providing an understanding of the foods from a specific region of Mexico and the role of historical events, climate, and topography in the development of a cuisine. On a typical trip, students (limit 10 to 15) attend six or seven classes, each two to four hours in length, and participate in such food-related activities as exploring markets, sharing meals in the homes and restaurants of local families, and other gastronomic excursions. Facilities vary, depending upon the location, and the teaching format ranges from demonstration with limited participation to full participation. The 1993 featured trip is to the state of Vera Cruz in January. A trip to Oaxaca is scheduled for February, with a shorter explorer trip to Puebla planned in between that can be taken either as an extension or separately. Most trips include an overnight stay and class in Mexico City. Trips for professionals, limited to five chefs and other experienced cooks, feature classes with Ms. Kennedy at her ecologically-constructed hillside home in Michoacan.

Specialties: Regional Mexican cuisine.

Faculty: Mexican cooking authority Diana Kennedy, author of *The Art of Mexican Cooking, The Cuisines of Mexico,* and *Mexican Regional Cooking*; María Dolores Torres Izábal of the Instituto de Cultura Gastronomica, an organization of Mexican women who are dedicated to preserving traditional Mexican cookery; traditional Zapotec Indian cook Abigail Mendoza; Socorrita Zorrilla, Oaxaca; Raquel Torres, Veracruz; and other local cooks.

Costs, Accommodations: The cost ranges from approximately $1,000 to $2,500, which includes most transportation in Mexico, double occupancy lodging in small hotels popular with Mexican families, and daily meals that emphasize the diversity of the regional cuisine. Participants may share a room or pay an additional fee for single occupancy. A $300 deposit, of which $100 is nonrefundable, must accompany application with balance due at least one month prior to tour. Cancellations more than two weeks prior forfeit $300 of the balance unless space is filled; no refunds thereafter.

Location: The Veracruz trip centers around the highland capital of Xalupa, with visits to the port city of Veracruz; the small port of Tlacotalpan on the "River of Butterflies"; Papantle, "The Place of Birds", a major center for growing the bean of vanilla orchid; and El Tajin, the ruins of the sacred city of the Totanac Indians. The Oaxaca trip is based in the city of Oaxaca and includes a class in a Zapotec Indian home in the weaving center of Teotitlan del Valle and visits to the ancient Indian cities of Mitla and Monte Alban.

Contact: Marilyn Tausend, Culinary Adventures, Inc., 6023 Reid Dr. N.W., Gig Harbor, WA 98335; (206) 851-7676, Fax (206) 443-9816.

GOURMET AMERICAS
Oaxaca, Mexico and Prague, Czechoslovakia
May-August, December

This tour organization offers culinary and cultural tours that include daily cooking demonstrations in homes and restaurants, dining at traditional restaurants, and tours to sites of culinary and historic interest. One-week Oaxaca tours include seven classes, where participants are taught how to make the seven moles and a variety of Oaxacan appetizers, breads, starches, legumes, soups, main courses, drinks, and desserts. Other activities include shopping at local markets, visits to food factories, tours of museums, craft villages, churches, and area ruins, and special events, such as the Guelaguetza dance festival, held in July. The one and two-week Prague tours include daily cooking demonstrations and lectures, visits to breweries and taverns, historical tours, attendance at concerts, operas, theatrical performances, and the Prague Spring Festival, held in May. Students are taught multi-ethnic Czech and Slovak cuisine.

Specialties: Oaxacan regional cuisine; Czech and Slovak cuisine.

Faculty: Local home cooks and restaurant chefs.

Costs: Cost of the Oaxaca tour is $1,575, which includes round trip airfare from San Francisco, deluxe double occupancy lodging at the Caleza Real or Hotel Senorial in downtown Oaxaca, most meals, and all planned activities. Cost of the Prague tour ranges from approximately $1,900 to $2,900, which includes round trip airfare from San Francisco, double occupancy lodging in modern deluxe hotels or the option of staying with a Czech family, most meals, and all planned activities. A $300 deposit is required with balance due six weeks prior to departure. Cancellation penalty ranges from $300 (45 to 55 days prior) to 50% of cost (30 to 44 days prior); no refunds thereafter.

Location: The Oaxaca tour includes Mitla, Monte Alban, Etla, Matatlan, Teotitlan del Valle, and Tialixtac de Cabrera. The Prague itinerary includes five areas: Hradcany, Mala Strana, Stare Mesto, Josefov, and Nove Mesto.

Contact: Ronald Thomas Kent, Director, Gourmet Americas, 908 Fremont Pl., Ste. 2, Menlo Park, CA 94025; (800) 992-3783 *or* (415) 321-8661, Fax (415) 321-5801.

KAY PASTORIUS SCHOOL OF CUISINE (page 13)

SILVIA ZEA COOKING SCHOOL
Mexico City, Mexico

September-June

Since 1981, Silvia Zea has offered demonstration courses (limit 35 students of all levels) in international cuisine, with emphasis on French, Oriental, and Mexican, and participation courses (limit 15 advanced students) in professional techniques for chocolate, cake decoration, breadmaking, and microwave and convection cookery. The three-hour morning sessions meet weekly in a fully-equipped kitchen classroom with overhead mirror and video equipment.

Specialties: A variety of topics, including international cuisines, microwave cookery, and special techniques.

Faculty: Silvia Zea de Gomez has an international chef diploma from the Universidad Iberoamericana in Mexico and is sponsored by microwave applicance manufacturer Sharp de Mexico. She has four experienced assistants.

Costs: Monthly tuition is $75 for demonstration s, $170 for participation courses.

Location: South downtown Mexico, near the floating gardens of Xochimilco and five minutes from the Paraiso Radisson Hotel.

Contact: Silvia Zea, Siracusa #95, Residencial Acoxpa, Mexico, D.F. 14300; (525) 684-7611.

MOROCCO

LA CARAVANE ADVENTURES IN FOOD AND TRAVEL
Morocco

Annual tour in February or November

Since 1983, Kitty Morse has conducted two-week tours (limit 20 participants) of Morocco that emphasize local gastronomy. The itinerary, which includes several days spent along the Kasbah Trail on the edge of the Sahara, features cooking demonstrations by local experts and special meals in private homes or historic locales. Ms. Morse also gives Moroccan culinary demonstrations at schools in California and around the U. S. and was this year invited to lecture on the subject at the Smithsonian Institution.

Specialties: Moroccan cuisine and culture.

Faculty: Kitty Morse was born in Casablanca, Morocco, and is author of *Come with me to the Kasbah: A Cook's Tour of Morocco*. She is a columnist for the *Los Angeles Times* San Diego edition and and is a member of the Southern California Culinary Guild and the Newspaper Food Editors and Writers Association.

Costs, Accommodations: Approximate cost of the guided tour is $3,000, which includes round-trip airfare from New York, land transportation, double occu-pancy deluxe and first class lodging, two meals daily, and all planned activities. A $500 deposit is required.

Location: Tour includes the coastal cities of Casablanca and Essaouira, the historic Imperial cities of Fez, Marrakesh, Meknes, and Rabat, the desert kasbahs of Erfoud, Rissani, Ouarzazate, Taliouine, and Taroudant, and a special excursion to Mirzouga sand dunes.

Contact: Kitty Morse, La Caravane Adventures, P.O. Box 433, Vista, CA 92085-0433; (619) 758-8631.

NETHERLANDS

LA CUISINE FRANCAISE
Amsterdam, Netherlands

September-June

Established in 1980, this school offers demonstration classes (limit 25 students) in French, Italian, and Oriental cuisines. Although classes are generally conducted in Dutch, sessions in English are available for groups of 15 to 25, on request. The class features fresh vegetables, a main course fish dish, and dessert, which are then served in the private dining room.

Specialties: International cuisines.

Faculty: School owner and instructor Patricia I. van den Wall Bake-Thompson was born in Great Britain and studied home economics at Harrow Technical College. She serves as a consultant to food companies.

Costs: Each session is $45, payable in advance. Credit cards accepted.

Location: Situated in an 18th century canal house, which also houses a private restaurant overlooking the gardens of the Herengracht and Keizersgracht, the school is close to the center of town.

Contact: La Cuisine Francaise, Herengracht 314, 1016 CD Amsterdam, Netherlands; (31) 20 6278725, Fax (31) 20 6203491.

NEW ZEALAND

THE EPICUREAN COOKSCHOOL
Auckland, New Zealand

Year-round

Established in 1989 in conjunction with The Epicurean Workshop's specialty cookware store, this school offers approximately 80 demonstration classes (limit 30 students) on a variety of topics, including ethnic cuisines, classics, techniques, and guest chef specialties. Classes are scheduled from 10 am to noon or 6:30 to 8:30 pm in the Workshop's teaching kitchen with overhead mirrors and are single sessions with the exception of a six-session basics course. Hands-on practical classes have recently been established in such specialty subjects as pasta, pastry and bread making. Participation classes for children (limit 10) are also offered.

Specialties: A variety of topics; guest chef specialties; classes for children.

Faculty: Directors Catherine Bell and Anne Moginie are graduates of Leith's School in London.

Costs: Single sessions are NZ$50, basics course is NZ$275.

Location: The school is in Newmarket, a major shopping center in Auckland, New Zealand's largest city.

Contact: The Epicurean Workshop, 27 Morrow St., P.O. Box 9255, Newmarket, Auckland, New Zealand; (64) 9 524 0906, Fax (64) 9 524 2017.

PORTUGAL

THE WANDERING SPOON (page 202)

SCOTLAND

TASTE OF TUSCANY (page 223)

TOP TIER SUGARCRAFT
Balloch, Inverness, Scotland

February-November

This school, established by Janet Munslow and Diana Turner in 1986, offers day, evening, and weekend sugarcraft courses. Each course is limited to eight students, who have individual work areas in the school's comfortable classroom. The teaching format is demonstration followed by practical work in the various aspects of cake decoration, including sugarpaste, royal icing, florals, chocolate, piping, marzipan, pastillage, ribbon work, and designing. Classes can be custom-designed to individual or group needs. Day classes are scheduled in the morning (10 am to noon) or all day (10 am to 3 pm); evening classes meet from 7 to 9 pm. The weekend course is held from 10 am to 3 pm on Saturday and Sunday.

Specialties: All aspects of sugarcraft, for the beginner to the professional level; personalized instruction in wedding cakes.

Faculty: Principal teacher Janet Munslow is a graphic designer, British Sugarcraft Guild member, and a judge. Diana Turner is also a member of the British Sugarcraft Guild and has more than ten years of experience in sugarcraft work. Both have won prizes at national and regional competitions.

Costs: The all-day class begins at £25, the two-day course begins at £36, and the two-day professional course begins at £150; the weekend course begins at £35; private instruction by prior arrangement. A full refund is granted those who cancel at least one month prior to class.

Location: A mile from Culloden Battlefield, five miles from Inverness. Local attractions include the Loch Ness monster, Cawdor Castle, Fort George, Nairn.

Contact: Top Tier Sugarcraft, 10 Meadow Rd., Balloch, Inverness, IV1 2JR, Scotland; (44) 463 790456.

SOUTH AFRICA

SILWOOD KITCHEN
CORDONS BLEUS COOKERY SCHOOL
Rondebosch, Cape, South Africa

Year-round

This school for career cooks, founded in 1964, offers three courses for professional cooks: the one-year Certificate course, the one-year Diploma course (for those who've completed the Certificate course), and the one-year Grande Diploma (for those who've completed the Diploma course). All courses begin in January. Students attend practical and theoretical classes from 8:30 am to 3 pm each day and, at the end of each academic year, must pass practical and theoretical examinations. The school is located in a 200-year-old coach-house that was transformed into a demonstration and experimental kitchen to which have been added three more kitchens, a demonstration hall, and a library.

During the first-year Certificate course, students take courses in the theory of cooking and baking, practical cooking and baking, practical icing, nutrition, art of the table, French and Afrikaans menu reading, floral art, wine appreciation, confections, and international cookery. The course is limited to 40 students who are divided into four groups of ten. The Diploma course, for those selected on the basis of merit, is a practical year in which the students participate in running the school and take outside catering and foodservice assignments. During the third year the student is required to go out and apply the knowledge learned the previous two years.

Specialties: Three one-year courses for professional cooks.

Faculty: The 11-member faculty includes school proprietor Mrs. Lesley Faull, cookery instructor Alicia Wilkinson, nutrition instructor Dorothy White, menu reading instructor Ailsa Smith, and practical supervisors Louise Faull, Lee Barty, Sue Durr, Lynette McDonald, Joan Pare, Ansie Kemp, and Shirley Henderson.

Costs: Tuition for those who pay in full by the first day of class is R9,200 for the Certificate course, R3,800 for the Diploma course, and R400 for the Grande Diploma. Quarterly and monthly payment options are available at a higher tuition. A R600 deposit must accompany application and those who cancel before January 1st receive a refund of R100.

Location: East of Cape Town at the intersection of Riverton Rd. and Silwood Rd.

Contact: Mrs. Lesley Faull, Director, Silwood Kitchen, Silwood Rd., Rondebosch, Cape, South Africa; (27) 21 686 4894.

SPAIN

ALAMBIQUE SCHOOL — JUAN ALTIMIRAS
Madrid, Spain

October-June

Established in 1973 by Clara Maria Amezúa, this school offers courses and culinary tours. The 2¹/₂-hour demonstrations (limit 35 students), scheduled in the morning or afternoon once weekly for two to four weeks, cover Sephardic, French, Spanish, and Spanish regional cuisines, rice, pasta, etiquette, protocol, and wine appreciation. Participation sessions are devoted to breadmaking, butchering, and haute cuisine. Chef Alain Gigant conducts several four-session basic and advanced cooking courses and demonstrations for professional cooks during November and two-session basic and advanced Christmas cooking courses in December. Classes for children are also offered. The two teaching kitchens are equipped with microwave, gas, and electric ovens and overhead mirrors.

Alambique also sponsors custom tours for groups of North American visitors. A six-day tour features three morning cooking demonstrations and lunches, dinner and demonstration at one of Madrid's fine restaurants, a restaurant kitchen tour, tour and tastings at a gourmet shop, a private tour of the Royal Palace, visits to the homes of Marquess of Velada and Marquess of Santa Rita, excursions to the fashion design gallery and the Prado Museum, and a Flamenco performance.

Specialties: Spanish and Spanish regional cuisines, French, Mediterranean, and Sephardic cuisines, rice, pasta, cakes and pastries, menus for holidays and entertaining, microwave cookery; children's classes; wine appreciation.

Faculty: Includes Victoria Llamas, Gloria Zunzunegui, Georgette Sournac, Asuncion Dominguez Lopez Cobos, Marga Velasco, Isabel Maestre, Concha de la Rocha, Ana Bensadon, Milagros Balta, Letitia Casans, Tom Giuliano, and Chef Alain Gigant.

Costs: Two-session courses range from 8,000 to 10,000 Pts.; four-session courses range from 14,000 to 16,000 Pts.; children's four-session courses are 8,000 Pts.

Location: The school is in the old part of Madrid, close to many attractions and hotels. Alambique also has outlets in Vigo, Oviedo, Seville, Leon, and Santander.

Contact: Clara Maria Amezúa de Llamas, Alambique, S.A., Calle de la Encarnacion, 2, Madrid 28013, Spain; (34) 1 247 88 27.

ALTAMIRA TOURS — FOODS OF SPAIN
Madrid and Barcelona

July and September

Altamira Tours, founded in 1984, offers two cooking school programs each year in Spain. The eight-day Madrid trip in July, designed for a minimum of 10 students, concentrates on the regional foods of Spain and is held at the Alambique School (page 231), which was established by Chef Juan Altimiras. Students are taught a variety of paellas, tapas, and specialties from the Basque region in northern Spain and the wines that accompany these dishes. Four-hour demonstration and participation classes are held four days a week, usually followed by multi-course meals for participants and accompanying spouses or friends. Afternoons and evenings are reserved for visits to area markets, gourmet shops, special restaurants, and sights of interest.

The nine-day September program, which is devoted to Catalan cuisine and limited to 12 participants, is held at the Restaurant School of Barcelona. Students are assigned individual work spaces for the four 4-hour morning sessions each week. Three course menus are prepared, including desserts, and lunches are served after class in the school's restaurant area. Additional activities include trips to markets, dinners at local Catalan restaurants, and a one-day excursion to the wine country to learn the process of making both sparkling and still wines and how to identify appropriate selections for various dishes.

Specialties: Spanish cuisine.

Faculty: Instructors are expert chefs from the regions represented.

Costs, Accommodations: The approximate cost of $2,500 for each trip includes first class double-occupancy hotel accommodations, and some meals. Single supplement is $250 for the July program, $350 for the September program. Cost of the July trip is based on a minimum of ten participants and there is a $150 supplement for groups of six to nine persons. Price for nonparticipant guests, including airfare, is $1,900. A $250 deposit must accompany reservation, with balance due 60 days prior to departure.

Location: Four-star hotel accommodations in Madrid and Barcelona are centrally located and convenient to the cooking schools.

Contact: Altamira Tours, 860 Detroit St., Denver, CO 80206; (800) 747-2869 *or* (303) 399-3660.

THAILAND

NAPA VALLEY COLLEGE CULINARY ARTS (page 16)

THE THAI COOKING SCHOOL AT THE ORIENTAL
Bangkok, Thailand
Year-round

Founded in 1986, this school offers five-day courses featuring authentic Thai dishes and preparation techniques together with simplified methods and substitute ingredients for ease of application outside Thailand. Facilities include classroom, participation-demonstration room, kitchen, eating area, and herbal garden. Participants arrive on Sunday, attend demonstration and participation sessions from 9 am to noon, Monday through Friday, and depart Friday afternoon. The daily topics are appetizers, salads, soups, fruit and vegetable carving, flower arrangement, curries and condiments, stir-fried, steamed, and fried dishes, desserts, menus, and how to order. Participants also receive information about the background and origin of Thai cuisine. In addition to classes, planned activities include a classical Thai dance performance, a tour of an open air market, guided visits to The Grand Palace and Temples, the Jim Thompson House and Suan Pakkard Palace, and dinners in selected Bangkok restaurants. Special afternoon classes from 2 to 5 pm are available upon request (minimum 15 students).

Specialties: Thai cuisine.

Costs, Accommodations: Cost of the programs, which includes five nights and six days at The Oriental Hotel, most meals, classes, guided trips, airport transfers, tax and service charges, is $1,965 double occupancy ($2,330 single), $1,330 for non-cooking guest; each additional night is $220. A riverboat cruise to Ayudhaya, the capital of ancient Thailand, is available at an additional cost. The $250 reservation deposit is fully refundable if cancellation is received more than one month prior to program. Full payment is due one month prior and those who cancel thereafter forfeit the deposit.

Location: The school, across from the Oriental Hotel and overlooking the Chao Phrya river, is in the city center and 10 to 20 minutes from the main business district and major attractions.

Contact: Manager, The Thai Cooking School at The Oriental, 48 Oriental Ave., Bangkok 10500, Thailand; (66) 236 0400 *or* Mandarin Oriental Hotel Group; (800) 526-6566.

WEST INDIES

COOKING WITH STEVEN RAICHLEN (page 68)

CURRENCY CONVERSION TABLE
(Exchange rates as of Sept. 10, 1992)

Country	Currency per U.S. $1
Australia (Dollar)	1.38
Canada (Dollar)	1.22
France (Franc)	4.84
Great Britain (Pound)	0.51
Ireland (Punt)	0.54
Israel (Shekel)	2.35
Italy (Lira)	1086.20
Mexico	3063.00
New Zealand	1.84
Netherlands (Guilder)	1.60
South Africa (Rand)	2.77
Spain (Peseta)	92.25

II

VOCATIONAL SCHOOLS & COMMUNITY COLLEGES

CULINARY APPRENTICESHIPS

CULINARY ARTS AND COOKING PROGRAMS
OFFERED BY JUNIOR AND COMMUNITY COLLEGES
AND VOCATIONAL-TECHNICAL SCHOOLS

In addition to those schools described on the previous pages, the following institutions offer programs that concentrate on the culinary arts and commercial cooking and baking. Each institution was asked to provide 18 vital statistics, which are arranged and abbreviated as follows (not all items were provided by each institution):

Name, department, address, and telephone number of institution

1) Year culinary program was established (last two digits, ie., 83 for 1983)
2) Length of program (y=years, s=semesters, m=months, w=weeks, d=days, h=hours)
3) Degree or certificate granted (Cert=Certificate, Deg=Degree, Dip=Diploma, AAS=Associate in Applied Science, AOS=Associate in Occupational Studies, AA=Associate in Arts, AS=Associate in Science, Appr=Apprenticeship)
4) Admission dates (Q=quarterly, F,W,S,Su=seasons; number of month, ie., 8 for August)
5) Total enrollment in program
6) Number of students per instructor
7) Is high school equivalency certificate accepted? (Y=Yes, N=No)
8) Is admission test required? (Y,N)
9) What percentage of applicants are accepted?
10) Can students enroll part-time? (Y,N)
11) Is financial aid available? (Y,N)
12) Are scholarships available? (Y,N)
13) Are paid externships provided? (Y,N)
14) Is job placement service available? (Y,N) What percentage of graduates obtain employment?
15) Annual tuition (IS, IC, ID=in-state, in-county, or in-district residents; OS, OC, or OD=out-of-state, out-of-county, or out-of-district residents; ch=credit hour; q=quarter; s=semester
16) Number of faculty members (FT=full-time, PT=part-time)
17) Accrediting bodies:

ACFEI	American Culinary Federation Educational Institute
CCA	Career College Association (NATTS and AICS)
MSA	Middle States Association of Colleges and Schools
NASC	Northwest Association of Schools and Colleges
NCA	North Central Association of Colleges and Schools
NEASC	New England Association of Schools and Colleges
SACS	Southern Association of Colleges and Schools
State	State Department of Education
WASC	Western Association of Schools and Colleges

18) Specialties or areas of emphasis

ALABAMA

Lawson State Community College
Commercial Food Preparation
3060 Wilson Rd., SW
Birmingham, AL 35221   Phone: 205-925-2515
(1)49 (2)21m (3)Cert (4)Q (6)23 (7)Y (8)Y (10)Y (11)Y (12)Y (14)Y 50% (15)IS $200 (16)2 (17)SACS

Wallace State Community College
Commercial Foods & Nutrition
P.O. Box 250
Hanceville, AL 35077-9080   Phone: 205-352-6403
(1)79 (2)18m/24m (3)Dip/Deg (4)10,1,4,7 (5)20 (6)15 (7)Y (8)N (10)Y (11)Y (12)Y (13)N (14)Y 98% (15)IS $1,100-$1,300 (16)2 (17)SACS

ALASKA

University of Alaska-Fairbanks
School of Career and Continuing Education
510 Second Ave.
Fairbanks, AK 99701   Phone: 907-474-5074
(1)78 (2)2y (3)Cert/AAS (4)F,S (5)25-30 (6)8-10 (7)Y (8)Y (9)85% (10)Y (11)Y (12)Y (13)Y (14)Y 95% (15)IS $51/ch;OS $140 (16)3 FT, 7 PT (17)NASC

ARIZONA

Pima Community College
Hospitality
1255 N. Stone Ave.
Tucson, AZ 85703   Phone: 602-884-6541
(1)72 (2)2y (3)Cert/AAS (4)1,5,8 (5)150 (6)30 (7)N (8)N (10)Y (11)Y (12)Y (13)N (14)Y (15)IS $22/ch, OS $28/ch (16)11 (17)NCA

Scottsdale Community College
Culinary Arts Program
9000 E. Chaparral Rd.
Scottsdale, AZ 85250   Phone: 602-423-6244
(1)85 (2)9m (3)Cert/AAS (4)8 (5)30 (6)7 (7)Y (8)N (9)60% (10)N (11)Y (12)Y (13)N (14)Y 90% (15)IS $1,100, OS $5,400 (16)2 FT, 2 PT (17)NCA

CALIFORNIA

Century Business College
Culinary Arts Dept.
2665 Fifth Ave.
San Diego, CA 92103   Phone: 619-233-0184
(1)82 (2)6-15m (3)Dip/AOS (4)Every 2w (5)300 (6)20 (7)Y (8)Y (9)90% (10)N (11)Y (12)Y (13)N (14)Y 82% (15)$6,500 (16)20 (17)CCA(NATTS) (18)Hospitality, business

Columbia College
Hospitality Management
P.O. Box 1849
Columbia, CA 95310 Phone: **209-533-5100**
(1)77 (2)2y (3)AS (4)8,1 (5)75 (6)10 (7)N (8)Y (9)99% (10)Y (11)Y (12)Y (13)N
(14)Y 100% (15)IS $120, OS $2,400 (16)2 FT, 5 PT (17)WASC (18)Fine cuis.

Contra Costa College
Culinary Arts
2600 Mission Bell Dr.
San Pablo, CA 94806 Phone: **415-235-7800, x311**
(1)62 (2)2y (3)Cert (4)8,1 (5)75-100 (6)20-25 (7)N (8)Y (9)90% (10)Y (11)Y
(12)Y (13)N (14)Y 90% (15)IS $100 (16)3 FT, 1 PT (18)Haute cuis., baking

Diablo Valley College
Culinary Arts Dept.
321 Golf Club Road
Pleasant Hill, CA 94523 Phone: **415-685-1230, x300**
(1)71 (2)2y (3)Cert/AA (4)8,1 (5)450 (6)24 (7)Y (8)N (10)Y (11)Y (12)Y (13)Y
(14)Y 100% (15)IS $60, OS $60+$105 (16)5 FT, 14 PT (17)WASC

Glendale Community College
Culinary Arts Dept.
1500 N. Verdugo Road
Glendale, CA 91208 Phone: **818-240-1000, x226/247**
(1)74 (2)2y (3)Cert (4)9,2 (5)235 (6)35-40 (7)N (8)N (9)95% (10)Y (11)Y (12)Y
(13)Y (14)Y 80-85% (15)IS $100, OS $2,700 (16)1 FT, 5 PT (17)State (18)Mgmt.

Grossmont College
8800 Grossmont College Drive
El Cajon, CA 92020 Phone: **619-465-1700, ext. 327**
(1)69 (2)1y/2y (3)Cert/Deg (4)8,1 (5)90 (6)20 (7)N (8)N (9)100% (10)Y (11)Y
(12)Y (13)Y (14)Y 100% (15)IS $60/s, OS $103/u (16)8 FT (17)WASC (18)Catering, dietetic, rest.

Laney College
Culinary Arts Dept.
900 Fallon St.
Oakland, CA 94607 Phone: **510-464-3407**
(1)48 (2)2y (3)Cert/AA (4)8,1 (5)200 (6)18 (7)Y (8)N (9)80% (10)Y (11)Y (12)Y
(13)N (14)Y 100% (15)$110 (16)5 FT, 4 PT (17)WASC

Lederwolff Culinary Academy
Admissions
3300 Stockton Blvd.
Sacramento, CA 95820 Phone: **916-456-7002**
(1)90 (2)41w(days),52w(eves) (3)Dip (4)Monthly(days),Bimonthly(eves)
(5)200 (6)15-25 (7)Y (8)Y (9)75% (10)Y (11)Y (12)Y (13)N (14)Y 100%
(15)$12,215 cooking, $7,095 baking (16)13 FT (17)CCA(NATTS) (18)Am. reg.
& classic. French cuis.

Los Angeles Trade-Technical College
Culinary Arts
400 W. Washington Blvd.
Los Angeles, CA 90015 Phone: 213-744-9480
(1)41 (2)2y (3)AAS/Cert (4)8,1 (5)200 (6)25 (7)N (8)Y (9)75% (10)N (11)Y
(12)Y (13)N (14)Y 80% (15)IS $250,OS $2,500 (16)7 (17)WASC (18)Baking,
cul. arts

Orange Coast College
Hospitality Dept.
2701 Fairview Blvd., Box 5005
Costa Mesa, CA 92628-5005 Phone: 714-432-0202
(1)64 (2)1y/2y (3)Cert/AA (4)8,1 (5)350 (6)15 (7)Y (8)N (9)100% (10)Y (11)Y
(12)Y (13)Y (14)Y 100% (15)IS $120/y, OS $102/u (16)15 (17)WASC, ACFEI
(18)Appren., baking, rest. mgmt.

Oxnard College
Hotel & Restaurant Management
4000 S. Rose Ave.
Oxnard, CA 93033 Phone: 805-488-0911
(1)85 (2)2y (3)Cert/Deg (4)8,1 (5)75-125 (6)20 (7)Y (8)N (9)100% (10)Y (11)Y
(12)Y (13)N (14)Y 95% (15)IS $5/u($50 max), OS $102/u (16)1 FT, 5 PT
(17)WASC (18)Cul. arts

San Joaquin Delta College
Culinary Arts Dept.
5151 Pacific Avenue
Stockton, CA 95207 Phone: 209-474-5020
(1)79 (2)1y/2y (3)Cert (4)Open (5)60 (6)20 (7)N (8)Y (10)Y (11)Y (12)Y (13)N
(14)Y 90% (15)IS $50, OS $96/u (16)3 (17)WASC

Santa Barbara City College
Hotel/Restaurant & Culinary Dept.
721 Cliff Drive
Santa Barbara, CA 93109-2394 Phone: 805-965-0581
(1)70 (2)2y (3)Cert/AS (4)F,S (5)120 (6)10-15 (7)Y (8)N (9)FCFS (10)Y (11)Y
(12)Y (13)N (14)Y 100% (15)IS $150, OS $96/u (16)2 FT, 6 PT (17)WASC

Santa Rosa Junior College
Consumer & Family Studies Dept.-Culinary Training
1501 Mendocino Ave.
Santa Rosa, CA 95401 Phone: 707-527-4395
(2)1Y (3)Cert (4)8,1 (5)25-40 (6)20-24 (7)N (8)N (10)Y (11)Y (12)Y (13)Y
(14)Y 100% (15)IS $60/s, OS $96/u (16)3 FT, 10 PT (17)WASC

Shasta College
Culinary Arts
P.O. Box 4960006,1065 N. Old Oregon Tr.
Redding, CA 96049-6006 Phone: 916-225-4600
(1)75 (2)1y/2y (3)Cert/AA (4)8 (5)125 (6)25 (7)Y (8)Y (10)Y (11)Y (12)Y (13)N
(14)Y 100% (15)IS $126/y, OS $94/u (16)1

COLORADO

Pikes Peak Community College
Culinary Institute of Colorado, Colorado Springs
5675 S. Academy Blvd.
Colorado Springs, CO 80906 Phone: 719-540-7371
(1)86 (2)2y (3)AAS/Appren/Cert (4)8,1,6 (5)25 (6)12 (7)Y (8)Y (9)100% (10)Y
(11)Y (12)Y (13)Y (14)Y 100% (15)IS $562/s, OS $2,110/s (16)2 FT (17)NCA,
ACFEI (18)

Warren Occupational Technical Center
Restaurant Arts
13300 W. Ellsworth Ave.
Golden, CO 80401 Phone: 303-988-3663
(1)74 (2)1s (3)Cert (4)8,1 (5)60 (6)20 (7)N (8)N (10)Y (11)Y (12)Y (13)Y (14)Y
95% (15)IS $658/s, OS $2,464/s (16)3 FT (17)State, NCA

CONNECTICUT

CBI Culinary Academy
7365 Main St.
Stratford, CT 06497 Phone: 203-380-1413
(1)88 (2)11-17w (3)Dip (4)9,11,1 (5)6-12 (6)6 (7)Y (8)Y (9)100% (10)Y (11)Y
(12)Y (13)N (14)Y 100% (15)$5,000 (16)1 FT, 2 PT

Manchester Community College
Culinary Arts Dept.
60 Bidwell Street
Manchester, CT 06040 Phone: 203-647-6000
(1)77 (2)1y (3)Cert (4)9,1 (5)54 (6)18 (7)Y (8)N (9)FCFS (10)Y (11)Y (12)Y
(14)Y 95% (15)IS $565/s, OS $1,130/s (16)6 (17)ACFEI (18)Cul. arts, baking

South Central Community College
Hospitality Management Program
60 Sargent Drive
New Haven, CT 06511 Phone: 203-789-7067
(1)88 (2)1y (3)Cert (4)9,1 (7)Y (8)Y (9)100% (10)Y (11)Y (12)N (13)Y (14)Y
100% (15)IS $585/s, OS $1,672/s (16)2 FT, 3 PT (17)State, NEASC (18)Baking,
nutrition

FLORIDA

The Art Institute of Ft. Lauderdale
Culinary Arts
1799 S.E. 17th St.
Ft. Lauderdale, FL 33316 Phone: 305-463-3000 x208
(1)91 (2)18m (3)AS (4)1,3,7,9 (5)120 (6)13 (7)Y (8)N (9)90% (10)N (11)Y (12)Y
(13)Y (14)Y 98% (15)$12,000 (16)7 FT, 3 PT

Atlantic Vocational Technical Center
Culinary Arts
4700 N.W. Coconut Creek Pkwy.
Coconut Creek, FL 33066 Phone: 305-977-2066
(1)76 (2)1,080h (3)Cert (4)Open (5)130 (6)15 (7)N (8)Y (9)90% (10)Y (11)Y
(12)Y (13)N (14)Y 85% (15)$700 (16)8 (17)SACS, ACFEI

Broward Community College
Restaurant Management
3501 Southwest Davie Rd.
Davie, FL 33314 Phone: 305-475-6892
(1)62 (2)2 1/2y (3)AS (4)F,S,Su (5)125 (6)60 (7)Y (8)N (10)Y (11)Y (12)Y (13)N
(14)Y 100% (15)IS $25/ch, OS $50/ch (16)2 (17)SACS

Daytona Beach Community College
Culinary Arts Dept.
P.O. Box 1111
Daytona Beach, FL 32015 Phone: 904-254-3051

Gulf Coast Community College
5230 W. U.S. Hwy 98
Panama City, FL 32401 Phone: 904-872-3850

Institute of the South for Hospitality & Culinary Arts
Fla. Community College at Jacksonville
4501 Capper Rd.
Jacksonville, FL 32218 Phone: 904-381-3555
(1)90 (2)1y (3)Cert (4)8,1,5 (5)100 (6)20 (7)N (8)N (9)100% (10)Y (11)Y (12)Y
(13)N (14)Y 95% (15)IS $832, OS $3,328 (16)3 FT, 4 PT (17)SACS

Mid-Florida Technical Institute
Commercial Cooking-Culinary Arts
2900 W. Oakridge Rd.
Orlando, FL 32809 Phone: 407-855-5880

North Technical Education Center
Commercial Foods & Culinary Arts
7071 Garden Rd.
Riviera Beach, FL 33404 Phone: 407-881-4600
(1)70 (2)1,800h (3)Cert (4)8,10,1,3,6 (5)40 (6)15-20 (7)N (8)N (9)100% (10)Y
(11)Y (12)Y (13)N (14)Y 90% (15)IS $170-$340 (16)1 (17)SACS (18)Basic
skills

Okaloosa-Walton Community College
Commercial Foods-Industrial Education
100 College Blvd.
Niceville, FL 32578 Phone: 904-678-5111
(1)73 (2)2y (3)AAS/AS (4)8,1,5 (5)25 (6)25 (7)Y (8)Y (10)Y (11)Y (12)Y (14)Y
92% (15)IS $21/SemHr, OS $42/SemHr (16)1 FT, 1 PT (17)SACS

Pinellas Technical Educational Center
Culinary Arts Dept.
6100 154th Ave.
N. Clearwater, FL 33516 Phone: 813-531-3531
(1)65 (2)18m (3)Dip (4)Every 9w (5)60 (6)15 (7)N (8)Y (9)100% (10)N (11)Y
(12)Y (13)N (14)Y 100% (15)IS $72/quin. (16)4 (17)ACFEI (18)Quantity foods

St. Petersburg Vocational Technical Institute
P.E.T.C. St. Pete Campus
901 34th St. South
St. Petersburg, FL 33711 Phone: 813-327-3671

Sarasota County Technical Institute
Culinary Arts
4748 Beneva Rd.
Sarasota, FL 34233 Phone: 813-924-1365
(1)67 (2)1,485h (3)Dip (4)Open (5)Varies (6)Varies (7)N (8)Y (9)90% (10)Y
(11)Y (12)Y (13)N (14)Y 100% (16)1 (17)SACS (18)Hosp. mgmt.

Seminole Community College
Culinary Arts/Food Service Management
100 Weldon Blvd.
Sanford, FL 32773-6199 Phone: 407-323-1450
(1)79 (2)1y/2y (3)Cert/AS (4)8,1 (5)50 (6)12 (7)Y (8)N (10)Y (11)Y (12)Y (13)Y
(14)Y 100% (15)$600/Cert, $1,664/AS (16)4 (17)State

Southeastern Academy
233 Academy Dr., Box 421768
Kissimmee, FL 34742-1768 Phone: 407-847-4444

Washington-Holmes Area Vocational Technical Center
Commercial Foods Prep. & Culinary Arts
209 Hoyt St.
Chipley, FL 32428 Phone: 904-638-1180
(1)84 (2)1,320h (3)Cert (4)Open (5)24 (6)12 (7)Y (8)N (9)98% (10)Y (11)Y
(12)Y (13)N (14)Y 100% (15)IS $300, OS $600 (16)2 (17)SACS (18)Fast food

GEORGIA

The Art Institute of Atlanta
School of Culinary Arts
3376 Peachtree Rd.
Atlanta, GA 30326 Phone:
(1)91 (2)18m (3)AAS (4)1,4,7,10 (5)213 (6)25 (7)Y (8)N (9)95% (10)N (11)Y
(12)Y (13)Y (14)Y (15)$7,950 (16)10 (17)SACS

Atlanta Area Technical School
Culinary Arts-Commercial Baking
1560 Stewart Ave. S.W.
Atlanta, GA 30310 Phone: 404-758-9451
(1)67 (2)18m (3)Dip (4)Q (5)50 (6)12 (7)Y (8)Y (10)Y (11)Y (12)Y (13)N (14)Y
92% (15)IS $400, OS $700 (16)6 (17)SACS

Augusta Technical Institute
Culinary Arts
3116 Deans Bridge Rd.
Augusta, GA 30906 Phone: 404-796-6900
(1)85 (2)4q/6q (3)Dip (4)S,F (5)20 (6)10 (7)Y (8)Y (9)95% (10)Y (11)Y (12)Y
(13)Y (14)Y 98%% (15)$192/q (16)2 FT (17)SACS (18)Catering

Savannah Technical Institute
Culinary Arts
5717 White Bluff Rd.
Savannah, GA 31499 Phone: 912-351-6362, x360
(1)81 (2)6q (3)Dip (4)Q (5)15 (6)12 (7)Y (8)Y (9)100% (10)Y (11)Y (12)Y (13)Y
(14)Y 85% (15)IS $186/q, OS $306/q (16)1 (17)SACS

HAWAII

Honolulu Community College
Commercial Baking
874 Dillingham Rd.
Honolulu, HI 96817 Phone: 808-845-9138
(1)20 (2)2y (3)Cert/Deg (4)F (5)50 (6)25 (7)Y (8)N (10)N (11)Y (13)Y (14)Y
100% (16)2 (17)WASC

Maui Community College
Culinary Arts Dept.
310 Kaahamanu Avenue
Kahului, HI 96732 Phone: 808-244-9181
(1)80 (2)2y/1y (3)AS/Cert (4)F,S (5)60-70 (6)12-15 (7)Y (8)N (9)100% (10)Y
(11)Y (12)Y (13)Y (14)Y 100% (15)IS $438, OS $2,598 (16)4 FT, 5 PT
(17)ACFEI, WASC (18)Cul. arts, baking

IDAHO

Boise State University
Culinary Arts Program
1910 University Dr.
Boise, ID 83725 Phone: 208-385-1957
(1)69 (2)1y/2y (3)Cert/AAS (4)8,1 (5)35 (6)10 (7)Y (8)Y (10)Y (11)Y (12)Y
(13)N (14)Y 98% (15)IS $652/s (16)3 FT

ILLINOIS

Black Hawk College-Quad Cities Campus
Culinary Arts Dept.
6600 - 34th Ave.
Moline, IL 61265 Phone: 309-796-1311
(1)88 (2)1y (3)Cert (4)9,1 (5)85 (6)15 (7)Y (8)Y (10)Y (11)Y (12)Y (13)N (14)Y
100% (15)ID $35/ch,OD $65/ch,OS $138/ch (16)8 PT (17)NCA

College of DuPage
Culinary Arts/Pastry Arts
22nd St. & Lambert Rd.
Glen Ellyn, IL 60137 Phone: 208-385-1011
(1)66 (2)1y/2y (3)Cert/AAS (4)9,1,3,6 (5)400 (6)15 (7)Y (8)N (9)100% (10)Y
(11)Y (12)Y (13)Y (14)Y 100% (15)ID $21/ch (16)4 FT, 10 PT (17)NCA, ACFEI

Elgin Community College
Culinary Arts Dept.
1700 Spartan Dr.
Elgin, IL 60123-7193 Phone: 312-687-1000
(1)74 (2)2y (3)AS (4)8,1 (5)160 (6)18 (7)Y (8)Y (10)Y (11)Y (12)Y (13)Y (14)Y
100% (15)IS $31, OS $93 (16)3 FT, 5 PT (17)NCA, ACFEI

Joliet Junior College
Culinary Arts/Hotel-Restaurant Mgt.
1216 Houbolt Ave.
Joliet, IL 60436-9352 Phone: 815-729-9020
(1)70 (2)2y (3)Cert/AAS (4)8,1,5,6 (5)200 (6)20 (7)Y (8)Y (9)98% (10)Y (11)Y
(12)Y (13)N (14)Y 95% (15)IS $982, OS $4,118 (16)9 (17)NCA, ACFEI
(18)Baking, pastry, buffet, banquet

Lincoln Trail College
Restaurant Mgt.-Culinary Arts
Route 3
Robinson, IL 62454 Phone: 618-544-8657
(1)70 (2)2y (3)AAS (4)8,1 (5)20-24 (6)10-12 (7)Y (8)Y (9)100% (10)Y (11)Y
(12)Y (13)Y (14)Y 100% (15)ID $900, OS $2,400 (16)1 FT, 1 PT (17)NCA
(18)Food serv. mgmt.

Triton College
Hospitality Industry Administration
2000 Fifth Avenue
River Grove, IL 60171 Phone: 708-456-0300
(1)70 (2)2y (3)AA (4)9 (5)150 (6)12 (7)Y (8)N (10)Y (11)Y (12)Y (13)Y (14)Y
97% (15)$1,000 (16)3 FT, 10 PT (17)NCA, ACFEI

Washburne Trade School
Chefs Training Program
3233 W. 31st St.
Chicago, IL 60623 Phone: 312-535-4422
(1)37 (2)88w (3)Cert (4)9,1,5 (5)150 (6)25 (7)Y (8)N (9)FCFS (10)N (11)Y (12)Y
(13)Y (14)Y 98% (15)IS $1,200, OS $4,000 (16)7

William Rainey Harper College
Hospitality Management
Algonquin & Roselle Rd.
Palatine, IL 60067-7398 Phone: 708-397-3000 Ext. 2874
(1)70 (2)1y/2y (3)Cert/AAS (4)8,1 (5)85 (6)15 (7)N (8)N (9)95% (10)Y (11)Y
(12)Y (13)Y (14)Y 100% (15)IS $33/ch, OS $170/ch (16)3 FT, 6 PT (17)NCA
(18)Breads, pastries, mgmt.

INDIANA

Indiana Vocational Technical College
Culinary Arts Dept.
3800 North Anthony Blvd.
Fort Wayne, IN 46805 Phone: 219-482-9171
(1)81 (2)2y (3)AAS (4)F,S (5)90 (6)12 (7)Y (8)Y (9)100% (10)Y (11)Y (12)Y
(13)Y (14)Y 100% (15)IS $1,835 OS $3,335 (16)2 FT, 5 PT (17)NCA, ACFEI
(18)Baking & pastry

Indiana Vocational Technical College-Central
Hotel & Restaurant Mgt./Culinary Arts
One W. 26th St.
Indianapolis, IN 46206 Phone: 317-921-4619
(1)86 (2)2y (3)AAS (4)F,S,Su (5)120 (6)10 (7)Y (8)Y (9)100% (10)Y (11)Y
(12)Y (13)Y (14)Y 98% (15)$1,500 (16)8 (17)ACFEI (18)ACFEI guidlines

Indiana Vocational Technical College-Gary
Hotel & Restaurant Mgt./Culinary Arts
1440 E. 35th Ave.
Gary, IN 46409 Phone: 219-981-1111
(1)81 (2)2y (3)Deg (4)1,5,8 (5)70 (6)12 (7)Y (8)N (9)90% (10)Y (11)Y (12)Y
(13)Y (14)Y 100% (15)IS $1,850, OS $3,300 (16)5 (17)NCA (18)Int. cuisines

Vincennes University
Culinary Arts Dept.
Vincennes, IN 47591 Phone: 812-885-5742
(1)85 (2)2y (3)AS (6)10 (7)Y (8)N (10)Y (11)Y (12)Y (13)Y (14)Y 100% (15)IS
$1,600, OS $4,400 (16) (17)NCA

IOWA

Des Moines Area Community College
Culinary Arts Dept.
2006 South Ankeny Blvd.
Ankeney, IA 50021 Phone: 515-964-6260
(1)75 (2)2y (3)AAS (4)F (5)125 (6)15 (7)Y (8)Y (9)100% (10)Y (11)Y (12)Y
(13)Y (14)Y 90% (15)IS $1,500, OS $3,000 (16)5 (17)NCA

Indian Hills Community College
Culinary Arts
525 Grandview
Ottumwa, IA 52501 Phone: 515-683-5195
(1)69 (2)18m (3)AAS (4)F,S (5)35 (6)12 (7)Y (8)Y (9)100% (10)Y (11)Y (12)Y
(13)N (14)Y 97% (15)IS $3,115, OS $3,640 (16)4 FT (17)NCA (18)Cul., baking

Iowa Lakes Community College-South Attendance Ctr.
Culinary Arts Dept.
3200 College Drive
Emmetsburg, IA 50536 Phone: 712-852-3554
(1)73 (2)2y (3)AAS (4)F (5)40 (6)20 (7)Y (8)Y (9)FCFS (10)Y (11)Y (12)Y
(13)Y (14)Y 95% (15)IS $2,500, OS $3,000 (16)2 (17)NCA (18)Mgmt.

Iowa Western Community College
Food Svc. Mgt./Culinary Arts/Retail Baking
2700 College Rd., Box 4-C
Council Bluffs, IA 51502 Phone: 712-325-3277
(1)74 (2)1y/2y (3)Dip/AAS (4)F,S (5)30-40 (6)10-12 (7)Y (8)Y (9)95% (10)Y
(11)Y (12)Y (13)Y (14)Y 95% (15)IS $1,470/y, OS $2,204/y (16)2 FT, 1 PT
(17)NCA (18)Cul. arts, baking

Kirkwood Community College
Culinary Arts Dept.
6301 Kirkwood Blvd., S.W.
Cedar Rapids, IA 52406 Phone: 319-398-5468
(1)72 (2)2y (3)AAS (4)F,S (5)87 (6)23 (7)Y (8)Y (9)100% (10)Y (11)Y (12)Y
(13)N (14)Y 97% (15)IS $42/ch, OS $79/ch (16)3 FT, 1 PT (17)NCA, ACF
(18)Rest. mgmt.

KANSAS

Johnson County Community College
Business & Technology Division
12345 College at Quivira
Overland Park, KS 66210-1299 Phone: 913-469-8500
(1)75 (2)2-3y (3)AOS (4)7,11 (5)350 (6)20 (7)Y (8)Y (9)80% (10)Y (11)Y (12)Y
(13)Y (14)Y 100% (15)IS $1,000, OS $3,000 (16)10 (17)NCA, ACFEI
(18)Appren.

Kansas City Ks. Area Vocational Technical School
Professional Cooking
2220 W. 59th St.
Kansas City, KS 66104 Phone: 913-334-1000
(1)75 (2)720h (3)Cert (4)Open (5)15 (6)15 (7)N (8)Y (9)100% (10)N (11)Y (12)Y
(13)Y (14)Y 88% (15)$616 (16)1 (17)State

Northeast Kansas Area Vocational Technical School
Quantity Foods Dept.
1501 W. Riley
Atchison, KS 66002 Phone: 913-367-6204
(1)69 (2)1y (3)Dip (4)Open (5)12 (6)12 (7)N (8)N (10)Y (11)Y (12)N (13)Y
(14)Y 100% (15)IS $724, OS $6,028 (16)1 (17)State

Wichita Area Vocational-Technical School
Food Service & Culinary Arts
324 N. Emporia
Wichita, KS 67202 Phone: 316-265-8666
(1)75 (2)9m (3)Cert (4)8,1 (5)20 (6)6 (7)Y (8)Y (9)95% (10)N (11)Y (12)N (13)N
(14)Y 95% (15)IS $1,500 (16)6 (17)State (18)Mid-mgmt.

KENTUCKY

Elizabethtown State Vocational Technical School
Commercial Foods
505 University Dr.
Elizabethtown, KY 42701 Phone: 502-765-2104
(1)75 (2)22m (3)Dip (4)7,10,1,4 (5)18 (6)18 (7)Y (8)Y (9)100% (10)Y (11)Y
(12)Y (13)Y (14)Y 95% (15)IS $500, OS $1,000 (16)1 (17)SACS (18)Rest.,
school, baker

Jefferson Community College
Culinary Arts Dept.
109 East Broadway
Louisville, KY 40202 Phone: 502-584-0181
(1)74 (2)2y (3)AAS (4)8 (5)22 (6)11 (7)Y (8)Y (10)N (11)Y (12)Y (13)Y (14)Y
96% (15)IS $680, OS $2,040 (16)2 FT, 1 PT (17)ACFEI, SACS

Kentucky Tech-Daviess County Campus
Commercial Foods
1901 Southeastern Parkway
Owensboro, KY 42303 Phone: 502-684-7211
(1)71 (2)2,640h (3)Dip (4)Q (5)30 (6)15 (7)Y (8)Y (10)Y (11)Y (12)N (13)N
(14)Y 92% (15) (16)2 (17)SACS

West Kentucky State Vocational Technical School
Culinary Arts
Blandville Rd., Box 7408
Paducah, KY 42002-7408 Phone: 502-554-4991
(1)79 (2)1 1/2y (3)Dip/Deg (4)7,10,1,3,6 (5)36 (6)18 (7)Y (8)Y (10)Y (11)Y
(12)Y (13)N (14)Y 80% (15)IS $150, OS $250 (16)2 (17)SACS

LOUISIANA

Baton Rouge Regional Technical Institute
Culinary Arts Dept.
3250 N. Acadian Thwy.
Baton Rouge, LA 70805 Phone: 504-359-9201
(1)80 (2)12m (3)Dip (4)Open (5)15 (6)15 (7)N (8)Y (9)100% (10)Y (11)Y (12)Y
(13)Y (14)Y 50% (15)IS $300, OS $600 (16)1 (17)SACS

Bossier Parish Community College
Culinary Arts Dept.
2719 Airline Drive North
Bossier City, LA 71111 Phone: 318-746-9851
(1)86 (2)9m (3)Cert (4)8 (5)25 (6)13 (7)Y (8)Y (9)98% (10)Y (11)Y (12)Y (13)N
(14)Y 100% (15)$3,100 (16)2 FT, 4 PT (17)ACFEI

Camelot Career College
P.O. Box 53326
Baton Rouge, LA 70805 Phone: 504-928-3005

New Orleans Regional Technical Institute
Culinary Arts Dept.
980 Navarre Ave.
New Orleans, LA 70124 Phone: **504-483-4626**
(1)84 (2)12m (3)Dip/Cert (4)Open (5)22 (6)11 (7)Y (8)Y (9)80% (10)Y (11)Y
(12)N (13)N (14)Y 90-100% (15)IS $300, OS $600 (16)2 (17)SACS (18)Instit.
cooking & baking

Sidney N. Collier Vocational Technical Institute
Culinary Arts
3727 Louisa St.
New Orleans, LA 70126 Phone: **504-942-8333**

MAINE

Southern Maine Technical College
Culinary Arts/Hotel, Motel & Rest. Management
2 Fort Rd.
S. Portland, ME 04106 Phone: **207-799-7303**
(1)56 (2)2y (3)Deg (4)Rolling (5)90 (6)11 (7)Y (8)Y (10)Y (11)Y (13)N (14)Y
88% (15)IS $1,728, OS $3,960 (16)6 (17)NEASC

MASSACHUSETTS

Berkshire Community College
Culinary Arts Dept.
1350 West St.
Pittsfield, MA 01201-5786 Phone: **413-499-4660**
(1)77 (2)1y/2y (3)Cert/AAS (4)F (5)15 (7)Y (8)Y (10)Y (11)Y (12)Y (13)Y (14)N
(15)IS $950, OS $3,990 (16)2 FT, 3 PT (17)NEASC

Bristol Community College
Culinary Arts Dept.
Fall River, MA 02720 Phone: **508-678-2811, x111**
(1)85 (2)1y (3)Cert (4)9,1 (5)22-24 (6)6 (7)Y (8)Y (9)80% (10)Y (11)Y (12)N
(13)N (14)Y 75% (15)IS $2,000, OS $5,800 (16)4 (17)NEASC (18)Basic cooking
& baking

Bunker Hill Community College
Hotel/Restaurant Management-Culinary Arts
New Rutherford Ave.
Charlestown, MA 02129 Phone: **617-241-8600, #336**
(1)78 (2)1y/2y (3)Cert/AAS (4)9,1 (5)125 (6)8-15 (7)Y (8)Y (10)Y (11)Y (12)Y
(13)N (14)Y 98% (15)IS $750/s, OS $1,995/s (16)6 FT

Essex Agricultural & Technical Institute
Culinary Arts Dept.
562 Maple Street
Hathorne, MA 01833 Phone: **508-774-0050**
(1)68 (2)2y (3)Cert/AAS (4)Rolling (5)75 (6)10-15 (7)Y (8)N (9)FCFS (10)Y
(11)Y (12)Y (13)Y (14)Y 100% (15)IS $1,016, OS $3,556 (16)7 (17)NEASC
(18)Int. cuis., baking

Massasoit Community College
Culinary Arts Dept.
1 Massasoit Blvd.
Brockton, MA 02402 Phone: 617-588-9100
(1)82 (2)2y (3)Deg (4)9 (5)60 (6)20-35 (7)Y (8)N (10)N (11)Y (12)Y (13)Y (14)Y
93.5% (15)IS $950, OS $1,900 (16)3 FT, 2 PT (17)State

Minuteman Tech
Foodservice/Hospitality Management
758 Marrett Road
Lexington, MA 02173 Phone: 617-861-6500
(1)73 (2)3y (3)Dip (5)90 (6)10 (7)N (8)Y (9)95% (10)Y (11)Y (12)Y (13)Y (14)Y
99% (15)IS $6,200

MICHIGAN

The Career Development Center
Culinary Arts
5961 14th St.
Detroit, MI 48208 Phone: 313-894-0610

Gogebic Community College
Culinary Arts Dept.
Ironwood, MI 49938 Phone: 906-932-4231

Grand Rapids Community College
Hospitality Education Division
151 Fountain, N.E.
Grand Rapids, MI 49503-3295 Phone: 616-771-3690
(1)80 (2)2y (3)AAAS (4)1,8 (5)210 (6)15-22 (7)Y (8)Y (9)95% (10)Y (11)Y
(12)Y (13)Y (14)Y 99.6% (15)IS $4,392, OS $5,400 (16)12 FT, 6 PT (17)ACFEI,
NCA (18)Cul. arts, food & bev. mgmt.

Henry Ford Community College
Culinary Arts/Hotel Restaurant Management
5101 Evergreen Rd.
Dearborn, MI 48128 Phone: 313-845-9651

Macomb Community College
Culinary Arts Dept.
44575 Garfield
Mt. Clemens, MI 48044 Phone: 313-286-2000
(1)72 (2)2y (3)AAS (4)F,S,Su (5)112 (6)16-35 (7)Y (8)N (10)Y (11)Y (12)Y
(13)N (14)Y 99% (15)IC $42/ch, OC $165/ch (16)3 FT, 2 PT (17)State

Monroe County Community College
Culinary Arts Dept.
1555 Raisinville Rd.
Monroe, MI 48161 Phone: 313-242-8957
(1)75 (2)2y (3)AOC/Cert (4)9 (5)36 (7)Y (8)Y (9)80% (10)Y (11)Y (12)Y (13)Y
(14)Y (15)IS $650, OS $962 (16)2 (17)NCA, ACFEI

Northwestern Michigan College
Culinary Arts Dept.
1701 East Front Street
Traverse City, MI 49684 Phone: 616-922-1010
(1)78 (2)2y (3)AAS (4)Open (5)75 (6)20 (7)Y (8)N (9)100% (10)Y (11)Y (12)Y
(13)Y (14)Y 90% (15)IS $43/ch, OS $48/ch (16)1 FT, 10 PT (17)ACFEI

Oakland Community College
Hospitality/Culinary Arts
27055 Orchard Lake Road
Farmington Hills, MI 48334 Phone: 313-471-7500
(1)78 (2)2y (3)AAS (4)9,1 (5)210 (6)15 (7)N (8)Y (9)98% (10)Y (11)Y (12)Y
(13)N (14)Y 90% (15)IC $1,800 (16)10 FT, 6 PT (17)ACFEI (18)Cul. arts, baking

Schoolcraft College
Culinary Arts
18600 Haggerty Rd.
Livonia, MI 48152-2696 Phone: 313-591-6400
(1)66 (2)2y (3)Cert/AAS (4)1,9 (5)144 (6)12 (7)Y (8)Y (9)100% (10)Y (11)Y
(12)Y (13)Y (14)Y 100% (15)$53/ch (16)6 FT, 6 PT (17)NCA (18)Cul. arts

Washtenaw Community College
Culinary Arts Dept.
4800 E. Huron River Dr.,Box D1
Ann Arbor, MI 48106-0978 Phone: 313-973-3601/3584
(1)72 (2)2y/1y (3)AAS/Cert (4)Q (5)80-120 (6)10 (7)Y (8)N (9)100% (10)Y
(11)Y (12)Y (13)Y (14)Y 90% (15)IS $1,800, OS $2,400 (16)3 FT, 10 PT
(17)NCA

Wayne County Community College
Culinary Arts Program
801 W. Fort St.
Detroit, MI 48226 Phone: 313-943-4000
(1)77 (2)2y (3)AAS (4)1,5,9 (5)80 (6)10 (7)Y (8)N (10)Y (11)Y (12)Y (13)N
(14)Y 70% (15)IS $35/ch, OS $70/ch (16)6 (17)NCA

MINNESOTA

Detroit Lakes Technical College
Commercial Cooking & Baking
Hwy. 34 East
Detroit Lakes, MN 56501 Phone: 800-492-4836
(1)65 (2)10m (3)Dip (4)8 (5)34 (6)17 (7)Y (8)Y (10)Y (11)Y (12)Y (13)N (14)N
(15)IS $34/ch, OS $68/ch (16)2

Dunwoody Institute
Baking Production & Management Technology
818 Dunwoody Blvd.
Minneapolis, MN 55403 Phone: 612-374-5800
(2)2y/1y (3)AAS/Dip (4)9,12,3 (5)45 (6)15 (7)Y (8)Y (10)Y (11)Y (12)Y (13)Y
(14)Y 100% (15)$3,264 (16)9 (17)CCA(NATTS)

Hennepin Technical Center-Eden Prairie
Culinary Arts Dept.
9200 Flying Cloud Drive
Eden Prairie, MN 55344 Phone: 612-944-2222
(1)72 (2)80ch (3)Dip (4)9,12,3 (5)35 (6)16 (7)Y (8)N (9)100% (10)Y (11)Y (12)Y
(13)Y (14)Y (15)IS $1,600, OS $3,200 (16)2 (17)ACFEI, NCA (18)Gourmet
cookery

Hennepin Technical College-Brooklyn Park Campus
Culinary Arts Dept.
9000 Brooklyn Blvd.
Brooklyn Park, MN 55445 Phone: 612-425-3800
(1)72 (2)80ch (3)Dip/Cert (4)F,W,S (5)60-65 (6)17 (7)N (8)N (9)100% (10)Y
(11)Y (12)Y (13)Y (14)Y 97-100% (15)IS $2,228, OS $4,456 (16)4 (17)NCA,
ACFEI (18)Gourmet cookery

Mankato Technical Institute
Culinary Arts
1920 Lee Blvd., P.O. Box 1920
North Mankato, MN 56002-1920 Phone: 507-625-3441, x229
(1)68 (2)11m (3)Cert (4)9,1,3,6 (5)25 (6)17 (7)Y (8)N (9)100% (10)Y (11)Y
(12)Y (13)N (14)Y 95% (15)IS $34/ch, OS $69/ch (16)3 (17)NCA

Moorhead Technical College
Chef Training
1900 28th Ave. S.
Moorhead, MN 56560 Phone: 800-426-5603
(1)66 (2)2y (3)Cert (4)Q (5)40-50 (6)20-25 (7)Y (8)N (10)Y (11)Y (12)Y (13)N
(14)Y 89% (15)Approx. IS $500/q, OS $600/q (16)2 (17)State

St. Paul Technical College
Restaurant-Hotel Cookery
235 Marshall Ave.
St. Paul, MN 55102 Phone: 612-221-1300
(1)67 (2)12m (3)Dip (4)9,12,3 (5)40-50 (6)14-16 (7)Y (8)Y (10)Y (11)Y (12)Y
(13)N (14)Y (15)IS $35/ch, OS $70/ch (16)3 (17)NCA (18)Cul. arts

MISSOURI

Penn Valley Community College
Lodging & Food Service Dept.
3201 S.W. Traffic Way
Kansas City, MO 64111 Phone: 816-932-7600
(1)67 (2)2y (3)AAS (4)6,8,1 (5)150 (6)10-15 (7)N (8)N (9)100% (10)Y (11)Y
(12)Y (13)Y (14)Y 98% (15)ID $39/ch, OD $64/ch, OS $92/ch (16)2 FT, 4 PT
(17)NCA

St. Louis Community College @ Forest Park
Culinary Arts Dept.
5600 Oakland Ave.
St. Louis, MO 63110 Phone: 314-644-9100
(1)76 (2)2y/3y (3)AAS/Appr (4)8,1 (5)250 (6)20 (7)Y (8)Y (10)Y (11)Y (12)Y
(13)Y (14)Y 98% (15)IS $950, OS $1,500 (17)NCA

MONTANA

Missoula Vocational Technical Center
Culinary Arts Dept.
909 S. Avenue West
Missoula, MT 59801-7910 Phone: 406-452-6811
(1)73 (2)1y/2y (3)Cert/AAS (4)8,1 (5)30 (6)15 (7)Y (8)Y (9)90% (10)Y (11)Y
(12)Y (13)N (14)Y 90% (15)IS $1,364, OS $2,634 (16)2 (17)ACFEI, NASC
(18)Resort hotel & lodging

NEBRASKA

Central Community College
Hotel, Motel, Restaurant Management
P.O. Box 1024
Hastings, NE 68902 Phone: 402-461-2458
(1)71 (2)2y (3)Cert/AAS (4)Open (5)40 (6)20 (7)Y (8)N (9)100% (10)Y (11)Y
(12)Y (13)N (14)Y 95% (15)IS $996, OS $1,536 (16)2 FT (17)NCA (18)Garde
manger

Metropolitan Community College
Culinary Arts
P.O. Box 3777
Omaha, NE 68103-0777 Phone: 402-449-8400
(1)76 (2)1-2y (3)Cert/Appr (4)9,12,3,6 (5)100 (6)10 (7)Y (8)N (9)100% (10)Y
(11)Y (12)Y (13)Y (14)Y 96% (15)IS $20/ch, OS $39/ch (16)2 FT, 10 PT
(17)NCA (18)Cul. arts

Southeast Community College, Lincoln Campus
Culinary Arts Dept.
8800 'O' St.
Lincoln, NE 68520 Phone: 402-471-3333
(1)87 (2)18m (3)AAS (4)10,3 (5)20 (6)10 (7)Y (8)Y (9)99% (10)Y (11)Y (12)Y
(13)Y (14)Y 98% (15)IS $22/ch, OS $29/ch (16)2 (17)NCA (18)Dietetic tech.

NEVADA

Area Technical Trade Center
Culinary Arts
444 West Brooks Ave.
N. Las Vegas, NV 89030 Phone: 702-799-8300

Clark County Community College
Culinary Arts Department
3200 East Cheyenne Ave.
North Las Vegas, NV 89030 Phone: 702-643-6060
(1)90 (2)1y/2y (3)Cert/Deg (4)Open (5)400 (6)18 (7)N (8)N (9)100% (10)Y
(11)Y (12)Y (13)N (14)Y 95% (15)IS $720, OS $2,220 (16)3 FT, 6 PT (17)NASC

Truckee Meadows Community College
Culinary Arts Dept.
7000 Dandini Blvd.
Reno, NV 89512 Phone: 702-673-7015
(1)80 (2)2y (3)AAS (4)1,9 (5)72 (6)18 (7)Y (8)N (10)Y (11)Y (12)Y (13)Y (14)Y
75% (15)IS $24/ch, OS $1,100+$24/ch (16)1 FT, 5 PT (17)State

NEW HAMPSHIRE

The Culinary Institute of New Hampshire College
2500 N. River Rd.
Manchester, NH 03106-1045 Phone: 603-644-3129
(1)83 (2)2y (3)Cert/AAS (4)9,1 (5)70 (6)15 (7)Y (8)N (10)Y (11)Y (13)Y (14)Y
98% (15)$8,460 (16)4 FT, 3 PT (17)NEASC, ACFEI

New Hampshire Technical College
Culinary Arts Dept.
2020 Riverside Dr.
Berlin, NH 03570 Phone: 603-752-1113
(1)66 (2)2y (3)Dip/Cert/AAS (4)Open (5)30 (6)15 (7)Y (8)N (10)Y (11)Y (12)Y
(13)Y (14)Y 100% (15)IS $1,950, OS $4,400 (16)2 (17)NEASC

University of New Hampshire-Durham
Thompson School of Applies Sciences-Food Svc Mgt.
Barton Hall, Rm. 105
Durham, NH 03824 Phone: 603-862-1073
(1)66 (2)24m (3)AAS (4)F,S (5)54 (6)10 (7)Y (8)N (9)75% (10)Y (11)Y (12)Y
(13)N (14)Y 90% (15)IS $2,590, OS $8,380 (16)4 (17)State (18)Food serv. mgmt.

NEW JERSEY

Hudson County Community College
Culinary Arts
161 Newkirk St.
Jersey City, NJ 07306 Phone: 201-714-2193
(1)83 (2)2y (3)Cert/AAS (4)9 (5)240 (6)15 (7)Y (8)Y (10)N (11)Y (12)N (13)Y
(14)Y 100% (15)IS $1,080, OS $2,160 (16)10 (17)MSA

Salem County Vocational Technical Schools
Culinary Arts
Box 350
Woodstown, NJ 08098 Phone: 609-769-0101
(1)76 (2)1y (3)Cert (4)9,1 (5)30 (6)15 (7)N (8)N (9)75% (10)Y (11)Y (12)Y
(13)N (14)Y 80% (15)$2,150 (16)20 (17)MSA (18)Baking, decorating

NEW MEXICO

Santa Fe Community College
Culinary Arts Dept.
P.O. Box 4187
Santa Fe, NM 87502-4187 Phone: 505-471-8200

(1)89 (2)2y (3)Cert/AAS (4)8,1 (5)60 (6)14 (7)N (8)N (9)100% (10)Y (11)Y (12)Y (13)Y (14)Y 100% (15)IC $17/ch, IS $20/ch, OS $45/ch (16)8 (17)NCA (18)Southwest cuis.

NEW YORK

Adirondack Community College
Commercial Cooking/Occupational Education
Bay Rd.
Queensbury, NY 12803 Phone: 518-793-4491
(1)69 (2)1y/2y (3)Cert/AAS (4)F,S (5)25 (6)10 (7)Y (8)N (10)Y (11)Y (12)Y (13)Y (14)Y 90% (15)$1,600 (16)1 FT, 1 PT (17)MSA

Erie Community College, City Campus
Hotel Management/Culinary Arts
121 Ellicott Street
Buffalo, NY 14203 Phone: 716-842-2770
(1)85 (2)2y (3)AOS (4)F (5)28 (6)28 (7)Y (8)Y (9)50% (10)N (11)Y (12)Y (13)N (14)Y 65% (15)IS $1,530, OS $3,600 (16)5 (17)MSA

Jefferson Community College
Hospitality & Tourism Dept.
Outer Coffeen Street
Watertown, NY 13601 Phone: 315-782-5250
(1)75 (2)2y (3)AAS/Cert (4)8,1 (5)95 (6)18 (7)Y (8)N (9)100% (10)Y (11)Y (12)Y (13)Y (14)Y 95% (15)IS $1,350, OS $2,700 (16)4 (17)MSA

Mohawk Valley Community College
Hospitality
Upper Floyd Ave.
Rome, NY 13440 Phone: 315-339-3470 x210
(1)78 (3)Cert/AOS (4)8,1 (5)40 (6)20 (7)Y (8)Y (10)Y (11)Y (12)Y (13)N (14)Y (15)IS $1,500, OS $3,000 (16)2 FT (17)MSA

Monroe Community College
Dept. of Food, Hotel, and Tourism Management
1000 East Henrietta Road
Rochester, NY 14623 Phone: 716-292-2000, ext 2586
(1)67 (2)2y (3)Cert/AAS (4)F,S (5)175 (6)18 (7)Y (8)N (9)80% (10)Y (11)Y (12)Y (13)Y (14)Y 96% (15)IS $2,000 (16)8-10 PT (17)MSA (18)Fd. svc. admin.

New York Food & Hotel Management School
154 West 14th Street
New York, NY 10011 Phone: 212-675-6655
(1)35 (2)6m (3)Cert (4)Every 4-6w (5)20-25 (6)12-30 (7)Y (8)Y (10)Y (11)Y (12)N (13)N (14)Y (15)$3,840 (16)5 (17)CCA(NATTS)

New York Institute of Technology
Culinary Arts Center, Bldg. #69
211 Carleton Ave.
Central Islip, NY 11722 Phone: 516-348-3232/3235
(1)87 (2)21m (3)AOS (4)F,S (5)120 (6)16 (7)Y (8)N (9)90% (10)N (11)Y (12)Y (13)N (14)Y 100% (15)$11,100 (16)9 (17)MSA

Niagara County Community College
Culinary Arts Dept.
3111 Saunders Settlement Rd.
Sanborn, NY 14132 Phone: 716-731-4101
(1)77 (2)2y (3)AA (4)9,1 (5)50 (6)15 (7)Y (8)Y (10)Y (11)Y (12) (13)Y (14)Y
90% (15)IC $1,780, OC $3,520 (16)2 FT, 1 PT (17)MSA

Onondaga Community College
Culinary Arts Dept.
Onondaga Hill
Syracuse, NY 13215 Phone: 315-469-7741
(1)79 (2)2y/1y (3)AAS/Cert (4)F,S (5)90-100 (6)16 (8)N (11)Y (12)Y (13)Y
(14)N (15)IS $1,350, OS $2,700 (16)2 (17)State

SUNY College of Agriculture & Technology
Food Service & Hospitality Administration
Cobleskill, NY 12043 Phone: 518-234-5011
(1)71 (2)2y (3)AOS (4)F,S (5)100 (6)15 (7)Y (8)N (10)Y (11)Y (12)Y (13)Y
(14)Y 98-100% (15)IS $2,984, OS $6,250 (16)11 (17)MSA

Schenectady County Community College
Hotel Technology & Culinary Arts
Washington Ave.
Schenectady, NY 12305 Phone: 518-346-6211
(1)69 (2)2y (3)Deg (4)9,1,5 (5) (6)22 (7)Y (8)N (10)Y (11)Y (12)Y (13)Y (14)Y
84% (15)IS $1,750, OS $3,500 (16)14 FT, 9 PT (17)MSA

Sullivan County Community College
Hospitality Division
LeRoy Rd., Box 4002
Loch Sheldrake, NY 12759-4002 Phone: 914-434-5750
(1)65 (2)2y (3)AAS (4)9,2 (5)146 (6)14 (7)Y (8)Y (10)Y (11)Y (12)Y (13)N
(14)Y 90% (15)IS $2,200, OS $4,050 (16)8 (17)MSA, ACFEI

NORTH CAROLINA

Asheville Buncombe Technical Community College
Culinary Technology
340 Victoria Rd.
Asheville, NC 28801 Phone: 704-254-1921
(1)68 (2)2y (3)AAS (4)9 (5)23 (6)12 (7)Y (8)Y (9)99% (10)Y (11)Y (12)Y (13)Y
(14)Y 80% (15)IS $644, OS $7,525 (16)2 FT, 1 PT (17)SACS (18)Cul. tech.

Central Piedmont Community College
Culinary Arts Dept.
P.O. Box 35009
Charlotte, NC 28235 Phone: 704-342-6721
(1)74 (2)2y (3)AAS (4)F,W,S (5)300 (6)12 (7)Y (8)Y (9)75% (10)Y (11)Y (12)Y
(13)Y (14)Y 98% (15)IS $800, OS $4,800 (16)25 (17)SACS, ACFEI (18)Cul.
competition

NORTH DAKOTA

North Dakota State College of Science
Chef Training & Management Technology
800 N. 6th St.
Wahpeton, ND 58076 Phone: 701-671-2201
(1)71 (2)18m (3)Dip/AAS (4)9,1 (5)30-35 (6)15 (7)Y (8)N (9)100% (10)Y (11)Y
(12)Y (13)N (14)Y 100% (15)IS $1,197, OS $2,897 (16)2 (17)NCA

OHIO

Cincinnati Technical College
Business Division
3520 Central Pkwy.
Cincinnati, OH 45223 Phone: 513-569-1500
(1)80 (2)2y (3)ASOB (4)Open (5)130 (6)15 (7)Y (8)Y (10)Y (11)Y (12)Y (13)Y
(14)Y 100% (15)IS $2,000, OS $3,800 (16)4 (17)ACFEI, NCA

Columbus State Community College
Hospitality Management Dept.
550 E. Spring St., Box 1609
Columbus, OH 43216-1609 Phone: 614-227-2579
(1)78 (2)3y (3)AAS (4)9,1 (5)60 (6)15 (7)Y (8)Y (9)100% (10)Y (11)Y (12)Y
(13)Y (14)Y 100% (15)IS $1,764, OS $3,816 (16)5 (17)ACFEI, NCA

Cuyahoga Community College
Hospitality Management
2900 Community College Ave.
Cleveland, OH 44115 Phone: 216-987-4081
(1)69 (2)2y (3)AAB (4)Q (5)175 (6)15 (7)Y (8)Y (9)85% (10)Y (11)Y (12)Y
(13)N (14)Y 95% (15)IS $32/ch (16)5 FT, 9 PT (17)NCA

Hocking Technical College
Culinary Arts Dept.
Nelsonville, OH 45764 Phone: 614-753-3591
(1)79 (2)2y (3)Cert/AAS (4)9,1,3,6 (5)150 (6)15 (7)Y (8)Y (10)Y (11)Y (12)Y
(13)Y (14)Y 95% (15)IS $1,500, OS $3,000 (16)5 (17)NCA

University of Akron
Hospitality Management
Gallucci Hall, #104
Akron, OH 44325 Phone: 216-972-7026
(1)68 (2)2y (3)Cert/AAS (4)F,S,Su (5)245 (6)18 (7)Y (8)Y (10)Y (11)Y (13)Y
(14)Y 95% (15)IS $2,430/y, OS $5,970/y (16)11 (17)State

University of Toledo
Food Svc. Mgt./Culinary Arts
Scott Park Campus
Toledo, OH 43606 Phone: 419-537-3112
(1)80 (2)2y (3)AAS (4)Q (5)30 (6)5 (7)Y (8)N (10)Y (11)Y (12)Y (13)Y (14)Y
(15)IS $2,610, OS $3,400 (16)1 FT, 1 PT (17)NCA

OKLAHOMA

Great Plains Area Vocational Technical Center
Commercial Food Svcs./Fast Foods Mgt.
4500 W. Lee Blvd.
Lawton, OK 73505 Phone: 405-355-6371
(2)18m (3)Cert (4)Open (5)36 (6)18 (7)Y (8)N (10)Y (11)Y (13)N (14)Y
(15)$300 (16)2 (17)NCA

Indian Meridian Vocational Technical School
Commercial Food Production & Mgmt.
1312 S. Sangre Rd.
Stillwater, OK 74074 Phone: 405-377-3333
(1)75 (2)1,050h (3)Cert (4)8 (5)36 (6)18 (7)N (8)Y (10)Y (11)Y (12)Y (13)N
(14)Y (15)ID $1,000, OD $2,000 (16)3 FT (17)State

Oklahoma State University-Okmulgee
Hospitality Services Technology Dept.
1801 E. 4th St.
Okmulgee, OK 74447 Phone: 918-756-6211
(1)46 (2)20m/16m (3)AAS/Dip (4)8,1,4 (5)90 (6)18 (7)Y (8)Y (9)90% (10)Y
(11)Y (12)Y (13)Y (14)Y 78% (15)IS $38, OS $131 (16)6 (17)NCA (18)Diet.
tech., baking

Pioneer Area Vocational Technical School
Commercial Foods
2101 N. Ash
Ponca City, OK 74601 Phone: 405-762-8336
(1)72 (2)1y (3)Cert (4)Open (5)36 (6)6 (7)Y (8)Y (10)Y (11)Y (13)Y (14)Y 100%
(15)$400 (16)3 (17)NCA

Southern Oklahoma Area Vocational Technical School
Culinary Arts
Rte. 1, Box 14M
Ardmore, OK 73401 Phone: 405-223-2070
(1)66 (2)2y (3)Cert (4)Open (5)40 (6)20 (7)Y (8)Y (10)Y (11)Y (12)Y (13)N
(14)Y (15)ID $0, OD $1,600 (16)1 FT, 2 PT (17)State

OREGON

Lane Community College
Culinary Arts Dept.
4000 E. 30th
Eugene, OR 97405 Phone: 503-747-4501
(1)78 (2)2y/1y (3)AAS/Cert (4)Open (5)50 (6)10 (7)Y (8)Y (10)Y (11)Y (12)Y
(13)Y (14)Y 90% (15)IS $1,035, OS $4,000 (16)3 FT, 3 PT (17)NASC

Linn-Benton Community College
Culinary Arts/Restaurant Mgt. c/o Aux. Serv.
6500 SW Pacific Blvd.
Albany, OR 97321 Phone: 503-928-2361

PENNSYLVANIA

Bucks County Community College
Business Dept.
Swamp Rd.
Newtown, PA 18940 Phone: 215-968-8246
(1)68 (2)2y/3y (3)AA (4)Open (5)180 (6)17 (7)Y (8)Y (10)Y (11)Y (12)Y (13)Y (14)Y 90% (15)IC $55/ch, OC $110/ch (16)2 FT, 4 PT (17)MSA

Community College of Allegheny County
Hospitality Mgt./Culinary Arts
595 Beatty Rd.
Monroeville, PA 15146 Phone: 412-327-1327
(1)67 (2)2y (3)AAS/Cert (4)Open (5)175 (6)15 (7)Y (8)N (10)Y (11)Y (12)Y (13)Y (14)Y 100% (15)IS $1,272, OS $2,544 (16)2 FT, 5 PT (17)MSA

Computer Tech
107 Sixth St.
Pittsburgh, PA 15222 Phone: 412-391-4197

Harrisburg Area Community College
Hotel, Restaurant, Institutional Management Dept.
3300 Cameron St. Rd.
Harrisburg, PA 17110 Phone: 717-780-2495
(1)65 (2)2y (3)Cert/AA (4)8,1 (5)250 (6)15 (7)N (8)Y (10)Y (11)Y (12)Y (13)Y (14)Y 100% (15)IS $100/ch, OS $150/ch (16)2 FT, 3 PT (17)MSA, ACBSP (18)Dietary mgmt.

Hiram G. Andrews Center
Voc. Supv. Culinary Arts Program
727 Goucher St.
Johnstown, PA 15905 Phone: 814-255-8288
(1)75 (2)4-18m (3)Dip (4)Every 4m (5)30 (6)15 (7)Y (8)Y (10)N (11)Y (12)N (13)N (14)Y 100% (15)$35/day (16)3 (17)CCA(NATTS) (18)Cook's & baker's helper

IUP Culinary School
125 South Gilpin Street
Punxsutawney, PA 15767 Phone: 814-938-8400
(1)90 (2)2y (3)Cert (4)9 (5)60 (6)12 (7)Y (8)Y (10)N (11)Y (12)Y (13)Y (14)Y 100% (15)$7,268 (16)5 (17)MSA (18)Fund. techniques

Orleans Technical Institute
Culinary Arts Dept.
1330 Rhawn St.
Philadelphia, PA 19111 Phone: 215-728-4488
(1)78 (2)6m (3)Dip (4)Open (8)Y (10)N (11)Y (12)Y (13)N (14)Y 85% (15)$3,950 (16)1-2

Pennsylvania College of Technology
Culinary Arts Dept.
One College Avenue
Williamsport, PA 17701-5799 Phone: 717-326-3761
(1)68 (2)2y (3)Deg/Cert (4)8 (5)90 (6)15 (7)Y (8)Y (9)100% (10)Y (11)Y (12)Y
(13)Y (14)Y 97% (15)IS $154/ch, OS $232/ch (16)6 FT, 3 PT (17)MSA, ACFEI
(18)Rest. mgmt.

Westmoreland County Community College
Culinary Arts Dept.
Armbrust Rd.
Youngwood, PA 15697 Phone: 412-925-4000
(1)81 (2)3y/2y (3)Appr/AAS (4)8,1 (5)120 (6)15-20 (7)Y (8)Y (10)Y (11)Y
(12)Y (13)Y (14)Y 100% (15)IC: $793/AAS,$1,248/Appr,OC: $1,586/$2,49
(16)4 FT, 18 PT (17)ACFEI (18)Baking & pastry

PUERTO RICO

Instituto del Arte Moderno, Inc.
Culinary Arts Dept.
Ave. Monserrate FR-5
Villa Fontana, Carolina, PR 00630 Phone: 809-769-7636
(1)87 (2)1,000h (3)Cert (4)1,8 (5)150 (6)25 (7)Y (8)N (10)N (11)Y (12)N (13)N
(14)Y (15)$2,900 (16)5 (17)CCA(NATTS)

Instituto de Educacion Univ.
Culinary Arts Dept.
Carr 3 Km 11.0 #7 APTDO.209
Carolina, PR 00628 Phone: 809-758-6410

Instituto Vocational y Commercial EDIC
Calle, Esquina 5 Urbanizacion Caguas Norte
Caguas, PR 00726 Phone: 809-744-8519

SOUTH CAROLINA

Greenville Technical College
Food Science Dept.
P.O. Box 5616, Station B
Greenville, SC 29606-5616 Phone: 803-250-8404
(1)77 (2)1y/2y (3)Cert/Deg (4)Q (5)60 (6)15 (7)Y (8)Y (10)Y (11)Y (12)Y (13)N
(14)Y (15)IC $222/q, OC $243/q, OS $381/q (16)1 FT, 2 PT (17)ACFEI, SACS

Horry-Georgetown Technical College
Culinary Arts Dept.
P.O. Box 1966
Conway, SC 29526 Phone: 803-347-3186
(1)85 (2)2y (3)Deg (4)2 (5)65 (6)12 (7)Y (8)Y (9)100% (10)Y (11)Y (12)Y (13)Y
(14)Y 100% (15)IS $450/s, OS $900/s (16)12 (17)SACS, ACFEI (18)Garde
manger, nutrition

Trident Technical College
Marketing Services
P.O. Box 10367; MK-C
Charleston, SC 29411 Phone: 803-572-6021
(1)86 (2)3s (3)Diploma (4)5,8,12 (5)20 (6)10 (7)Y (8)Y (10)Y (11)Y (12)Y (13)Y
(14)Y 100% (15)IC $1,215, OC $1,445, OS $2,277 (16)2 FT (17)SACS

SOUTH DAKOTA

Mitchell Area Vocational Technical School
Cook/Chef
821 N. Capitol
Mitchell, SD 57301 Phone: 605-995-3030
(1)68 (2)18m (3)Dip/Cert/AAS (4)9 (5)40 (6)18-20 (7)Y (8)N (10)Y (11)Y (12)Y
(13)N (14)Y 100% (15)$1,260 (16)2 (17)NCA

TEXAS

The Art Institute of Houston
Culinary Arts - Admissions
1900 Yorktown
Houston, TX 77056 Phone: 713-623-2040
(1)93 (2)18m (3)AAS (4)1,4,7,9 (6)20 (7)Y (8)N (9)65% (10)Y (11)Y (12)Y
(14)Y (16)$10,600 (17)CCA

El Centro College
Food & Hospitality Services Institute
Main at Lamar Streets
Dallas, TX 75202 Phone: 214-746-2202
(1)71 (2)2y (3)AAS (4)1,8 (5)450 (6)20-35 (7)Y (8)Y (10)Y (11)Y (12)Y (13)Y
(14)Y 80-90% (15)IC $400, IS $800, OS $2,000 (16)4 FT, 8 PT (17)SACS

Galveston College
Culinary Arts Dept.
4015 Avenue Q
Galveston, TX 77550 Phone: 409-763-6551
(1)87 (2)2y (3)Cert (4)1,9 (5)15-45 (6)15 (7)Y (8)Y (10)Y (11)Y (12)Y (14)Y
(16)2 FT, 8 PT

Houston Community College System
Consumer Services
1300 Holman
Houston, TX 77004 Phone: 713-630-1121
(1)73 (2)1y (3)Cert (4)9,1,5 (5)60 (6)20 (7)Y (8)N (10)N (11)Y (12)Y (13)Y
(14)N (15)IS $840, OS $2,900 (16)2 FT, 4-5 PT (17)SACS

Odessa College
Culinary Arts
201 W. University
Odessa, TX 79764 Phone: 915-335-6583
(1)90 (2)2y (3)Cert/AAS (4)Open (5)30 (6)10-15 (7)Y (8)Y (9)75% (10)Y (11)Y
(12)Y (13)Y (14)Y 100% (15)IS $550, OS $800-$1,000 (16)5

St. Philip's College
Hospitality Operations
2111 Nevada
San Antonio, TX 78203 Phone: 512-531-3315
(1)79 (2)2y/3y (3)AAS/Appr (4)8,1,6 (5)250 (6)50 (7)Y (8)Y (10)Y (11)Y (12)Y
(13)N (14)Y 85% (15)IS $500, OS $900 (16)5 (17)SACS

San Jacinto College North
Chef's Apprenticeship Training
5800 Uvalde
Houston, TX 77049 Phone: 713-459-7150
(1)86 (2)2y/3y (3)AAS (4)9,1 (5)20-30 (6)12 (7)Y (8)Y (9)90% (10)Y (11)Y
(12)Y (13)N (14)Y 50% (15) (16)3 (17)SACS (18)Commercial cooking

VIRGINIA

ATI Career Institute
School of Culinary Arts
7777 Leesburg Pike, Suite 100 South
Falls Church, VA 22043 Phone: 703-821-8570
(1)88 (2)30w (3)Cert (4)Every 6w (5)93 (6)8 (7)Y (8)N (9)30% (10)Y (11)Y
(12)Y (13)Y (14)Y 92% (15)$6,700 (16)10 (17)ACCET (18)Cul. & pastry arts

WASHINGTON

Edmonds Community College
Culinary Arts
20000 - 68th Ave. West
Lynnwood, WA 98036 Phone: 206-672-6329
(1)88 (2)6q (3)ATA (4)F,W,S (5)45 (6)20 (7)Y (8)N (9)100% (10)Y (11)Y (12)Y
(13)Y (14)Y 100% (15)IS $330/q, OS $1,250/q (16)2 FT, 2 PT (17)State
(18)Cooking & mgmt.

Lower Columbia College
Culinary Arts Dept.
Longview, WA 98632 Phone: 206-577-2300

North Seattle Community College
Culinary Arts Dept.
9600 College Way North
Seattle, WA 98103-3599 Phone: 206-527-3600
(1)70 (2)1y/2y (3)Cert/AAS (4)Q (5)80 (6)15 (7)Y (8)Y (10)N (11)Y (12)Y (13)N
(14)Y 90% (15)IS $288, OS $1,258 (16)4 (17)NASC (18)Rest. cooking

Olympic College
Commercial Cooking/Food Service
16th & Chester
Bremerton, WA 98310-1699 Phone: 206-478-4576
(1)78 (2)2y/3q (3)AAS/Cert (4)Open (5)25 (6)13 (7)Y (8)N (9)85% (10)Y (11)Y
(12)Y (13)N (14)Y 85% (15)$825 (16)2 (17)State (18)Rest. mgmt.

Renton Technical College
Culinary Arts Dept.
3000 N.E. Fourth Street
Renton, WA 98056 Phone: 206-235-2352
(1)68 (2)1,620h (3)Cert (4)Open (5)30 (6)12 (7)Y (8)Y (9)100% (10)Y (11)Y
(12)Y (13)Y (14)Y 100% (15)$400/q (16)2 FT, 5 Asst. (17)ACFEI, NASC
(18)Hands-on, guest chefs

Seattle Central Community College
Hospitality Mgt.and Culinary Arts Dept.
1701 Broadway, Rm. 2120
Seattle, WA 98122 Phone: 206-587-5424
(1)41 (2)5q (3)Cert/AAS (4)Q (5)100-125 (6)20 (7)N (8)Y (9)85% (10)N (11)Y
(12)Y (13)Y (14)Y 90% (15)IS $310/q, OS 1,234/q (16)7 FT, 2 PT (17) (18)Int.
cuisine, ice carving, banquets

Skagit Valley College
Culinary Arts-Restaurant Mgt.
2405 College Way
Mt. Vernon, WA 98273 Phone: 206-428-1211
(1)79 (2)1y/2y (3)Cert/AAS (4)Open (5)60 (6)20 (7)Y (8)Y (10)Y (11)Y (12)Y
(13)Y (14)Y 100% (15)IS $894, OS $3,402 (16)3 (17)State

South Puget Sound Community College
Food Service Technology
2011 Mottman Rd., SW
Olympia, WA 98502 Phone: 206-754-7711 x376
(1)89 (2)2y (3)ATA (4)9,1,4,6 (5)40 (6)20-25 (7)Y (8)Y (10)Y (11)Y (12)Y
(13)N (14)Y (15)IS $32/ch, OS $124/ch (16)2 FT (17)State

South Seattle Community College
Hospitality & Food Science Division
6000 16th Ave. S.W.
Seattle, WA 98106-1499 Phone: 206-764-5344
(1)75 (2)18m (3)Cert/AAS (4)9,1,3,6 (5)130-160 (6)15 (7)N (8)N (9)100% (10)Y
(11)Y (12)Y (13)N (14)Y 96-100% (15)IS $1,240, OS $4,936 (16)7 FT, 8 PT
(17)ACFEI, NASC (18)Classic. cuis., pastries

Spokane Community College
Culinary Arts Dept.
1810 N. Greene St.
Spokane, WA 99207 Phone: 509-536-7100
(1)62 (2)2y (3)AAS (4)9 (5)75-100 (6)20 (7)Y (8)Y (10)Y (11)Y (12)Y (13)N
(14)Y 85% (15)IS $867, OS $3,402 (16)4 (17)NASC

WEST VIRGINIA

Garnet Career Center
Commercial Foods
422 Dickinson St.
Charleston, WV 25301 Phone: 304-348-6127

West Virginia Northern Community College
Culinary Arts Dept.
College Square
Wheeling, WV 26003 Phone: 304-233-5900
(1)75 (2)2y (3)Cert/AAS (4)Open (5)26 (6)9 (7)Y (8)Y (9)100% (10)Y (11)Y
(12)Y (13)N (14)Y 85% (15)IS $42/ch, OS $120/ch (16)4 (17)NCA

WISCONSIN

Chippewa Valley Technical College
Restaurant & Hotel Cookery; Hospitality Mgt.
620 W. Clairemont Ave.
Eau Claire, WI 54701-1098 Phone: 715-836-3514
(2)2y (3)Deg (4)2 (5)36 (6)18 (7)Y (8)N (9)100% (10)Y (11)Y (12)Y (13)N (14)Y
(15)IS $45/ch, OS $295/ch (16)3 FT (17)NCA (18)Catering, deli mgmt.

Fox Valley Technical Institute
Culinary Arts Dept.
1825 N. Bluemound Dr.
Appleton, WI 54913 Phone: 414-735-5638
(1)72 (2)2y (3)Dip/Deg (4)F,W (5)100 (6)12 (7)Y (8)Y (9)90% (10)Y (11)Y
(12)Y (13)Y (14)Y 100% (15)IS $1,620, OS $10,000 (16)8 (17)NCA (18)Rest.
cooking & mgmt.

Madison Area Technical College
Culinary Arts Dept.
3550 Anderson St.
Madison, WI 53704 Phone: 608-246-6308
(2)1y/2y (3)Dip/Deg (4)F,S (5)80-100 (6)15 (7)Y (10)Y (11)Y (12)Y (13)N
(14)Y 80% (15)IS $1,500, OS $1,650 (16)6

Milwaukee Area Technical College
Restaurant & Hotel Cookery Program
700 West State Street
Milwaukee, WI 53233 Phone: 414-278-6255
(1)55 (2)2y (3)AAS (4)8,1 (5)150 (6)18 (7)Y (8)Y (9)50% (10)Y (11)Y (12)Y
(13)N (14)Y 98% (15)IS $2,260, OS $8,244 (16)11 (17)NCA, ACFEI

Waukesha County Technical College
Center for Hospitality Mgmt. & Cul. Arts Studies
800 Main St.
Pewaukee, WI 53072 Phone: 414-691-5254
(1)72 (2)1y (3)Dip/Appren (4)8,1 (5)38 (6)12 (8)N (9)100% (10)Y (12)Y (14)Y
95% (16)3 FT, 3 PT (17)NCA, ACFEI

VOCATIONAL-TECHNICAL SCHOOLS OUTSIDE THE U.S.

AUSTRALIA

Dandenong College
Hospitality Studies
121 Stud Rd.
Dandenong, Victoria, Australia 3175 Phone: 61-3-797-5610
(1)86 (2)2y FT, 4y PT (3)Cert (4)2 (5)200 (6)10-20 (7)Y (8)N (9)20% (10)Y
(11)N (12)N (13)N (14)N 100% (15)IS A$0, OS A$7,000 (16)20 FT, 10 PT
(17)State (18)Food & bev. mgmt.

Regency College of Technical & Further Education
Days Road
Regency Park, Australia 5010 Phone: (61) 8 348 4444

CANADA

Algonquin College
Hospitality Dept.
1385 Woodroffe Ave.
Nepean, ON, K2G 1V8, Canada Phone: 613-727-7761
(1)60 (2)1y/2y (3)Cert/Dip (4)9,1/9 (5)80/30 (6)20/15 (7)Y (8)N (9)50% (10)Y
(11)Y (12)N (13)N (14)Y 90% (15)C$856, Foreign C$5,000 (16)25 FT, 35 PT
(17)

Humber College of Applied Arts & Technology
School of Hospitality, Tourism, & Leisure
205 Humber College Blvd.
Etobicoke, ON, M9W 5L7, Canada Phone: 416-675-3111
(1)75 (2)1-3y (3)Cert/AS (4)9,1 (5)150 (7)Y (8)Y (9) (10)Y (11)Y (12)Y (13)Y
(14)Y 95% (15)IS C$900, Foreign C$5,000 (16)12 FT, 5 PT (17) (18)Cul. &
pastry arts, cont. ed.

Niagara College of Applied Arts and Technology
Hospital and Tourism Division
5881 Dunn St.
Niagara Falls, ON, L2G 2N9, Canada Phone: 416-374-1663
(1)89 (2)2y (3)Dip (4)3 (6)24 (7)Y (8)N (9)50% (10)N (12)N (13)N (14)Y 100%
(15)IS C$1,000, OS C$7,400 (16)4 FT, 2-4 PT (17)State (18)Classic. cuis.

Southern Alberta Institute of Technology
Hospitality Careers Dept.
1301 - 16th Ave., N.W.
Calgary, AB, T2M 0L4, Canada Phone: 403-298-8612
(1)57 (2)2y (3)Dip (4)8 (5)100 (6)13 (7)Y (8)N (9)75% (10)Y (11)N (12)Y (13)N
(14)Y 87% (15)IS C$1,322, OS C$3,350 (16)35 FT, 3 PT (17) (18)Cafeteria,
formal dining

NATIONAL APPRENTICESHIP TRAINING PROGRAM FOR COOKS
American Culinary Federation Educational Institute (ACFEI)

The ACFEI's culinary apprenticeship program, established in 1976, offers career-oriented cooks an alternative to private culinary institutions and vocational-technical schools. Apprentices, who generally range in age from 18 to 40 (average age 24), receive three years (6,000 hours) of on-the-job training while earning an income. The first 500 hours are a probationary period, after which the apprentice is eligible to join the ACFEI and become registered with the Department of Labor. In addition to a 40-hour work week, the apprentice receives 192 hours per year in related classroom instruction. Salary is based on a ratio of a journey-worker's wage with step increases.

To qualify for the program, applicant must be at least 17 years of age, have a high school diploma or equivalent, and have passed all entry-level academic and aptitude examinations as prescribed by the Apprenticeship Committee of the ACFEI. Consideration is given to those who have had high school food service training or on-the-job experience. A five-step screening process includes an orientation seminar, documentation of prior experience, and personal interviews. The successful applicant signs an Apprenticeship Contract.

The program is planned in six semi-annual stages, which can be shortened or lengthened according to the individual's ability. The apprentice keeps a weekly Log Book in which recipes and food preparation techniques are recorded. Those who successfully complete the apprenticeship can: prepare, season, and cook soups, sauces, salads, meats, fish, poultry, game, vegetables, and desserts; produce baked goods and pastries; fabricate meat portions from primal cuts; prepare a buffet dinner; select and develop recipes; plan, write, and design complete menus; plan food consumption, purchasing, and requisitioning; operate a working budget in food and labor costing; recognize quality standards in fresh vegetables, meats, fish, and poultry; demonstrate supervisory abilities and interrelate with other departments in a food operation; and demonstrate basic artistic culinary skills, including ice carving, tallow sculpturing, cake decorating, and garniture display work.

In addition to actual work skills, the apprentice completes 30 hours minimum class time at an accredited post-secondary institution in each of 12 areas of related instruction: 1) Introduction to Food Service (Industry Survey); 2) Sanitation and Safety; 3) Basic Food Preparation (Introduction to Cooking); 4) Business Math (Food Cost Accounting); 5) Food and Beverage Service; 6) Nutrition; 7) Garde Manger; 8) Menu Planning and Design; 9) Baking; 10) Purchasing; 11) Supervisory Management; 12) Advanced Food Preparation.

Upon completion of the program, the apprentice is identified as a Certified Cook and may be offered employment at the training establishment or recommended for job placement. More than 13,500 apprenticeships have been completed since the program was established and approximately 2,600 apprentices are currently enrolled in 39 states, the District of Columbia, Puerto Rico, and Nassau, Bahamas.

Contact: Stephen C. Fernald, CWC, ACFEI Apprentice Director, American Culinary Federation, P.O. Box 3466, 10 San Bartola Rd., St. Augustine, FL 32085; (800) 624-9458 *or* (904) 824-4468, Fax (904) 825-4758.

The following is a list of the 118 ACFEI apprenticeship programs in effect on August 14, 1992.

ALABAMA

ACF Birmingham Chapter *
Janie Green
Jefferson State Comm. College
2601 Carson Rd.
Birmingham, AL 35215
Work Phone: 205-853-1200

ACF Greater Huntsville Chapter
Ron Casey
P.O. Box 12364
Huntsville, AL 35815

ACF Gr. Montgomery Chapter*
Mary Ann Ward, CEC, CCE
Trenholm State Technical College
1225 Air Base Blvd.
Montgomery, AL 36108
Work Phone: 205-262-4728
Home Phone: 205-272-7245

ACF Metro Mobile Chefs Assn.
Levi Ezell, CEC, CCE, AAC
Carver Technical College
414 Station St.
Mobile, AL 36603
Work Phone: 205-473-8692

ARIZONA

Chefs Assn. of Greater Phoenix *
Walter Leible, CMC
Paradise Valley C.C.
7101 N. Tatum Blvd.
Paradise Valley, AZ 85253
Work Phone: 602-840-8100, x275

Chefs Assn. of Southern AZ, Tucson *
Bob Shell, CWC, CCE
P.O. Box 13895
Casa, AZ 85732
Work Phone: 602-327-3594

ARKANSAS

ACF, Little Rock Chapter
Rolf Tinner, CEC, AAC
The Excelsior Hotel
3 Statehouse Plaza
Little Rock, AR 72201
Work Phone: 501-375-5000, x3024

BAHAMAS

Bahamas Culinary Assn.*
Addimae Rolle-Farrington,CWC
Bahamas Hotel Training College
P.O. Box N 4896
Nassau, Bahamas
Work Phone: 809-326-5860

CALIFORNIA

ACF Chefs Assn. San Joaquin Valley
John Chiminello
Chiminello Catering Co.
2221 N. Weber Ave.
Fresno, CA 93705
Work Phone: 209 233-4634

ACF Monterey Peninsula Chefs
  Assn.
Katherine Niven
Dir. Culinary Arts/Cabrillo College
6500 Soquel Dr.
Aptos, CA 95003

ACF Southwest Assn. of Chefs
  & Culinarians
Bob Green
126 Hermes St.
Simi Valley, CA 93065
Work Phone: 805-527-9663, x208
Home Phone: 805-582-9291

* There is a possibility of a pastry apprenticeship.

California Capitol Chefs Assn.
Joe Kriess
1608 Oakview Dr.
Roseville, CA 95661
Work Phone: 916-338-5800
Home Phone: 916-784-0226

Chef de Cuisine of Bakersfield
William Coyle
Bakersfield College-Food Service
1801 Panorama Dr.
Bakersfield, CA 93305
Work Phone: 805-395-4345

Chefs Assn. of the Pacific Coast*
Kay Stickney
Rest. & Hotel Apprentice &
    Training Program
1650 S. Amphlett Blvd., Ste. 312
San Mateo, CA 94402
Work Phone: 415-341-2941

Chefs Assn. of San Diego*
Paul Boutris, CEC
1924-31st St.
San Diego, CA 92102
Work Phone: 619-297-2251
Home Phone: 619-232-7009

Chefs de Cuisine Assn of California *
Ernest W. Green
14842 Raquel Ln..
Canyon Country, CA 91351

Northern California Chefs Assn.
Michael Piccinino
6945 Pine Dr.
Anderson, CA 96007
Work Phone: 916-225-4829
Home Phone: 916-241-6162

Orange Empire Chefs Assn.*
Joe Orate, CC
P.O. Box 1214
Orange, CA 92668
Work Phone: 714-661-6918
Home Phone: 714-558-4126

Santa Barbara Chefs Assn.
Blake Montag
Santa Barbara City College-
    Culinary Educ.
721 Cliff Dr.
Santa Barbara, CA 93109
Work Phone: 805-965-0581, x2458
Home Phone: 805-685-5310

Santa Clara Valley Chapter
Saliem W. Thomas
2239 Seacliff Dr.
Milpitas, CA 95035
Work Phone: 408-268-4653
Home Phone: 408-263-0227

Southern California Inland
    Empire Chefs Assn.
Paul Melchior/Brad Toles
Red Lion Inn/Ontario
222 N. Vineyard
Ontario, CA 91764
Work Phone: 714-983-0909

COLORADO

ACF Colorado Chefs Assn.*
Michael Campe, CEC
838 Symes Bldg., 820 16th St.
Denver, CO 80202
Work Phone: 303-893-3333, x67107

ACF Pikes Peak Chapter, Inc.*
Matt Ziegler
1023 W. Pikes Peak Ave.
Colorado Springs, CO 80904
Work Phone: 719-540-7371

DELAWARE

ACF Delmarva Peninsula Chap.
Mark S. Mayers, CEC
12917 Riggin Ridge Rd.
Ocean City, MD 21842
Work Phone: 301-289-5182
Home Phone: 301-289-7370

ACF First State Chefs
William C. Martin, Jr.
R.D.#2, Box 78-F
Peace Dale Rd.
Landenberg, PA 19350

DISTRICT OF COLUMBIA

ACF Nations Capitol Chefs
Rolf Stroeh
6215 Wilmington Dr.
Burke, VA 22015
Work Phone: 703-769-4693
Home Phone: 703-239-1062

FLORIDA

ACF Bay Culinarians
Travis Herr, CCE
Gulf Coast Community College
5320 W. Hwy. 98
Panama City, FL 32401

ACF Central Florida Chapter
Major Jarman, CEC
348 Tangerine St.
Altamonte Springs, FL 32701
Work Phone: 407-831-0945
Home Phone: 407-830-1911

ACF Gr. Ft. Lauderdale Chapter
Chris Becker
2409 N.E. 27th Ave.
Ft. Lauderdale, FL 33305
Work Phone: 305-977-2072
Home Phone: 305-561-1687

ACF Gr. Jacksonville Chapter*
Stephen C. Fernald, CWC
American Culinary Federation
P.O. Box 3466
St. Augustine, FL 32085
Work Phone: 904-824-4468

ACF Gulf to Lakes Chefs Chapter
Jim Aro
P.O. Box 1179
Eustis, FL 32727
Work Phone: 904-357-8222, x253

ACF Miami Chapter
John Mondone, CEC
4234 S.W. 72nd Way
Davie, FL 33314
Work Phone: 305-347-2119
Home Phone: 305-472-6619

ACF Palm Beach County Chefs*
Ron Zabkiewicz
513 Reo Dr.
Jupiter, FL 33458
Work Phone: 407-369-7000, x7119

ACF St. Augustine Chapter
Howard Holanchock
St. Augustine Technical Ctr.
Collins Ave. @ Del Monte
St. Augustine, FL 32086
Work Phone: 904-824-4401

ACF Treasure Coast Chapter
Charles Castilyn/V.A.C.E.
Martin Co. Adult Educ.
500 E. Ocean Blvd.
Stuart, FL 34994
Work Phone: 407-287-6400, x345

Disney World (In-house)
Tim Rosendahl
Walt Disney World Co.-
    Culinary Development
P.O. Box 10000
Lake Buena Vista, FL 32830-1000
Work Phone: 407-824-5233

Gulf Coast Culinary Assn.
Gus Silivos
Skopelos Seafood & Steak Rest.
670 Scenic Hwy.
Pensacola, FL 32503

There is a possibility of a pastry apprenticeship.

Sarasota Bay Chefs Assn.
Heinz Schellenberger, CCE
4748 Beneva Rd.
Sarasota, FL 34232
Work Phone: 813-924-1365

Sea World (In-house)
David Nina, CWC
7007 Sea World Dr.
Orlando, FL 32821
Work Phone: 407-351-3600, x191

Southwest Florida Chefs Assn.
William Brower, CEC, AAC
5330 Bayside Ct.
Cape Coral, FL 33904
Work Phone: 813-542-5501

Tampa Bay Chefs Assn.
Steve Struzinski
5034 Dickens Ave.
Tampa, FL 33629
Work Phone: 813-831-4982

Volusia County Chefs & Cooks*
Brian Clarke
2114 India Palm Drive
Edgewater, FL 32141

West Central Florida Prof.
 Chefs & Cul.
Dennis Montileone, CEC
484 F. Santa Cruze Pl., NE
St. Petersburg, FL 33703

GEORGIA

ACF Inc., Gr. Atlanta Chapter*
John Brantley, CEC
3571 Forrest Glen Tr.
Lawrenceville, GA 30244
Work Phone: 404-381-8618

Golden Isles of Georgia Culinary
 Assn. * (In house)
Louis Borochaner, CEPC
205 Palm St.
St. Simons Isl., GA 31522
Work Phone: 912-638-3611, x5640

HAWAII

Chefs de Cuisine Assn. of Hawaii *
William Trask
Ilikai Hotel
1777 Ala Moana Blvd.
Honolulu, HI 96816
Work Phone: 808-949-3811
Home Phone: 808-735-5641

Maui Chefs Assn.*
Christopher Speere
29 Kokomo Rd.
Haiku, HI 96708
Work Phone: 808-242-1225
Home Phone: 808-575-2353

IDAHO

ACF Idaho State Chefs Assn.
John Fisher
2025 N.W. 12th
Meridian, IN 83642
Work Phone: 208-342-4622 *or*
        800-243-4622

ILLINOIS

ACF Chicago Chefs of Cuisine*
Alexander Dering
1030 N. State St., Unit 9B
Chicago, IL 60610
Work Phone: 312-787-3997
Home Phone: 312-943-4412

ACF Heart of Illinois Prof.
 Chef Assn.
Mark Buckley, President
104 Leonard Dr.
Chillicothe, IL 61523
Work Phone: 309-829-8092

INDIANA

ACF Greater Indianapolis Chapter
Bill O'Brien
Marriott Food Svs.-I.U.P.U.I.
620 Union Dr.
Indianapolis, IN 46202
Work Phone: 317-274-5082

ACF South Bend Chapter
Denis F. Ellis, CEC.AAC
Univ. of Notre Dame, So. Dining Hall
Notre Dame, IN 46556
Work Phone: 219-239-5416
Home Phone: 219-271-9171

ACF Tri-States Chefs Chapter
Robert Bird
Vincennes University-Culinary
 Arts Dept.
Vincennes, IN 47591
Work Phone: 812-885-5858
Home Phone: 812-886-6714

IOWA

ACF Chef de Cuisine/Quad Cities
Anthony Kowalczyk, CEC, AAC
Davenport Club, 200 E. Third St.
Davenport, IA 52801
Work Phone: 319-324-8920
Home Phone: 309-755-3990

KENTUCKY

ACF Bluegrass Chefs Assn.
Robert Karisny
1352 Deer Lake
Lexington, KY 40502
Work Phone: 606-263-6611
Home Phone: 606-253-1916

LOUISIANA

ACF Greater Baton Rouge Chapter
Bruce Cain
Baton Rouge C.C.
8551 Jefferson Hwy.
Baton Rouge, LA 70809
Work Phone: 504-965-5466

ACF New Orleans Chapter*
Iva Bergeron
Delgado Community College
615 City Park Ave.
New Orleans, LA 70119
Work Phone: 504-483-4208

MARYLAND

ACF Cumberland Valley Chapter
Raymond Antoniuk
8620 Pinecliff Dr.
Frederick, MD 21701

Central Maryland Chefs Assn.
Elaine Heilman
420 Ednor Rd.
Silver Springs, MD 20904
Work Phone: 301-997-4562
Home Phone: 301-774-3703

MWRCAC
Judith Knapp
7113 Ambassador Rd.
Baltimore, MD 21207
Work Phone: 301-298-4698

MASSACHUSETTS

ACF Cape Cod & The Islands*
Robert Trainor
Chatham Bars Inn
Shore Rd.
Chatham, MA 02633
Work Phone: 508-945-0096

ACF Greater Worcester Chefs Assn.
Chip Dufalt
74 Loxwood St.
Worcester, MA 01604
Work Phone: 508-753-4925
Home Phone: 508-753-1986

Epicurean Club of Boston
Christopher Leu
Westin Hotel, 10 Huntington Ave.
Boston, MA 02116
Work Phone: 617-424-7524

Massachusetts Culinary Assn.
John Nicas
The Castle Restaurant
1230 Main St.
Leicester, MA 01524
Work Phone: 508-892-9090
Home Phone: 508-892-8000

There is a possibility of a pastry apprenticeship.

MICHIGAN

ACF Capitol Professional Chefs
  Assn.
John Farris
Lansing Community College
419 W. Capital
Lansing, MI 48910
Work Phone: 517-483-1563, x11
Home Phone: 517-321-0334

ACF Michigan Chefs de Cuisine
  Assn.*
Kevin Enright, CEC, CCE
Oakland Community College
27055 Orchard Lake Rd.
Farmington Hills, MI 48018
Work Phone: 313-471-7500

ACF of Northwestern Michigan
Steven Richard Berkshire
425 George St.
Traverse City, MI 49684
Work Phone: 616-938-2100, x3369
Home Phone: 616-946-3198

MISSOURI

ACF Gr. Kansas City Chefs Assn.*
Patrick Sweeney
Johnson County Community
  College
12345 College @ Quivira
Overland Park, KS 66210
Work Phone: 913-469-8500, x3611

ACF Chefs & Cooks of
  Springfield/Ozark
Jim Hintz
Heart of Ozarks Comm. Tech. Coll.
P.O. Box 5958
Springfield, MO 65801

Chefs de Cuisine of St. Louis*
Robert Schultz
Adams Mark Hotel
4th & Chestnut
St. Louis, MO 63102
Work Phone: 314-241-7400

MONTANA

Chefs & Cooks of Montana
Jack Hemsing, CEC
Billings Petroleum Club
Box 1957
Billings, MT 59103
Work Phone: 406-252-6702
Home Phone: 406-652-1149

NEBRASKA

ACF Professional Chefs of Nebraska
Gerrine Schreck, CEC, CWC
5619 Huntington, #6
Lincoln, NE 68507
Work Phone: 402-471-3333, x219
Home Phone: 402-423-5165

ACF Professional Chefs of Omaha
Jim Trebbien
Metropolitan Community College
P.O. Box 3777
Omaha, NE 68103-0777
Work Phone: 402-449-8394

NEVADA

ACF Colorado River Chefs Assn.
Jerry Thompson
Harrahs Casino, 2900 S. Casino Dr.
Laughlin, NV 89029

The Frat. of Exec. Chefs of Las Vegas
Claude Lambertz
University of Nevada-Las Vegas
4505 Maryland Pkwy.
Las Vegas, NV 89154
Work Phone: 702-739-3503

High Sierra Chefs Assn.
Terence Woodard
P.O. Box 624401
South Lake Tahoe, CA 96154
Home Phone: 916-542-9205

NEW HAMPSHIRE

Greater North New Hampshire
  Chapter
Phil Learned, CEC
The Balsams Resort Hotel
Dixville Notch, NH 03576
Work Phone: 603-255-3400

NEW JERSEY

ACF Tri-Country Chapter
William White
Burlington County College
County Rte. 530
Pemberton, NJ 08068
Work Phone: 609-894-931, x441
Home Phone: 609-784-5656

Professional Chefs of South Jersey *
John Carbone, CCE,CE, AAC
P.O. Box 157
Port Republic, NJ 08241
Work Phone: 609-652-1726
Home Phone: 609-646-4950

NEW MEXICO

ACF Chefs of Santa Fe*
Richard Ortiz
Santa Fe Community College
S. Richards Ave., P.O. Box 4187
Santa Fe, NM 87502-4187
Work Phone: 505-471-8200

ACF "Paso Del Norte" Chapter
Ralph Hadley
10605 Rushing Rd.
El Paso, TX 79924
Home Phone: 915-821-6501

ACF Rio Grande Valley Chapter*
Doug Dunning, CE
Albuquerque Tech-Voc Inst.
525 Buena Vista S.E.
Albuquerque, NM 87106
Work Phone: 505-224-3731

NEW YORK

ACF Albany Chapter
Donald Sacca, CEC
111 Industrial Park Rd., Apt.3
Troy, NY 12180
Work Phone: 518-449-8090
Home Phone: 518-861-6207

ACF of Greater Buffalo
Samuel J. Sheusi
5084 Dana Dr.
Lewiston, NY 14092
Work Phone: 716-731-4101
Home Phone: 716-297-4551

Chefs of Westchester & Lower
  Connecticut
Brian Martin
Black Goose Grille, 972 Post Rd.
Darien, CT 06820
Work Phone: 203-655-7107
Home Phone: 914-667-0984

NORTH CAROLINA

ACF Charlotte Chapter
Richard Price
6316 Rocklake Dr.
Charlotte, NC 28214
Work Phone: 704-892-4633

ACF Fayetteville/Ft. Bragg Chefs
G. Martin Lassiter
P.O. Box 1602
Buries Creek, NC 27506

ACF Outer Banks Culinary Assn.
Beat Zuttel
300 Dogwood Tr.
Southern Shores, NC 27949
Work Phone: 919-261-2764
Home Phone: 919-261-8780

Professional Chefs of the Carolinas
Fredi Morf
1316 Hickory Hollow Ln.
Raleigh, NC 27610
Work Phone: 919-839-0691

* There is a possibility of a pastry apprenticeship.

Triad Professional Chefs Assn.
Wayne Odachowski
Four Seasons Town Centre
3121 High Point Rd. @ I-40
Greensboro, NC 27407
Work Phone: 919-292-9161, x193

Western N. Carolina Culinary Assn.
Hubert Treiber
Grove Park Inn & CC
290 Macon Ave.
Asheville, NC 28804

OHIO

ACF Akron Chapter
Jay Baker
1325 Coraham Rd.
Cuyahoga Falls, OH 44224
Work Phone: 216-688-6066
Home Phone: 216-928-2535

ACF Cleveland Chapter
Richard Fulchiron, CEC
Cuyahoga Community College
2900 Community College Ave.
Cleveland, OH 44115
Work Phone: 216-987-4087

ACF Columbia Chefs Chapter*
Carol Kizer, CCE
Columbus State Community College
550 E. Spring St.
Columbus, OH 43215
Work Phone: 614-227-2579
Home Phone: 614-488-8907

Maumee Valley Chefs
Benita Wong, CWC
Univ. of Toledo Comm/Tech College
Scott Park Campus
Toledo, OH 43606
Work Phone; 419-537-3114

OKLAHOMA

ACF Tulsa Chapter
Reno Jungo
OSU-Technical Branch
Okmulgee, OK 74447
Work Phone: 918-756-6211, x262

Culinary Society of Oklahoma*
Genni Thomas
4337 Dahoon Dr.
Oklahoma City, OK 73120
Work Phone: 405-755-1515
Home Phone: 405-752-1279

OREGON

ACF Southern Oregon Chapter
Russell Rickert
164 Almeda
Ashland, OR 97520
Work Phone: 503-776-5057
Home Phone: 503-482-8704

Chefs de Cuisine Society of Oregon *
Anthony Danna
75 N.E. Dekum
Portland, OR 97211
Work Phone: 503-223-2119
Home Phone: 503-289-4532

PENNSYLVANIA

ACF Laurel Highlands Chapter*
Mary Zappone
Westmoreland Cty. Community
    College-Cul. Arts
Armbrust Rd.
Youngwood, PA 15697-1895
Work Phone: 412-925-4000

Central Pennsylvania Chefs Assn.
Michael Harants
201 E. Green St.
Mechanicsburg, PA 17055
Work Phone: 717-691-7376

Chefs Assn. of Pittsburgh*
Willie Stinson, CEC
Community College of Allegheny
    Cty.-Cul. Arts
808 Ridge Ave.
Pittsburgh, PA 15212
Work Phone: 412-237-2698

Delaware Valley Chefs Assn.*
Thomas Macrina
3104 Jolly Rd.
Norristown, PA 19401
Work Phone: 215-925-7000
Home Phone: 215-279-9577

Delaware Valley Chefs Assn.
Richard Zettlemoyer, Jr.
Holiday Inn
4700 Street Rd.
Trevose, PA 19053
Work Phone: 215-364-2000

PUERTO RICO

ACF Puerto Rico Chefs Assn.
Jose Mora
P.O. Box 37879, Luis Marin Airport
Isla Verde, PR 00937-0837
Work Phone: 809-791-0305

RHODE ISLAND

ACF Rhode Island Chapter
Theodore Butzbach
14 D Caddy Rock Rd.
North Kingston, RI 02815
Work Phone: 401-828-7800, x264
Home Phone: 401-294-4174

Newport Chapter ACF
Bruce Hoerauf/Sous Chef
Newport Marriott Hotel
25 America's Cup Ave.
Newport, RI 02840
Work Phone: 401-849-1000

SOUTH CAROLINA

South Carolina Upstate Prof. Chefs
Keith Gardiner
12 Brookway Dr.
Greenville, SC 29605
Work Phone: 803-233-1621
Home Phone: 803-370-2201

TENNESSEE

ACF Greater Memphis Chapter
John Fatino, CEC, CCE
108 N. Auburndale, Apt.116
Memphis, TN 38104
Work Phone: 901-278-8200, x29

ACF Middle Tennessee Chapter
Stanley Jensen
116 Connie Dr.
Hendersonville, TN 37075
Work Phone: 615-264-1436

Opryland Hotel (In house)
Richard Gerst
2800 Opryland Dr.
Nashville, TN 37214
Work Phone: 615-889-1000

TEXAS

ACF Capitol of Texas Chefs
Thomas Ciapi, CWC
11605 Fruitwood Pl.
Austin, TX 78758
Work Phone: 512-323-2511

TCA-Austin
Larry Forth
Huston-Tillotson College
1820 E. Eighth St.
Austin, TX 78702
Work Phone: 512-476-7421

TCA-Corpus Christi
Scott Almy
Holiday Inn-Emerald Beach
116 Holly Rd.
Portland, TX 78374
Work Phone: 512-883-5731, x2231

TCA-Dallas*
James Goering, CCE, CEC
El Centro College
Main @ Lamar
Dallas, TX 75202-3604
Work Phone: 214-746-2217
Home Phone: 214-241-4487

There is a possibility of a pastry apprenticeship.

TCA-Houston
Fritz Gitschner
Houston C.C., 1 Potomac Dr.
Houston, TX 77057

TCA-Rio Grande Valley
Isaac Pina, CEC
Palm Management, Inc.
415 S. International Blvd.
Weslaco, TX 78596-9204
Work Phone: 512-969-2411, x274

TCA-San Antonio
Steve Martin
St. Philips College
2111 Nevada
San Antonio, TX 78213
Work Phone: 512-531-3315

Texas Chefs Assn.*
William Phipps, CEC
8206 Cattle Bend
Converse, TX 78109
Work Phone: 512-822-8722, x163

UTAH

ACF Beehive State Chefs Chapter
Jeff Dejong
Salt Lake Community College
4600 S. Redwood Rd.
Salt Lake City, UT 84130
Work Phone: 801-581-2202

VERMONT

North Vermont Chefs &
  Cooks Assn.
Kevin Draper
RD1, Box 2620
Waterbury Center, VT 05677
Work Phone: 802-888-3030
Home Phone: 802-244-5851

VIRGINIA

Blue Ridge Chefs Assn.
Witt Ledford
Sheraton Hotel-Charlottesville

2350 Seminole Tr.
Charlottesville, VA 22901

Colonial Williamsburg Fdn.*
  (In house)
Steve Maiorana
223 E. Ottawa Rd.
Virginia Beach, VA 23462

The Trellis Restaurant (In house)
Andrew O'Connell
Duke of Gloucester
P.O. Box 287
Williamsburg, VA 23187-0287
Work Phone: 804-229-8610

Virginia Chefs Assn.*
Mark Kimmel, CEC
7212 Bennington Rd.
Richmond, VA 23225
Work Phone: 804-782-9432
Home Phone: 804-745-1647

WASHINGTON

Washington State Chefs Assn.
David Estes
30218 Second Ave. S.
Federal Way, WA 98003
Work Phone: 206-433-2524
Home Phone: 206-946-4466

WISCONSIN

ACF Chefs of Milwaukee, Inc.
Knut Apitz
Grenadier's Restaurant
747 N. Broadway @ Mason
Milwaukee, WI 53202
Work Phone: 414-276-0747

ACF Fox Valley Chapter
Albert Exenberger, CEC
Fox Valley Technical Inst.
1825 N. Bluemound Dr.,
P.O. Box 2277
Appleton, WI 54913-2277
Work Phone: 414-735-5600

III

CULINARY & ACCREDITING ORGANIZATIONS

AMERICAN CULINARY FEDERATION (ACF)
St. Augustine, Florida

This professional, educational, and fraternal association of chefs and cooks, founded in 1929 to further the advancement of the culinary profession, is organized into more than 250 local chapters across the U. S. and the Caribbean. Its membership of more than 20,000 chefs, pastry chefs, and cooks ranges from culinary students to accomplished, experienced chefs. As the oldest and only nationwide professional cooks' association recognized by other leading foodservice organizations, the ACF's objective is to offer a means for culinarians to gain experience, training, education, and fellowship.

The American Culinary Federation Educational Institute (ACFEI), a subsidiary of the ACF, recognizes exemplary culinary schools through accreditation by its Accrediting Commission (eligibility requirements and list of accredited institutions follows), grants certification to chefs on the basis of knowledge and experience, and provides a U.S. Department of Labor recognized three-year National Apprenticeship Training Program for Cooks (page 256). Certification categories include Certified Cook/Baker, Certified Working Chef and/or Pastry Chef, Certified Culinary Educator, Certified Executive Chef and/or Executive Pastry Chef, and the highest level, Certified Master Chef/Certified Master Pastry Chef. Culinary students who meet certain criteria are eligible for ACFEI loans or scholarships. Another subsidiary of the ACF, The American Academy of Chefs, is the honor society of American chefs and admits those who are recognized by their colleagues as leaders in the field of culinary arts.

Membership benefits of the ACF include: educational seminars at the National ACF Convention and regional meetings; a subscription to the ACF's monthly magazine, *The National Culinary Review*, which contains information on new trends, activities, meetings, and employment opportunities for chefs; and the opportunity to compete for gold, silver, and bronze medals in ACF-approved culinary arts shows sponsored by local chapters. The ACF and the National Restaurant Association jointly sponsor the United States Culinary "Olympic" Team that represents the American culinary profession in the largest and oldest of all international cooking competitions, the Culinary "Olympics" held every four years in Frankfurt, Germany. Membership dues vary from chapter to chapter. Individuals who live more than 50 miles from a chapter can become members-at-large for $65 per year.

Contact: The American Culinary Federation, P.O. Box 3466, St. Augustine, FL 32085; (800) 624-9458 *or* (904) 824-4468, Fax (904) 825-4758.

AMERICAN CULINARY FEDERATION
EDUCATIONAL INSTITUTE (ACFEI) ACCREDITING COMMISSION
St. Augustine, Florida

Accreditation by the American Culinary Federation Educational Institute Accrediting Commission, the educational arm of the American Culinary Federation, is a review process that evaluates the quality of an educationally-accredited postsecondary institution's program in culinary arts and foodservice management. The program's objectives, staff, facilities, policies, curriculum, instructional methods, and procedures are examined to determine if they meet ACFEI

Standards, which were developed to meet the requirements for entry-level culinarians. To be eligible, a program must contain a majority of required competencies; must be offered by a school that is accredited by an agency recognized by the U.S. Department of Education and Council on Postsecondary Accreditation; must be full-time, include at least 1,000 contact hours, and result in a certificate, diploma, or degree; must have a full-time coordinator who has been ACFEI Certified as a Culinary Educator, Executive Chef, or Executive Pastry Chef *or* has earned a master's degree in an appropriate discipline; and must have been in continuous existence for at least two years and have graduated a sufficient number of students in order to be evaluated. In addition, application for accreditation must be authorized by the Dean of the department and 50% of the full-time faculty in the technical phase of the program must have credentials equivalent to an ACFEI Certified Culinary Educator, Working Chef, or Pastry Chef. On June 1, 1990, the ACFEI was officially recognized by the U. S. Department of Education for a three-year term as an accrediting agency.

Contact: For a current list of accredited programs: The Educational Institute, American Culinary Federation, P.O. Box 3466, St. Augustine, FL 32085; (904) 824-4468. For accreditation application: The American Culinary Federation Educational Institute Accrediting Commission, 959 Melvin Rd., Annapolis, MD 21403; (410) 268-5659.

ACFEI-Accredited Schools as of August 5, 1992:

ALABAMA
Jefferson State Comm. College, 267

ARIZONA
Scottsdale Culinary Institute, 3

CALIFORNIA
California Culinary Academy, 5
Diablo Valley College, 239
Orange Coast College, 240

COLORADO
Pikes Peak Community College, 241

CONNECTICUT
Manchester Community College, 241

FLORIDA
Atlantic Vocational Tech. Center, 242
Florida Culinary Institute-
   New England Tech., 33
Pinellas Vo-Tech Institute , 243
Southeast Inst. of Culinary Arts, 35

HAWAII
Maui Community College, 244

IDAHO
Boise State University, 244

ILLINOIS
College of DuPage, 245
Elgin Community College, 245
Joliet Junior College, 245
Kendall College, 40
Triton College, 245

INDIANA
Indiana Vo-Tech College,
   (Indianapolis & Ft. Wayne), 246

IOWA
Des Moines Area Comm. College, 246
Kirkwood Community College, 247

KANSAS
Johnson County
   Community College, 247

KENTUCKY
Jefferson Community College, 248
National Center for Hospitality
   Studies at Sullivan College, 48

LOUISIANA
Bossier Parish Community College, 248
Delgado Community College, 271

AMERICAN INSTITUTE OF BAKING (AIB)
Manhattan, Kansas

This nonprofit educational and research organization was established in 1919 to promote the cause of education in nutrition and in the science and art of baking, bakery management, and the allied sciences. Located in a $5 million, 75,000 square foot facility on thirteen acres overlooking the Kansas State University campus, the AIB employs 105 full-time personnel and is supported by the contributions of more than 550 member companies.

The AIB's School of Baking has trained more than 15,000 individuals since classes began in 1922. Current programs include the twice yearly 16-week Baking Science and Technology course for those desiring supervisory positions in the baking industry, the twice-yearly 10-week Bakery Maintenance Engineering program, and a variety of short courses and seminars that offer the opportunity for updating technical knowledge and sharpening baking skills. Correspondence courses include the 50-lesson Science of Baking course, the 46-lesson Food Science and Technology course, the 16-lesson In-store and Retail Baking Technology course, the 26-lesson course in Bakery Maintenance Engineering, the 15-lesson course in Food Plant Sanitation, and the 12-lesson course in Warehouse Sanitation. The AIB's Certified Baker Program provides companies with a training program that can be implemented while employees are on the job. Scholarships and financial aid are available.

The AIB's research department laboratories develop new knowledge and problem-solving techniques; the Technical Assistance group provides detailed information on scientific, technical, and regulatory subjects; the Department of Sanitation Education offers educational training and in-plant inspection; the Department of Safety Education offers educational training and in-plant audits; and the Library responds to requests for information from all over the world.

Contact: American Institute of Baking, 1213 Bakers Way, Manhattan, KS 66502; (800) 633-5137 *or* (913) 537-4750.

THE AMERICAN INSTITUTE OF WINE & FOOD (AIWF)
San Francisco, California

This nonprofit educational organization, with more than 7,000 members and 33 chapters across the country and overseas, was founded in 1981 by Julia Child, Robert Mondavi, Richard Graff and others to advance the understanding, appreciation, and quality of wine and food. Its objective is to facilitate the broad exchange of information and ideas for the benefit of all who care about wine and food, to stimulate greater scholarly interest in food and drink, and to foster expanded research and educational opportunities in these fields.

Membership benefits include *The Journal of Gastronomy* yearly publication, *American Wine & Food* newsletter, invitations to AIWF national and Chapter programs, special prices on national educational conferences and seminars, and savings on wine and food publications. The Institute sponsors the annual Conference on Gastronomy, maintains the AIWF Collection of gastronomic literature, and is developing a food and wine resource database. AIWF chapters in Arizona (Phoenix), Atlanta, Boston, Chicago, Colorado, Connecticut, Dallas/ Fort Worth, Delaware Valley (Philadelphia), France (Paris), Inland Empire (Redlands), Hawaii, Kansas City, Los Angeles, Mississippi, Milwaukee, Monterey Bay, New Orleans, New York, North Carolina (Piedmont), Northern California, Northern Ohio, Orange County (CA), Rhode Island, Sacramento, San Diego, Santa Barbara, Seattle, Silicon Valley (San Jose), Southern Arizona (Tucson), South Florida (Miami), Washington, D.C., and Vermont sponsor local educational events and provide members with the opportunity to meet others who share their interests. Chapters are scheduled to open in such other major areas as Eastern Ohio, Las Vegas, Ann Arbor, Detroit, Wichita, Richmond, New Jersey, Toronto, and New Zealand. Student chapters, which organize their own educational events as well as participate in regular chapter activities, are currently active at the French Culinary Institute, the California Culinary Academy, Cornell University, the Culinary Institute of America, New England Culinary Institute, and the University of California at Pomona. Student chapters will soon open at UCLA, Johnson & Wales University, and Widener University.

Annual tax-deductible membership dues are $35 for student members; $60 for dedicated consumers— those with a serious interest in wine and food; $125 for those professionally involved in wine, food, and related fields; and $500, $1,000, and $2,500 for corporate businesses.

Contact: The American Institute of Wine & Food, 1550 Bryant St., San Francisco, CA 94103; (415) 255-3000.

LES AMIS DU VIN
Silver Spring, Maryland

This international food and wine society, with 400 chapters in the United States and abroad, is open to individuals who are devoted to the appreciation of fine wine and the art of leisurely dining. Its objective is to provide active, continuing education, enabling those who have just become interested in wine to become connoisseurs and connoisseurs to become specialists. The society provides a list of more than 200 experts who are available to speak at chapter tastings nationwide.

Membership benefits include: a subscription to the bimonthly *The Friends of Wine Magazine*, which contains articles written by wine experts and vintage tasting reports; discounts on wine purchases from affiliated wine shops; group tastings, gourmet dinners, and other wine related events sponsored by individual chapters; and specially priced travel excursions accompanied by wine experts.

Single or family membership is $30 for one year, $55 for two years, $80 for three years, and $300 for life. *The Friends of Wine Magazine* subscription (without membership) is $18 per year, $24 outside the U.S., $38 overseas airmail.

Contact: Les Amis du Vin, 2302 Perkins Place, Ste. 202, Silver Spring, MD 20910; (301) 588-0980.

CAREER COLLEGE ASSOCIATION (CCA)
Washington, D.C.

This educational organization was established in 1991 as a consolidation of the National Association of Trade and Technical Schools (NATTS) and the Association of Independent Colleges and Schools (AICS), both sponsors of accrediting commissions that evaluate private career schools and accredit those that meet certain standards. CCA represents almost 2,000 private post-secondary vocational institutions in the U. S. and abroad.

Contact: Career College Association, 750 First St., NE, Ste. 900, Washington, DC 20002; (202) 336-6700.

CCA-Accredited Schools as of September 1, 1992:

ARIZONA
Scottsdale Culinary Institute, 3

CALIFORNIA
California Culinary Academy, 5
Century Business College, 238
Lederwolff Culinary Academy, 239

CONNECTICUT
CBI Culinary Academy, 241

FLORIDA
Art Institute of Ft. Lauderdale, 241
Johnson & Wales University, 111
New England Institute
   of Technology at Palm Beach, 33
Southeastern Academy, 243

ILLINOIS
Cooking and Hospitality
   Institute of Chicago, 39

KENTUCKY
Sullivan College, 48

LOUISIANA
Camelot Career College, 248
Culinary Arts Inst. of Louisiana, 50

MARYLAND
Baltimore International
   Culinary College, 55, 207

MASSACHUSETTS
The Cambridge School
   of Culinary Arts, 59

CONFRÉRIE DE LA CHAINE DES RÔTISSEURS
Houston, Texas

This international gastronomic organization, originally founded in Paris in 1248 as a guild of masters in the art of roasting geese for the royal table, was disbanded in 1791 and was reincorporated in 1950 by three amateurs and two professionals who wanted to restore the pride in culinary excellence lost during a period of wartime shortages. Its purpose is to encourage diverse educational functions and promote fellowship among amateur and professional individuals with a serious interest in good wine and cuisine. Professionals, who make up approximately 30% of the membership, include well-known authors, lecturers, and critics, individuals involved in food preparation, service, and administration in hotels and restaurants, and suppliers of wine, food, and equipment. The nonprofit, tax-exempt Chaine Education Fund supports a number of educational and charitable programs.

In the U.S. the Chaine has approximately 130 local chapters with more than 7,000 members and associates. Membership benefits at the local level include competitions and participation in various gastronomic functions throughout the year, usually four to six formal dinners supplemented by two to four smaller events, such as wine and food tastings, barbecues, or receptions. On a regional and national level, members can join in Chaine-sponsored excursions, attend the national convention, and share, by invitation, the activities of other chapters. Members who travel outside the U.S. can participate in a variety of activities, conventions, and reunions.

In areas where a chapter has been established, membership is normally by invitation only. Usually at least two members must endorse an application, which must be forwarded to the National Office with annual dues and initiation fee. Interested individuals who do not know a member are encouraged to contact the

National Office for information. Recommended applications are sent to Paris for further review and acceptance and members are accorded privileges in both the National and International Societies. Special dues reductions are offered to spouses, individuals under the age of 30, full-time culinary arts students, and culinary instructors.

Contact: Confrérie de la Chaine des Rôtisseurs, 4299 San Filipe, #110, Houston, TX 77077; (713) 877-1046.

COUNCIL ON HOTEL, RESTAURANT AND INSTITUTIONAL EDUCATION (CHRIE)
Washington, D.C.

Founded in 1946 as a nonprofit organization, CHRIE's mission is to "foster the international advancement of teaching, training, learning, research and practice in the field of hospitality and tourism management, and to encourage and facilitate the professional development of its members". Both a trade and a professional organization, CHRIE's more than 2,200 members from 45 countries include administrators, educators, industry professionals, and association and government executives involved in education, training, and human resource development. Membership benefits include an annual conference (August 4-7, 1993, in Chicago, July 27-30, 1994, in Palm Springs) and several publications: *The CHRIE Communique* bi-weekly newsletter, the *Hospitality & Tourism Educator* interdisciplinary quarterly, the three times yearly *Hospitality Research Journal*, and the annual *Hosteur Magazine*, an internationally distributed career and self-development magazine for the more than 60,000 students at CHRIE-member schools. The *Annual Directory of CHRIE Members* contains biographical data on individual members and *A Guide to College Programs in Hospitality & Tourism* includes information on curriculum, size of program, admission requirements, and availability of scholarships and internships.

Contact: CHRIE, 1200 17th St., N.W., Washington, DC 20036-3097; (202) 331-5990, Fax (202) 785-2511.

COUNCIL OF REGIONAL CULINARY ORGANIZATIONS (CORCO)

This organization was formed in 1987 to help regional culinary groups to better communicate and exchange information and ideas. Its more than 20 member organizations include, for example, the New York Women's Culinary Alliance, the Northwest Culinary Alliance of Seattle, the Chicago Culinary Guild, and the San Francisco Professional Food Society. Official meetings, scheduled during the annual IACP conferences, provide a forum for organization representatives to network and discuss topics relating to events and programs, membership categories and dues, committee and board structure, and bylaws.

Contact: Jane Hibler, CORCO, 282 Northwest Macleary Blvd., Portland, OR 97210; (503) 228-4740.

THE EDUCATIONAL FOUNDATION OF THE
NATIONAL RESTAURANT ASSOCIATION
Chicago, Illinois

Established in 1987, the Educational Foundation of the NRA is a nonprofit organization created to advance the professional standards of foodservice management through education. The Foundation develops courses, video training, seminars, and other comprehensive training programs that help managers gain proficiency in a variety of areas. Programs include the SERVSAFE Risk Management Series, Customer Service Training, and Managing Human Resources. The organization offers the Foodservice Management Professional (FMP) credential to industry professionals who meet specific work and education requirements and who pass the certification exam. The Foundation awards more than 250 scholarships, grants, and fellowships to students, educators, and professionals who want to pursue industry educations. Free brochures include *Careers in Foodservice* and *A Guide to Two- and Four-Year Foodservice/Hospitality Programs*.

Contact: The Educational Foundation of the National Restaurant Association, 250 S. Wacker Dr., Ste. 1400, Chicago, IL 60606; (312) 715-1010.

INTERNATIONAL ASSOCIATION
OF CULINARY PROFESSIONALS (IACP)
Louisville, Kentucky

This not-for-profit professional association, which began as the Association of Cooking Schools, was founded in 1978 to link culinary educators in a worldwide network. Governed by an 11-member Board of Directors with more than 1,600 members representing over 20 countries, IACP's objectives and projects include: providing continuing education and professional development through regional and international conferences, publications, and the annual IACP Cookbook Awards; promoting the exchange of culinary information among members of the professional food community; and establishing professional and ethical standards through a certification program for culinary professionals and endorsement of cooking schools. Funding for scholarships and culinary research is provided by IACP's Foundation for Cooking Advancement and Research Education Foundation (CAREF).

There are five categories of membership: Professional Members are individuals who derive their income from food-related activities; Cooking School Members are vocational or avocational schools that focus on culinary education; Business Members are small, entrepreneurial food-related service businesses; Corporate Members are companies and organizations that produce or promote food and cooking-related products on a larger scale; and Student/Apprentice Members are individuals enrolled in a program leading to a culinary career. Member benefits include the annual IACP Conference (Apr. 14-18, 1993, in New Orleans); newsletters and research reports; the annual IACP *Membership Directory*; a certification program through which members may earn the status of Certified Culinary Professional (CCP), Approved Teacher, Approved Food Writer, or Approved Caterer and cooking schools may obtain IACP endorsement (see next page). Annual dues are $125 (plus $30 one-time fee) for Professional Members, $250 (plus $50) for Cooking School Members, $300 (plus $50) for Business Members; $500 (plus $100) for Corporate Members, and $50 for Student/Apprentice Members.

Contact: International Association of Culinary Professionals, 304 W. Liberty St., Suite 201, Louisville, KY 40202; (502) 581-9786, Fax (502) 589-3602.

INTERNATIONAL ASSOCIATION OF CULINARY PROFESSIONALS (IACP) ENDORSED COOKING SCHOOLS

Endorsement by the International Association of Culinary Professionals is a review process that is open to all Business members. To be endorsed, a school must have been in business for at least 20 months and have accumulated a minimum of 800 teaching hours, of which 50% are currently performed by IACP-Approved Teachers or Certified Culinary Professionals (CCPs). The school must also adhere to certain equipment, safety, and curriculum requirements and is subjected to an on-site inspection during class hours. Endorsement is renewable annually.

IACP-Endorsed Schools as of September 1, 1992:

Ballymaloe Cookery School, 205
Everyday Gourmet School
  of Cooking, 128
Giuliano Bugialli's
  Cooking in Florence, 214
L'Academie de Cuisine, 53
La Varenne, 200
Leith's School of Food-Wine, 172

Les Gourmettes Cooking Sch., 1
Peter Kump's New York
  Cooking School, 95
Ada Parasiliti
  Cooking School, 209
Le Cordon Bleu London, 165
The Kitchen Shoppe, 107
Zona Spray Cooking School, 102

THE JAMES BEARD FOUNDATION, INC.
New York, New York

The nonprofit James Beard Foundation was established in 1986 to honor the father of American gastronomy and establish his home as the first historical culinary center in North America. According to Julia Child, who conceived the idea of saving his home, "The Foundation is part of an effort by many of us in the business — food writers, cooks, teachers, restaurateurs, purveyors, and wine growers — to establish gastronomy as a recognized art, a bona fide discipline, and a profession." The Foundation's mission is to keep alive the ideals and activities that made James Beard the acknowledged "Father of American Cooking". It fosters appreciation and development of gastronomy through preserving and promulgating our culinary heritage and recognizing and promoting excellence in all aspects of the culinary arts. A scholarship and apprenticeship program are a growing aspect of the Foundation. The library is currently being restored and developed as a resource via telephone and fax for food writers and food enthusiasts. While its primary focus is on Beardiana, it also maintains an extensive biographical file on contemporary chefs and other culinary artists and welcomes requests for information regarding recipes, restaurants, and cooking schools.

Membership benefits include discount prices on the more than 200 events held annually (usually dinners featuring well-known American chefs), continuing food art exhibits, workshops, classes, and wine tastings. A series of Saturday morning workshops (limit 20 members) features a two-hour demonstration by a well-known guest chef, followed by a light lunch of the foods prepared. Members receive a monthly 24-page newsletter, *News From the Beard House*, and professional members are listed in the Foundation directory. The annual James Beard Awards, including book, journalism, chefs, and restaurant awards, plus conferences for chefs and writers, attracts a large gathering of fine food and beverage professionals the first weekend in May during "Beard Birthday Fortnight". The Beard House also provides a meeting place for nonprofit culinary organizations.

Tax-deductible annual membership dues begin at $50 for nonprofessionals and $100 ($200 for those living within 75 miles of Manhattan) for professionals.

Contact: The James Beard Foundation, Inc., 167 W. 12th St., New York, NY 10011; (212) 675-4984, Fax (212) 645-1438.

NATIONAL RESTAURANT ASSOCIATION
Washington, D.C.

Established in 1919, this organization is the leading national trade association for the foodservice industry, providing its 18,000 members with a wide range of educational, research, communications, convention, and government affairs services.

Member services range from individual advice on recipes to representation of the industry to the federal government and the public. The ideals and interests of the foodservice industry are promoted through interaction with federal legislators and political leaders, a media relations program, and a speech bank. Publications include *Restaurants USA*, a monthly magazine devoted to ideas and trends; *Washington Weekly*, a weekly political report; *Current Issues Reports*, in-depth coverage of specific topics; and operations and "how to" manuals. Members can also utilize the toll-free Member Hotline, which accesses the Information Service and Library. The not-for-profit National Restaurant Association's Educational Foundation, located in Chicago, was created to advance professional standards of foodservice hospitality management through education. The Restaurant, Hotel-Motel Show, the industry's largest trade show, offers a full program of educational events conducted by industry leaders. The show is held in Chicago each May and is free to members.

Any entity that operates facilities and/or supplies meal service on a regular basis for others is eligible to join. Dues, which are based on total annual foodservice and beverage volume, begin at $125 for annual sales under $250,000.

Contact: National Restaurant Association, 1200 - 17th Street, N.W., Washington, DC 20036-3097; (202) 331-5900, Fax (202) 331-2429.

IV

APPENDIX

SPECIALTY INDEX

AMERICAN REGIONAL
Baron of Barbeque (KS), 47
Captiva Cooking School (FL), 31
Chef Allen's (FL), 32
Cookin' Cajun Cooking School (LA), 49
Jane Butel Tex-Mex (NY), 73
Kay Pastorius Sch. of Int'l Cuisine (CA), 13
Marriott's Grand Hotel Ck. School (GA), 1
New Orleans School of Cooking (LA), 51
Pacific Northwest Field Sem's. (WA), 130
Santa Fe School of Cooking (NM), 74

BAKING, PASTRIES, DESSERTS
L'Academie de Cuisine (MD), 53
Baltimore Int'l Culinary College (MD), 55
California Culinary Academy (CA), 5
Carole Bloom Patissiere (CA), 7
Chocolate Gallery (NY), 76
Clark College Culinary Arts (WA), 127
Cleveland Restaurant Ck. School (OH), 99
Cooking/Hospitality Inst. Chicago (IL), 39
Cooking School of the Rockies (CO), 26
Le Cordon Bleu - London (England), 165
Le Cordon Bleu - Paris (France), 186
Le Cordon Bleu Paris School (Can.), 151
Culinary Arts at the New School (NY), 80
Culinary Institute of America (NY), 82
Ecole de Gastronomie Francaise Ritz-
    Escoffier (France), 190
Ecole Lenotre France (France), 192
Espace Friand Ecole de Gastronomie
    (France), 192
European Educ. Ctr./Park Hotel (MD), 207
Florida Culinary Institute (FL), 33
George Brown College (Canada), 153
Healy-Lucullus Sch. French Ck. (CO), 26
Johnson & Wales Univ./Cul. Arts (RI), 111
Mary Beth Clark - Ck. School (NY), 219
Master Classes/M. & V. Hazan (NY), 218
National Ctr. Hospitality Studies (KY), 48
Peter Kump's New York Ck. Sch. (NY), 95
Restaurant School (PA), 109
Scuola di Arte Culinaria Cordon Bleu
    (Italy), 221
UCLA Ext. Div. Culinary Arts (CA), 23
La Varenne (DC), 200

CAKE DECORATING, CANDIES, CHOCOLATE
Amy Malone Cake Decorating (CA), 4
Cake Cottage, Inc. (MD), 57

Cake Icing Course (England), 160
Chocolate Gallery (NY), 76
Clea's Castle Cooking School (IL), 38
Country Kitchen (IN), 45
Ecole Lenotre France (France), 192
Espace Friand Ecole de Gastronomie
    (France), 192
Exquisite World of Chocolates (VA), 147
Food in France (England), 193
George Brown College (Canada), 153
Hotel Hershey Weekends (PA), 105
Kake Kreations (CA), 12
King's Chocolate House (NY), 89
McCall's Cake Decoration, (Can.), 156
Squires Kitchen CakeDecor. (Eng.), 177
Sugar 'n Spice Cake Decor. Sch. (CA), 21
Top Tier Sugarcraft (Scotland), 230
Wilton School of Cake Decorating (IL), 44
Woodnutt's Cake Decor. (England), 181

CATERING
L'Academie de Cuisine (MD), 53
La Bonne Cuisine School (TX), 117
Clea's Castle Cooking School (IL), 38
Council Adult Education (Australia), 137
Culinary Arts at the New School (NY), 80
Ecole Lenotre France (France), 192
Napa Valley College Cul. Arts (CA), 16
Peter Kump's New York School (NY), 95
UCLA Ext. Div. of Culinary Arts (CA), 23

ENGLISH, IRISH, SCOTTISH, WELSH
Alix Gardner Cookery Sch. (Ireland), 204
Ballymaloe Cookery School (Ireland), 205
Bonne Bouche School (England), 159
Catherine Blakeley (England), 162
Cookery Centre of Ireland (Ireland), 206
Cooking at Verity (England), 164
Frances Kitchin Cooking (England), 169
Manor School Fine Cuisine (England), 174
Tante Marie Sch. Cookery (England), 177

FAR EASTERN
China Advocates (CA), 158
Chinese Cookery, Inc. (MD), 57
Chopsticks Cooking (Hong Kong), 202
Elegance School (Hong Kong), 203
Elizabeth Chong (Australia), 140
Exploring Kitchens of Asia/Joyce Jue
    (CA), 134
George Brown College (Canada), 153

Harry's Chinese Cooking (Australia), 142
House of Rice Store (AZ), 2
Japanese Cooking Classes (Australia), 143
Karen Lee Cooking Classes (NY), 88
Ken Lo's Memories of China (Eng.), 171
Kisetsu Japanese Cooking (Australia), 144
Lily Loh's Chinese Cooking (CA), 15
Linda Quo School (Australia), 144
Marge Cohen (MA), 61
Norman Weinstein's School (NY), 93
Oriental Food Market /School, Inc. (IL), 43
Say Hi (TX), 121
Siamese Princess Restaurant (CA), 20
Thai Cooking/The Oriental (Thailand),233
Uwajimaya Cooking School (WA), 130
La Venturé (IL), 43
What's Cooking (IL), 44
Yan Can International School (CA), 25

FISH & SEAFOOD
Sonia Stevenson (England), 176
Sydney Seafood School (Australia), 146

FOOD WRITING & STYLING
De Gustibus at Macy's (NY), 84
Napa Valley College Cul. Arts (CA), 16

FRENCH
L'Academie de Cuisine (MD), 53
Andre Daguin Hotel France (France), 183
Bonne Bouche School (England), 159
A La Bonne Cocotte (NY), 75
California Culinary Academy (CA), 5
Cambridge School Culinary Arts (MA), 59
Casseroles du Midi (France), 183
Chateau Country School (France), 184
Chateau de Saussignac Sch. (France), 184
Chillingsworth Inn (MA), 60
Cookery at the Grange (England), 163
Cookhampton (NY), 77
Cooking at the Abbey (France), 185
Cooking With John Doherty at the Waldorf (NY), 78
Cooking School of the Rockies (CO), 26
Cooking at Verity (England), 164
Le Cordon Bleu - London (England), 165
Le Cordon Bleu - Paris (France), 186
Le Cordon Bleu Paris School (Can.), 151
Country Kitchens of Gascony (MA), 187
La Cucina (Australia), 138
La Cuisine Francaise (Netherlands), 229
La Cuisine Sans Peur (NY), 79
Cuisine-Islands of W. Meditt. (NY), 225
Cuisinieres du Monde (France), 188

Dubrulle French Culinary School (Canada), 152
Ecole des Arts Culinaires (NY), 188
Ecole de Cuisine (WI), 132
Ecole de Gastronomie Francaise Ritz-Escoffier (France), 190
Ecole Lenotre France (France), 192
Epicurean Cooking School (CA), 9
Food in France (England), 193
French Culinary Institute (NY), 85
French Kitchen (Australia), 140
Gourmet School of Cooking (CA), 10
Gretta Anna School (Australia), 141
Hexham School of Cookery (Eng.), 170
Holidays in sun/south France (France), 194
Jane Thompson Cooking School (NY), 87
Memphis Culinary Academy (TN), 115
Michael's Waterside (CA), 15
Miller Howe Cookery Courses (Eng.), 175
Paris Cooks (DC), 30
Paris en Cuisine (France), 194
Pasquaney Inn Cooking School (NH), 69
Peter Kump's New York Ck. Sch. (NY), 95
La Petite Cuisine (England), 196
Postilion School of Culinary Art (WI), 133
Princess Ere 2001 (France), 196
Raymond Blanc's Le Petit Blanc Ecole de Cuisine (TX), 176
Sara Monick Culinary Tours (MN), 197
Sauce for the Goose, Etc. (CA), 19
Summer House Cooking School (TX), 62
Tante Marie School (England), 177
Traditional Family Cooking in the Quercy (France), 198
Le Trou Restaurant/Cooking Sch. (CA), 22
Two Bordelais (CA), 199
Vacances Cuisine (France), 199
La Varenne (DC), 200
La Venture (IL), 43

HERBS & SPICES
Caroline Holmes - Herbs (England), 161
Cookbook Cottage (KY), 48

INDIAN
Julie Sahni's Indian Cooking (NY), 88
Neelam Kumar's N. Indian Cuisine (Canada), 157

ITALIAN
Ada Parasiliti Cooking School (Italy), 209
L'Amore di Cucina Italiana (NY), 209
Anna Teresa Callen Italian Cooking School (NY), 74
Badia a Coltibuono (TX), 210

TRAVEL AND VACATION PROGRAMS

PROFESSIONAL PROGRAMS

CHILDREN'S PROGRAMS

RESTAURANTS

SCHOOL RANKINGS BY TUITION COST

Use this index for approximate guidance only. Programs are indexed by total tuition for those that are less than nine months and by annual tuition for those that are nine months or more. Additional costs, such as housing, food, fees, books, supplies, and transportation, are not included. Schools whose in-state (in-county, in-district) and out-of-state (out-of-country) tuition costs fall in different categories are indicated by IS (IC, ID) or OS (OC) following the state or country. Consult individual listings for more specific information.

TOTAL TUITION FOR PROGRAMS OF LESS THAN NINE MONTHS

$2,500 TO $4,999

Epicurean Cooking School (CA), 9
Alix Gardner's Cookery Sch. (Ireland), 204
Boston Univ. Sem's.-Culin. Arts (MA), 58
Cookery Centre of Ireland (Ireland), 206
Cooking-Hospital. Inst. of Chicago (IL), 39
Dubrulle French Culinary Sch. (Can.), 152
Le Trou Rest. & Cooking School (CA), 22
New York Food-Hotel Mgt. Sch. (NY), 255
Orleans Technical Institute (PA), 259
Warren Occup. Tech. Ctr. (CO OS), 241

$5,000 TO $9,999

ATI Career Institute (VA), 262
Ballymaloe Cookery School (Ireland), 205
CBI Culinary Academy (CT), 241
Century Business College (CA), 238
Connecticut Culinary Institute (CT), 27
Peter Kump's New York Ck. Sch. (NY), 95

$10,000 OR OVER

Eastbourne Coll. Food-Fashion (Eng.), 168
Ecole de Gastronomie Francaise
    Ritz-Escoffier (France), 190
Ecole des Arts Culinaires (France), 188
New York Restaurant School (NY), 92
Tante Marie's Cooking School (CA), 21

ANNUAL TUITION FOR PROGRAMS OF NINE MONTHS OR LONGER

LESS THAN $1,000

Algonquin College (Canada IS), 265
Asheville Buncombe Tech. Comm. Coll.
    (NC IS), 256
Atlanta Area Technical School (GA), 243
Atlantic Vocational Tech. Ctr (FL), 242
Augusta Technical Institute (GA), 244
Baton Rouge Regional Tech. Inst. (LA), 248
Berkshire Community Coll. (MA IS), 249
Broward Community College (FL IS), 242

Central Community College (NE IS), 253
Central Piedmont Comm. Coll. (NC IS), 256
Clark Cty. Community Coll. (NV IS), 253
College of DuPage (IL ID), 245
Columbia College (CA IS), 239
Contra Costa College (CA), 239
Cuyahoga Community College (OH), 257
Dandenong College (Australia IS), 265
Diablo Valley College (CA), 239
Edmonds Community Coll. (WA IS), 262
El Centro College (TX IS), 261
Elgin Community College (IL), 245
Elizabethtown State Voc. Tech. School
    (KY IS), 248
George Brown College (Canada IS), 153
Glendale Community College (CA IS), 239
Great Plains Area Voc. Tech. Ctr. (OK), 258
Greenville Technical College (SC IC), 260
Grossmont College (CA IS), 239
Horry-Georgetown Tech. Coll. (SC IS), 260
Houston Community College (TX IS), 261
Humber College of Applied Arts
    & Technology (Canada IS), 265
Inst. of the South for Hospitality
    & Culinary Arts (FL IS), 242
Jefferson Community College (KY IS), 248
Joliet Junior College (IL IS), 245
Kansas City Ks. Area Vocational Technical
    School (KS), 247
Laney College (CA), 239
Lawson State Community Coll. (AL), 238
Lincoln Trail College (IL ID), 245
Los Angeles Trade-Tech. Coll. (CA IS), 240
Massasoit Community Coll. (MA IS), 250
Maui Community College (HI IS), 244
Metropolitan Commun. Coll. (NE IS), 253
Monroe County Commun. Coll. (MI), 250
New Orleans Reg. Technical Inst. (LA), 249
North Seattle Comm. Coll. (WA IS), 262
North Technical Education Ctr. (FL), 242
Northeast Kansas Area Vocational
    Technical School (KS IS), 247
Odessa College (TX OS), 261
Okaloosa-Walton Comm. Coll. (FL IS), 242

Oklahoma State Univ. Okmulgee (OK), 258
Olympic College (WA), 262
Orange Coast College (CA IS), 240
Oxnard College (CA IS), 240
Penn Valley Commun. Coll. (MO ID), 252
Pima Community College (AZ), 238
Pinellas Technical Educ. Ctr. (FL), 243
Pioneer Area Voc. Tech. Sch. (OK), 258
San Joaquin Delta College (CA IS), 240
Santa Barbara City College (CA IS), 240
Santa Fe Community College (NM IC), 254
Santa Rosa Junior College (CA IS), 240
Savannah Technical Institute (GA OS), 244
Seattle Central Comm. Coll. (WA IS),263
Seminole Community College (FL), 243
Shasta College (CA IS), 240
Skagit Valley College (WA IS), 263
South Puget Sd. Comm. Coll. (WA IS),263
Southeast Comm. Coll., Lincoln (NE), 253
Southeast Inst. of Culinary Arts (FL IS), 35
Southern Okla. Voc. Tech. (OK ID), 258
Spokane Community College (WA IS), 263
St. Louis Comm. College (MO IS), 252
St. Philip's College (TX OS), 262
Stratford Chefs School (Canada IS), 157
Truckee Meadows Coll. (NV IS), 254
Washington-Holmes Voc. Tech. (FL), 243
West Kentucky State Voc. Tech. (KY),248
Westmoreland Comm. Coll. (PA IC),260
William Rainey Harper College (IL IS), 245

$1,000 TO $1,999

Adirondack Community College (NY), 255
Black Hawk College-Quad Cty.(IL ID), 244
Boise State University (ID), 244
Broward Community College (FL OS), 242
Bucks County Commun. Coll. (PA IC), 259
Bunker Hill Community Coll. (MA IS), 249
Central Community College (NE OS), 253
Chippewa Valley Tech. Coll. (WI IS), 264
Clark College Culinary Arts (WA), 127
Columbus State Comm. Coll. (OH IS), 257
Community Coll. Allegh. Cty.(PA IS), 259
Des Moines Area Comm. Coll. (IA IS), 246
Detroit Lakes Technical Coll. (MN IS), 251
Elizabethtown St. Voc. Tech. (KY OS), 248
Erie Community College, City (NY IS), 255
Essex Agric. & Tech. Institute (MA IS), 249
Fox Valley Technical Institute (WI IS), 264
Greenville Technical College (SC OS), 260
Hennepin Tech.-Eden Prairie (MN IS), 252
Hocking Technical College (OH IS), 257
Horry-Georgetown Tech. (SC OS),260
Hudson County Comm. Coll. (NJ IS), 254

Indian Meridian Voc. Tech. (OK ID), 258
Indiana Vocational Tech. Coll. (IN IS), 246
Indiana Voc. Tech. Coll.-Central (IN), 246
Indiana Voc. Tech. Coll.-Gary (IN IS), 246
Iowa Western Commun. Coll. (IA IS), 247
Jefferson Community College (NY IS), 255
Johnson Cty. Community Coll. (KS IS), 247
Kirkwood Community College (IA IS), 247
Lane Community College (OR IS), 258
Macomb Community College (MI), 250
Madison Area Technical College (WI), 264
Manchester Community Coll. (CT IS), 241
Mankato Technical Institute (MN IS), 252
Massasoit Community Coll. (MA OS), 250
Metropolitan Commun. Coll. (NE OS), 253
Missoula Voc. Tech. Center (MT IS), 253
Mitchell Area Voc. Tech. School (SD), 261
Mohawk Valley Comm. Coll. (NY IS), 255
Moorhead Technical College (MN OS), 252
New Hampshire Tech. Coll. (NH IS), 254
Niagara Coll. Arts/Tech. (Can. IS), 265
Niagara County Comm. Coll. (NY IC), 256
North Dakota State Coll. Sci. (ND IS), 257
North Seattle Commun. Coll. (WA OS), 262
Northwestern Michigan College (MI), 251
Oakland Community College (MI IC), 251
Okaloosa-Walton Coll. (FL OS),242
Onondaga Community Coll. (NY IS), 256
Pikes Peak Community Coll. (CO IS), 241
Renton Technical College (WA), 263
Santa Fe Community Coll. (NM OS), 254
Schenectady Cty. Comm. Coll.(NY IS), 256
Schoolcraft College (MI), 251
Scottsdale Community Coll. (AZ IS), 238
Seminole Community College (FL), 243
South Central Commun. Coll. (CT IS), 241
South Seattle Commun. Coll. (WA IS), 263
Southeast Institute of Culinary Arts (FL), 35
Southern Alberta Inst. Tech. (Can. IS), 265
Southern Maine Tech. Coll. (ME IS), 249
St. Louis Comm. Coll. (MO OS), 252
St. Paul Technical College (MN IS), 252
Trident Technical College (SC IC), 261
Triton College (IL), 245
Truckee Meadows Coll. (NV OS), 254
Univ. of Alaska-Fairbanks (AK IS), 238
Vincennes University (IN IS), 246
Wallace State Commun. Coll. (AL IS), 238
Warren Occup. Tech. Ctr. (CO IS), 241
Washburne Trade School (IL IS), 245
Washtenaw Community Coll. (MI IS), 251
Wayne County Commun. Coll. (MI IS), 251
West Virginia N. Comm.Coll. (WV IS), 264
Wichita Area Voc.-Tech. School (KS), 247

$2,000 TO $2,999

Bristol Community College (MA IS), 249
Cincinnati Technical College (OH IS), 257
Clark County Comm. Coll. (NV OS), 253
Columbia College (CA OS), 239
Comm. Coll. Allegheny Cty. (PA OS), 259
Detroit Lakes Tech. College (MN OS), 251
El Centro College (TX OS), 261
Glendale Comm. College (CA OS), 239
Grossmont College (CA OS), 239
Hennepin Tech. Coll.-Brkln. (MN IS), 252
Houston Community College (TX OS), 261
Hudson County Comm. Coll. (NJ OS), 254
Instituto del Arte Moderno, Inc. (PR), 260
Iowa Lakes Comm. Coll. (IA IS), 246
Iowa Western Comm. College (IA OS), 247
Jefferson Comm. College (KY OS), 248
Jefferson Comm. College (NY OS), 255
Kirkwood Comm. College (IA OS), 247
Lincoln Trail College (IL OS), 245
Los Angeles Trade-Tech. (CA OS), 240
Manchester Comm. College (CT OS), 241
Mankato Technical Institute (MN OS), 252
Maui Community College (HI OS), 244
Milwaukee Area Tech. Coll. (WI IS), 264
Missoula Vocational Tech. (MT OS), 253
Monroe Community College (NY), 255
North Dakota State Coll. Sci. (ND OS), 257
Onondaga Comm. College (NY OS), 256
Orange Coast College (CA OS), 240
Oxnard College (CA OS), 240
Penn Valley Comm. College (MO OS), 252
SUNY Coll. Agric./Tech. (NY IS), 256
Salem Cty. Voc. Tech. Schools (NJ), 254
San Joaquin Delta College (CA OS), 240
Santa Barbara City College (CA OS), 240
Santa Rosa Junior College (CA OS), 240
Shasta College (CA OS), 24
St. Paul Technical College (MN OS), 252
Sullivan Cty. Comm. College (NY IS), 256
Trident Technical College (SC OS), 261
University of Akron (OH IS), 257
University of New Hampshire (NH IS), 254
University of Toledo (OH IS), 257
Washtenaw Comm. College (MI OS), 251
Wayne County Comm. Coll. (MI OS), 251

$3,000 TO $4,999

Atlantic Community College (NJ), 70
Berkshire Comm. College (MA OS), 249
Black Hawk Coll.-Quad Cities (IL OS), 244
Bossier Parish Comm. College (LA), 248
Bunker Hill Comm. College (MA IS), 249

Centr. Piedmont Comm. Coll. (NC OS), 256
Cincinnati Technical College (OH OS), 257
Columbus State Comm. Coll. (OH OS), 257
Des Moines Area Comm. Coll. (IA OS), 246
Dunwoody Institute (MN), 251
Edmonds Comm. College (WA OS), 262
Erie Community College, (NY OS), 255
Essex Agric. & Tech. Inst. (MA OS), 249
Grand Rapids Comm. College (MI IS), 250
Harrisburg Area Comm. College (PA), 259
Hennepin Tech.-Eden Prairie(MN OS), 252
Hennepin Tech.-Brklyn. Pk. (MN OS), 252
Hocking Technical College (OH OS), 257
Indian Hills Comm. College (IA OS), 246
Indiana Voc. Tech. College (IN OS), 246
Indiana Voc. Tech. Coll.-Gary (IN OS), 246
Inst. of South-Hosp./Cul. Arts (FL OS), 242
Iowa Lakes Comm. Coll. (IA OS), 246
Johnson County Comm. Coll. (KS OS), 247
Joliet Junior College (IL OS), 245
Indian Hills Comm. College (IA IS), 246
Lane Community College (OR OS), 258
Memphis Culinary Academy (TN), 115
Mohawk Valley Comm. Coll. (NY OS), 255
New Hampshire Tech. Coll. (NH OS), 254
Pennsylvania Coll. Tech. (PA IS), 260
Pikes Peak Comm. College (CO OS), 241
Schenectady Comm. Coll. (NY OS), 256
Seattle Central Comm. Coll. (WA OS), 263
Silwood Kitchen Sch. (South Africa), 231
Skagit Valley College (WA OS), 263
South Central Comm. College (CT OS), 241
South Puget Sd. Comm. Coll. (WA OS), 263
South Seattle Comm. Coll. (WA OS), 263
Southern Alberta Inst. Tech. (Can. OC), 265
Southern Maine Tech. Coll. (ME OS), 249
Spokane Comm, College (WA OS), 263
Stratford Chefs School (Canada OS), 157
Sullivan County Comm, Coll. (NY OS), 256
University Alaska-Fairbanks (AK OS), 238
University of Toledo (OH OS), 257
Vincennes University (IN OS), 246
Washburne Trade School (IL OS), 245
West Va. No. Comm. Coll. (WV OS), 264

$5,000 TO $7,449

Algonquin College (Canada OC), 265
Bristol Community College (MA OS), 249
Cooking and Hosp. Inst. of Chicago (IL), 39
Dandenong College (Australia OC), 265
George Brown College (Canada OS), 153
Grand Rapids Comm. College (MI OS), 250
Humber College Arts/Tech. (Can. OC), 265
IUP Culinary School (PA), 259

Lederwolff Culin. Acad. (CA Baking), 239
Minuteman Tech (MA), 250
National Ctr. Hospitality Studies (KY), 48
Niagara Coll. Arts/Tech. (Canada OS), 265
Northeast Kansas Voc. Tech. (KS OS), 247
Pennsylvania Coll. of Tech. (PA OS), 260
SUNY College Agric./Tech. (NY OS), 256
Scottsdale Comm. College (AZ OS), 238
University of Akron (OH OS), 257
William Rainey Harper Coll. (IL OS), 245

$7,500 TO $9,999

Art Institute of Atlanta (GA), 243
Asheville Buncombe Tech. (NC OS), 256
Baltimore In'tl. Culinary College (MD), 55
Cambridge Sch. of Culinary Arts (MA), 59
Chippewa Valley Tech. Coll. (WI OS), 264
Culinary Inst. of New Hampshire (NH), 254
Le Chef Culinary Arts School, (TX), 117
Milwaukee Area Tech. Coll. (WI OS), 264
Natural Gourmet Cookery School (NY), 90
Newbury College (MA), 61
Paul Smith's College (NY), 94
Scottsdale Culinary Institute (AZ), 3
University New Hampshire (NH OS), 254

$10,000 OR OVER

Art Institute of Ft. Lauderdale (FL), 241
California Culinary Academy (CA), 5
Centre de Form. Tech. Ferrandi (Fr.), 194
Culinary Arts Instit. of Louisiana (LA), 50
Culinary Institute of America (NY), 82
Culinary School of Kendall College (IL), 40
Florida Culinary Institute (FL), 33
Fox Valley Technical Instit. (WI OS), 264
French Culinary Institute (NY), 85
Johnson-Wales Univ. (FL, RI, SC, VA), 111
L'Academie de Cuisine (MD), 53
Le Chef Culinary Arts School, (TX), 117
Le Cordon Bleu - Paris (France), 186
Lederwolff Culinary Academy (CA), 239
Leith's Sch. of Food & Wine (England), 171
New England Culinary Institute (VT), 122
New York Instit. of Technology (NY), 255
Pennsylvania Inst. Culinary Arts (PA), 108
Restaurant School (PA), 109
Tante Marie School of Cookery (Eng.), 177
Western Culinary Institute (OR), 103

SCHOOL RANKINGS BY % APPLICANTS ACCEPTED

The following schools provided the approximate percentage of applicants that are accepted to their programs. Schools that accept all applicants up to a certain limit are indicated by FCFS (first-come, first-served) following the state or country.

LESS THAN 50% OF APPLICANTS ARE ACCEPTED

ATI Career Institute (VA), 262
Boston Univ. Sem's. Culin. Arts (MA), 58
Dandenong College (Australia), 265
Le Trou Rest. & Cooking School (CA), 22
New England Culinary Institute (VT), 122
Stratford Chefs School (Canada), 157

50% TO 75% OF APPLICANTS ARE ACCEPTED

Algonquin College (Canada), 265
Art Institute of Houston (TX), 261
Dubrulle French Culinary Sch. (Can.), 152
Erie Community College, City (NY), 255
Le Chef Culinary Arts School, (TX), 117
Milwaukee Area Technical Coll. (WI), 264
Newbury College (MA), 61
Niagara Coll. Arts/Tech. (Canada), 265
Scottsdale Culinary Institute (AZ), 3

75% TO 89% OF APPLICANTS ARE ACCEPTED

Bristol Community College (MA), 249
California Culinary Academy (CA), 5
Central Piedmont Comm. Coll. (NC), 256
Clark College Culinary Arts (WA), 127
Cooking-Hospital. Inst. of Chicago (IL), 39
Cuyahoga Community College (OH), 257
Ecole des Arts Culinaires (NY), 188
Florida Culinary Institute (FL), 33
Johnson-Wales Univ. (FL, RI, SC, VA), 111
Johnson County Commun. Coll. (KS), 247
Laney College (CA), 239
Lederwolff Culinary Academy (CA), 239
Los Angeles Trade-Tech. Coll. (CA), 240
Monroe Community College (NY), 255
Monroe County Commun. Coll. (MI), 250
National Ctr. Hospitality Studies (KY), 48
New Orleans Regional Tech. Inst. (LA), 249
Odessa College (TX), 261

Olympic College (WA), 262
Paul Smith's College (NY), 94
Peter Kump's New York Ck. Sch. (NY), 95
Salem County Voc. Tech. Schools (NJ), 254
Seattle Central Commun. Coll. (WA), 263
Southern Alberta Inst. of Tech. (Can.), 265
University of Alaska-Fairbanks (AK), 238
University of New Hampshire (NH), 254
Western Culinary Institute (OR), 103

90% TO 100% OF APPLICANTS ARE ACCEPTED

Atlantic Comm. College (NJ), 70
Art Institute of Atlanta (GA), 243
Art Institute of Ft. Lauderdale (FL), 241
Asheville Buncombe Tech. Coll. (NC), 256
Atlantic Vocational Tech. Ctr. (FL), 242
Augusta Technical Institute (GA), 244
Baltimore Int'l. Culinary College (MD), 55
Baton Rouge Regional Tech. Inst. (LA), 248
Bossier Parish Community Coll. (LA), 248
CBI Culinary Academy (CT), 241
Cambridge Sch. of Culinary Arts (MA), 59
Central Community College (NE), 253
Century Business College (CA), 238
Chippewa Valley Technical Coll. (WI), 264
Clark County Community Coll. (NV), 253
College of DuPage (IL), 245
Columbia College (CA), 239
Columbus State Commun. Coll. (OH), 257
Contra Costa College (CA), 239
Culinary Arts Instit. of Louisiana (LA), 50
Des Moines Area Commun. Coll. (IA), 246
Edmonds Community College (WA), 262
Elizabethtown State Voc. Tech. (KY), 248
Essex Agric./Tech. Inst.(MA FCFS), 249
Fox Valley Technical Institute (WI), 264
Glendale Community College (CA), 239
Grand Rapids Community Coll. (MI), 250
Grossmont College (CA), 239
Hennepin Tech.-Eden Prairie (MN), 252
Hennepin Tech.-Brooklyn Park (MN), 252
Horry-Georgetown Tech. Coll. (SC), 260
Indian Hills Community College (IA), 246
Indiana Vocational Tech. Coll. (IN), 246
Indiana Voc. Tech. Coll.-Central (IN), 246
Indiana Voc. Tech. Coll.-Gary (IN), 246
Inst. of South-Hospit./Culin. Arts (FL), 242

Iowa Lakes Comm. Coll.-(IA FCFS), 246
Iowa Western Community Coll. (IA), 247
Jefferson Community College (NY), 255
Joliet Junior College (IL), 245
Kansas City Ks. Voc. Tech.Sch. (KS), 247
Kirkwood Community College (IA), 247
L'Academie de Cuisine (MD), 53
Leith's School of Food & Wine (Eng.), 171
Lincoln Trail College (IL), 245
Manchester Comm. Coll. (CT FCFS), 241
Mankato Technical Institute (MN), 252
Maui Community College (HI), 244
Metropolitan Community Coll. (NE), 253
Minuteman Tech (MA), 250
Missoula Vocational Tech. Ctr. (MT), 253
Natural Gourmet Cookery School (NY), 90
New York Inst. of Technology (NY), 255
Norman Weinstein Cooking Sch. (NY), 93
North Dakota State Coll. of Sci. (ND), 257
North Technical Education Ctr. (FL), 242
Northwestern Michigan College (MI), 251
Oakland Community College (MI), 251
Oklahoma State Univ-Okmulgee (OK), 258
Orange Coast College (CA), 240
Oxnard College (CA), 240
Penn Valley Community Coll. (MO), 252
Pennsylvania Coll. Technology (PA), 260
Pikes Peak Community College (CO), 241
Pinellas Technical Educ. Ctr. (FL), 243
Renton Technical College (WA), 263
Restaurant School (PA), 109
San Jacinto College North (TX), 262
Santa Barbara City College (CA FCFS), 240
Santa Fe Community College (NM), 254
Sarasota County Technical Inst. (FL), 243
Savannah Technical Institute (GA), 244
Schoolcraft College (MI), 251
South Central Community Coll. (CT), 241
South Seattle Community Coll. (WA), 263
Southeast Comm. Coll., Lincoln (NE), 253
Tante Marie's Cooking School (CA), 21
Washburne Trade School (IL FCFS), 245
Washington-Holmes Voc. Tech. (FL), 243
Washtenaw Community College (MI), 251
Waukesha County Tech. Coll. (WI), 264
West Virginia No. Comm. Coll. (WV), 264
Wichita Area Voc. Tech. School(KS), 247
William Rainey Harper College (IL), 245

MASTER INDEX